I0868327

THE GHOST BEHIND THE MASKS

Victorian Literature and Culture Series

JEROME J. MCGANN AND HERBERT F. TUCKER
EDITORS

THE GHOST BEHIND THE MASKS

THE VICTORIAN POETS AND SHAKESPEARE

W. David Shaw

University of Virginia Press
CHARLOTTESVILLE AND LONDON

University of Virginia Press
© 2014 by the Rector and Visitors of the University of Virginia
All rights reserved
Printed in the United States of America on acid-free paper

First published 2014

1 3 5 7 9 8 6 4 2

LIBRARY OF CONGRESS CATALOGING-IN-PUBLICATION DATA

Shaw, W. David (William David)
The ghost behind the masks : the Victorian poets and Shakespeare /
W. David Shaw.
pages cm. — (Victorian literature and culture series)
Includes bibliographical references and index.
ISBN 978-0-8139-3544-7 (cloth : alk. paper) — ISBN 978-0-8139-3545-4 (e-book)
1. English poetry—19th century—History and criticism. 2. Aesthetics, Modern—19th century. 3. Shakespeare, William, 1564–1616—Influence. 4. Poetics—History—19th century. 5. Great Britain—History—Victoria, 1837–1901. I. Title.
PR595.A34S53 2014
821'.8'0938—dc23
2013023499

In memory of my daughters, Margaret and Alyssa,
who hold all who loved them in a strong toil of grace

Contents

Acknowledgments

For their learning and sharp accuracy of judgment, I am indebted to the two scholars who read my manuscript for the University of Virginia Press. I am also grateful to the Press's Humanities Editor, Cathie Brettschneider, for her generous counsel and support, and to Colleen Romick Clark for her careful editing of the text. I owe most to the intellectual acumen and imaginative insight of my wife, Carol, a scholar whose grace of mind and manner has made the advancing years a climax, and marriage a harvest of memories in common. I owe a more distant debt of gratitude to the graduate students at the University of Toronto who twenty years ago in a seminar on Victorian poetry persuaded me to offer extra sessions on the Victorians and Shakespeare. Since that time the poetry I have committed to memory has been alive with the sound of Clough quoting *Hamlet,* Hopkins echoing *King Lear,* and Lady Macbeth talking through Christina Rossetti. I keep overhearing Othello and Hamlet in Tennyson, and a host of Shakespearean voices in Browning.

My most long-standing debt of gratitude is to the late Harvard scholar Reuben Brower. In the tutorials I conducted for him and in a graduate seminar on John Dryden, he showed me that literary history is the exact opposite of what I thought it was: not a museum of inert ideas but a playhouse of dramatic tones and contending voices. He taught me how a history of literary influence can encourage rather than suppress critical intelligence. For a young student raised as an undergraduate on historical scholarship alone, as for many other sons and daughters of Ben, this was a great enlightenment. His bounty as scholar and mentor had no winter in it. It was an autumn that grew the more for reaping.

Introduction

TO THINK LIKE SHAKESPEARE AND THE GREAT VICTORIANS IS NOT to know but to see wonder, mystery, and the unknown everywhere, especially at the heart of what we think we know. Swaying between opposing possibilities and wavering between worlds, Shakespeare and the Victorian poets both express and nourish a genius for speculative wonder and debate. Though I do not pretend to offer a single argument about Shakespeare and the Victorians, my exploration of such topics as the contest between man-made law and natural right, Stoic fatalism and self-reliance, the sanity of lunatics, lovers, and poets and the madness of commonplace minds supports the claim that the Victorian poets follow Shakespeare in substituting for the closed dome of an age of belief the unsealed dome of the Pantheon. Marked by perplexed persistence and doubt, the Shakespeare Victorians value and emulate is a master of the antiphonal style displayed in Hamlet's tortuous soliloquies, in Brutus's soliloquy in the garden, and in the great unresolved debates over individual will and the claim of Platonic universals in *Troilus and Cressida.*

Like Lear, who tells Cordelia he must wipe his hand first, for "it smells of mortality" (*King Lear* 4.6.136), Tennyson never seems to get over the taste of death in the new geology of Robert Chambers and Charles Lyell. But as Tennyson's Ulysses passes through untraveled worlds, whose margins fade forever and forever as he moves, it is hard for him to see death as a boundary, since it is precisely his knowledge of death's "closing all" that propels him through and beyond boundaries. Though "death is terrible, disruptive, and final," it is our awareness of death, "more than the experience of death itself," that constitutes "the unique burden of being human" (Kushner, 1996, 154–55).[1] Instead of indoctrinating a reader or raising some scaffold of belief as Milton or Dante do, the lofty edifice Shakespeare raises, like the dome of Hamlet's "excellent canopy, the air," replaces boundaries with horizons. The problem with belief is that it sets a boundary to vision. The Shakespeare whose greatness once assumed flesh for a corps of Victorian disciples is a skeptic and a visionary, an apostle of higher ignorance like Montaigne.

❁ ❁ ❁

In the first section of the book, "Poetic Beginnings," I show how Tennyson in *The Princess,* his inimitable mock-heroic imitation of *Love's Labor's Lost,* is able to mature as a writer of songs and lyrics, just as Shakespeare, amid his verbal gymnastic and poetic antics, is able to learn his art as a playwright. In the second chapter, I trace a similar development in Browning, who once told J. S. Mill that he owed his origins as a poet to a performance of Edmund Kean as Richard III. After the success of *Dramatic Lyrics,* Browning might easily have gone on to exploit the popular success of theatrical masterpieces like "My Last Duchess," just as Shakespeare could have gone on to produce more *Richard the Thirds.* But instead of prostituting their poetic gifts to theatrical popularity, Browning turned to the more challenging task of resurrecting historical personages like Andrea del Sarto and Fra Lippo, while Shakespeare learned to represent contending, self-divided states of mind in soliloquies by Richard II, Brutus, and Hamlet, whom Stephen Greenblatt hails as a "prince of the inward insurrection" (2004, 303).

The second section of the book, "Hamlet's Afterlives," opens with a chapter exploring Dickens's art of incongruously combining in Pip, the hero of *Great Expectations,* the tragic fate of Hamlet and the darkly comic fate of Malvolio. In the second chapter of this section, I compare Tennyson's portrait of man, the cosmic accident and tragic misfit of *In Memoriam,* with Hamlet's famous discourse on the paragon of animals. Juxtaposing the two passages, a reader may see how, after astronomy and physics have turned the universe into a machine without a will, Kant's starry heavens, an image once of God's presence, begin to pale in grandeur beside the consciousness of speakers like Hamlet and Tennyson's mourner, the new ghosts in the machine. Hamlet's angel of dust, a god in exile, shapes the dual vision of Tennyson's elegy, which sees man both as a monster, "a dream, a discord," and as the roof and crown of things, the summit of creation.

In the third section of the book, "Shades of King Lear," I show how the voice that tolls most insistently in Victorian poets and prose writers, even in the anguished mourner of *In Memoriam* (section 12), is the voice, not of Hamlet, but rather of dispossessed outcasts from Shakespeare's darkest tragedy, *King Lear.* Edmund's worship of nature as his goddess, together with a familiar passage from *The Winter's Tale,* shapes Victorian debates over nature as a moral norm (chapter 5). A pervasive presence in *Tess of the d'Urbervilles* and Hardy's elegies (chapter 6), *King Lear* also informs the jeering commentary of Dagonet and Tristram in Tennyson's "The Last Tournament," which combines the raillery of Shakespeare's Thersites and Timon with the jests of Lear's Fool (chapter 7). Aspiring to be Lear on the heath, Browning's Childe Roland finds that his confrontation with an end-of-the-line sublimity leaves him as dazed as Kent and Edgar after the deaths of Cordelia and her father. In chapter 8, I show how G. M. Hopkins, afraid of falling off mountains of the mind, seems bound upon his own wheel of fire in the sonnet "No worst, there is none," which echoes Edgar's cry in *King Lear* (4.1.27–28).

The fourth section, "Grace and Death," opens with a chapter examining the power of Shakespeare and Tennyson to celebrate in the beauty of the dead Cleopatra and Maud a "strong toil of grace." The next chapter contrasts Shakespeare's fear that death may bring in its wake an infinity of torments with the Victorian fear that death will simply annihilate us. In the book's penultimate chapter, I juxtapose passages in *In Memoriam* and Shakespeare's sonnets in order to show how the ravages of time the devourer pass like great shock waves through both works. Awed by "the terrible Muse" of Chambers and Lyell, for whom "the dark backward and abysm of time" (*The Tempest* 1.2.50) have obliterated all but a few traces of the earth's natural history, Tennyson shares his "passion of the past" with Shakespeare, whose sonnets record the ravages wrought by Ovid's *tempus edax rerum.* No alms for oblivion can moderate or tame the undertow of Ovid's terrifying Muse, the power of hungry time to pull down mountains, raise oceans, and devour every creature on the planet.[2]

Like Erik Gray in his study *Milton and the Victorians,* I find it liberating to escape occasionally from criticism that looks exclusively to Victorian thought when seeking to illuminate the literature of that era. By concentrating on a Shakespearean grid of thought and feeling that makes possible the writing of some great Victorian poems, I try to recover what T. S. Eliot calls "the presence of the past." In his erudite and lively book *Victorian Poets and the Changing Bible,* Charles LaPorte convincingly argues that the tendency of scholars to dismiss "Victorian hermeneutics" as "a dull interlude between Romantic and twentieth-century theories of interpretation" is obsolete and misleading (2011, 5). Just as Victorian literary theory, which was once rejected as a hinterland, has proved to be a remarkably diverse and productive field, so, as LaPorte amply demonstrates, developments in theology and biblical scholarship help shape what Northrop Frye might call the "secular scriptures" of five Victorian poets: Elizabeth and Robert Browning, Tennyson, Clough, and George Eliot. LaPorte's book makes a signal contribution to Victorian poetics, critical theory, and the history of ideas. More than most books in the field, it also substantiates G. B. Tennyson's claim that "aesthetics and theology do not in the nineteenth century grow in alien soils; they are branches of the same tree" (1981, 61). In the last chapter of this book, I supplement LaPorte's synchronic approach to Victorian poetry and biblical culture by showing how theories of words and the Word reach down through time, shaping what T. S. Eliot calls "three voices of poetry" in both Shakespeare and his Victorian descendants.

Adrian Poole's volume in the Arden Shakespeare series studies Shakespeare in a Victorian context. My study reverses his emphasis by placing Victorian poets in the context of Shakespeare. Concentrating on the Victorians' understanding and reception of Shakespeare, Poole writes a penetrating source study, grounded in allusion and thematic influence. His counterpart in Shakespearean scholarship is Stephen Greenblatt, who in *Shakespearean Negotiations* and *Will in the World* shows how Shakespeare's poems and plays engage with cultural currents of his own age. More ambitious is Harold Bloom's claim in *The Invention of the Human* that Shakespeare invented the kind of consciousness we now all share. In most of the book, when exploring Shakespeare's influence on Victorian culture, I follow the lead of Greenblatt and Poole. But in the penultimate chapter, when examining Victorian sonnets written on Shakespeare, I show how Browning in his sonnet "The Names" anticipates Bloom's grander claim that Shakespeare is a creator and sustainer of worlds. If his art is godlike, it is because it is a majestic and daunting "invention of the human." In Browning's view, to compass Shakespeare's influence is to circumscribe a power second in majesty only to the God who brooded over creation, and who in Hebrew tradition—as Elohim or the tetragrammaton—is too sublime to name. Trying to take Shakespeare's measure is like passing judgment on the polestar, whose worth's unknown although its height be taken.

Browning is Shakespearean because of his passion for secrecy, his need to keep a mask in place. Tennyson's poetry is Shakespearean, not by virtue of its style, and not because of its frequent allusions to Shakespeare, but because it shares with Shakespeare what John Keble calls a "master passion," a "passion of the past." In style and manner Tennyson is more Miltonic, less Shakespearean, than Browning and Hopkins, or even than Christina Rossetti, whose reserve and profound simplicity are often more Shakespearean. "Pray you, undo this button," like Rossetti's "Give me the lowest place," is an example of natural simplicity, whereas Tennyson usually achieves only a mannered semblance of it. One discovery I did not foresee (though it was foreseen by Erik Gray in his study of Milton) is that the visibility of a precursor's influence on the Victorian poets and the degree of their engagement with that precursor often exist in inverse ratio. Though this discovery may seem paradoxical,

John Keble's theory of displaced passions in his influential *Oxford Lectures on Poetry* both anticipates and helps explain it.

According to Keble, the most permanently interesting features of poetry—Lucretius's "passion for the Infinite" or Virgil's "master passion" for pastoral celebration (1912, 2:334, 417)—are so artfully veiled that we can glimpse them only indirectly, out of the corner of the eye. Keble's theory of displaced "master passions" has a wide application to Victorian monologues, which appropriate a multitude of Shakespearean voices, often as many as Caliban hears in the harmonies orchestrated by Prospero. Even in a series of narrative poems like *Idylls of the King,* Tennyson never wholly suppresses a lyric "passion of the past," which makes him, as T. S. Eliot says, "a Virgil among the Shades, the saddest of all English poets, among the Great in Limbo" (1932, "In Memoriam," 337).

To say Shakespeare's plays are the work of a ghost is not to say they were written by Francis Bacon. Shakespeare, the ghost behind the masks, has withdrawn from his creation. Since he is as close to Iago as to Imogen, *Othello* and *Cymbeline* are works of a ghostly playwright, but not a ghost writer. Staining the white radiance of eternity, Shakespeare rarely turns up as any one color on the spectrum. Though a master light of all our seeing, he is all colors and hence no color. Like the Elgin Marbles, the Shakespeare the Victorians encounter is the shadow of a magnitude. Shakespeare's Muse is the ghost of a ghost, the shadow of Proteus, a god who is himself a transient shadow or trace. A presence like the air, Shakespeare is the medium that makes possible what many Victorians see, even when like Proteus he is not quite visible himself. Nineteenth-century writers feel crippled and distorted by the narrow functions and role-playing society imposes. Just as Browning in "One Word More" admires the complete Renaissance man, the Dante who could paint an angel and the Raphael who could write a century of sonnets, so Keats admires Shakespeare, a god of many masks, for being Iago as well as Imogen, a poet of a wide and comprehensive soul. Browning's Aristophanes prophetically ascribes to Shakespeare the same capacity to see life steadily and see it whole that Arnold ascribes to Sophocles. Taking "in every side at once, / And not successively," the great genius of the "Tin-islands" will be "hailed superior" to the Greeks, Aristophanes predicts, because he combines "High and Low" in equal measure and in tragedy and comedy alike (*Aristophanes' Apology,* lines 142–46).[3]

Right about what he implicitly denies but wrong about what he explicitly asserts, Arnold claims in a letter to Clough, "Shakespeare, Shakespeare, you are as obscure as life" (1932, 63). If Shakespeare sometimes sounds obscure, it is because the thought he is trying to formulate is genuinely difficult, not because it is obscurely expressed. The force of Arnold's complaint lies in what it implicitly denies. Since Shakespeare, even in his sonnets, is never a transparent, confessional poet, and since he has retreated in his plays behind multiple personae, the ghost behind the masks is invisible. Who has ever seen Shakespeare plain, unmasked, or naked to the eye?[4]

Shakespeare has all the Baconian requirements: his wide reading in Ovid, Plutarch, and Montaigne makes him a full man; his mastery of rhetoric and logic, an exact man; and his delight in witty repartee, a ready man. Through all his wisdom, wit, and logic there shine the warmth, simplicity, and loving-kindness that endeared "gentle Will" to his contemporaries. Shakespeare and his Victorian heirs think most originally in lyrics and sonnets, in monologues, soliloquies, and dramatic dialogues. I have written this work of academic criticism, not for students of theater and performance, but for readers who enjoy the language of poets whose happiest thoughts, though no less exacting or exploratory, are more fortuitous, less deliberate, than the inquiries of philosophers.

PART I

POETIC BEGINNINGS

1

Word and Love Games

BEROWNE AND IDA'S PRINCE

IN *LOVE'S LABOR'S LOST,* SHAKESPEARE SHOWS WHAT HAPPENS WHEN the Princess of France and a bevy of her ladies visit the little academy of Navarre, a stronghold of young male courtiers and pedants resolved to woo their female guests with displays of extravagant erudition and wit. The young playwright celebrates his love affair with words while poking fun at their potential absurdity and excess. The play's most brilliant adaptation, Tennyson's *The Princess,* is an aspirant's discovery of his own genius as a lyric poet. Tennyson also delights in the adolescent pranks of male transvestites, and gently satirizes the grand pretentiousness of Ida's schemes for educational reform. Since the pretensions of Ida and her female colleagues are no less absurd than the pranks of the transvestite Prince and his fellow intruders, Tennyson, like Shakespeare, is able both to mock what he values and to celebrate what he mocks.

Like Mercutio's Queen Mab speech in *Romeo and Juliet,* Berowne's discourse on light in *Love's Labor's Lost* is a spontaneous display of intellectual exuberance and wit. Ida's exquisite songs and lyrics in *The Princess* function as the emotional counterpart of such esprit. They are specimens of "word-music," a phrase one critic uses to describe verse "with a minimum of meaning... (but of maximum emotional value... to the character that has to speak it)" (Granville-Barker, 1946–47, 2:418). Tennyson's satire on women's rights and educational reform is now as dated as Shakespeare's attack on academic pedantry. But just as *The Princess* lives today in the acknowledged beauty of its songs and lyrics, so many of the dead jokes and lost topical allusions in *Love's Labor's Lost* are redeemed by flashes of poetic exuberance and wit. Amid his verbal gymnastics and brilliant antics as a poet, Shakespeare is learning his art as a dramatist. Tennyson's very limits as a writer of satiric narrative and mock-epic verse also help him mature as a writer of songs and lyrics. In each case the weakness of the aspiring satirist is the strength of the evolving playwright or poet.

❖ ❖ ❖

The most artful youth in the retinue of Navarre's king is Berowne, whose overflow of high spirits is both an exercise in sophisticated wit and a criticism of wit's excess. Even in praising the female eye, Berowne is trapped in a toil of narcissism.

> Why! all delights are vain, but that most vain
> Which with pain purchas'd doth inherit pain:
> As, painfully to pore upon a book
> To seek the light of truth; while truth the while
> Doth falsely blind the eyesight of his look.
> (*Love's Labor's Lost* 1.1.72–76)

Addicted to couplets and snared by his use of four rhymes in two lines, Berowne is more enamored of the idea and language of love than of love itself. To fall in love with words that lack the light of reason and invention is to woo the mirror reflection of love, its shadow not its substance. In a riot of self-destructive wit, Berowne uses multiple meanings of light to show that the eye made blind by study beholds neither light nor knowledge but only darkness.

> Light seeking light doth light of light beguile:
> So, ere you find where light in darkness lies,
> Your light grows dark by losing of your eyes.
> Study me how to please the eye indeed,
> By fixing it upon a fairer eye.
> (1.1.77–81)

Though the sixfold play on "light" is "the sheer exuberance of an athlete who has discovered that he can play what game he likes with words," G. B. Harrison believes the speech is still important. "It is the answer of the 'upstart crow' whose Latin was little and whose Greek was less to those intellectual snobs who believed all learning lived in books" (1947, 890).

Berowne never loves any woman as ardently as the Prince comes to love Ida in Tennyson's version of *Love's Labor's Lost.* In truth, Berowne's climactic speech, purportedly a celebration of love's victory over learning, is little more than a triumph of special pleading and paradox. As Harold Bloom says, the speech "is superbly free of any concern for Rosaline, ostensible object of his passion" (1998, 130).

> O! we have made a vow to study, lords,
> And in that vow we have forsworn our books:
> For when would you, my liege, or you, or you,
> In leaden contemplation have found out

Such fiery numbers as the prompting eyes
Of beauty's tutors have enrich'd you with?

(4.3.315–20)

More in love with learning than with women, Berowne confesses to forswearing books only because he finds in "the prompting eyes" of women better tutors of beauty than Plato or the love poets he studies. A scholar's praise of love begets an infinite regress, since he finds in women's eyes new libraries in which endlessly to study and extend his learning by giving "to every power a double power, / Above their functions and their offices" (4.3.328–29). Within each power or faculty, a male admirer of women sees a double (or reflex) image of that power. Abounding in the same exaggerated tropes and conceits of courtly love that Romeo uses before falling in love with Juliet, Berowne's witty discourse serves only to confirm and reinforce a pervasive male narcissism.

Using the mirror trope chiasmus—"a word that all men love," "a word that loves all men"—Berowne appeals to the biblical paradox that we must lose our life to find it. Since St. Paul claims that charity fulfills the law, and since charity is only another name for love, it follows with the force of a syllogism that we men should forsake our studies for the love of women.

It is religion to be thus forsworn;
For charity itself fulfils the law;
And who can sever love from charity?

(4.3.360–62)

Shakespeare complicates the natural order of thoughts by introducing chains of syllogistic reasoning, artificial resemblances between words like "grace" and "disgraced" (1.1.3), and even a tautology designed to clinch an argument: "And who can sever love from charity?" (4.3.362). Such artifice has more affinity with Mercutio's volatile discourse on Queen Mab than with the fire that ignites Romeo and Juliet and blasts the lovers into a new dimension. As an art of spontaneous combustion, the pyrotechnics of Berowne and Mercutio has no efficient cause. After burning a combustible world in one small space, both speakers finish in a flare, leaving only "airy nothings" in their wake. As Coleridge says, Berowne makes "the words themselves the subjects and materials of . . . surplus action." The language "agitates our limbs and forces our very gestures into states of high excitement" (1930, 1, 96).

Late in the play, this acrobat of language decides to renounce the "taffeta phrases," "silken terms precise," and "three-piled hyperboles" (5.2.406–10) that make his head a grave rather than a treasure-house of learning. But as Peter Hyland notes, the speech in which Berowne renounces an affected style (5.2.394–415) is itself affected, consisting "of five quatrains and a final rhyming couplet," and whose "last fourteen lines constitute a sonnet" (1996, 116).

Like Shakespeare's academy, institutes of learning are too often Pentagons of pedantry that chain rather than liberate the muses. C. L. Barber believes that "the most delightful touch in the whole play is the exchange that concludes Berowne's reformation, in which he playfully betrays the fact that his mockery of sophistication is sophisticated, and Rosaline underscores the point as she deftly withdraws the hand she has taken" (1972, 108).

> And to begin: wench, so God help me, law!
> My love to thee is sound, sans crack or flaw.
> Rosaline. Sans "sans," I pray you!
>
> (5.2.414–16)

It is easier for Berowne and his male companions to renounce romance than their love affair with word games and wit.

The extravagant conceits Berowne vows to censure are a symptom of Romeo's distemper when, like Berowne, he falls in love with the idea of being in love. Instead of wooing his shadowy mistress, "the fair Rosaline," Romeo retires from the world as sick at heart as an invalid who has just been diagnosed with a serious attack of courtly love.

> Here's much to do with hate, but more with love.
> Why then, O brawling love! O loving hate!
> O anything, of nothing first create!
> O heavy lightness! serious vanity!
> Misshapen chaos of well-seeming forms!
> Feather of lead, bright smoke, cold fire,
> sick health!
>
> (*Romeo and Juliet* 1.1.182–87)

Witty but mannered, and punctuated by no fewer than seven exclamation points, this outburst by Romeo is not the idiom of heartfelt love. Lacking the gravity and pith of the Prince's paradoxes ("See what a scourge is laid upon your hate, / That heaven finds means to kill your joys with love" [5.3.293–94]), the oxymorons of "brawling love" and "loving hate" imitate the overflow of Berowne's heady high spirits. No youth deeply in love would dissipate his fire in a volley of antonyms as effervescent yet coldly labored as "feather of lead, bright smoke, cold fire, sick health" (1.1.187). The moment the god descends and pierces Romeo's heart with passion for a warm and ardent teenage girl, the lover demands to know Juliet's name. Instead of retreating from the world, he seizes the first opportunity to speak to her.

Like Berowne, the conceited Osric is another Shakespearean prototype of the Victorian aesthete. His praise of Laertes, a vapor of airy nothings, fails to condense into any meaning Horatio can discern.

> ... indeed to speak feelingly of him, he is the card
> or calendar of gentry, for you shall find in him the
> continent of what part a gentleman would see.
> (*Hamlet* 5.2.113–16)

Instead of wrapping his subject in raw breath, Osric conceals it in silken phrases—"card or calendar of gentry," "continent of what part"—whose euphuistic pairings are emptier of content than even the flights of fancy favored by Mercutio or Berowne. Since any praise Osric has to offer is lost in a maze of words, Horatio wonders if it might be possible to understand him "in another tongue."

Coruscating on a thin ice of verbal artifice, the symbolism of some Pre-Raphaelite poets and aesthetes is as "unconsummated" as the aborted love-making in *Love's Labor's Lost.* D. G. Rossetti's "cup of three in "The Wood-spurge" (line 16), his "feast-day of the sun" in "The Hill Summit" (line 1), and William Morris's strange choosing cloths in "The Defense of Guenevere" have all the hallmarks of a conventional symbolism except one: an assigned connotation. Whereas T. S. Eliot's "blue" in "Ash Wednesday" has a symbolic meaning, "blue of larkspur, blue of Mary's color" (4.10), the significance of Morris's "blue" in "The Defence of Guenevere" is purely arbitrary, a triumph of caprice over logic, of surprise over expectation.

> "And one of these strange choosing cloths was blue,
> Wavy and long, and one cut short and red;
> No man could tell the better of the two.
>
> "After a shivering half-hour you said:
> 'God help! heaven's color, the blue:' and he said, 'hell.'"
> ("The Defence of Guenevere," lines 34–38)

In *The Merchant of Venice* words rhyming with "lead"—"bred," "head," and "nourishéd"—guide Bassanio to his choice of the proper lead casket.

> Tell me where is fancy bred,
> Or in the heart or in the head?
> How begot, how nourishéd?
> Reply, reply.
> (*The Merchant of Venice* 3.2.63–66)

But in Morris's poem, the rhyme of "said" with "red," which would have led to the right choice of color, is too oblique to be helpful. In the suppressed rhyme of "blue" with "true," fate seems to be misleading Guenevere by mixing the clues. It is possible, of course, that Morris expects Guenevere to know that blue, originally a symbol of fidelity in love, came in the Middle Ages to represent its own opposite. As Johan Huizinga explains, "by a very curious transition, blue, instead of being the color of faithful love, came to mean infidelity, too, and next, beside the faithless wife, marked the dupe. In Holland the blue cloak designated an adulterous woman, in France the "cote bleue" denotes a cuckold. At last blue was the color of fools in general" (1949, 292).

Like Berowne and Osric, some Victorian poets favor sound over sense. Tennyson's "moan of doves in immemorial elms / And murmur of innumerable bees" (*The Princess* 7.206–7) is a triumph of alliterative virtuosity. But it is too contrived to succeed completely as imitative harmony. More effective is the restrained alignment of sound with sense in the opening lines of "Oenone": "There lies a vale in Ida, lovelier / Than all the valleys of Ionian hills" (lines 1–2). The alliteration is sinuous. The unstressed feet wind their way through peaks of accented consonants and open vowels with as much tenacity and grace as the vale of Ida and other valleys wind their way through Ionian hills. But too often Victorian alliteration has to be rescued from the wreckage of sound left littered in its wake by a "maze of monotonous murmur, / Where reason roves ruined by rhyme" (Swinburne, "Poeta Loquitur," lines 9–10). Rivaling Osric's virtuosity and Berowne's play on six forms of "light," Swinburne in "The Garden of Proserpine" revels in a volley of triple feminine rhymes and a ripple of seven alliterating w's, which imitate the trembling of the lip in the initial stages of weeping.

> Wan waves and wet winds labour,
> Weak ships and spirits steer;
> They drive adrift, and whither
> They wot not who makes thither;
> But no such words blow hither,
> And no such things grow here.
> (lines 19–24)

We know that as a Cambridge undergraduate Tennyson took part in the Apostles' performance of several of Shakespeare's plays. And as Linda H. Peterson has shown, the poet was also "part of an artistic coterie" that in the late 1820s and early 1830s "used Shakespeare's heroines as a vehicle for commenting on modern womanhood" (2009, 28). Indeed, in his youthful correspondence Tennyson is as addicted to lighthearted allusions to Shakespeare as Berowne is addicted to the extravagant idioms of love poetry. Alfred's offhand, often witty references range from allusions to *Measure for Measure* and *As You Like It* to quotations from *Pericles, Hamlet,* and *Othello.* Punning on the name of the Milnes' family seat in Bantry, Tennyson tells Brookfield that "as Shakespeare says, 'We must be married or we live in Bawtry (*As You Like It* 3.3.99), wherefore being a batchelor [*sic*] am I settled here" (1981, 142). Equally exuberant, if less flippant, is the young Shakespearean's generous tribute to Edward FitzGerald, whom he calls "as just a man / As e'er my conversation coped withal" (*Hamlet* 3.2.59; Tennyson, 1981, 132). In early letters to his friends a Shakespearean comparison comes as naturally to Tennyson as a biblical or classical allusion comes to Milton.[1]

In *The Princess,* Tennyson reverses the action of *Love's Labor's Lost* by allowing the Prince and a group of young male friends to invade a college established by Princess Ida for the education of women. In Tennyson's version of *Love's Labor's Lost,* the Prince finds the protocols of Ida's academy as charming but absurd as Berowne comes to find the word and love games of the academy at Navarre. Cross-dressing, a familiar device in Shakespeare's comedies, takes advantage of the use of boy actors in an all-male cast. The Prologue pokes fun at this device in the draping of Sir Ralph in female silks. The reversal of sexual roles takes a more alarming turn when the women push the transvestites from rocks and try to drown them in brooks. At first there are no real objects of sexual desire in an all-female academy, and it is natural that the Prince should turn to Florian, and Ida to Psyche. The transition from these ennobling but limited friendships to love between the Princess and the Prince is the kind of growth that takes place in Tennyson's life after Hallam's death and his marriage to Emily Sellwood. Like Shakespeare in *Love's Labor's Lost,* Tennyson deftly balances absurdities in the academy with qualities that are immensely appealing. Though the "lucid marbles" and "ample awnings gay" (2.10–11) strain for a mock-epic Miltonic effect, their luxury also highlights the exquisite slightness of the ritual. The point of comparing the brightly attired intruders in their academic silks to "rich moths" emerging from "dusk cocoons" (2.5) lies in the wit of the simile's beautiful diminution.

Like the Prince's timidities and seizures, Ida's repressed sexuality taps a deeper psychic life than any psychology Shakespeare chooses to explore in *Love's Labor's Lost.* Struggling in the stream, Ida is first compared to a "blossomed branch / Rapt to the . . . fall"; a moment later the figurative branch becomes the literal branches of a tree which the Prince catches and drags down (4.161–62). The Prince's sexual fantasy is almost immediately confirmed in the description of the gates, those "valves / Of open-work" that bear the mark of the hunter's "rash intrusion, manlike"—a bawdy mock-epic touch, also oddly Miltonic (4.184–86). The next moment the branches of the tree, now the limbs of Ida struggling in the stream, turn into the horns of Actaeon, transfixed into a stag, "grimly spiked," his punishment for gazing on Diana (4.188). Gradually the suppressed psychic forces begin to surface in ten inserted songs and lyrics that chart in the unquiet hearts of Ida and the Prince the deeper feelings Shakespeare explores in comedies like *As You Like It* and *Twelfth Night.*

The song "Ask me no more" from *The Princess* is charged with more feeling than any encounter in *Love's Labor's Lost.* The woman in the song, though resisting love, is also dying of it. She repeats the words "Ask me no more," not to tranquilize herself, but to charge the phrase with more and more feeling. The surprising force of the lyric comes partly from metrical bareness and partly from the swift progression in intimacy: "fond," "friend," "dear love" (lines 4, 8, 14). Until the surrender of the last stanza, question and petition—"when have I answered thee? / Ask me no more" (4–5); "Ask me no more: what answer should I give?" (6)—continue to echo and re-echo in a finely balanced chiasmus of sound and sense.

The artifice of Berowne's word games is to the heartfelt wooing of Ida's Prince what an operatic comedy is to a real-life romance. In the lyric "O Swallow, Swallow" (4.75–98), which preserves a strangely charming blend of pastoral simplicity and human insight, the lover pleads with the swallow to intervene with the woman who is deaf to his suit. In the lyric "Now sleeps the crimson petal" (7.161–74), the true marvel occurs in a blending so complete that the lily loses itself in the lake. In the penetration of the male form by the lily, Tennyson appropriately reverses the sexual metaphor. The receiving element is first equated with the woman—"the Earth all Danaë" (167) to the stars—and then with the man, "the bosom of the lake" that enfolds the lily (172). By the end of the lyric, the male and female elements, representing the Prince and Ida, no longer consciously embrace but slip into each other, lost in a coupling of pronouns—"my dearest, thou" (173)—and a grammatical identity of persons.

An important feature of Shakespeare's sensuous music is the strong sense of empathy it achieves with the aid of active verbs and concrete images. When Shakespeare writes of "daffodils / That come before the swallow dares, and take / The winds of March with beauty" (*The Winter's Tale* 4.3.118–20), he takes away the reader's breath, just as the daring flowers catch and take away the breath of the winds. A force of nature that daunts the swallows is "taken" in a double sense: it is ravished by the bold beauty of the flowers, but also made captive by them. Such is the "natural magic" of these words that, as Matthew Arnold says in his essay "Maurice de Guerin," "we feel ourselves to be in contact with the essential nature" of the daffodils and March winds. "No longer bewildered and oppressed by them," we "have their secret, and [are] in harmony with them; and this feeling calms and satisfies us as no other can" (1964, 61).

In *The Merchant of Venice,* Shakespeare gives ballast to the lightweight Lorenzo by attuning his ear to the same exalted music of the spheres that Milton celebrates in his ode "At a Solemn Music."

> How sweet the moonlight sleeps upon this bank!
> Here will we sit and let the sounds of music
> Creep into our ears. Soft stillness and the night
> Become the touches of sweet harmony.
> (*The Merchant of Venice* 5.1.54–57)

Weighing the quantity of every vowel he breathes, Lorenzo makes each accented syllable coincide with a long quantity, except for the vowels in "sit" and "let." Though music dominates, its sounds are gently reinforced by sensations of touch, taste, and sight. The touches of both harmony and moonlight are said to be sweet, and like the unheard melodies in Keats's "Ode to a Grecian Urn," the music is tactile in its very capacity to be still. As a cushion to the ear, silence is described as "soft": "Soft stillness and the night / Become the touches of sweet harmony." Adorned "with patines of bright gold," Heaven is visually alive and luminous. Its floor of thickly inlaid disks supports the tread of choiring spheres. And as these heavenly orbs sing to the cherubim in defiance of the laws of modern astronomy, only our deafness, the "muddy vesture of decay," prevents our hearing their music even now.[2]

Equally magical is the lover's lyric of welcome to the advent of night in *The Princess.* As the nocturnal fire-fly replaces the waving cypresses and winking goldfish, a yearning awakens in the young lover. He becomes more a seer than a painter of landscape, and under his eye a transformation takes place that is as marvelous as "the Celtic aerialness and magic" that lighten Lorenzo's words in *The Merchant of Venice.*

> "Now sleeps the crimson petal, now the white
> Nor waves the cypress in the palace walk
> Nor winks the gold fins in the porphyry font.
> The fire-fly wakens; waken thou with me.
>
> Now droops the milk-white peacock like a ghost,
> And like a ghost she glimmers on to me.
>
> Now lies the Earth all Danaë to the stars,
> And all thy heart lies open unto me.

> Now slides the silent meteor on, and leaves
> A shining furrow, as thy thoughts in me.
>
> Now folds the lily all her sweetness up,
> And slips into the bosom of the lake.
> So fold thyself, my dearest, thou, and slip
> Into my bosom and be lost in me."
>
> (*The Princess* 7.161–74)

In an unbroken chain of visual mergings, the beloved, the meteor, and the stars join together in cosmic space, with the lover as one of the marveling participants. The man and the woman, the stars and the earth, the lily and the lake become mirror images of each other. Fish and peacocks are made insubstantial by shimmering verbs: "winks" and "glimmers" (163, 166). Meteors slide down to earth, and earth itself is ploughed into "a shining furrow" (170), gleaming fitfully across a nighttime sky. The discrete photographic details of the opening stanza—the microscopic charm of the winking "fin" and "firefly" (163–64)—are allowed to fuse in a blending of the drooping peacock with the glimmering ghost, and of the sliding meteor with a shining plough. Other images join heaven to earth and approximate in the sleeping petal and folding flower a water-lily painting by Monet. Though Lorenzo's lines on music never allude to a lover's sigh, they clearly breathe it: indeed, a sigh suffuses every syllable he speaks. Though Tennyson's lover never mentions sexual union with his mistress, every image of his lyric celebrates a consummation of their love.

Shakespeare's belief that ideal young manhood unites masculine and female qualities appears to have shaped Tennyson's praise of "manhood fused with female grace" in both *In Memoriam* (109.17) and *The Princess* (7.263–64): "Yet in the long years liker they must grow; / The man be more of woman, she of man." Though Tennyson "prizes that soul where man and woman meet," and celebrates the wife who combines "all the charms of woman" with "all the breadth of man" in "Locksley Hall Sixty Years After" (line 48), he is equally critical of the effeminacy of the water-fly Osric and the dandy, Bulwer-Lytton, who affects an effeminate manner. Shakespeare's Adonis combines male strength and beauty with the modesty of a charming young virgin. As in *The Tempest,* where Prospero delays the sexual union of Ferdinand and Miranda, Shakespeare also protests against "too early initiation into sexual experience . . . 'Who plucks the bud before one leaf put forth?'" (Goddard, 1951, 21). Seeking a blend of male and female qualities, Tennyson shares Shakespeare's view that "the imagination . . . is an hermaphrodite; in proportion as men and women become imaginative they tend, without losing the dominant characteristics of their own sex, to take on those of the other. Adonis is a far-off prophecy of Ariel" (Goddard, 1951, 22).

Behind the great lyric Ida reads aloud, "Come down, O maid," we hear Shakespeare's virgin Perdita, who shocks the audience by casually dropping the verb "breed."

> No more than were I painted, I would wish
> This youth should say 'twere well: and only therefore
> Desire to breed by me.
>
> (*The Winter's Tale* 4.4.101–3)

Though fiercely virtuous like Perdita, Ida realizes that snow-pure virginity is barren. Her "white ravine" and "firths of ice" (7.190–91) are as terrifying to any aspiring suitor or Alpine mountaineer as Wordsworth's "spots of time" in *The Prelude.*

> Come down, O maid, from yonder mountain height,
> What pleasure lives in height (the shepherd sang),
> In height and cold, the splendor of the hills?
> But cease to move so near the heavens, and cease
> To glide a sunbeam by the blasted pine,
> To sit upon a star upon the sparkling spire;
> And come, for Love is of the valley, come,
> For Love is of the valley, come thou down
> And find him.
>
> (*The Princess* 7.177–85)

Like the frigid mountain, a virgin anxious to keep men at a distance must learn to balance the desolation of the Jungfrau against reassuring impressions of community and pastoral warmth. Like Mercutio's virtuoso performance in *Romeo and Juliet* and some of Shakespeare's most ravishing lyrics, the songs and lyrics in *The Princess* may have little, except as emotional poems, to tell us. But if they are "airy nothings," they are also, like Shakespeare's songs, among the most beautiful in the language.

2

The Trespass of Intimacy

ARTISTS IN CRIME

TO SHAKESPEARE BROWNING OWES HIS VERY ORIGINS AS A POET. He told J. S. Mill that a performance of Edmund Kean as Richard Crookback led him to write *Pauline,* his first attempt to realize a childish scheme "to *act,* as well to make verses, music, and God knows . . . what castles in Spain" (1981, 1, 1021). Part of the magic Browning shares with Shakespeare in this "Fool's Paradise" is an ability to "assume and realize" different characters. It includes an uncanny power to make an audience intimate with dupes, charlatans, and villains. By constantly explaining to an audience the traps he is setting, Richard Crookback makes his victims seem obtuse. But the purpose of his explanation is not just to diminish Anne or Prince Edward but to draw in the playgoer. By taking us "completely into the destroyer's confidence as if we were trusted accomplices" (Harbage, 1963, 355), a villain like Richard, Iago, or Browning's own Duke of Ferrara is allowed to encroach on our trust. Enforced intimacy invades our comfort zone. It comes uncomfortably close to breaking down taboos.

Shakespeare's portrayal of Richard Crookback is marked by what one critic calls "juvenility and genius. Nothing Shakespeare ever wrote was apparently done with more gusto" (Goddard, 1951, 35). The "sense of triumph in power, in exuberance of invention" is equally evident in Browning's Duke and the Spanish monk. At once juvenile and diabolical, they play with the Duchess's portrait or with the monk's enemy, Brother Lawrence, as a delinquent child might play with a toy. After the success of *Dramatic Lyrics* and *Richard III,* Browning and Shakespeare might easily have continued to exploit the early popularity of artists in crime like the Duke of Ferrara or Richard Crookback. But instead of inventing any fictional character he chooses, Browning, like Shakespeare, comes under a different spell: the lure of historical re-creation. Not content with mere pretense, Browning deepens his art in *Men and Women* and *Dramatis Personae* by resuscitating historical or literary personages, Renaissance artists like Fra Lippo Lippi and Andrea del Sarto, whose histories are recorded in Vasari's *Lives of the Artists,* or else fictional characters like Shakespeare's own Caliban.[1] In the same way, Shakespeare himself has to balance the illusions of an easy theatrical success like *The Comedy of Errors* with the demanding concern for fact of historical plays like the three parts of *King Henry VI.* As Harold Goddard paradoxically reflects, "It may have been history that saved him from the theatre" (1951, 56).

Browning's transition from an early theatrical masterpiece like "My Last Duchess" to the psychological and intellectual complexities of monologues by Cleon, Karshish, and St. John marks an important development in his effort to portray "action in character" rather than "character in action." It parallels Shakespeare's growing mastery of an irresolute, antiphonal style, which exists in an oddly crude and wooden form in Crookback's last soliloquy in *Richard III.* Shakespeare's attempt to "hammer out" what Stephen Greenblatt calls "a kind of inner theatre" (2004, 300) is better achieved in Richard II's elegant prison soliloquy and (most notably) in the less polished but intellectually more supple soliloquy in which Brutus debates with himself the reasons for and against killing Caesar.

A prototype of Browning's aesthetic criminals, Richard adorns his villainy with grotesque aesthetic touches. When he murders Henry, he says his blood-stained sword sheds "purple tears" for "the poor king's death" (*3 Henry VI* 5.6.63–64). Claiming that he "came into the world with [his] legs forward" (71) in order to waste no time removing relatives with better claims to the throne, Richard boasts that the teeth he is born with has allowed him to "snarl and bite and play the dog" in a progressive decline from the human to the animal. Though Richard's skill with words shows he is a poet, he realizes that poetry, like love, requires some consonance or harmony of souls. But since Richard is "[himself] alone" (83), he is both one of a kind and solitary. He has "no brother" and is "like no brother" (80). Being loveless and unique, he rhymes and chimes with nothing.

Constantly watching and marveling at his brilliance as an actor and a villain, Richard turns his self-advertised deformity and wickedness into a subject for art. Since the hunchbacked Richard cannot win at love, he will win as an artist of crime, as an imaginative villain. A dog himself who is barked at by other dogs as he limps past them, Richard's only delight is to see his shadow in the sun. Eclipsed by the son of York, a sun that leaves his younger brother in the shade, Richard must make his own deformed shape, both physical and moral, the haunt and the main region of his song.

His second soliloquy is a marvel of self-invention in which Richard gloats over his murder of Prince Edward and his successful wooing, against all odds, of the prince's widow, Anne. Alternating between self-deception about his attractiveness as a lover and a candid anatomy of his physical deformities, Richard conveniently elides the fact that Anne loathes the Duke and yields to his suit only because she is forced to. He chides Anne for preferring his own deformities and dissembling looks to the handsome Edward, "Young, valiant, wise, and, no doubt royal" (*Richard III* 1.3.245), just as Hamlet rebukes his mother for failing to see that his father is to Claudius what Hyperion is to a satyr. Like an actor experimenting with different roles in his repertory, Richard at one moment takes pleasure in exaggerating his misshapen form and at the next moment concedes he has "crept" into "favor with [himself]," whom he now regards as a "marvelous proper man." Affecting a vain pride in his appearance, he has even bought a glass, he says, "That I may see my shadow as I pass" (264).

Only in his third and last soliloquy does Richard's theatrical artifice and wit desert him. Engulfed in calamity, the artist in villainy no longer has leisure to view himself with an actor's detachment. Unable to decide whether he loves or hates himself, Richard's soliloquy is riddling without being witty and convincing as psychology without being fully intelligible as art. Oscillating between love of the ambitious duke and hatred of the murderer, Richard is too panic-stricken to be lucid. "I am a villain: yet I lie, I am not / Fool, of thyself speak well; fool, do not flatter" (5.3.191–92). The psychology itself is easier to understand than the artlessly confused way in which Shakespeare uses simple oppositions to express it. The psychology is too intractable and the self-pity too blatant for artifice. Still the admiring spectator of his own criminal deeds, Richard becomes at the end a single-minded, avenging power, like the three ghosts of his nightmare.

In developing the pull of a two-way antiphonal style, Brutus's soliloquy in the orchard in *Julius Caesar* represents a notable advance over *Richard III*. Though his motive in killing Caesar is more grotesque and less intelligible than Cassius's motive, which is understandable personal animus, the self-divided Brutus is more lucid and dispassionately reflective than the disintegrating Richard Crookback.

> It must be by his death; and for my part,
> I know no personal cause to spurn at him
> But for the general.
>
> (*Julius Caesar* 2.1.10–12)

What exactly will be satisfied by Caesar's death: the envy or ambition of his rivals; the animus of Brutus; the political welfare of Rome? As in a Browning monologue, an internal debate is already under way. But far from hastening to a conclusion, Brutus is delayed by second thoughts: "I know no personal cause," he concedes at the outset. In substituting general principle for personal conviction, Brutus is already surrendering to that intolerable love of abstraction condemned by A. N. Whitehead as a major vice of the intellect.

As the Euclid of a new moral geometry, unique to the Stoics and himself, Brutus wants to prove Caesar's assassination is necessary. Assigned the task, he sets out like a good logician to prove it. All dictators threatening to destroy the Roman republic must be removed; Caesar poses such a threat; therefore Caesar should be killed. Though the conclusion follows with logical rigor, Brutus half realizes that both the major and minor premises of the syllogism harbor serious material fallacies. There are surely other ways of blocking or removing Caesar than by murdering him. And though some dictators might abuse their power, Caesar is unlikely to do so, since he has betrayed no imperial ambition in the past. Brutus's wise-sounding aphorism that pretense of humility is a ladder on which ambition climbs to power owes less to logic than to hearsay. It qualifies as "common proof" (2.1.21) only in the sense that, like most aphorisms, it encapsulates a form of half-intuitive wisdom, of ready application in emergencies, which is precisely how Edmund Burke defines prejudice. As Brutus tosses to and fro, caught between surges of indictment and receding waves of counterargument and concession, it is impossible not to chart an undertow of deep reluctance and self-doubt in his soliloquy.

The least artful way for a soliloquist to enlist a playgoer as an ally or accomplice is to address him directly. Better suited to comedies than tragedies, such a trespass on a playgoer's intimacy is the actor's equivalent of a stand-up comedian's aside or the knowing wink of an ironist. Whereas "an audience looks at a tragedian," Wilde says only "a comedian looks at his audience" (1968, 125). Though actors may use the device to woo an audience or make it laugh, there is seldom textual warrant for it in Shakespeare's plays. The principal exception occurs in Shakespeare's early comedy *The Two Gentlemen of Verona,* where Launce briefly shatters the dramatic illusion by asking the audience to act as his advocate and judge. When his dog, Crab, pisses under the Duke's table, Launce saves Crab from a whipping by confessing to the deed himself. "You shall judge," Launce tells the audience, whether or not his dog would have been hanged if he had not taken the blame personally (4.4.17–18). He cannot resist adding pleasure to his joke by immediately sharing it with the playgoer.

A subtler way for a character to trespass on our intimacy is to enter our consciousness. Hamlet manages to inhabit our soul. We share too many of his angelic apprehensions to see him only as an avenger. We are touched by too many generous and humane impulses in Macbeth, a murderer with the imagination of a poet, to see him only as a villain. It is as hard for a playgoer to surrender his ties to Macbeth as it is for Macbeth himself to renounce the higher angels of his nature. He retains a keen sense of the graces "which should accompany old age, / As honor, love, obedience, troops of friends," although he knows he "must not look to have" them (*Macbeth* 5.3.24–26). Trapped in several different perceptions of himself, Macbeth has established too many bonds with the audience to have them broken completely once he settles on the course of a relentless (if repentant) murderer, the only choice that seems to serve his ends after killing Duncan. When Macbeth dies, something dies in the consciousness of each playgoer, too.

No Victorian monologue takes the reader as directly into the poet's confidence as Launce takes the audience in *The Two Gentlemen of Verona*. It is true that Browning's Bishop Blougram crosses his auditor's comfort zone when he keeps calling him his "friend." "We're two college friends, suppose," he tells the skeptic ("Bishop Blougram's Apology," line 145). In becoming more intimate with Gigadibs than the skeptic wants, he even insinuates that Gigadibs, instead of despising the bishop, would like to be a confidant and friend. But intimacy with an auditor is not to be confused with trespassing on the privacy or comfort zone of a reader. In "Bishop Blougram's Apology," the closest Browning comes to intruding on our space is when he removes his mask in the epilogue and tells us in a metafictional aside that the Bishop "said true things, but called them by wrong names" (line 996).

Less overt are Browning's two attempts to invade the reader's space in "Fra Lippo Lippi." On one occasion the poet speaks over Fra Lippo's head in a direct homiletic address to the reader (lines 156–57). On a later occasion Fra Lippo abruptly emerges from a corner of his own painting, where one least expects to find him (361). This reversal of perspective repeats the pattern established in the opening line, where the monk steps through a frame to involve the reader directly in his own world: "I am poor brother Lippo, by your leave!" By carefully aligning himself with the reader and with the police officers who arrest him—"You speak no Latin more than I, belike" (281)—Fra Lippo converts his argument against the ascetic life into a partly ad hominem argument against its unprepossessing advocate, the Prior. Like one of Matthew Arnold's "hangdog" terms, "Latin" is a pejorative label that Fra Lippo uses to mock the Prior's pretentious vocabulary of "spiritual" motivation: "Give us no more of body than shows soul!" As purely conceptual language, it lacks the rich tonalities of those passages in which Fra Lippo celebrates an incorruptible impulse to glorify God and His creation. But unless the monk returns with a jolt to his sensual base ("I'm a beast, I know" [270]), his poem will cease to be a dramatic monologue—an attempt by Fra Lippo to secure some personal advantage from the officers—and will turn into a homily instead.

More alarming is Thackeray's invasion of our space in his sermon on death in *Vanity Fair.* Instead of charming or seducing the reader, the homilist drags him without warning into the dismal fellowship of the dead. This trespass of intimacy is Thackeray's version of Donne's injunction "Ask not for whom the bell tolls; it tolls for thee."

> However much you may be mourned, your widow will like to have her weeds neatly made—the cook will send or come up to ask about dinner—the survivors will soon bear to look at your picture over the mantelpiece, which will presently be deposed from the place of honour, to make way for the portrait of the son who reigns. (chap. 61)

At first Thackeray uses the second-person pronoun as an innocuous synonym for "one" or Everyman: "What a memento of Life, Death, and Vanity it is—that arch and stair—if you choose to consider it" (chap. 61). But the next time the pronoun is used, it is we, the readers, who have died, and our heirs who have taken possession of our house. As in Johnson's poem "The Vanity of Human Wishes," the form distorted appears to justify the fall, and detestation rids the indignant wall. The portrait's removal, which is the Fall of man in miniature, is *our* fall, and not just the fall of a stern, unloved patriarch in a Victorian novel.

The failure of a dramatic speaker to establish intimacy with an auditor may be a necessary though not sufficient condition of a monologue's capacity to establish intimacy with the reader. Precisely because Browning's Englishman in Italy talks too much about himself to woo Fortu, he seduces *us,* who are intrigued by his covert power plays and thinly disguised sexual fantasies about towering mountains and "soft plains" cowering below them (lines 181–91). Similarly, though Andrea del Sarto talks too much about himself to engage Lucrezia's interest, his habit of revealing more about himself than he is conscious of revealing makes him highly successful in seducing the reader.

It is easier to establish intimacy with a reserved ironist like Fra Lippo Lippi, who pretends to be worse than he is, than with a saintly self-promoter like Tennyson's Simeon Stylites, who pretends to be holier than he is. As a painter of the flesh, which is God's best gift, Fra Lippo is a holy man who conceals his holiness. The masks that veil sanctity help explain the close connection between intimacies of consciousness and the disguises assumed by a champion of reserve like the poet who travels incognito in "How It Strikes a Contemporary." In that monologue the most intimate details of the poet's domestic life with his dog and maid are an object of the speaker's intrusive gaze. But because the poet, as God's deputy, passes through the world incognito, he is more intimate with other people's secrets than they are with his.

He is the ultimate voyeur and spy, who returns the speaker's gaze by gazing on everyone else.

A reader is less gripped by Andrea del Sarto in a purely empathetic way, far less carried away by him, than by the raucous swearing song of the Spanish monk or by the hypnotic incantations of the court lady in "The Laboratory." Yet Browning himself never felt particularly close to these last two speakers. He dismisses his early monologues as "scenes and song-scraps," "mere and very escapes of [his] inner power" (letter of 11 Feb. 1845; 1969, 1:17). In "Andrea del Sarto," by contrast, a poem Browning deeply cared for, the viscera and pulses are much less involved. The less physically swayed he is, the more Browning can create conditions of deep caring and concern. Risking a generalization, we may say that the self-annihilating kind of empathy and the more intimate forms of identification and concern exist in inverse ratio.

In his most intimate monologues, Browning draws us into the orbit of painters like Andrea del Sarto and Fra Lippo Lippi, who are about to be displaced by superior rivals. The sudden volley of short questions at the end of "Andrea del Sarto"—"Must you go? / That Cousin here again? he waits outside?" (lines 219–20)—is like the volley of questions fired off by a bewildered Gloucester at the beginning of *King Lear.* Andrea is breathless, panting to keep up with yesterday's news. Events are overtaking him, just as they are overtaking Gloucester. Though not exactly obscure, Fra Lippo and Andrea pale in the presence of their famous contemporaries. Their plight becomes clearer if we compare them with the protest of Browning's "pictor ignotus," a Salieri among painters, rapidly being eclipsed by a Renaissance Mozart. Pictor ignotus is a Casaubon figure: we can feel the chill descend on his fantasies of greatness, like a touch of death. Just as he feels pushed to the side of his life by the youthful painter who should have sat as a grateful apprentice at the older painter's feet, so Fra Lippo foresees the greatness of hulking Tom, the youth named Guidi, who will soon overtake and eclipse him.

Few Shakespearean soliloquies or Victorian monologues exceed in psychological subtlety Browning's "Andrea del Sarto," whose speaker is closer to Shakespeare's Richard II than to a villain like Iago. As an offstage performer, Andrea is continually inventing roles for himself like Shakespeare's actor-king. After first playing the part of an unappreciated genius, Andrea tries his hand as the faithful husband who places perfection of his domestic life with the disloyal Lucrezia above perfection of his work and loyalty to his patron. Andrea also experiments with the role of the thrifty son whose hard work excuses hardness of heart toward improvident parents. In shifting blame from himself to God and Lucrezia, Andrea is not just being evasive. Like the hard-hearted daughters in *King Lear,* he is also acting in bad faith, and the person he tries hardest to deceive is himself.

Instead of reaching self-understanding, Andrea keeps acting out fantasies that hide his true desires and needs. The little understanding Andrea manages to achieve blocks further understanding. By insulting and finally dismissing Lucrezia, Andrea behaves as if he does not really expect or even want his wife to spend the evening with him. What Andrea half conceals from himself, Browning manages to convey to the reader. It is more satisfying for Andrea to construct a past in which Lucrezia is responsible for the painter's neglect of his parents, his crimes against King Francis, and even his failures as an artist, than it is for him to have a faithful wife or—what is more to the point—to know the truth about himself.

Like Andrea del Sarto's fantasies, Hamlet's hide more than they reveal. In flirting with Ophelia then obscenely abusing and rejecting her, Hamlet is subject to a conflict of desires that deflect onto Ophelia his ambivalent feelings about his mother. Though Gertrude clearly loves Claudius, she ought also to loathe him as the assassin of her first husband, whom Hamlet calls "Hyperion to a satyr." If Ophelia were to have sex with Hamlet, her father's killer, she would be repeating the crimes of Gertrude, who in marrying the killer of Hamlet's father is also committing incest with her brother-in-law. Does Hamlet suspect that "the satyr Claudius [is] his phallic father" (Bloom, 2011, 66)? How far back exactly does Gertrude's incest go? Hamlet borrows deceiving references to murderous impulses and incestuous desires that he can only vicariously experience. As an actor borrows costumes from a wardrobe, so the loan of varied parts from a rich dramatic repertory leads both Hamlet and Andrea into fantasy and possible error rather than the knowledge each is seeking.

Since most of us will be pushed to the side of our lives if we live long enough, Shakespeare's soliloquies, like Browning's monologues, often make us feel closer than we want to feel to old, cast-aside speakers like Gloucester and Lear, who "smells of mortality." Instead of passing with Lear into another world in the full glory of his love for Cordelia, we are afraid of being pushed off the stage or withering dismally into oblivion like Gloucester and his bastard son. Equally appalling is the prospect of being captivated by Iago, whose soliloquies we inhabit at our peril. Iago's virtuosity as an artist of intrigue presumes upon our intimacy. It trespasses on our space. Just when Iago's casuistry is beginning to assume a brain-numbing plausibility, he tears off the mask of wise counselor and friend by disclosing his "divinity of hell" for what it is: "When devils will the blackest sins put on, / They do suggest at first with heavenly shows, / As I do now" (2.3.357–59). We have no desire to be Iago's confidant or friend, and his soliloquies tell us more than we want to hear.

As in Mantegna's portrait of the dead Christ, whose torso and pierced feet are thrust into an observer's face by a daring use of linear perspective, we are brought closer to Iago than we want to come.

No passage in Shakespeare is more intoxicated than the chilling prophecy in which Iago the sorcerer casts his spell over Othello.

> Not poppy, nor mandragora,
> Nor all the drowsy syrups of the world
> Shall ever medicine to thee that sweet sleep—
> Which thou ow'dst yesterday.
>
> (*Othello* 3.3.330–33)

Possessed by thoughts that gnaw the sorcerer's mind like poison, Iago uses Desdemona's ill-fated handkerchief as a drug to incite jealousy, the "green-eyed monster that doth mock the meat it feeds on." As Othello says of the handkerchief, "There's magic in the web of it" (3.4.69).

> My medicine, work! Thus credulous fools are caught;
> And many worthy and chaste dames even thus,
> All guiltless, meet reproach.
>
> (4.1.46–48)

By "quasi-musical, quasi-magical means," as one critic says, Iago's medicine produces in Othello a "rawness of passion, a conflict between innocently suicidal inquiry and a rage almost beyond words" (Kermode, 2000, 178). Wearing his rage as armor, Othello allows Desdemona's pleas to break like waves upon the stubborn stupidity of his repeated demand for "the handkerchief."

> *Othello.* The handkerchief!
> *Desdemona.* I pray talk me of Cassio.
> *Othello.* The handkerchief!
> *Desdemona.* A man that all his time
> Has founded his good fortunes on your love,
> Shar'd dangers with you—
> *Othello.* The handkerchief!
> *Desdemona.* I' faith, you are to blame.
> *Othello.* 'Zounds!
>
> (3.4.93–98)

Othello's unflinching demand acquires the steely strength of a shield. "Rage beyond words," Kermode observes, "was not something the early Shakespeare would have thought of aiming at." Though inarticulate when consumed by rage, Othello is also as lucid as a logician when explaining to Iago in the preceding scene that "I'll see before I doubt; when I doubt prove; / And on the proof" climb a ladder of deduction to a just and sound conclusion (3.3.190–91). Whether the conclusion be jealousy or love, it will be as foolproof, Othello thinks, as a demonstration in Euclidian geometry: QED. But now, as Othello barely articulates his unyielding demand for the handkerchief, "a long experience of theatre has taught Shakespeare a new way of writing poetry" (Kermode, 2000, 178). Willing to forgo eloquence for dramatic effect, and rhetoric for a graceless pause or awkward silence, Shakespeare is a playwright first in *Othello* and a poet second.

All but buried under Iago's unconvincing motive-hunting and implausible pretexts for hating Cassio are a few words that flare out like lightning with the flash of truth. Like Marvell's lover in "To His Coy Mistress," Iago may hear time's winged chariot drawing near, and under the pressure he says something so true that it takes our breath away.

> If Cassio do remain,
> He hath a daily beauty in his life
> That makes me ugly.
>
> (5.1.18–20)

Jealous of a daily beauty in Cassio's life, Iago is offended by anything that seems godlike or genuinely superior to him. Like Judas's betrayal of Christ, Iago's betrayal of Othello "involves a kiss, indeed a same-sex kiss that he fabricates to churn up Othello's jealous suspicions about his wife" (Gubar, 2009, 181). "According to Iago's scheming story, the dreaming Cassio—thinking his bedfellow was Desdemona—would 'kiss me hard / As if he plucked up kisses by the roots / That grew upon my lips'" (*Othello* 3.3.424–26; Gubar, 2009, 381). Oscar Wilde says that all men kill the thing they love. In a better world, Iago might have loved Cassio and been his friend in deed, and not just in pretense. Forced like Judas to witness the master's love and preference for a rival, Iago cannot prevent the raw humanity of jealousy and disappointment from breaking through. In the end, however, Iago's hate cannot be explained, since it is as gratuitous as love. Iago has Judas in his soul. A master of intrigue, who loves entrapment for its own sake, Iago is more than a mere thwarted artist. We cannot understand either Iago or Judas until we understand the mystery of a corrupted human will. Shakespeare, it seems, has a temperamental aversion to Puritans. He dislikes virtuous severity when coupled in Malvolio with a mean mind. The "honest" Iago never does evil so fully and cheerfully as when pretending to act out of conscience for Othello's own welfare. Intolerant of beauty, Iago's ugliness is the darkness that hates light. "The torchbearer turned incendiary," as one critic calls him, Iago is "Lucifer fallen," the "moral pyromaniac" (Goddard, 1951, 462). Even as Iago sets others on fire, his own blood remains cold as ice.

Worship of Desdemona is Othello's religion. To renounce her is to renounce "the seals and symbols" of his faith. As a sign of closure, a seal secures and fixes something. By contrast, a symbol is luminous and expansive: as Coleridge says, it is a translucence of the eternal in and through the temporal.

> And then for her
> To win the Moor, [were't] to renounce his baptism,
> All seals and symbols of redeemed sin,
> His soul is so enfettered to her love,
> That she may make, unmake, do what she list.
> (*Othello* 2.3.348–52)

William Empson explains that the double noun construction—"all seals and symbols of redeemed sin"—is "a reflection about the character of a *symbol:* that it depends on the fixture or *sealing* down of an association, and is thus analogous to an act of faith" (1961, 90).

Asked to explain itself, all evil can say is what Iago says in his first soliloquy. He hates Othello as he does "hell-pains, / Yet for necessity of present life, / [He] must show out a flag and sign of love, / Which is indeed but sign" (1.1.155–58). As Othello's ensign or standard-bearer, Iago's duty, Denis Donoghue explains, is "to show forth true colors, flags, signs that refer truthfully beyond themselves to meanings at large in the world" (1998, 147). Denying that Platonic universals exist, however, and that words like honesty and love are more than mere "word-words" or names, Iago, an Ockham among semioticians, betrays his calling as an ensign. He forgets that a sign that refers to nothing beyond itself betrays its function.

> Which is indeed but sign. That you shall surely
> find him
> Lead to the Sagittary the raised search;
> And there I will be with him.
> (1.1.158–60)

In a single overcrowded line (158), bursting with thirteen jostling syllables, Iago jams together both a desire to conceal his animus and a desire to reveal it by betraying Othello.

Aligning Shakespeare with Tennyson are memorable "moments of suspension" when both poets pause to "reflect or comment on their own medium." Hillis Miller calls such a pause or break in their poetry a form of "parabasis," "a breaking of the illusion that language is a transparent medium of meaning" (1985, xiv). In the climactic ninety-fifth section of *In Memoriam,* Tennyson pauses to ask what precise portion of his visionary experience he can hope to convey in "matter-moulded" forms of speech. If "words, like nature, half reveal and half conceal the soul within," then their veiled lucidity must be a major concern of any poet who is also a secretary or keeper of secrets. In the debate over Platonic universals in *Troilus and Cressida,* as in ensign Iago's discourse on signs, Shakespeare is also musing on his linguistic resources as a playwright. If a rose by any other name would be as sweet, then only a nominalist, a manipulator of thing-words like Iago (as opposed to Othello, who is bewitched by Platonic universals), can accurately convey the true nature of a rose, even a rose that is as cankered and defiled as Iago claims Desdemona is. Denis Donoghue suggests that *Othello* dramatizes a conflict over Greek and Senecan styles. Whereas Othello's ceremonial style is Greek, epic, and noble, Iago's style is Senecan: "It is a style that delights in setting words free from their standard duty toward objects and referents" (1998, 151).

"The (noun) and (noun) of (noun)" construction is common in Shakespeare, who usually assigns the whole unit a singular verb. Empson believes that the first two nouns in the construction—"flag" and "sign"—are both early attempts (the result of two casual shots) at saying the same thing" (1961, 90). What can be extracted from "flag" and "sign" as their highest common factor is something Iago should be able to expound. Yet by combining two opposite ideas (dishonest show and hidden malice), the nouns cancel each other out. A flag or banner chooses to dwell on the outward sign of an emotion. Ruskin finds an example in *Macbeth:* "Where the Norweyan banners flout the sky, / And fan our people cold" (1.2.51). "The outward shiver and coldness of fear is seized on," and attributed, as Ruskin says, "to the drift of the banners" (1972, 23). In *Othello,* however, Shakespeare refuses to stay outside the signs and banners. Moving instead into the cold heart of Iago, Shakespeare dwells on the fearful chill that freezes Iago's heart and makes him hate sex and loathe women.

The ostentation of a banner waving in the breeze, declaring its meaning to the world, cannot be reconciled with the opacity of a sign that half conceals the hatred of sex and women that turns Iago to ice. Betraying an obsessive interest in what people do in bed, Iago is a congenital voyeur. He prefers to watch them perform the sex act than do it himself. Unlike the gallant and courteous Cassio, who is sexually free and easy with women, Iago cannot conceal his contempt for them. He hates and fears women for being sexed, and is jealous of men like Cassio who delight in their company. In a homosexual fantasy that is also a patent lie designed to trap Othello, Iago tells the Moor that he recently shared a bed with Cassio. While dreaming, Iago's lusty partner kissed Iago's "hand" and "laid his leg / Over [his] thigh" (3.3.413), mistaking his bedfellow for Desdemona. Just as Othello's love is a seal of faith, so Iago's love is a flag of outward show and pretense. If Iago's sign seals anything, it is the mystery of an obsessive malice too gratuitous—too motiveless and deeply rooted—to be understood or labeled. Though publicly announced and transparent to every playgoer, the depth of Iago's evil is also a buried seed, a mystery still waiting to be solved when the play is over. As Northrop Frye observes, "A book may be public property and still sealed, as the evil in Macbeth is to kids who read it in grade nine" (2000, 554).

Iago is an actor's actor, who can play any part demanded of him. He is also a surrogate playwright, a second Shakespeare, brooding over his plot, as A. C. Bradley suggests, "drawing at first only an outline, puzzled how to fix more than the main idea, and gradually seeing it develop and clarify as he works upon it or lets it work" (1957, 189). As Shakespeare's double, Iago is a tireless genius in evil, who lets the dark daemon speak through him as it will. Dwelling in a world of fertile invention, he looks forward to snaring his victims, not in Desdemona's toil of grace, but in the net of a subtly sinister magician.

> *Iago* [*Aside.*] He takes her by the palm; ay, well said,
> whisper; With as little a web as this will I ensnare
> as great a fly as Cassio. Ay, smile upon her, do.
> (2.1.168–70)

"O excellent!" exclaims Coleridge. "The importance given to fertile trifles, made fertile by the villainy of the observer" (1930, 1, 52). Iago falls into the mind trap, not of a motive-hunter who wants to believe "the lusty Moor" has cuckolded him, but of an artist in crime. He is a sorcerer like Prospero, who, lacking a proper medium for the exercise of his art, uses deceit and villainy as a substitute.

Though Iago may not know why he hates Cassio and Othello, it is possible, of course, that Shakespeare knows. The most persuasive explanation I have encountered comes from Denis Donoghue. "A modern low style of speech," found in Iago, he says, "sets out to destroy an ancient style that it discerns in itself" (1998, 163). By "ancient style" Donoghue means the "high, noble, epic style" of Othello, whose disgusting grandeur repels Iago, especially since he can overhear a trace of that style in himself. As an instance of such "Othello music," Donoghue cites the intoxicating speech in which Iago declares that "not poppy, nor mandragora, / Nor all the drowsy syrups of the world" will bring peace again to Othello. Iago hates in himself an Othello-like style that "has a posthumous air about it." Its values, he thinks, are already a dead time's exploded dream. Style is ingratiation. Hamlet's introspective style finds a soul mate in Horatio. But the high poetry of Othello only chills the heart of the prosaic Iago. By destroying Othello, Iago kills the style he hates, then "is destroyed in turn by the ceremony of the play, the force that makes for integrity and truth and finds its true voice of feeling in Desdemona" (Donoghue, 1998, 163).

In *Troilus and Cressida,* where a high style seems archaic and outmoded once anarchy is loosed upon the world, Shakespeare deflates martial glory by using the pun on "Hector's strumpet" to remove some of the grace and flourish from "Hector's trumpet" (4.4.142). Setting the imagination free, an irreverent use of puns allows Shakespeare to indulge in an indecorous overflow of intellectual high spirits and word play. But even after the ceremony of innocence is drowned, Shakespeare strains to keep a grand manner alive in the lofty speeches of Hector and Ulysses. He uses a fluid and vigorous blank verse to mount Hector's defense of value and Ulysses's plea on behalf of order and degree.

Granville-Barker suggests that Shakespeare's "natural bent may well have been toward the grace of rhyme. He gives this ample trial, varies it by quatrains, by a sonnet occasionally; and never quite abandons the rhymed couplet" (1960, 49). This is equally true of Browning, who is seduced by couplets in "My Last Duchess," even when he tries hard to conceal them. The rhymes are subterranean, as smooth as the Duke's manner and as deep as his motives. Though the long blank-verse monologues in *The Ring and the Book* often become mechanical and dull, as do "long lifeless screeds" of blank verse in Shakespeare, Granville-Barker rightly claims that blank verse is "open, as no other [verse form] is, to variety and individuality of expression" (49). When imagination catches fire, and Tennyson enters the soul of Tithonus and Lucretius, or Browning enters the mind of Andrea del Sarto or Fra Lippo Lippi, as Shakespeare takes possession of Richard II's soul or King Lear's, "the intensity of the possession keeps [the blank verse] tense and strong" (49). It is true that Tennyson's "Ulysses" owes more to the slow majestic march of Milton's blank verse line than to Shakespeare's. And the dovelike lamentation of the blank verse in "Oenone" sounds less like Shakespeare than Keats. But when sense of form and strength of character unite, the blank verse of many of the best Victorian monologues—Tennyson's "St. Simeon Stylites" and "Lucretius," Browning's Caliban upon Setebos" and "Cleon"—reminds us most of Shakespeare.

Many of Browning's villains—the court lady in "The Laboratory," the Spanish monk, the Duke in "My Last Duchess"—are not only men or women of action but also artists in crime like Iago, the playwright of an intricate plot in whose "conception and execution . . . he experiences the tension and joy of artistic creation" (A. C. Bradley, 1957, 188).[2] The exhilaration experienced by artists in evil is contaminating. Their "combination of unusual intellect with extreme evil is . . . more than startling, it is frightful. It is rare, but it exists; and Shakespeare represents it in Iago" (189, 194). Just as we experience Iago's genius for invention as a virus or cancer, so we keep thirsting, like addicts, for new disclosures of malign audacity in Browning's Duke of Ferrara, even as we sink and sicken with each new discovery we make. The most important secret he shares is not the most sensational one: his probable murder of his last duchess. "This grew, I gave commands; / Then all smiles stopped together" (lines 45–46). More puzzling than the fact he has murdered his wife or removed her to a nunnery is the Duke's reason for sharing his story with the envoy. He occupies the same position in Browning's canon as Hamlet does in Shakespeare's. His power as a dramatic character resides in his endless suggestiveness, and in a play of forces that continue to seduce and confound his subtlest critics.

A silent auditor like the envoy in "My Last Duchess" may feel momentarily privileged to share some of the Duke's confidences. He may even experience the same uneasy awareness as Shakespeare's playgoer when soliloquies by Iago and Edmund allow him to share unsettling information about plots to destroy Othello or Edgar. Like Hamlet, however, the Duke also withholds as much as he reveals. Perhaps the most open, least secretive of Shakespeare's plays is *The Comedy of Errors,* where the introduction of a second pair of twins makes the play four times as ingenious but also four times as transparent as Plautus's comedy *The Menaechmi.* By contrast, as Shakespeare matures as a playwright, he comes to value mysteries of identity and hidden motives over transparent duplication of a theme. In addition to being a deviser of clever plots, he also wants to be riddling and enigmatic, like Browning's Duke, even if it means breaking the playwright's first rule by having a complex character like Hamlet withhold secrets from the audience.

Cunningly inventive like Iago, Browning's Duke is also as secretive and self-withholding as Hamlet. Just before he dies, Hamlet hints that the secret most worth imparting is still to be revealed. "Had I but time . . . O, I could tell you / But let it be" (*Hamlet* 5.2.339–43). As Harold Bloom says, "Hamlet utters a total of almost twenty more lines after that 'let it be,' so that one can experience a certain frustration at not being told part, at least, of what is hinted" (2003, 114). Every one of Hamlet's soliloquies withholds more than it discloses. In his soliloquy "O, what a rogue and peasant slave am I," there are sound tactical reasons Hamlet might have adduced to justify his delay in avenging his father's ghost. Better reasons also exist for Hamlet's deciding not to commit suicide than a fear of what may happen to him after death. There are also more compelling reasons for not killing Claudius at prayer than Hamlet's ignoble wish to send his uncle's soul to hell. More intriguing than anything Hamlet says is what he refuses to say. "Riddling in so many ways," as Christopher Ricks says of William Empson's poems, Hamlet's soliloquies and Browning's "My Last Duchess" are openly secretive, publicly so as poems, not privately as autobiography. One remembers Empson's remark about Hamlet: "he successfully kept a secret by displaying he had got one" (1987, 181).

Complicating the Duke of Ferrara's monologue in "My Last Duchess" is a clash between two contradictory motives—the Duke's desire for a large dowry and his need to dazzle and impress the envoy. If the envoy's master, the Count, has a shred of humanity, he is unlikely to offer up his daughter on the altar of a Bluebeard. Nor do we believe the Duke for a moment when he protests that his object is the Count's "fair daughter's self," not her dowry.

> I repeat,
> The Count your master's known munificence
> Is ample warrant that no just pretence
> Of mine for dowry will be disallowed;
> Though his fair daughter's self, as I avowed
> At starting, is my object.
>
> (lines 48–53)

There is no warm and breathing beauty in the Duke's description. His abstract phrases, hedged round with alliterating Latin words and double negatives, do nothing to delight the heart or express affection. Yet surprising as it sounds, the Duke is not being totally deceptive in claiming a dowry is of secondary importance. His primary aim is to amplify and correct before a submissive auditor traumatic memories from his domestic past that the envoy's marriage mission has revived. The Duke even drops a hint he might prefer to hide: his last duchess was instinctively warm and spontaneous, and would never allow the curtain to be drawn over her in life.

In identifying himself with the lusty Neptune and casting the woman as the mule, the Duke is trying to heal the psychic wound that triggers his compulsion to be lordly and despotic, always in control. His ceremonious rhetoric, matchlessly contrived to secure, from the first lordly gesture to the final impudent levity, a breathtaking progression of dramatic shocks, reveals that the Duke is performing for the benefit of the envoy, whom he is trying to seduce and control as a surrogate wife. "Contentious and self-justifying," as Geoffrey Hartman says, "Browning's people direct their will at a hidden God. The poet is their advocate, caught in the same condition, and he refuses to give the game away" (1970, 245–46). Like Browning, the Duke worships his gods in silence. His secret and furtive end is to dramatize his complete possession of the Duchess's smile, which he takes keen delight in turning on and off by merely pulling a rope, like a child absorbed with a toy.

In charming and seducing the envoy, the speaker in "My Last Duchess" also seduces the reader. Artfully drawn in by this spellbinder, we, the audience, feel more like a marveling accomplice than a censor. In a sweep of godlike omnipotence, the Duke's opening lines "call" into being, as if by a fiat of divine creation, an acknowledged "wonder."

> I call
> That piece a wonder, now; Fra Pandolf's hands
> Worked busily a day, and there she stands.
> (lines 2–4)

Like Belinda's echo of Genesis in "The Rape of the Lock" ("Let Spades be trumps! She said, and trumps they were"), the oracular grammar invites a biblical parody. In extending his civilities to the envoy, this autocratic spellbinder, while choosing "never to stoop" himself, becomes a subtle social parody of the Christian God of Browning's St. John, who "stoops . . . to rise . . . Such ever was love's way" ("A Death in the Desert," line 134). St. John's paradox of "stooping to rise" reminds us that "everything good . . . descends: harmony in music, order, the Incarnation" (Frye, 2000, 486). The Duke's pretense to "stoop," not out of love, but only out of a selfish desire to dramatize his own importance, would be less striking and audacious if its resonance with oracular passages in *The Ring and the Book* and "Saul" did not also harbor deep jokes and ironies at the speaker's expense. When Browning's Duke tells the envoy, "Nay we'll go / Together down, sir," it is hard not to hear an echo of Richard II's overture to the usurper, Bolingbroke, which combines courtesy and irony in equal measure: "In the base court? Come down? Down, court! down, king! (*Richard II* 3.3.182). Only Shakespeare could have turned a stage direction into a pun; and only Browning could have brought to life the lethal pun in "dies" (line 19). The paint that dyes the Duchess's portrait is also the faint half blush that dies or expires along her throat.

The profession of feeling in "Will't please you sit" is offset by the Duke's self-important quotation of himself ("I said") and by the studied artifice of "by design." No sooner does the Duke invite the envoy and the reader to draw close, as if they were confidants, than he pushes them away. Intimacy is displaced by the phrase "strangers like you" and by the cool rationality of the causal "for." It is as if we and the envoy were merely another statistic, our response an anticipated stage effect, something predicted by the Duke with scientific accuracy. "Will't please you sit?," "Will't please you rise?," "Nay, we'll go / Together down, sir" (lines 5, 47, 53–54). The Duke is in no sense "stooping" to the envoy or to us, but merely pulling strings, as if we were puppets. In extending courtesies, the speaker never ceases to dramatize his self-importance. Like the bellows on an accordion, professed intimacy and ducal hauteur keep contracting and expanding the distance between speaker and audience with the same delight in control and the same exercise of power that the Duke displays in drawing the curtain back and forth over his wife's portrait.

Just as the Duke has trapped a faithful wife he accuses of being promiscuous, so he now sets a second trap for himself and a third one for the envoy. The trap set for the envoy is obvious enough. If the envoy tells his master, the Count, that the Duke is a Bluebeard, the marriage mission may fail. At the very least it will be put in jeopardy. But if the envoy succeeds in his mission by lying about the Duke, his master's daughter is likely to suffer the fate of the Duke's other wives. The trap the Duke sets for himself is less obvious. If he is to secure a large dowry, he must suppress painful memories of his last marriage. But how can he do this while "stooping" to the distasteful task of negotiating another marriage, this time with a mere Count's daughter, his social inferior? To avoid humiliation and preserve his dignity, the Duke must exercise authority and power over the envoy. Though few stage plays can accommodate characters as complex as Hamlet, Hamlet is a simple character compared with Browning's Duke. Only a dramatic monologue can accommodate a speaker whose method of controlling his auditor is as subtle and daring as the Duke's.

Adrian Poole has noticed that the arch villain of *The Ring and the Book,* Count Guido, combines the motiveless malignity of Iago with the jealousy of Othello. Of equal importance in *The Ring* are the gold and leaden caskets in *The Merchant of Venice,* which throw light on Browning's parable of the ring. Gold, the most prized but least useful of metals, is Browning's image for "fact." Incapable of intelligent selection, the narrator at the beginning of *The Ring* is as impressed by antiquarian glamour as are Portia's first two suitors. Speaking in the comically inflated vein of Chaucer's Knight—"How history proves . . . nay, read Herodutus!" (*The Ring and the Book* 1.297)—the narrator indulges in the same fatuous apostrophes as the Princes of Morocco and Arragon before making their unlucky choice of a casket. Like gold, historical fact possesses the mere surface appearance of value. Only when the dramatized narrator turns to address his British public directly does he speak for Browning, the implied author, just as Bassanio, the suitor who chooses the proper lead casket, speaks for Shakespeare. If Browning retains "fact" as the prize word of Victorian positivists like H. T. Buckle, who tries to make history into a statistical science, so gold remains the idol of the shallow, luxury-loving society of Shakespeare's Belmont. But Browning also cleverly alters the connotation of "gold" to include "fancy," the imaginative sense of fact as well as the crude residue itself: "Fancy with fact is just one fact more" (1.464).

The narrator assures the British public that "fancy" is a "fact." "Fancy" is the "gold" that his audience has always supposed to be the opposite of "fact."

This reversal has a certain "shock value," and to justify it Browning reminds us that fancy and fact, the lead alloy and the gold, remain distinct only until the final spurt of acid dissolves the alloy. Then the perfect ring that remains can express both the particular truths of history, which are the gold cherished by the fact-loving British public, and Browning's own values, the alloy of poetry and imaginative re-creation, which recast the story of Caponsacchi's rescue of Pompilia as a replay of Perseus's rescue of Andromeda from a sea monster and of Browning's rescue of Elizabeth from a tyrannical father. In her great speech on mercy, Portia momentarily towers above the twists and turns of the legal rhetoric she has carefully rehearsed as a jurist and doctor of law. Her sublime poetry takes even the legally trained Portia by surprise. By making the alloy of lead "justifiably golden," Browning, too, hopes to surpass or excel the central dramatic act of his life. But like Portia's divine words on mercy, the daring rescue of a damsel in which Browning himself is cast as the dashing young deliverer can be immortalized only when embalmed and treasured up as the precious life blood of "R.B., a poem," the confessional masterpiece of a master spirit, epic in its sweep.

As Shylock threatens to extract a pound of flesh from Antonio, so Guido views his marriage to Pompilia as a bond that legalizes murder after he convicts his wife of adultery. As a cross between Portia and the ill-fated Antonio, however, Pompilia, like her Shakespearean prototype, knows how to tower. Caponsacchi, her soldier-saint, is also her Muse, who (like Portia's in her "quality of mercy" speech) "reverberates the truth" and flashes "the word God gave him, back to man": "God stooping shows sufficient of his light / For us i' the dark to rise by. And I rise" (7.1796–97, 1843–45). The final understatement overcomes the radical failure of language to say explicitly what is in the full heart. Her last three words, "And I rise," achieve the fullest possible meaning consonant with the simple words this saint must use.

Like Shylock, whose hate is his answer to the world's scorn, and like Bassanio, the charming suitor who marries Portia as much for her money as for her patrician demeanor and grace of mind, Guido is part fortune-hunter and part misanthrope, an inveterate scoffer and blasphemer. Yet in Guido's own eyes there is nothing to differentiate his enterprise in crime from the performance of any other "hypocrite," which in Greek is just a synonym for actor. When the rules change during the middle of the game, and the rituals that Guido mistook for a puppet-play acquire the same significance that they acquire for Shylock and Antonio in Portia's court of law, why, Guido asks, should he rather than someone else be punished? Shakespeare poses the same question in *The Merchant of Venice.* How does Shylock differ from Antonio or from any other Gentile? "I am a Jew. Hath not a Jew eyes?" Is Antonio, the merchant who devotes his life to launching argosies and making profit through trade, any less culpable or mercenary than Shylock, the money-lender? As Harold Goddard says, "Shakespeare seizes one of the most exciting moments of the play (when the dramatic tension is so high that nobody will notice) to drive home this truth, the instant when Portia, disguised as a Young Doctor of Laws, enters the courtroom. 'Which is the merchant here and which the Jew?' she inquires in almost the first words. All she wants, of course, is to have the defendant and plaintiff identified. But the Shakespearean overmeaning is unmistakable. Merchant and Jew! Noble trader of Venice and despicable money-changer, at what poles they appear to stand! Yet—which is which?" (1951, 89).

Though Shakespeare and Browning withhold secrets from mass audiences that want their prejudices confirmed, they also share secrets with more discriminating readers. "De te fabula," Browning says at the end of "The Statue and the Bust." Is virtue too high a price to pay for "the unlit lamp and the ungirt loin"? Or is Victorian "virtue" sometimes vice in disguise? *Henry V,* a patriotic play that glorifies war, has managed to survive in spite of—or perhaps because of—its chauvinism. But it is a lesser play than *Troilus and Cressida,* which portrays the horror of war, or than *Henry IV,* which balances the heroic postures of Hotspur and Hal with the great antiwar soliloquies of Falstaff. Even in *Henry V,* ostensibly Shakespeare's most patriotic play, we overhear the poet behind the playwright subverting the Archbishop's exaggerated praise of England's military greatness.

> To fill King Edward's fame with prisoner kings,
> And make her [England's] chronicle as rich with praise
> As is the ooze and bottom of the sea
> With sunken wrack and sunless treasuries.
>
> (*Henry V* 1.2.162–65)

"The somber image, which comes through in spite of the speaker's shallow conscious insights[,] . . . suggests the injustice and horror of the war, the misery to be inflicted on both France and England by a spoiled child of fortune, and, above all, the ultimate futility of the whole enterprise" (Frye, 1990, 57–58). "A poet-playwright," one critic contends, "is a contradiction in terms. But a poet-playwright is exactly what Shakespeare is. And so his greater plays are one thing as drama and another as poetry, one thing on the outside, another within" (Goddard, 1951, 83). Even as Hamlet heaps praise on Fortinbras for risking all for "an egg-shell," for a plot of land "not tomb enough and continent / To hide the slain" (*Hamlet* 4.4.64–65), a playgoer who listens carefully can hear the death knell and the censure of folly tolling just below the surface tribute.

The subtlest attack against Shakespeare's vaunted morality is launched by John Keats, who argues that unlike Wordsworth, the great moral poet of mankind, Shakespeare is a nonmoral chameleon. Empathizing as readily with artists in crime like Iago as well as with saints like Imogen, Shakespeare embraces everything and nothing: he appears to have no value or standard of his own. If we carry Keats's argument to its logical conclusion, we have to question whether any dramatic poet can be moral. Unless he delivers his own homily in a chorus, how can we expect a playwright to be as unambiguously instructive or directly moral as the poet of *Paradise Lost* or *The Prelude*?

Shakespeare's characters, even when existential in tone and temper, are seldom "beyond good and evil." They are not to be confused with Browning's Johannes Agricola, a grim elect soul who thinks grace is the winning ticket in a lottery conducted by Setebos, the cruel and capricious god of Shakespeare's Caliban. Nor are Shakespeare's characters to be mistaken for serenely blind optimists like Browning's Pippa, whose faith that "God's in his heaven— / All's right with the world!" (*Pippa Passes* 1.227–28) is a Pelagian parody of grace. The case for a moral Shakespeare is put most forcibly by Iris Murdoch. The same light "which illuminates the atmosphere of the Platonic dialogues . . . is to be found," she argues, "in Shakespeare's plays. They "*shine* with a positive sense of goodness," which is "shown rather than explicitly or laboriously said" (1992, 142). Indeed, it is as hard to think of Shakespeare as a nonmoral chameleon as it is to think of Spinoza as an atheist.[3] Even the evil Macbeth is a *moral* criminal, driven to extremes of remorse and despair by his guilt. Though Lady Macbeth makes her husband feel that murder of Duncan is necessary, almost a duty, it conspires against all the forces of Macbeth's habitual good nature. Murder requires an act of will working against the tenor of his conscience, against his regard for a "renown and grace" that are lost forever the moment he kills Duncan. Shakespeare makes bearable the terrible scene in *King Lear* where Gloucester's eyes are put out only because he is in his own unique and profound way a moral poet who revolts strongly against the horror of the scene. As Frye says, what Shakespeare presents "is not the paralyzing horror of a real blinding scene, but an exuberant horror, full of the energy of repudiation" (1963, 41).

The most Shakespearean moment in Browning's *Pippa Passes* is the disintoxicated moment feared by the drug addict. It is the disenchanted moment of moral revulsion when Sebald declares he would kill again, even kill the world, if only he could restore to life the man he has murdered. Would a less repentant (hence less moral) assassin resolve to expiate his crime in so shocking and immoral an avowal?

> Ottima, I would give your neck,
> Each splendid shoulder, both those breasts of yours,
> That this were undone! Killing! Kill the world,
> So Luca lives again!
>
> (1.124–27)

An Italian Lady Macbeth, Ottima is as fiercely proud of her lover's ruthless capacity to kill as her Shakespearean counterpart is ashamed of the human kindness flowing like milk instead of blood through the veins of her partner in crime.

> Well, then, I love you better now than ever,
> And best (look at me while I speak to you)—
> Best for the crime.
>
> (1.155–57)

For his part, Sebald would wring his mistress's neck, sever her shoulder, even cut off her breasts, to undo what he has done. Browning expects us to recall the great moment in *Macbeth* when the assassin wishes he could run time back on its tracks and die an hour before the murder is committed.

> Had I but died an hour before this chance,
> I had lived a blessed time; for, from this instant,
> There's nothing serious in mortality.
> All is but toys; renown and grace is dead.
>
> (*Macbeth* 2.3.96–99)

As A. C. Bradley says, "This is no mere acting. The language here has none of the false rhetoric of his merely hypothetical speeches. It is meant to deceive, but it utters at the same time his profoundest feeling. And this he can never hide from himself for long" (1957, 300–301). Later, when Sebald threatens suicide, Ottima says he should kill *her.* If anyone has to be sacrificed on the altar of his moral imagination, it should be Ottima herself, the chief architect of their crime.

Vico says we should interpret persons in such a way as to preserve their humanity. All the evil characters in *King Lear* violate this principle. They treat Gloucester and the king as animals incapable of introspection, of consistent desires, or of planning for their future. As Ovidian in his own metamorphoses as Io or Actaeon, Shakespeare, as Keats discerns, can be Iago as well as Imogen. But even when the character he impersonates is on the verge of losing his humanity, and is barely a person, Shakespeare often makes the character as articulate as Shakespeare. After Macbeth murders Duncan and Iago incites a murderous jealousy in Othello, they disappoint expectations we normally have of hosts and friends. Their status as humans is under pressure. But just as Io struggles to make clear her identity by using her hoof to stamp her name in the dust, so even the inhuman Edmund, for whose sake Goneril and Regan are either poisoned or slain, struggles to assert his lost status as a person by asserting over the women's dead bodies, "Yet Edmund was beloved!" (*King Lear* 5.3.239). Seldom in Shakespeare is the metamorphosis of the human into the inhuman so complete that it effaces a person's identity. The terrifying jealousy that overtakes Leontes in *The Winter's Tale* may seem unmotivated and inhuman. But Shakespeare has endowed Leontes so completely with his own gift for speech that, like the antlers of the great stag Actaeon, the horns which the self-styled cuckold begins to grow and display affirm rather than destroy his human identity. In Shakespeare, as in Ovid, we can usually see how the outer animal disguise and the inner human person fit together. Yet just as Shakespeare maintains a fine Ovidian balance between a person's animal and human qualities, so his restrained response to Christianity seems also to reflect a subversive delight in the negative and ironic aspects of metaphor. The claim that Christ or Caesar is both god and man is the kind of metaphor Ovid playfully but consistently erodes by collapsing a god's personality into a purely natural object. An Ovidian metamorphosis typically signals a breakdown of metaphor.

If one happens to be a master of negative capability like Keats, Browning, or Shakespeare, the best disguise may be no disguise at all. Like John Buchan's criminal in *The Thirty-Nine Steps,* Browning's poet in "How It Strikes a Contemporary" is so unremarkable in outward appearance, and so adept at blending into any environment he is in, that he can assume an incognito without donning a mask. When Keats expresses his fear that because the artist of roles "is everything" he is therefore "nothing" and strictly speaking "has no character" (1958, 2:81), he is ignoring the counter-truth that impersonation always implies some separation, some distance to be crossed. Far from making us hollow at the core, empathy is an indispensable agent of moral growth. No impersonator can lack the authority of a presiding personality who gives "generously" of herself even while taking back from others. When such authority is lacking, the poet becomes what W. J. Fox calls a mere "poetical harlequin," a chameleon like Keats's poet of negative capability. His Muse so devours the poet's personality that he may gain the whole world but lose his own soul.

Iago's malignity, like Satan's, is motiveless. But so are Cordelia's mercy and love. If begging for mercy is a sin because it suspends a law demanding a brother's death, then in *Measure for Measure,* Isabella is willing to accept the sin and confess it in her morning prayer. The most eloquent appeal for mercy comes from Portia, who places it above justice and "the sceptred sway" of kings. The law that allows Shylock to extract his pound of flesh may be more perfect because more binding than any moral obligation to be merciful.

But what is more perfect in the legal sense may be less perfect in the moral sense, which appeals to people as free, assenting beings, without constraining them like robots.

For Portia, mercy is to justice what the Beatitudes are to the Ten Commandments. In fulfilling the law, the Sermon on the Mount also abolishes the law. John Stuart Mill expounds this paradox in the fifth chapter of his book *Utilitarianism.* A right conferred by law imposes an obligation that Mill calls "perfect" or legally binding, like the contract Antonio signs with Shylock. Moral obligation, by contrast, is imperfect. Involving no legal obligation, it drops "as the gentle rain from heaven." As Mill says, Antonio has no "moral right" to Shylock's "generosity or beneficence" (1965, 247). But his "imperfect" moral claim on Shylock therefore seems worthier and more admirable than the so-called perfect obligation of a legal contract, precisely because the law does not require the "rarer action" that is found "in virtue" [rather] than in vengeance" (*The Tempest* 5.1.27–28).

A mystery of identity or motive cannot be solved like a puzzle in logic. Any effort to explain why Iago destroys Othello, why Brutus murders Caesar, why Browning's Duke makes damaging admissions to the envoy, cannot quite solve the mystery of their motives: "No cause, no cause." Why does Hamlet delay killing Claudius? Why does Andrea keep insulting his wife when his ostensible motive in addressing her is to persuade her to stay at home with him? The mystery comes, not from what is unknown about these characters, but from what is illimitable in them. If the height of Cordelia's goodness is unimaginable, the depth of Iago's evil is unfathomable. As Frye notes, "Unmotivated evil has something bafflingly inscrutable about it. When Iago is asked why he deliberately destroyed the lives and happiness of Othello and Desdemona, who had trusted him and never done him any harm, he replies only with obstinate silence. He doesn't know why himself" (1990, 281). Motive-hunting never compasses anything so gratuitous as pure evil or sainthood. Searching for motives in Cordelia or Edmund is too often a mind trap. It snares the searcher while allowing the saint or villain to go free.

PART II

HAMLET'S AFTERLIVES

3

Toils of Fate

DICKENS, HAMLET, AND MALVOLIO

"GREAT WITS ARE SURE TO MADNESS NEAR ALLIED," CLAIMS DRYDEN in *Absalom and Achitophel* (line 163); and we may say the same of tragedy and comedy. Thin partitions divide calamity from farce in *Othello,* where the Moor is both a tragic victim of betrayed love and a sexual dupe, the laughing-stock of what Thomas Rymer notoriously calls a "bloody farce, without salt or savor" (1971, 164). In *Great Expectations,* weird incantations and ritual repetitions make Pip the victim of a fate that seems at first tragic. There are forces at work in his world that he, like Hamlet, only half understands and registers only subliminally. But in his vain love for Estella, as in Malvolio's absurd wooing of his mistress, Pip is also a comic dupe. Like Malvolio, who is told that some are born to greatness, some achieve greatness, and others have greatness thrust upon them, Pip must learn to distrust and devalue his "great expectations." In Dickens's novel I want to test Stephen Booth's idea that comic and tragic structures have more in common than we first suspect, and that, "whatever we may consciously believe, we feel cheated by comedies and grateful to tragedies" (Booth, 1983, 77).

Despite Wopsle's unintentionally comic performance of *Hamlet,* which has precedent in Fielding's humorous treatment of the play in *Tom Jones,* Pip himself is an apparently tragic Hamlet. Just as the ghost of Hamlet's father summons him to take revenge on his murderer, so Pip is forced to detach himself from the world when the father who has adopted him turns out to be, not the fairy godmother he expected, but the ghost of a grisly old convict instead. In the opening scene in the graveyard, the convict reminds Pip of a pirate who came to life from the gibbet on which he was hanged, and who went back to the scaffold to hook himself up again. The cattle seem just as terrified of this ghostly pirate as Pip. Instead of running into objects in the mist, objects are said to run into Pip. He is invaded by forces that impinge on him from mysterious other worlds, like the ghost of Hamlet's father, who rises unbidden from the underworld or purgatory.

Unlike *Hamlet, Great Expectations* is more concerned with memory than revenge. The vengeful motives of Miss Havisham and Magwitch preoccupy us less than our attempts to remember and make sense of repeating phrases, widely separated in space and time. On the fateful night of his return, when Magwitch cross-examines Pip about his income—"As to the first figure now, Five?" (chap. 30)—a host of authority figures can be heard talking through this ghost. We hear Pumblechook posing multiplication tables, his waistcoat heaving with windy arithmetic: "Seven times nine, boy! . . . Seven? And four? And eight? And six?" (chap. 8); Jaggers interrogating Pip about the amount of money he wants: "How much? Fifty pounds? . . . Five pounds?" (chap. 24); and Trabb's commanding his apprentice to bring the appropriate rolls of cloth for Pip's inspection: "Give me Number four, you!" and "Are you bringing numbers five and eight?" (chap. 19). Joe's purblind deciphering of the letters "J" and "O" in Pip's half-literate script are accepted as "astonishing" proof of Pip's scholarship (chap. 7). Later in chapter 39, in the grim deciphering of the convict's identity, Pip finds equally astonishing proof that his strange visitor is a riddling master of mysteries: "As to the first letter of that lawyer's name now. Would it be J?" With its elided words and subliminal meanings, the whole novel resembles one of Pip's barely decipherable letters or Mrs. Joe's pictograph for Orlick.

Throughout the novel the reader has an uncanny sense of having heard before a mysteriously resonant use of "I saw," "I saw," or "I knew," "I knew," without being able to recall the precise time and place. Flashes of déjà vu light up the landscapes for an instant, then gutter out before recognitions can fuse. Something encountered in the past—a gesture, a look, a fragment of speech—is on the tip of our tongue. Why can't we remember it? Pip has the same experience of a look repeated or a gesture half remembered but not precisely placed when Estella waves to him from the carriage near Newgate prison (chap. 32). "The nameless shadow" that passes before him is a subliminal recollection of Molly's hand; and the prison air Pip tries to exhale has a closer connection with Estella, the convict's daughter, than his conscious mind allows him to acknowledge. Ritual incantations and suppressed meanings create a strong sense of fate, hidden but inexorably impending, which only a deceived fool or an unwary reader would presume to say he understood or foresaw.

Wopsle's ill-fated performance as Hamlet is preceded by his sermon on swine, his performance of Mark Antony's oration over the body of Caesar, and his recitation of the tragedy of George Barnwell. In each instance

Wopsle illogically indicts Pip for some misdemeanor or crime. "Swine were the companions of the prodigal," Wopsle preaches. "What is detestable in a pig, is more detestable in a boy." Pumblechook observes that Pip might have been born as a pig and ended life as a pork pie. His gratuitous remark sounds less absurd if we remember the pork pie Pip stole to help a criminal and his inadvertent poisoning of Pumblechook with tar water poured into a half-emptied jug to conceal his theft of the wine taken to Magwitch. With his grotesque Roman nose, turned-up cuffs, and stiff standing hair, Wopsle makes a grotesque Mark Antony. Yet as a deft indictment of Brutus and his fellow conspirators, Antony's famous funeral oration in *Julius Caesar,* which Wopsle recites before Pip, has the effect of implicating his captive auditor in a comparable crime.

The case against Pip reaches a climax in the third of Wopsle's performances—his recitation of George Barnwell's tragedy, which prompts Pumblechook's remonstrance: "Take warning, boy, take warning!, as if . . . I contemplated murdering a near relation" (chap. 15). When fully understood, Pumblechook's unspoken prophecy is also a surprising disclosure of the novel's Oedipal displacements. For Pumblechook, like Wopsle, is obliquely linking Pip with Oedipus as the unwitting cause of an adopted father's death and of the death of a surrogate mother, Mrs. Joe—as well as of a putative mother by adoption, Miss Havisham. By chapter 39 there are already hints that Magwitch's adopted son wants to marry his second father's daughter, with the result that son and daughter may someday become husband and wife. Collapse enough intermediate terms, and the remaining identities are bound to seem incestuous and Oedipal.

The most daunting and dismal of Wopsle's performances is his fourth and final one as Hamlet. As if conspiracy in the court of Denmark were not complicated enough, a conspiracy exists among friends of the actor who plays Claudius. They hire a heckler to interrupt Wopsle and spoil his performance as Hamlet. Such is the conspiracy within Pip's own family, where his fairy godmother turns out to be a malicious witch, his godfather a criminal, and his daughter the icy and vacuous beauty Pip foolishly falls in love with. When conspiracy in *Hamlet* transfers itself to the politics of the play's production, the crossover of embarrassments from stage play to real life encourages the reader to explore connections between Wopsle's Hamlet and countless mishaps that overtake Pip during the course of the novel. Just as Pip is alternately dismissed by Pumblechook as an ungrateful felon and patronized by him as a gentleman, so the elegant gesture with which Wopsle's Hamlet uses a white napkin to wipe Yorick's skull is construed by an unkind audience as the role playing of a waiter. When the royal phantom has difficulty reading its lines, the cough reminds the audience of the ghost's infirmity and its untimely removal to the underworld. Gertrude "the Kettledrum" is as grotesquely rotund as Miss Havisham is withered and gaunt. And in her slow musical madness, Ophelia proves as great a trial as Estella. Just as the royal dais is a kitchen chair, and Ophelia's coffin an empty box whose lid rolls off, so the play itself is a pretentious production that elicits, alas, none of the goodwill rewarding the simple but honest efforts of the mechanicals who perform Peter Quince's play in *A Midsummer Night's Dream.*

The most important event foreshadowed by Wopsle's performance as Hamlet is Magwitch's return in the discovery scene. In Alexander Welsh's words, "The principal ghost in *Great Expectations* returns personally to deliver his stunning revelation of the facts to Pip . . . and apparently moves in to stay" (2001, 128). Unlike the ghost of Hamlet's father, who removes himself from the action except for a few troubling moments in the closet scene, Magwitch returns from the Australian underworld to make demands of his adopted son and to perform the duties of a stage manager and director from the near side of the grave. In asking Pip to avenge his "godfather," he is also inviting him to bring ruin on that father and on other members of the family. What is merely absurd in Wopsle's recitation of the tragedy of George Barnwell will become urgent and exacting when Barnwell's fate of going to the scaffold at Newgate threatens to become the fate of Pip's "godfather," and when other "near relations" of this Victorian Hamlet—Miss Havisham, a withered version of the mad Ophelia, and Mrs. Joe—come to comparably violent ends.

A subtler and (I think) greater bearing of Shakespeare's play on Pip's fate is its grotesque tripling and quadrupling of dramatic roles. "The noble boy in the ancestral boots was inconsistent; representing himself, as it were in one breath, as an able seaman, a strolling actor, a grave-digger, a clergyman, and a person of the utmost importance at a court fencing-match" (chap. 31). The unintended comedy is a result of collapsing too many identities. The economy that makes possible the noble boy's performance of five different roles anticipates the curious combination of absurdity and nightmare in the scene of the ghostly benefactor's return. Who would have dreamed that a grisly old ghost combining such widely separated parts as Estella's father and Pip's father by adoption, as the convict on the marsh and the long-silent benefactor, would rise from the grave to haunt Pip as the ghost of his father haunts Hamlet?

Later that night, the humor of conflating too many parts troubles Pip's sleep. He dreams he is a distraught Wopsle playing Hamlet to Miss Havisham's ghost, having to perform before twenty thousand people while knowing fewer than twenty words of his part. The incongruous running together of separate identities—some in real life, some in fiction, others in Shakespearean drama—accurately reflects Pip's own dilemma. Just as Claudius's address to Gertrude as "our sometimes sister, now our queen" broaches the taboo subject of incest, so Pip falls in love with a woman who is also his half-sister, the daughter of his second father. Miss Havisham, the fairy godmother of his dreams, is also a would-be mother-in-law, the woman who has adopted the person he wants to marry. But as the mother to a half-sister, she is also a second mother. As Alexander Welsh observes, the prospect of marriage to Estella promises "a kind of incest between the only begotten and the chosen child" of Magwitch (2001, 128). Since there are too few people to fill too many roles, merged identities are bound to seem incestuous.

So far I have treated Pip as a helpless victim trapped like Hamlet in the toils of a fate he is powerless to control. I want to consider now how far Pip is able to dupe others in transparently fantastic and funny snares, and how far he is a comic dupe like Malvolio, who walks into traps he might easily have avoided. Like Maria and her cohorts in *Twelfth Night,* Pip manages to dupe Mrs. Joe and Pumblechook almost as cleverly as Miss Havisham dupes Pip. Seldom has so charming a tissue of make-believe been cast over two gaping dupes as in the tall tale Pip concocts about his first visit to Satis House.

> "She was sitting," I answered, "in a black velvet coach."
>
> Mr. Pumblechook and Mrs. Joe stared at one another—as well they might—and both repeated, "In a black velvet coach?"
>
> "Yes," said I. "And Estella—that's her niece, I think—handed her in cake and wine at the coach-window, on a gold plate. And we all had cake and wine on gold plates. And I got up behind the coach to eat mine, because she told me to."
>
> "Was anybody else there?" asked Mr. Pumblechook.
>
> "Four dogs," said I.
>
> "Large or small?"
>
> "Immense," said I. "And they fought for veal-cutlets out of a silver basket." (chap. 9)

As his own version of Bottom's dream, Pip's fairy-tale fantasy is a delightful exercise in the art of gulling. Introduced by successive "ands," three incredible marvels are allowed to tumble one over the other. Amazed at his own power to deceive and charm, Pip punctuates each new fantasy as it rolls off his tongue with an incredulous "said I," "said I." Pip's vision is as prophetic as it is funny. The dogs who fight for veal cutlets are yelping little Pockets, fighting for scraps of Miss Havisham's fortune. And when Pip climbs into the gold coach at the rich lady's request, he is half consenting to become a victim of his own fairy-tale delusions. In surrendering to her spell, Pip, it seems, is half taken in by his own power to deceive. Exchanging roles with the fairy princess in her glass coach, Pip consents to become a male Cinderella himself. After his ball in London, Pip will find that a fate more grotesque than comic has transformed his glass coach into a pumpkin and his fairy godmother into a ghostly godfather who, like Hamlet's father, has returned from the grave to haunt him.

Even in being indentured to Joe, Pip lets himself be fettered ceremoniously to a fate he could easily have made less gruesome. Since Pip is adept at gulling Pumblechook and Mrs. Joe, and since he realizes Pumblechook is a pompous fraud and Miss Havisham a sinister contriver, why does he allow these same authority figures to control him? A more resourceful youth could surely have prevented Pumblechook from turning a "great festival" into a ritual of shame by pushing Pip through the crowd as if he were a felon who had just picked a pocket or set fire to a rick. We want Pip to control his fate as cleverly as Joe does on the few occasions he manages to outwit his wife. When Mrs. Joe demands to know how much money Miss Havisham has given Pip, Joe artfully reveals the amount slowly, in three separate stages. He placates his wife by giving an impressive ritual quality to his disclosures. The suspense he creates turns him into an authority figure—the equal of Jaggers and Magwitch when they later quiz Pip about larger sums of money.

After Pip receives news of his great expectations, he patronizes Biddy and takes delight in saying farewell to a dull rural world with as much hauteur and disdain as Malvolio displays when condescending to speak to his fellow servants after being told by letter that some have greatness thrust upon them. As Malvolio adopts strange mannerisms and modes of attire designed to please Olivia, so Pip in his exalted new station dreams of winning the favor of another great lady, Estella. Like a condescending Malvolio, Pip is never more supercilious than when dreaming of future greatness, chiding Joe with being a slow learner, and accusing Biddy of being jealous.

No one dupes Pip as palpably as Maria and her cohorts gull Malvolio in *Twelfth Night.* But an avenger just as resourceful as Maria and her fellow conspirators does appear in *Great Expectations* in the form of a relentlessly comic mimic, Trabb's boy, who mocks Pip on a return visit to the village.

> Casting my eyes along the street at a certain point of my progress I beheld Trabb's boy approaching, lashing himself with an empty blue bag. Dreaming that a serene and unconscious contemplation of him would best beseem me, and would be most likely to quell his evil mind, I advanced with that expression of countenance, and was rather congratulating myself on my success, when suddenly the knees of Trabb's boy smote together, his hair uprose, his cap fell off, he trembled violently in every limb, staggered out into the road, and crying to the popu-

> lace, "Hold me! I'm so frightened!" feigned to be in a paroxysm of terror and contrition, occasioned by the dignity of my appearance. As I passed him, his teeth loudly chattered in his head, and with every mark of extreme humiliation, he prostrated himself in the dust. (chap. 30)

The wiggling of the boy's body and elbows recalls Uriah Heeps's obsequious writhing in *David Copperfield.* But far from being a toady like his master Mr. Trabb, who keeps rubbing his hands as he shows Pip to the door of his shop, Trabb's boy contorts himself in a paroxysm of irreverent mockery. He pretends that Pip, in his transformed state, is too lofty to be recognized. At the same time, the lowly mimic takes pains not to be snubbed by Pip: "Don't know yah!" he is the first to say; "don't know yah, pon my soul don't know yah!" The sinister prophetic force of "not knowing" someone will clarify later when Pip fails to recognize the convict who returns from Australia or to realize that this convict is also his benefactor. Like Polonius's comic resolve in *Hamlet* to use "indirections [to] find direction out" (2.1.63), the mockery of Pip by Trabb's boy is what Frank Kermode in another context has called a "little parodic scherzo." It is "the tune" of the novel—the theme of not knowing someone—"played in a farcical variation" (2000, 110).

"To be rubbed out" is also to be effaced—annihilated. Pip's sense of who he is is effectively effaced by Trabb's sycophantic rubbing of his hands, by Pumblechook's excessive handshaking, by the merciless mockery of Trabb's apprentice, and by the later return of the benefactor as a reformed criminal. Such twists of fate Pip has to construe as grim practical jokes. As surely as Maria's cruel joke feeds Malvolio's illusions, so Pumblechook's preposterous flattery and the heartless ridicule of Trabb's boy feed Pip's. After Magwitch's return, Pip's distress is no less acute than Malvolio's when confined to a cell and treated for an imaginary fit of madness. Pip's torment reaches its climax during the night he is forced to spend alone at the Hummums.

> Not long before, I had read in the newspapers, how a gentleman unknown had come to the Hummums in the night, and had gone to bed, and had destroyed himself, and had been found in the morning weltering in blood. It came into my head that he must have occupied this very vault of mine, and I got out of bed to assure myself that there were no red marks about; then opened the door to look into the passage, and cheer myself up with the companionship of a distant light, near which I knew the chamberlain to be dozing. (chap. 45)

Like frames in a horror flick, the short principal clauses launch a march of horrors. But as Jonathan Bishop argues, this "phantasmagoric night in the Hummums" is only a "Dickensian purple patch." Instead of dramatizing a dark night of the soul, it achieves only a local atmospheric effect of cold soot, hot dust, and clusters of insects trapped in a dirty netting thrown over a bed. Though "the 'night-fancies' of suicide accompanying this spooky interlude" are memorable enough, "nothing important is resolved through this experience, for Pip or for Dickens. It is only an image, a performance" (Bishop, 1972, 182). Is Pip, then, only an immovable comic butt, too flat and rigid to reform? Or does he have the potential to grow, like Hamlet, who shows a wise maturity of judgment in the graveyard scene that is not discernible earlier in the play?

Unlike Dickens, who creates for the most part mere caricatures or masks, Browning and Shakespeare create three-dimensional personae fully possessed of evolving identities and attributes. It is difficult to satirize Pumblechook, Miss Havisham, or even Pip, for to do so Dickens has to produce a caricature of a caricature. Malvolio and Shylock, by contrast, are round rather than flat characters; and it is all too easy to mock and satirize them beyond limits that seem tolerable or fair. Most audiences jeer at Malvolio and laugh him off the stage. But there will always be playgoers like Charles Lamb for whom Malvolio is a victim of some stature and dignity. When Pip slights Joe or Malvolio snubs his fellow servants, each deserves to be mocked. Since Pip's pride in his expectations is no less spurious or affected than Malvolio's pride, the mockery to which Trabb's boy subjects Pip is no crueler and no less deserved than the torture Maria and her cohorts inflict on Malvolio. But Pip's ability to keep his head during his night in the Hummums is also evidence of mental stability. Equally (if not more) impressive is Malvolio's power to maintain composure when confined to a dark room and treated as a lunatic. Just as Malvolio loses none of his dignity when he charges his mistress Olivia with having done him a grievous wrong, so Pip loses none of his stature or sense of worth when he becomes conscious of the terrible wrongs inflicted on him by the mad Miss Havisham. The dark house in which Malvolio is imprisoned is no less dark and sinister than Satis House, the spooky abode of Miss Havisham, an eternally unsatisfied, vindictive ghost, who feeds like a vampire off the life blood of her adopted daughter and Pip.

Early in the novel, when Pip tries to express original moral insights in language that resists and is slow to accommodate them, his words become contoured and nuanced, edged with possible double meanings. Like Macbeth's hallucination of the dagger covered with blood, Pip's vision of the file coming toward him through the door or of the stranger taking aim at him with an invisible gun (chap. 10) objectifies the guilt he feels about aiding a criminal. Though Pip brings the convict the file and food out of fear, not pity, he also feels some loyalty to Magwitch. An honest thief like Falstaff, Pip is betrayed by language. Too scrupulous to be a criminal, he is torn between allegiance to his convict and fear of the law.

> "So," said my convict, turning his eyes on Joe in a moody manner, and without the least glance at me; 'so you're the blacksmith, are you? Then I'm sorry I've eat your pie."
>
> "God knows you're welcome to it—so far as it was ever mine, "returned Joe, with a saving remembrance of Mrs. Joe. "We don't know what you have done, but we wouldn't have you starved to death for it, poor miserable fellow-creatur,—Would us, Pip?"
>
> The something that I had noticed before, clicked in the man's throat again, and he turned his back. The boat had returned, and his guard were ready, so we followed him to the landing-place made of rough stakes and stones, and saw him put into the boat, which was rowed by a crew of convicts like himself. No one seemed surprised to see him, or interested in seeing him, or glad to see him, or sorry to see him, or spoke a word, except that somebody in the boat growled as if to dogs, "Give way, you!" which was the signal for the dip of the oars. By the light of the torches, we saw the black Hulk lying out a little way from the mud of the shore, like a wicked Noah's ark. (chap. 5)

Unlike Joe, Pip cannot put into words what he feels for the convict. But in observing that Magwitch is careful not to glance at him, Pip is sensitive enough to register the convict's tactful concern and gratitude. Pip now calls Magwitch "*my* convict," and apparently endorses Joe's sentiment that he would not have the convict starve to death, "poor miserable fellow-creatur" that he is—"Would us, Pip?" The young Pip appreciates Magwitch's generous attempt to absolve him of guilt in the theft of the file and food. More important, when Pip observes that something kept clicking "in the man's throat," he is tacitly acknowledging a symptom of emotion in the convict, even some sign of throttled affection or remorse. Dickens introduces a long chain of correlative conjunctions and repeated pronouns—"or interested in seeing him," "or glad to see him," "or sorry to see him," "or spoke a word"—to signal Pip's withholding of the normal compassion for a friend's plight that, under different circumstances, he would like to have expressed, if not verbally, then at least parenthetically by some gesture or deed. Trapped in the language he inherits, however, as surely as Magwitch is fettered by his chains, Pip feels impelled to distance himself from the convict's prison-ship, which he describes as a vessel fit only for dogs, a foul hulk lying out from shore "like a wicked Noah's ark."

I find the language adventurous, even daring, in its struggle to express moral insights in words that refuse to accommodate them and that result in a distortion or betrayal of what Pip wants to say. In any conflict of private conscience and public authority, abetting a criminal is immoral, because it violates a prevailing moral code or law. But Magwitch on the marsh is like Lear's fool on the heath. To withhold fellow feeling and food from a starving wretch dissolves the bonds of their shared humanity. It is better to be an ethical immoralist like Pip than an unethical moralist like the self-serving Pumblechook. A close parallel is found in Mark Twain's *Huckleberry Finn,* where Huck, like Pip, is a prisoner of language inherited from his culture. If escape from hell means betraying Jim, then Huck is prepared to go to hell. If escape from guilt means betraying a friend, then Pip is prepared to accept and bear that guilt. As C. S. Lewis observes in one of his finest letters, "The scene in which Huck decides to be 'good' by betraying Jim, and then finds he can't and concludes that he is a reprobate, is really unparalleled in humor, pathos, and tenderness. And it goes down to the very depth of all moral problems" (2007, 67).

We can say of the passage from Dickens just quoted what Samuel Johnson says of Gray's "Elegy": if Dickens had written always thus, "it had been vain to blame and useless to praise him." But we must not make *Great Expectations* a better novel than it is. Shakespeare would never have consented to eighteenth-century attempts to provide *King Lear* with a happy ending. Dickens, by contrast, is deeply divided about how his novel should end. His acceptance of Edward Bulwer-Lytton's advice to change the original ending so that Pip and Estella could marry is proof of a deep crack or fault line in the novel. Is Pip any worthier of Estella than Malvolio is of Olivia? Or does the return of his second father, like a ghost from the grave, mature Pip and make him the wiser and sadder man Hamlet becomes after the return of his father's ghost?

To help Magwitch escape is to get rid of Pip's benefactor under the pretext of trying to free him. It anticipates the concluding chapters of *Huckleberry Finn,* where Huck and Tom Sawyer substitute for an adult moral drama a child's game of freeing a slave already freed by his owner. Instead of maturing Pip, as the return of his father's ghost matures Hamlet, the experience in court allows Pip to be "generous and noble," as one critic says, without any "personal cost" (Bishop, 1972, 183). Pip, unlike Hamlet, is redundant. He is a brother instead of a husband to Estella, and a kind of infant to Biddy, who is always more his mother or stepmother than the wife he wants her to become. After his fever he wakes up in Biddy's lap. Instead of marrying her, he returns to the womb that bore him, to a second mother. Mrs. Joe was always more an overbearing tyrant than a sister, and the second Mrs. Joe is more a mother than the wife she might have become. Like Oedipus, Pip is left without a lifeline. If Tess's marriage bed is a deathbed, Pip's marriage bed is only a cradle. It is "no wonder," concludes Jonathan Bishop, that "Dickens could not decide whether Pip deserved to marry Estella. There is really no question: he is not old enough" (1972, 184).

As evidence of Dickens's limitation as a novelist, Richard Poirier cites the failure of Pip's entertaining language to become suppler and more mature as he grows up. As a youth Pip is more absorbed by the lozenge shape of the tablets in the graveyard, each about a foot and a half long, than by the premature union in death that the slabs memorialize. Similarly, the convict who scares Pip with stories of a young man who creeps his way to a boy's heart and tears it open has less in common with the ghost in *Hamlet* than with a camp counselor who understands child psychology and knows how to entertain and scare his charges. In Poirier's words, "the style given to Pip" from the first paragraph is "more socially accommodating, funny, and entertaining than any man could possibly afford to be who has already passed through the horrendous experiences he is ready to talk about. His mode of speech is that of a theatrical entertainer or recitalist, a very clubbable fellow. This is at least one case where the man who suffers is not the man who writes, or narrates, and Dickens wants us simply to overlook the discrepancy" (1987, 152). Poirier's case is not unassailable. There is, after all, such a device as free indirect discourse, which allows a narrator like the mature Pip to enter as readily into the mind of his childhood self as into the mind of any other character in the novel. Poirier's case against Dickens becomes more convincing when we recognize that the amiable amble of Pip's speech—his digressive, sauntering way of speaking—never changes. He is the same entertaining narrator at the end of the novel as he is at the beginning. Without the strength to carry the powers of childhood alive into the strength of manhood, Pip never grows up. Cased in the unfeeling armor of a shellfish, Estella, by contrast, is never young. Making love to Estella is like eating lobster with the shell on.

A comic fate may be hard at first to distinguish from a tragic one. The intriguing similarities and perplexing differences are well formulated by Stephen Booth. Their "real but superficial likeness," he argues, "is demonstrated by the following pair of superficially similar propositions about 'the nature of things' and human folly. . . . Comedy operates from—and demonstrates—the proposition that there is a way things are and fools forget what it is. Regrettably, however, no one is always or altogether immune from occasional fits of foolish forgetfulness. Tragedy operates from—and demonstrates—the proposition that there is a way things are and that fools assume it is knowable and known. Regrettably, however, no one is or can be exempt from the moment-to-moment, day-by-day necessity of assuming that the ways of things are as previous experience leads us to expect them to be" (1983, 78).

Twelfth Night is a comedy because it affirms there is a limit to human possibilities (wealthy women do not marry their servants), and Malvolio forgets this is so. *Hamlet* is a tragedy because it affirms there is no limit to human possibilities (man is infinite in faculty and angelic in apprehension); and only a fool like Rosencrantz or Guildenstern thinks he knows what the possibilities are. Mocked for his pretensions by Trabb's boy and gently reproved for them by Biddy, Pip has more in common with a fool like Malvolio than with a cipher like Rosencrantz or a nonentity like Guildenstern, who mistakenly believe they can extract information from their old school chum Hamlet, even though he is a more practiced master of secrecy and reserve than Jaggers. When Miss Havisham and Magwitch are seen from far out, as superintending powers mysteriously in control of the fates of Estella and Pip, they seem as powerful as gods. The toils in which they trap their victims arouse tragic emotions of pity and fear. Seen close up, as a mad witch and a deluded convict, these same characters appear merely warped and grotesque: the snares they use to catch their prey arouse comic emotions of laughter or scorn.

Tragedy breaks through boundaries and expands our vision. It prompts us to marvel like Hamlet when he tells Horatio there are more things in heaven and earth than are dreamt of in his philosophy. Hamlet cannot believe that the ladder of creation should stop with him. Like "this excellent canopy, the air," his world must be unbounded. In comedy, by contrast, we are forced to exercise what Stephen Booth calls "a faith in limits." When Maria and her cohorts gull Malvolio, we "retreat," as Booth says, "to a bastion at a comfortable distance from the particular point where some particular rigidity"—Malvolio's conviction of his superior worth, for example—"has proved brittle" (1983, 77). Despite his frequent astonishment and wonder, Pip's horizons are never enlarged beyond limits appropriate to an English gentleman. A comic genius like Dickens delights in what separates people rather than what unites them. The genius who wrote *Hamlet* is the exact opposite: he is drawn like a magnet to what Yeats considers the essentially disinterested, inclusive pole of a tragic vision. Because we want Pip to grow up as a man, and Dickens as an artist, we feel as cheated by the comedy of his failed encounters as we feel grateful for the growth into wisdom of a tragic hero like Hamlet.

4

The Angel of Dust

A GOD IN EXILE

SOMETIMES SHAKESPEARE'S MOST AUTHORITATIVE WORDS RISE UNbidden in the mind of a speaker who is preoccupied with other matters. Such is Hamlet's great aside "What a piece of work is man," which originates as a screen to hide his secret thoughts and suspicions from Rosencrantz and Guildenstern, who have been sent to spy on him.[1] Instead of speaking intimately, as a confidant or friend, Hamlet talks with the remote authority of an oracle. Lofty words tower above his offhand banter, and are more impressive for emerging out of the casual, sauntering movement of the prose.

> I have of late—but wherefore I know not—lost
> all my mirth, foregone all custom and exercise;
> and indeed it goes so [heavily] with my disposi-
> tion that this goodly frame, the earth, seems to
> me a sterile promontory, this most excellent can-
> opy, the air, look you, this brave overhanging
> [firmament] this majestical roof fretted with
> golden fire, why, it appears no other thing to me
> than a foul and pestilent congregation of vapours.
> (*Hamlet* 2.2.305–15)

Despite his professed indifference, the splendors of heaven swell in a triad of appositions: "this most excellent canopy, the air," "this brave overhanging" firmament, "this majestical roof fretted with golden fire." Though the earth itself may seem to Hamlet only a "sterile promontory," its "excellent canopy" and "majestical roof" are transformed into an edifice of great grandeur. But even as he marvels at the splendor of this edifice, Hamlet protests that he is unable to worship at its altar. The only congregation with which he has any affinity is "a foul and pestilent congregation of vapours."

Geoffrey Tillotson observes that Hamlet's prose is strikingly different from the prose being written at the time. "That Hamlet was of the Court went without saying, but to the courtly he added at least an equal amount of the academical—he was also of the University. The prose he spoke was . . . appropriate for writers trying to think about the new matter then coming into man's ken, and whose writings were mainly addressed to the aristocracy" (1968, 86). Though Hamlet's prose is sometimes as terse and aphoristic as Bacon's, when moved by a sense of "all coherence gone," or perplexed by contradictions in the new astronomy, he can soar as high as Sir Thomas Browne or John Donne. Once launched into impulsive prophecy, Hamlet's imagination catches fire, stirred by the query of the eighth psalm: "What is the son of man that thou dost care for him?"

Having marveled at the glory of God's handiwork in fashioning the firmament, Hamlet wants to know why the creator of this masterpiece should be mindful of so lowly a creature as Hamlet. He is puzzled why God should have exalted man in giving him dominion over beasts of "the field, birds of the air, and fish of the sea." The Psalmist's implied answer is that man's "glassy essence," his soul, is a mirror of the God-given glory it reflects. Out of his despair Hamlet rises to a celebration of human dignity that has few rivals outside the Bible.

> What a piece of work is a man! How noble in
> reason! How infinite in faculty, in form and
> moving! How express and admirable in action!
> how like an angel in apprehension! How like a
> god! The beauty of the world! The paragon of
> animals! And yet, to me, what is this quintes-
> sence of dust?
>
> (2.2.315–20)

Hamlet's hymn of praise to man is not an argument but a prayer. But it is a forceful prayer, one that shines and spreads like a great fireworks display, before evaporating and falling to earth, ending up as a small mound of dust. The invocations mount at first in a ritual of supplication. The syntax is fluid, and modifiers can shift from one invoked faculty to another. Man is "express and admirable" in "form and moving" as well as in action. And he is angelic "in action" as well as in apprehension," an attribute that is as appropriate to a god as to an angel. Out of Hamlet's loss of mirth and his forgoing of exercise, a vision is emerging. Or is it only the dream of an unreal glory Hamlet no longer believes in? Having evoked man's most admirable qualities, attributes that make him "the beauty of the world" and "the paragon of animals," Hamlet refuses to claim them for himself. Instead, his whole angelic catalogue collapses suddenly, like a fallen meteor or extinguished rocket, into an ash heap, the merest "quintessence of dust," which leaves the eye of the beholder cold and indifferent.

The brief, one-sentence supplications—"How noble in reason!" "How infinite in faculty . . . !"—allow each exalted attribute to sink into the mind like an oracle, authoritative in its detachment. Even the appalling question "And yet, to me, what is this quintessence of dust?" is more than rhetorical, since it may invite a different response from Rosencrantz or the playgoer than it does from Hamlet. Adjectives are protean, and turn easily into their opposites: "goodly" becomes "sterile," and epithets like "excellent" and "majestical" change into "foul" and "pestilent." "Beauty" is a complex attribute, including both the architectural glory of the firmament, its "roof fretted with golden fire," and the intellectual beauty of a being "infinite in faculty" and "noble in reason." To each glory glimpsed through "this most excellent canopy, the air," which is the unsealed dome of starry heaven itself, Hamlet gives devotion and allegiance. Faced with a crisis of attitude that is also a problem of altitude, Hamlet has the choice of looking either up or down. "Promontory" brings Hamlet to a cliff edge, inviting him either to peer into an abyss or to raise his eyes to the height of a great canopy or dome.

Touching God behind a veil of skepticism, Hamlet finds that the more speculative his flights of prose become, the more they sound like a blank verse poem. Prose accords well enough with his levity and wit. But if we scan as verse the passage beginning, "What a piece of work is man!," we are struck by the casually expansive run-ons, the meditative caesural pauses, and the two alignments of a sentence ending with the termination of what might be a blank verse line. Occurring after "how like a god!," which is Hamlet's boldest claim, and after "how infinite in faculty," which raises humanity above the rest of creation, these alignments allow Hamlet to wear his glory as a cloak. Few speeches in Shakespeare better support Coleridge's claim that even the playwright's "prose has in the lowest *dramatis personae,* a cobbler or a Hamlet, a rhythm so felicitous and so severally appropriate, as to be a virtual meter" (Coleridge, 1930, 1, 13).

Wallace Stevens associates these "glorious" lines from *Hamlet* with nobility. "The quotation from Shakespeare," he tells Elsie Moll, "is particularly serviceable to me now, for I have lately had a sudden conception of the true nobility of men and women." People are to be judged, like Hamlet, "by the valor of their spirits, by their conquest of the natural being, by their victories in philosophy" (1996, 143–44). Despite its exaltation, however, Hamlet's speech is pervaded by ennui and doubt. If his levity is the despair of self-distrust, his wit is the mask of playful irony and skepticism. The difference between the paragon of animals and the quintessence of dust, between the excellent canopy and the congregation of vapors, is the difference between a daydream and a vision. The daydream comes by accident, as the indulgence of a poetic imagination. Perhaps Hamlet as poet even surrenders too easily to liturgical eloquence, ever eager like the psalmist to praise creation. By contrast, his vision of the vapors and the dust comes reluctantly to Hamlet, and by way of deep shock. He surrenders to the poetry as he surrenders to the vagaries of a wayward dream. But he is deepened and made wiser by the prose of his vision.

Like Matthew Arnold, Hamlet wanders between two worlds, one dead, the other powerless to be born. If Arnold is a High Church agnostic, who admires everything about Catholicism except its Christianity, Hamlet is a skeptic who admires everything about the classical wisdom and Christian faith of Renaissance Humanism except the inhumanity of its revenge codes. How can a ghost who comes from purgatory exhort a being angelic in action and godlike in apprehension to commit so inhuman a deed as murder? Hamlet disbelieves in everything, including his role as an avenger. Yet his doubt cannot save him, because it comes, not from the higher angels of his nature, but from a divided will that, even in invoking celestial powers, devotes them to infernal ends.

> Haste me to know't, that I, with wings as swift
> As meditation or the thoughts of love,
> May sweep to my revenge.
>
> (1.5.29–31)

"Wings, meditation, love," as one critic notes: "what inappropriate equipment for a deed of blood! As so often in Shakespeare, the metaphors undo the logic and tell the truth over its head" (Goddard, 1951, 349).

Equally unstable is the dignity to which "the paragon of animals" aspires in *Measure for Measure.*

> but man, proud man,
> Dress'd in a little brief authority,
> Most ignorant of what he's most assur'd,
> His glassy essence, like an angry ape,
> Plays such fantastic tricks before high heaven
> As makes the angels weep who, with our spleens,
> Would all themselves laugh mortal.
>
> (2.2.117–23)

The blank verse veers so erratically between extremes of self-confidence and ignorance, laughter and tears, that it anticipates by well over a century Alexander Pope's famous couplets on humanity's fractured legacy in *An Essay on Man.* It is often assumed that if man has an essence, it is to discover essences. As one philosopher wryly notes, "The notion that our chief task is to mirror accurately, in our own Glassy Essence, the universe around us is the complement of the notion, common to Democritus and Descartes, that the universe is made up of very simple, clearly and distinctly knowable things, knowledge of whose essences provides the master-vocabulary which permits commensuration of all discourses" (Rorty, 1979, 357). Though man assumes his soul reflects this universe as in a mirror, his glassy essence is so fragile and brittle, so riddled with cracks and flaws, that the ghostly antics he performs with his optical toy are an offense to heaven. "Authority" is immediately qualified by the adjectives "little" and "brief." It is further eroded by the fact that "proud man" presumes to wear his authority as a garment, which is only an accident of his attire, not an essential quality bequeathed to him at birth, as immortality is said to be conferred on angels and gods.

Just as divided as Shakespeare's assessment of man's angelic and apelike nature in *Measure for Measure* is Tennyson's grand appraisal of man's dual status as paragon and misfit in section 56 of *In Memoriam.* Often called a Victorian *Essay on Man, In Memoriam* strikes more dissonant chords than Pope's poem. Stranding man on the isthmus of a middle state, Pope merely rides upon a rocking horse, as Keats says, and calls it Pegasus.

> Created half to rise, and half to fall;
> Great lord of all things, yet a prey to all:
> Sole judge of Truth, in endless Error hurled:
> The glory, jest, and riddle of the world!
> (*An Essay on Man* 2:15–18)

By contrast, Tennyson, like Hamlet, wrecks such harmonies forever. Qualities of "purpose," "trust," and "love" that exalt man, that make him, as Hamlet says, "noble in reason," "infinite in faculty," angelic "in apprehension," "the beauty of the world," "the paragon of animals," also make him, as the lowliest "quintessence of dust" (*Hamlet* 2.2.315–19), the great anomaly in creation. The psalm rolled to wintry skies by this damaged god or angel made of dust strikes a noble discord in the music of the spheres.

> And he, shall he,
>
> Man, her last work, who seemed so fair,
> Such splendid purpose in his eyes,

> Who rolled the psalm to wintry skies,
> Who built him fanes of fruitless prayer,
>
> Who trusted God was love indeed
> And love Creation's final law—
> Though Nature, red in tooth and claw
> With ravine, shrieked against his creed—
>
> Who loved, who suffered countless ills,
> Who battled for the True, the Just,
> Be blown about the desert dust,
> Or sealed within the iron hills?
>
> (*In Memoriam* 56.8–20)

In the first two quatrains, a familiar feature of the appositional sublime, the use of widely spaced anaphora—"Who built," "Who trusted," "Who loved"—gives man, God's noblest work, a spacious dwelling place in language. But, far from confirming that nobility, the run-ons between stanzas suspend man over an abyss of dizzying duration and depth. If God is not love, how can Feuerbach and George Eliot insist that love is godlike? In the last four lines, the relative pronouns modifying "man"—"who loved," "who suffered," "who battled"—begin huddling together. "Who hath the oracle of [man's] ashes," asks Thomas Browne, or where they are to be scattered? (1967, 245). Diffused as dust or imprisoned in iron, the bleak predicates of the quoted question—"Be blown about . . . / Or sealed within"—mount to a crescendo of panic and fear. Normally *In Memoriam*'s self-contained tetrameter quatrains provide the mourner with a safe platform on which to stand. But now that floor is opening up. At the bottom of the altar-stairs that slope through darkness up to God lies a false floor. And through that floor, man, the cosmic misfit, can fall in an apparently endless descent far lower than the rest of the creation. Hamlet's "paragon of animals" turns out to be as far below the dinosaurs as he was once thought to be above them as "the roof and crown of things."

In the last two stanzas of section 56, the fear that the most godlike of animals is not only an angel of dust but also a self-divided and grotesque monster of discord collapses the expansive appositions into word heaps that are barely grammatical.

> No more? A monster then, a dream,
> A discord. Dragons of the prime
> That tare each other in their slime,
> Were mellow music matched with him.
>
> O life as futile, then, as frail!
> O for thy voice to soothe and bless!

What hope of answer, or redress?
Behind the veil, behind the veil.

(56.21–28)

The final fearful decline into fragments without verbs—"No more? A monster then, a dream / A discord"—destroys the harmony of the "mellow music" (24). Do dreams of cosmic harmony, as Thomas Hardy believes, tragically unfit Hamlet's "paragon of animals" for life and love in a theater of war described by Erasmus Darwin as "one vast slaughter house"? Biologically considered, dragons of the primeval slime are better suited to a gladiatorial combat "red in tooth and claw" (11) than Hamlet's damaged and ineffectual angel. A noble discord in the scale of being, he is a creature infinite in faculty and godlike in apprehension who dreams of glories unknown to his Creator. Though such a Creator is not malicious, he may not, as Einstein thought, be subtle either, but simply the "Vast Imbecility" that Hardy fears in "Nature's Questioning" (line 13), a God who produces minds but lacks one himself—a monstrous paradox. The section ends in a cacophony of disintegration, subsiding in the final breathless phrases "Behind the veil, behind the veil" to a momentary stasis of chord and discord, expectation and distress.

How, we might ask, can poets like Tennyson or Robert Frost conscript a Darwinian world of accidental variation and random change into the service of art, where design of some kind must prevail? Tennyson accomplishes this paradoxical feat by showing that design is stubborn. It persists in the highly patterned quatrains of *In Memoriam,* a poem that questions the very existence of design. It survives, too, in Frost's exquisitely designed little sonnet "Design," even when its speaker dares to doubt "if design govern in a thing so small" as a moth's destruction by a spider. No poet, I suspect, can dispense with arguments from design as thoroughly as Darwin and still remain a poet. A poem without design is merely a bad poem. Even in expressing his fear that God may be a wild poet, creating without conscience or an aim, Tennyson in *In Memoriam* manages to subdue that fear by ascribing the wildness, not to God himself, but to a creature acutely conscious of indifference and cruelty in God's creation.

Unlike Iago's and Edmund's soliloquies, which anticipate or explain what later happens in *Othello* and *King Lear,* Hamlet's soliloquies often offer a glimpse of alternative scripts for the play. In "To be, or not to be," for example, Hamlet might have committed suicide, but does not. Later, Hamlet might easily have killed Claudius at prayer, but does not. In each case the soliloquist writes a rough outline for a script Shakespeare decides to lay aside or reinvent.

> Now might I do it pat, now he is praying:
> And now I'll do it: and so he goes to heaven:
> And so am I revenged. That would be scanned.
> (*Hamlet* 3.3.73–75)

Since Claudius's betrayal of guilt during the play scene has confirmed the truth of the Ghost's accusation, this would surely be the perfect moment for Hamlet to dispatch Claudius, a murderous adulterer and usurper. Justifying his action later, Hamlet would doubtless be welcomed into the arms of a people who love the prince and despise his uncle. But alas, as A. C. Bradley says, Hamlet "scans" his words; "and the sword that he drew at the words, 'And now I'll do it,' is thrust back into its sheath" (1957, 107). Instead of suppressing all reference to the plot Hamlet wipes from his mind, Shakespeare allows traces to show through. His willingness to share with the playgoers an alternative script for the play is Shakespeare's version of Tennyson's practice of "reinventing" his poems.

Recasting his lines even as he writes them, just as Shakespeare reinvents *Hamlet,* the grieving Tennyson of the epistle to Dufferin makes no attempt to censor subversive thoughts about the comprehensive wrongness of a son's dying before his father.

> To question, why
> The sons before the fathers die,
> Not mine! and I may meet him soon.
> ("To the Marquis of Dufferin and Ava,"
> lines 46–48)

Even in rejecting his right to ask the question, Tennyson lets it stand, crying out for an answer. Shakespeare must have asked the same question after the death of his son, Hamnet.

In his verse epistle to James Spedding, Tennyson, like Hamlet, allows first thoughts to stand, before amending them.

> I will not say, "God's ordinance
> Of Death is blown in every wind";
> For that is not a common chance
> That takes away a noble mind.
> ("To J.S.," lines 45–48)

"I will not say," the poet says, even as he says it. So eager is he to have his first thoughts conform to his own corrected notions that he admits a moment later, "I wrote I know not what" (57). Tennyson allows his self-corrections to stand because, as the sign of a self-divided mind like Hamlet's, they sanction his use of other two-way meanings in the elegy: "Lie still, dry dust, secure of change" (76). Is the dead Spedding assured of change, secure in the knowledge that nothing is exempt from change but change itself? Or is he now protected from change, as secure in his grave as a prisoner in his cell?

Like a palimpsest's partially effaced script, Tennyson's Hamlet-like impulse to scrutinize his first thoughts and then revise them can be glimpsed in section 10 of *In Memoriam.* Allowing the submarine nightmare of the corpse engulfed by "roaring wells" to correct the unreal pastoral picture of the dead man resting "beneath the clover" (lines 17, 13), Tennyson registers both his fond illusions and his sobering corrections, the thoughts he voices and the more affecting and disturbing ones he often leaves unsaid.

Hamlet is the play the Victorian poets quote most often, not because it is Shakespeare's greatest tragedy, but because its hero, in the manner of many Victorians, is immobilized in his sphere of action. Like Hamlet, Browning's speaker in "Two in the Campagna" has one foot in infinity and the other in time. Why should his aggressive sexual appropriation of the body of nature—of its "small orange cup" and "primal naked forms of flowers" (lines 16, 28)—be all erotic foreplay, without the expected consummation? Why, having touched the woman close, must he stand away, like Joyce's Gabriel Conroy in "The Dead," as if he were about to see and touch a ghost?

Browning's lover wants to compass "Infinite passion" in a single moment of time. But he forgets that Hamlet's paragon of animals, however infinite in faculty and angelic in apprehension, is also doomed to simplify his endless desires into specific wants which he then finds inadequate.

> Just when I seemed about to learn!
> Where is the thread now? Off again!
> The old trick! Only I discern—
> Infinite passion, and the pain
> Of finite hearts that yearn.
> ("Two in the Campagna," lines 56–60)

Though endless repetition may exalt a celebrant of "Infinite passion," for the sensual Don Juan who wants a single pleasure, sex, an infinite number of times, it spells only boredom and defeat.

The hedonist in "Two in the Campagna" unwittingly betrays his misgivings about free love by allowing a tentative wavering tone to enter the first lines he speaks: "I wonder do you feel today / As I have felt?" (1–2). The lingering uncertainty is made more tenuous by the *ababa* rhyme scheme, in which the final *a* rhyme abides like an unsettling echo, just when we assume we have heard the last of it. Even when the aspiring lover adapts Renan's argument that nature knows nothing of chastity, the ugly mounting of the small orange cup by five groping beetles does nothing to promote his cause. What should be a culminating appeal to the woman ("How is it under our control / To love or not to love?" [34–35]) becomes a turning point instead. Sensing like Hamlet that a "king of infinite space" can never "be bounded in a nutshell" (*Hamlet* 2.2.260–61), Browning's self-critical speaker starts out to say, "How can I help loving you?" but ends by confessing, "How can I help not loving you," my little nutshell, who "are just so much" to me, "no more" (37)? No sooner has the lover experienced a pang of the soul's incurable loneliness than he protects himself against loss by teaching himself both to care and not to care about being finite and shell-bound. Instead of dwindling into a predictable Don Juan, who wants one thing an infinite number of times, Browning's lover prefers to be an unsatisfied Hamlet or Faust. He would rather be denied an infinite number of things all at once.

In a notorious 1871 review of D. G. Rossetti's *Poems,* Robert Buchanan casts leading Victorian poets for roles in *Hamlet.* He offers the part of Hamlet to Tennyson and Browning, who are to play the prince on alternate nights. The sage and serious Matthew Arnold will play Horatio to their Hamlet, while poor Rossetti is cast as Osric. As for Swinburne and Morris, these other members of "the Fleshly School of poetry" will have to content themselves with minor parts as Rosencrantz and Guildenstern. In Buchanan's malicious caricature, Pre-Raphaelite poets are suited only for walk-on parts. But they will resort, he predicts, to "what is technically known as 'gagging.'" They will "make themselves fully as prominent as the leading character, and . . . indulge in soliloquies and business strictly belonging to Hamlet himself" (888). Despite Tennyson's many quotations from *Hamlet,* however, and Browning's introspective bent, the true Prince of Denmark among the poets is surely not Buchanan's first two choices for the role, or any of his Pre-Raphaelite Pretenders, but Arthur Hugh Clough, the Victorian poet whose skepticism most resembles Hamlet's.

Though Adrian Poole makes no mention of Clough in his fine study of Shakespeare and the Victorians, it is Clough, I think, more than any other poet or novelist, who justifies Poole's claim that "if there is a presiding spirit over the Victorian Shakespeare, and what the Victorians made of Shakespeare, it is Hamlet" (2004, 8). Sicklied over like Hamlet with the pale cast of thought, Clough's hero in *Amours de Voyage* combines a subtle and incessant intellectual activity with an incapacity to decide or do anything. If there is "something rotten in the state of Denmark," there is something equally corrupt in the consciousness of Clough's Victorian England, which values thoughtless compliance over Emerson's conviction that prayer is too often a disease of the will, creed too often a disease of the mind. The epitaph Browning plants on his grammarian, "This man decided not to Live but Know," might also have been planted on Clough's hero, Claude, whose name in Latin, "claudus," means "lame," and who is permanently maimed by speculations that unfit him for action. Clough's Claude is Hamlet's most bemused Victorian heir. Of their high intelligence, which makes them intellectuals to the core, we may say what Freud says of religion: intellection is also the disease it claims to cure.

If Hamlet, like Aristotle, thought death were the end, he might commit suicide. But he avoids self-slaughter because, for all he knows, death is a sleep, and in that sleep someone who has killed himself might have bad dreams. At the moment he dies, Hamlet tells Horatio "the rest is silence." The dead prince will be silent, not because he knows there will be nothing to tell Horatio, but because death is an undiscovered country. No traveler has ever returned from its borders. Hamlet's last words are self-concealing and elusive. He uses his remaining breath, not to lighten the burden of the mystery, but to ask Horatio to speak wisely on his behalf. Claude's great temptation is to betray Hamlet's skepticism and reserve by making the truth less provisional and uncertain than it is.

> I will look straight out, see things, not try to evade
> them;
> Fact shall be fact for me, and the Truth the Truth
> as ever,
> Flexible, changeable, vague, and multiform, and
> doubtful.—
> Off, and depart to the void, thou subtle, fantastical
> tempter!
> (*Amours de Voyage* 5.5.100–103)

The ill genius he would banish from his deathbed is a temptation to profess something he does not believe.

> O ill genius thou! I shall, at my life's dissolution,
> (When the pulses are weak, and the feeble light of the
> reason
> Flickers, an unfed flame retiring slow from the socket),
> Low on a sick-bed laid, hear one, as it were, at the
> doorway,
> And looking up see thee, standing by, looking emptily
> at me;
> I shall entreat thee then, though now I dare refuse
> thee,—
> Pale and pitiful now, but terrible then to the dying.—

> Well, I will see thee again: and while I can will repel
> thee.
>
> (5.5.105–12)

Claude is afraid of what will happen at the end of his life when the "light of reason" can barely drag itself across a line-ending to flicker precariously, as it does at the head of line 107, before starting to gutter down at the second-syllable caesura. Though reluctant to surrender the menacing "unfed flame retiring slow," which acquires the supernatural power of a Miltonic phantom framed between the adjective "unfed" and the solemn epithet "retiring slow," Claude still wants to repel from his sick-bed the specter of any forced profession of belief. But just as Hamlet defies augury not a whit, so Claude says he believes in Providence, "at least in part" (5.8.176). About to lapse into a mindless optimism, Claude is embarrassed by his dishonest facility with words and immediately edits his confession: "Ah, no, that isn't it" (5.8.178).

In *Adam Bede,* George Eliot says it is "very hard . . . to say the exact truth even about your own immediate feelings—much harder than to say something fine about them which is *not* the exact truth" (chap. 17). Claude is always trying to elude the ill genius that tempts him to say something eloquent and fine that falsifies what he feels. Unlike Shakespeare's John of Gaunt, who thinks truth lies upon the lips of dying men, Claude fears that people are more likely to fake their last testaments. Last words are not always authentic. Instead of concentrating the mind, death may distract or confuse it. If Claude is to remain like Hamlet in a state of perpetual uncertainty, he has to admit he is uncertain whether his skepticism will desert him at the hour of his death. Will he resist the temptation of many dying people to say, not what they feel, but what they think they ought to say?

Like Hamlet, Claude dwells too exclusively in the life of the mind. Leaping over his anticipated married life with Mary, he imagines his own death and funeral even before he decides to track down his future wife and woo her. In Claude's mind the prospect of a train terminus turns into the terminus of life itself. He cannot think of marriage and his wedding trip without imagining the progress of his own funeral train. Indeed, unless he foresaw his own funeral train, he could not marry Mary, because he needs the assurance that no contract lasts forever. His interest in Mary, he muses, is a mere quirk of placement or accident: "it is only juxtaposition,— / Juxtaposition, in short; and what is juxtaposition?" (1.11.225–26). Clough uses juxtaposition to write eloquently about the heartbreaking waste of Claude's imaginative gifts. Aspiring "evermore to the Absolute only" (5.4.59), Claude is prevented from bringing his love to any satisfactory conclusion. The decline of Hope, the second of Paul's three Christian virtues, into hope ("As for Hope, to-morrow I hope to be starting for Naples" [5.10.203]) charts the decline of the man without "Hope," mastered by mere whims of the moment. Notoriously unmethodical in tracking Mary down, Claude possesses not the purposive sense of a successful lover, but the negative capability that Keats associates with the dramatic art of Shakespeare. Claude's decisions to act are no more effective in banishing indecision than are Hamlet's attempts to use conspiracy to achieve a conspirator's ends. Like Hamlet's digressions, which unfit him for his role in a revenge tragedy, Claude's speculations about art, theology, politics, and religion are the evasions of someone who seems to have forgotten what a poem entitled *Amours de Voyage* is ostensibly about. Breaking down his options and then multiplying his resolutions to act, Claude imagines outcomes for events that have not yet occurred and will probably never occur. Like Hamlet, Claude keeps running away from what he seems to be running toward. He even tries to run away from the knowledge that he is running.

George Meredith's sonnet sequence *Modern Love,* an anatomy of marriage and its discontents, is a cross between Clough's *Amours de Voyage* and Shakespeare's sonnets. It combines the false starts and contretemps of Clough's *Amours* with the reprisals and banter that wreck harmony between Shakespeare's lover and the dark lady of the sonnets or between Petruchio and Katherina in *The Taming of the Shrew.* As wittily ironic and detached as Clough, Meredith builds on the form of the Italian rather than the English sonnet. Capturing the overflow effect of the sixteen-line sonnet in which Romeo and Juliet extend courtesies at the masked ball, Meredith adds two extra lines to make the sonnet a structure of four quatrains rhymed *abba.* The powerful concluding sonnet combines tense, dramatic syntax with sprung rhythms reminiscent of Hopkins.

> Thus piteously Love closed what he begat:
> The union of this ever-diverse pair!
> These two were rapid falcons in a snare,
> Condemned to do the flitting of the bat.
> Lovers beneath the singing sky of May,
> They wandered once; clear as the dew on flowers;
> But they fed not on the advancing hours:
> Their hearts held cravings for the buried day.
> Then each applied to each that fatal knife,
> Deep questioning, which probes to endless dole.
> Ah, what a dusty answer gets the soul
> When hot for certainties in this our life!—
> In tragic hints here see what evermore
> Moves dark as yonder midnight ocean's force,

> Thundering like ramping hosts of warrior horse,
> To throw that faint thin line upon the shore!
>
> (sonnet 50, *Modern Love*)

Instead of making the advancing years a climax, and marriage a harvest of memories in common, time starves and embitters Meredith's aging couple. They never learn the secret of negative capability, the ability to remain in uncertainties like Keats, Clough, and Shakespeare, without irritably searching after some vexed certainty or hotly contested truth. In the beautiful concluding simile, the successive triple and quadruple stresses of "faint thin line" and "midnight ocean's force" capture the heavy tread of powers that thunder across the earth, as in Carlyle's "Natural Supernaturalism," before dissipating their force like the clouds in *The Tempest,* which leave not a rack behind.

In a second minor masterpiece of Hamlet-like indecision and doubt, *Dipsychus,* Clough allows a Spirit to mock the fertility with which contradictions and antinomies proliferate in his protagonist's mind. As the Spirit invades the mind and becomes increasingly a region of it, Dipsychus finds that only in some saving action can forces of doubt and mental paralysis be appeased. All minds possess a Dipsychus and a Spirit, and the two impulses—the impulses to know and to act—are locked together, as in Hamlet, in a life-and-death embrace. Quoting lines from *As You Like It,* the Spirit reminds Dipsychus that Shakespeare is as much the advocate of sexual license and ribaldry as of mid-Victorian innocence and purity (1.3.129–31). As one critic says, "The lesson here is not that the great literary and artistic tradition of Western Europe provides Dipsychus with insufficient ammunition to fight his moral battles; it is that the Spirit can draw from the same literary stockpile" (LaPorte, 2011, 140).

Clough would unquestionably find more to admire in the skeptic than in his critical opponent in J. W. Ben Gough's spirited parody "The Higher Criticism."

> I saw a Higher Critic, looking scholarly and cool,
> As he stood beside the portals of the new Negation
> school;
> As I passed he stopped me by a motion of his hand,
> Saying, "Pray don't look so much at ease—you do
> not understand.
>
> . . . .
>
> "You're in error if you think that David wrote the
> so-called Psalms,
> Or see a Messianic sense in the sacrifice of lambs;

> And your comforting assurance that the Canon is
> exact
> Is in painful contradiction to the Higher Critic fact.
> (lines 1–4, 21–24)

Though Clough, like Hamlet, shares the skepticism of a Higher Critic, he is also a fideist who in the impotence of his reason is prepared to take refuge in faith.

In a review of "Recent English Poetry" published in the *North American Review* (July 1853), Clough contrasts Alexander Smith's forthright Spasmodic verse with the tortuous thought of Arnold's Empedocles. Smith is to Othello what Arnold is to Hamlet. The latter is "all thoughtful, discriminating selection and rejection," and the former "frank and bold acceptance of what lies around [him]" (quoted in Houghton, 1959, 401). In the mirror of Arnold's Hamlet-like Empedocles, Clough sees reflected his own overly scrupulous Claude. In an exuberant parody, Clough half concedes the defects of Claude's ambivalent manner and invites the reader to consider an alternative. "Will you be content, O reader, to plod in German manner over miles of a straight road, that seems to lead somewhere, with the prospect of arriving at last at some point where it will divide at equal angles, and lead equally in two opposite direction, where you may therefore safely pause, and thankfully set up your rest, and adore in sacred doubt the Supreme Bifurcation? Or do you hold, with Voltaire, who said (apropos of the question then debated among French wits, whether there were or were not a God) that 'after all, one must take a side'?" (Houghton, 1959, 401).

Clough is as skeptical a critic as he is a theologian. Taking Shakespeare to task for diverting us "from the natural course of thought, feeling, and narrative, to see how curiously two trifles resemble each other" (Houghton, 1959, 402), Clough, like Keats, believes Shakespeare is an intelligent but too easily diverted master of negative capability. We know a great deal, yet nothing essential, about him. The more facts we collect, the greater our ignorance. Disappearing like a ghost behind a multitude of masks, Shakespeare entertains a host of ideas without embracing any of them. To claim we have reached a definitive understanding of him is not just a factual or historical mistake: it is also a literary and critical one. What, after all, is literary understanding of Shakespeare but a willingness to remain in uncertainties, like Hamlet, Montaigne, or Clough's skeptically quizzical Claude?

Othello is deceived about what Desdemona and Cassio may have done in the recent past, and Hamlet cannot muster enough resolve to act upon what he knows. He is the failed hero of a revenge tragedy because he broods too much about the past to lead his life forward. This contrast between understanding life backward and leading it forward lends force to A. C. Bradley's famous remark that if Hamlet and Othello had exchanged roles, there would have been no tragedy. The forthright Othello would have dispatched Claudius without delay, and the shrewd Hamlet would have seen through Iago in an instant.

Though incessant intellection unfits Claude for action, he is as quick to discern and as quick to feel as Hamlet, who thinks with the aid of ever-shifting metaphors. Arnold calls Clough a mere "depth-hunter" in poetry. But he is wrong about Clough, whose poetry has worn better than his own. As Barbara Hardy says, "Clough writes intellectual poetry, but it is poetry in which the passions and sensations are inseparable from the intellect. . . . Clough has the rare ability to stand back from his strong passion without excess of irony. Where there is irony, it is the very rare kind that can live with strong feeling and does not shrivel it up by ridicule or criticism" (1969, 266).

Although T. S. Eliot's Prufrock declines the honor and protests, "No! I am not Prince Hamlet, nor was meant to be" ("The Love Song of J. Alfred Prufrock," line 112), he belongs to the same tradition as Hamlet and Claude. Incapable like Hamlet or Prufrock of decisive action, Clough's Claude can still be admired for his skeptical reserve. It is a quality that draws him into the orbit of those lukewarm or Laodicean angels whom Dante consigns to limbo, in an antechamber of hell, but whose great refusal seems strangely heroic, even endearing, to such uncommitted ironists as Clough, Pater, and Oscar Wilde. In positing forms of Denis Donoghue's "adversary knowledge," which "puts in parenthesis, for the duration of the reading, the claims that the world makes upon us" (Donoghue, 1995, 316, 318), Hamlet and Claude perfect a "rhetoric of pleasure, delay, and antinomian care" that Donoghue associates with the legacy of Pater and of his intellectual heirs, Joyce and Yeats. As Eliot says, the polished, unperturbed skepticism of a Hamlet or a Clough is "a highly civilized trait, though, when it declines into pyrrhonism it is weakness: for we need not only the strength to defer a decision, but the strength to decide" (1948, 29). Like Hamlet, Claude has a queasy sense of groping in the dark, of trying to believe in something like purgatory or the God of the agnostic theologians, neither of which may actually exist. If the ghost of Hamlet's father demands that his son commit a sin, how can the ghost come from purgatory, a place for purging old sins, not for committing new ones? And if Clough is unable to embrace the fideism of his tutor, W. G. Ward, how can he avoid unbelief or atheism? Clough's faith, like Shakespeare's, seems to have been gutted. Taking no sides in conflicts and resolving no exacting issues, he is one of the undogmatic skeptics who locate themselves like Hamlet in the middle world of Thomas Hardy's Laodicean, the lovable and elusive Paula Power.

Watching the shadow of the fifth century fall upon the sixteenth in chapter 3 of *Apologia Pro Vita Sua,* John Henry Newman briefly glimpses a ghost. Even when it disappears, like the ghost of Hamlet's father, he protests that "he who has seen a ghost, cannot be as if he had never seen it. The heavens had opened and closed again" (1968, 99). Has Newman had a glimpse into heaven or merely been enchanted? Is he a Prospero upon whom riches have dropped? Or is he a Hamlet, disturbed by what he has seen, uncertain of the status of a ghost that has vanished almost as soon as it appeared? When Newman peers into the mirror of historical analogy, he is appalled to see staring back at him the face of a heretic, a Monophysite. But worse than seeing a heretic is the experience of seeing no face at all. This is what happens in chapter 5 when, looking into the mirror of "this living busy world," he sees reflected no image of its Creator.

At first glance it might seem that Newman's epic survey of hopelessness and disillusion in the last chapter of *Apologia Pro Vita Sua* is as remote from Shakespeare as St. Paul is from Hamlet. But the theologian's dismay is no less visceral than Hamlet's when he tells Horatio "how ill's all here about my heart" (*Hamlet* 5.2.223). The prospect of being stranded on a desolate South Sea island, "having no hope and without God in the world," inflicts a terrible wound on Newman. It assaults him like an attack of headache or nausea. Newman's feelings overflow. Like Hamlet after the visitation of his father's ghost, he is in spiritual extremity, driven into straits from which there is no obvious escape. Either God does not exist, or "the human race is implicated in some terrible aboriginal calamity. It is out of joint with the purposes of its Creator."

> To consider the world in its length and breadth, its various history, the many races of man, their starts, their fortunes, their mutual alienation, their conflicts; and then their ways, habits, governments, form of worship; their enterprises, their aimless courses, their random achievements and acquirements, the impotent conclusion of long-standing facts, the tokens so faint and broken of a superintending design, the blind evolution of what turn out to be great powers of truth, the progress of things, as if from unreasoning elements, not towards final causes, the greatness and littleness of man, his far-reaching aims, his short duration, the curtain hung over his futurity, the disappointments of life, the defeat of good, the success of evil, physical pain, mental anguish, the prevalence and intensity of sin, the pervading idolatries, the corruptions, the dreary hopeless irreligion, that condition of the whole race, so fearfully yet exactly described in the Apostle's words,

> "having no hope and without God in the world,"—all this is a vision to dizzy and appall; and inflicts upon the mind the sense of a profound mystery, which is absolutely beyond human solution.
>
> (Newman, 1968, 186–87)

This long paragraph consists of a single intimidating sentence. Searching every state and canvassing every prayer, its protracted indictments have the authoritative weight and majesty of Samuel Johnson's poem "The Vanity of Human Wishes." But Newman's language is both simpler and more tortured than Johnson's. For Newman's taste, Johnson's style is too mannered and patterned. "Much as I love and revere the personal character and intellectual vigor of Dr. Johnson," Newman says, "I cannot deny that his style often outruns the sense and the occasion, and is wanting in that simplicity which is the attribute of genius" (1959, 275).

Though a subtle thinker, Newman shares with Shakespeare a love of simplicity not always apparent in Johnson. A rugged writer who scales the truth by "some inward instinct, or some obscure meaning," like "a clamberer on a steep cliff" (1887, 257), Newman is also drawn in prayer to the simplest expressions and plainest phrases. He needs "regular words," Owen Chadwick reminds us, "short, simple, easy to use and never so elaborate that they overoccupy the mind or tempt it into formality. He loved, and revived the use of, the Private Prayers of Lancelot Andrews. . . . Newman once defined his own ideal thus: 'the lowliest, awfullest, calmest, concisest language we can'" (1983, 11). Though a cardinal of his church who travels to Rome to receive a red hat, Newman is as opposed to formality in dress as he is to formal language. Preferring a dingy cassock to a prelate's robes, Newman was once turned away from St. Paul's Cathedral by an officious verger, partly because he looked too shabby to enter. "Put me into official garb and I am worth nothing," Newman writes to a friend. "Leave me to myself, and every now and then I shall do something" (Chadwick, 1983, 10).

Ever practical and empirical, Newman has as much affinity with David Hume as with the speculative genius of Plato and the Church Fathers, whom he loved to read and edit. Too English to be a hedgehog, a builder of big systems like Aristotle or Aquinas, Newman is a fox, adept at making sly, agile moves. Though Hume may seem an odd ally, Newman accepts the great skeptic's distinction between strong and abiding sensory impressions and weak ideas of sense. The most lively ideas of a theologian's "notional assent" are still inferior, feeble copies of those vivid impressions that inform and animate the "real assent" of a believer. Just as Berkeley simplifies his theory of knowledge by banishing material substance as an unnecessary postulate, so Hume rejects as a fiction any spiritual substance in which a ghostly succession of sense impressions might be thought to inhere. Newman agrees with Hume, however, that only a philosopher in his study could think that the world is a theater of fleeting phantoms that continually pass, re-pass, and glide away. Hume posits causality, not because he can show it exists, but because the moment he forsakes his study he must have faith in it to preserve the world's coherence and stability. Newman embraces faith for the same reason: to make his world intelligible. It is the last refuge of a skeptical mind.

In the passage from Newman I have just quoted at length, a reader waits, endlessly it seems, for a grammatical completion of its opening infinitive phrase, "to consider." Though man's aims are far reaching, the duration of man himself is pitiably puny and "short." As in Hamlet's appeal to the "paragon of animals," the "beauty of the world," man's drive toward noble ends is thwarted by "pervading idolatries" and superstitions. The greatness of a creature angelic in apprehension and infinite in faculty is offset by his stupefying "littleness." Since his designs are everywhere thwarted, good is defeated and evil appears to thrive. Unlike Hamlet, however, whose indictment of Denmark's rottenness is too often an invective of intemperance and imbalance, Newman produces a despairingly honest and balanced picture. His words are as frank as they are harsh, and possess the authority of unwilling testimony. Drawn from the depth of Newman's conscience, his words seem wrenched out of him against his will.

Even when writing lasting works of theology, Newman makes his speculations sound as tentative as possible. Like Hamlet, he has "so profound a sense of the mysteries of the universe" that, in Owen Chadwick's words, he is "skeptical of anyone's success in probing. A man's mind may come to shadows of truth, and probabilities, and sudden poetic flashes of insight." But there is so much more in heaven and earth than Newman, Hamlet, or Horatio can dream of that he finds "little purpose in toiling away to build a tower of the intellect which will only cramp reality and imprison truth" (1983, 15). In his despair Newman is as addicted as Hamlet to the doubling of epithets and the conjoining of opposites, "the greatness and littleness of man, his far-reaching aims, his short duration, . . . the defeat of good, the success of evil, physical pain, mental anguish." Though Newman would be familiar with the spawning of such antithetical and parallel constructions in the Psalms and the Book of Common Prayer, he sounds more like Shakespeare's prince than the psalmist. Like Hamlet in his soliloquy "O what a rogue and peasant slave am I," Newman taxes the mind by doubling and tripling his examples. Trying to conjoin what threatens to fly apart, he creates, like Hamlet, what Frank Kermode calls a "small wilderness of mirrors" (2000, 113). In Kermode's words,

"The meaning of the whole depends upon a kind of unnaturalness in the doubling," bordering in Newman's case on hysteria, and introducing "unease and mystery" into his prose (102).

To read the paragraph is to suffer torture on a rack. It is to move through a long catalogue of grammatical objects, only to be brought up short by an emphatic dash, which eventually provides a principal clause for a sentence that has been spilling over sixteen lines of print. It is impossible not to experience Newman's own trauma and confusion. Part of the writing's shock value and power lies in its oddly appropriate use of the long-delayed verb "inflicts." "The sense of a profound mystery" is not usually "inflicted" upon the mind. But Newman's sensation is as sharp as pain and as acute as an attack of migraine or nausea. His way of concluding the paragraph illustrates what he has just observed about the "impotent conclusion of long-standing facts." The catalogue produces a lengthy list of incontrovertible truths. But the conclusion itself is impotent because it concludes or solves nothing.

In the end, a calamity either destroys its victim or restores some trace of sanity, some "calm of mind, all passion spent," by disclosing a design that the tragedy conceals. We are never sure if Troilus will survive his nightmare of a world divided, of bonds severed and dissolved. "His heart's hope is his soul's despair," as R. P. Blackmur says of Henry Adams (1980, 13). But unlike Hamlet, who despairs of grace, Newman asks what the calamity of man's fall has to teach him. He seeks an answer by pushing steadily into the depth of his subject. Like Hamlet, Newman senses that in the paragon who is also the quintessence of dust there is both greatness and insufficiency, a mystery "too glorious and too profound," as Chadwick says, "for the tidiest minds to limit" (1983, 58). The vestige of a nobility that is impossible to attain in a fallen state is anticipated several times by Shakespeare. As Christ goes about his Father's business, so Florizell's father in going about his own paternal business tells his son that nothing Perdita "does or seems / But smacks of something greater than herself, / Too noble for this place" (*The Winter's Tale* 4.4.157–59). A more distant but equally haunting presentiment of noble origins is found in *Twelfth Night,* when Olivia inquires about Viola's parentage, and the latter replies that it is "Above [her] fortunes" (1.5.296). But despite the shadow Shakespeare casts on Newman, only Newman could have written *Apologia Pro Vita.* For as Newman himself remarks in the chapter on literature in *The Idea of a University,* "We might as well say that one man's shadow is another's as that the style of a really gifted mind can belong to any but himself. . . . His thought and feeling are personal, and so his language is personal" (1959, 269). If the style of a great writer "follows him about *as* a shadow" (269), then any encounter of Newman with Shakespeare can seldom be more than a chance intersection of passing shades.

At first, the possibility of a terrible divide that splits apart a parent and his children is present to Newman only as a haunting echo. He entertains it, as does Shakespeare, in the fable of a handsome and refined youth, without memory of his childhood, disinherited, as it seems, by parents he has shamed. The fable deftly corrects certain defects in the stark dilemma Newman had originally posed, which too carelessly implied that in discarding his children God left behind no tokens of his presence. The tokens are there, but they point toward a desolating disjunction, a great divide between "the promise and the condition" of man's being. Hamlet and Newman both surrender to despair. But Newman's despair is temporary. His shock is followed by intensified perception, because his vision of insurrection and calamity retains intact a vestige of design. He has relived a disaster and begun to understand it.

PART III

SHADES OF KING LEAR

5

Thou, Nature, Art My Goddess

THE GARDEN AND THE HEATH

THE ETHICS OF SHAKESPEARE'S EDMUND IN *KING LEAR* IS THE ethics of naturalism, embraced in the Victorian age by Darwin, Herbert Spencer, and Tennyson's fool Dagonet in "The Last Tournament." When Edmund invokes Nature as his goddess in his first soliloquy in *King Lear,* he is introducing a distinction between "natural right" and "man-made law" that harks back to the thought of the Greek sophists. Coming after the straight prose of Goneril and Regan, the perfect medium for two practical schemers, Edmund's lift into lively blank verse lends force to his claim to be an imaginative villain who possesses natural capacities and innate talents lacking in his brother.

> Thou, Nature, art my goddess; to thy law
> My services are bound. Wherefore should I
> Stand in the plague of custom, and permit
> The curiosity of nations to deprive me,
> For that I am some twelve or fourteen moonshines
> Lag of a brother? Why bastard? Wherefore base,
> When my dimensions are as well compact,
> My mind as generous, and my shape as true,
> As honest madam's issue?
>
> (*King Lear* 1.2.1–9)

In the litany of Edmund's grievances, "base" keeps sounding as an insistent groundswell or basso ostinato: "Why brand they us / With base? with baseness? bastardy? base, base?" (1.2.9–10). He protests that the base behavior predicted of him by his father is both illogical and unloving. As it turns out, the law's branding Edmund a bastard degrades an intelligent and resourceful son into a monster more unrestrained and aggressive than any "lusty stealth of nature" that begot him. In the end Edmund proves more heartless than his father in his worst nightmare could possibly imagine.

Edmund the base
Shall top th' legitimate. I grow, I prosper.
Now, gods, stand up for bastards.
(*King Lear* 1.2.20–22)

No prophecy in Shakespeare is more darkly fulfilled.

Reviving the etymology gone dead in "legitimacy," a word that traces its origin back to "lex" or man-made law, Edmund plays as flippantly with Edgar's claim to be "legitimate" as with his own base "bastardy."

Well, then
Legitimate Edgar, I must have your land.
Our father's love is to the bastard Edmund
As to th' legitimate. Fine word, "legitimate."
Well, my legitimate . . .
(1.2.15–19)

The Nature Edmund invokes as his goddess is not the well-cultivated garden that Polixenes fashions out of nature in *The Winter's Tale.* It is the brutalized world of Lear on the heath, a "nature red in tooth and claw." Polixenes believes that, if art is man's nature, nature itself is the art of God. Nothing could clash more jarringly with the Nature Edmund worships as his goddess. His Nature is not just a collective name for everything that is, but a name for everything that takes place without voluntary human agency. Edmund's goddess sanctions a Hobbesian view of life: one that is poor and solitary, nasty, brutish, and short.

No two speeches better illustrate the distance separating the heath from the garden than Edmund's angry invocation to his goddess, Nature, and the gardener's elegant speech on horticulture in *Richard II.* For the brusque, colloquial candor of the villain Edmund, the gardener substitutes a formal, highly conceited style that has less in common with Machiavelli's *The Prince* than with a medieval allegory on flowers.

Go, bind thou up yon dangling apricocks,
Which, like unruly children, make their sire
Stoop with oppression of their prodigal weight;
Give some sustenance to the bending twigs.
Go thou, and like an executioner,
Cut off the heads of too fast growing sprays,
That look too lofty in our commonwealth.
(*Richard II* 3.4.29–35)

Lopping off the heads of light and flexible sprays that grow too fast like rebellious subjects, a prudent gardener will prop up ponderous fruits that droop and dangle, weighed down by polysyllabic nouns like "oppression" or by adjectives like "prodigal."

One critic suggests that "the first thought of a modern audience is: what a ridiculous way for a gardener to talk. The first thought of an Elizabethan would have been: what is the symbolic meaning of those words, spoken by this king of the garden, and how does it bear on the play?" (Tillyard, 1957, 143–44). The gardener is not implying that nature is opposed to art, or the natural to the artificial. He is saying rather that the art of good government is the cultivation of a kingdom's natural fertility. A king should assist the growth of wholesome crops. As J. S. Mill explains in his essay "Nature," "A ship floats by the same laws of specific gravity and equilibrium, as a tree uprooted by the wind and thrown into the water. The corn which men raise for food, grows and produces its grain by the same laws of vegetation by which the wild rose and the mountain strawberry bring forth their flowers and fruit" (1938, 729). Like successful horticulture, navigating the ship of state is a refinement of natural laws governing the weather, the tides of the sea, and the cycle of the seasons.

The regal and moral function of good gardening affords a total contrast to the desolation of Lear on his heath, where, stripped of pomp and state, he reveals the lowest ebb to which human life may sink. As a "poor, bare, forked animal," "unaccommodated man" is lowlier than a silk-producing worm or a wool-bearing sheep. The garden world of horticulture bears the same relation to the uncultivated wilderness of Lear on his heath as art bears to nature. As Sir Thomas Browne reflects in *Religio Medici,* "Nature is not at variance with art, nor art with nature; they both being the servants of [God's] providence; Art is the perfection of Nature: Were the world now as it was the sixth day, there were yet a Chaos: Nature hath made one world, and Art another. In brief, all things are artificial, for nature is the Art of God" (1967, 23). If nature is held up as a moral and aesthetic norm only because it is art on a higher level, then all arguments about "naturam sequi," from the Stoics down, are necessarily circular. Are the Stoics not exhorting us to follow X only because a non-X has already been converted into X? Since art is man's nature, then there is nothing about social contracts, laws, and religious institutions that are unnatural to man, however unnatural they may seem to the rest of nature.

The passage from Shakespeare most cited in Victorian poetic theory and its critical literature is the one from *The Winter's Tale* in which Polixenes tries to resolve the claims of two traditions: a classical Aristotelian tradition, which asserts that art imitates nature, and an idealizing Baconian tradition, which claims that art is feigned history. Instead of merely imitating nature, art may add to nature. But contrary to what Bacon and many idealizing Romantic theorists argue, art does not truly improve on nature. The art "which you say adds to Nature" is "an art that Nature makes." This is because art reveals the final and formal causes already immanent in nature's material causes.

> Yet Nature is made better by no mean
> But Nature makes that mean; so, over that art
> Which you say adds to Nature, is an art
> That Nature makes. You see, sweet maid, we marry
> A gentler scion to the wildest stock,
> And make conceive a bark of baser kind
> By bud of nobler race. This is an art
> Which does mend Nature, change it rather, but
> The art itself is Nature.
>
> (*The Winter's Tale* 4.4.89–97)

When Aristotle calls art an imitation of nature, he is including in his doctrine of immanent teleology those final and formal causes that art's function is not only to imitate but also to realize and make manifest. As an art of immanent ends, horticulture brings forth and refines the final and formal causes already residing in a plant's material cause. Far from supplanting or superseding nature, the gardener who grafts a new and gentler scion onto a wild tree's stock is both assisting and amending a natural method of propagating mixed races, hybrid plants, or new species of trees. As Polixenes explains to Perdita, the art that seems to mend or change nature is an art employed by "great creating Nature" herself.

In David Masson's review of E. S. Dallas's *Poetics: An Essay on Poetry* (London, 1852) and of Alexander Smith's *Poems* (London, 1853), Polixenes's speech from *The Winter's Tale* is used to support (quite misleadingly, in my view) an idealizing Baconian theory of art instead of a theory of art's immanent ends. Masson's review originally appeared as an essay, "Theories of Poetry and a New Poet," in the *North British Review* (vol. 19 [August 1853]: 297–344), and was published as the ninth chapter of his *Essays Biographical and Critical, Chiefly on English Poets* (Cambridge, 1856).[1] Despite Victorian attempts to romanticize Aristotle, and to assimilate classical theories of art to theories that owe more to Keats than to Shakespeare, the theory Polixenes expounds is more Aristotelian than Baconian. Since it represents a natural, not a merely painted or imaginary, world, Shakespeare's garden in *The Winter's Tale* has more in common with Spenser's garden of Adonis than with the artificial paradise of Tennyson's lotos-eaters or with his garden of the Hesperides.

Endorsing a traditional argument for God's existence, William Paley in his *Natural Theology* argues that only a super-craftsman could have created an organism so perfect as the human eye or brain. But David Hume excises such a fiction with the same deft efficiency as he excises the fiction of a necessary cause or connection between two events that occur consecutively. The constant association in our minds of A and B produces the idea that A causes B. By transforming an objective event into a merely subjective one, Hume both anticipates and explains Darwin's reversal of Paley's position. "Where Paley has taken intelligence to be the cause and adaptation the result," as Dwight Culler observes, "Darwin had shown that adaptation was the cause and survival the result—survival of the fittest" (1968, 228). Hume's reversal is more radical than Darwin's, "for it asserts that it is not design which implies a designer but the appearance of design which gives rise in our minds to the conception of a designer. In other words, it not only refutes Paley, which Darwin could not do, but it also explains how [Paley's] error arose" (230). Paley's argument that God is a super-craftsman or designer derives the provided beauty of a Creator from the achieved beauty of an artist. It fails to see that the beauty achieved in a play likc *The Merchant of Venice* or a sonnet like "The Windhover" and the beauty provided by a moonlit bank or a falcon in flight are distinct types. Contrary to "naïve imitation theories of art, one is not derived from the other" (Frye, 2000, 708).

One might have expected Huxley, as Darwin's champion, to endorse an ethics of naturalism, like Darwin's other influential disciple, Herbert Spencer. What a shock, then, when Huxley strongly denounces such an ethic in his 1893 Romanes lecture, "Evolution and Ethics." It is as if an audience of Darwinists were being addressed by a champion of the church, a Bishop Wilberforce with strong ascetic leanings. Comparing ethics to a garden, Huxley argues that, like the gardens in *The Winter's Tale* and *Richard II,* the success of a humanizing ethical process depends on the taming and repression of aggressive instincts that may secure momentary victory in a state of nature, but which spell disaster for any civilized society. If left unchecked, rapacious appetites will prey on "humanity / Like monsters of the deep" (*King Lear* 4.2.49–50). Until the gardener learns to tame the heath, as ethics learns to master nature, everything will include itself "in power," as Shakespeare's Ulysses predicts,

> Power into will, will into appetite;
> And appetite, an universal wolf,
> So doubly seconded with will and power,
> Must make perforce an universal prey,
> And last eat up himself.
>
> (*Troilus and Cressida* 1.3.119–24)

Though Huxley cannot dispense with a horticultural metaphor, he finds it a useful servant but deceptive master. There are two implications of the metaphor he wants to disown. In extirpating weeds and noxious growths, Huxley's gardener is not promoting the survival of only the most attractive flowers. He looks instead for balance and contrasts in his garden. Huxley is not advocating eugenics or the cultivation of a master breed of plants. When neo-Darwinists speak of the survival of the fittest in a struggle for existence, they are forsaking the cooperative model of the garden for the competitive model of the heath. If horticulture abets competition, it is not a competition for the survival of only a few plants and the extinction of all the rest. It is a competition for balance and arrangement, where issues of survival are replaced by opportunities, not for mere life, but for a good and fulfilled life. Huxley concludes that "what is often called the struggle for existence . . . is a contest, not for the means of existence, but for the means of enjoyment." In such a struggle "the qualities which insure success are energy, industry, intellectual capacity, tenacity of purpose, and, at least, as much sympathy as is necessary to make a man understand the feelings of his fellows" (1948, 115–16).

A second implication of the horticultural metaphor is the doctrine of progress, which Huxley is also eager to expel. It is deceptive to think that a proper cultivation of nature will someday turn the whole earth into a garden. Alas, evolution has been accompanied by few modifications of "the physical, or the mental, characters of men who have been subjects of it. I have not met with any grounds for suspecting that the average Englishmen of today are sensibly different from those that Shakespeare knew and drew. We look into his magic mirror of the Elizabethan age, and behold, nowise darkly, the presentiment of ourselves" (114). In a resounding indictment of the hunger for utopias, Huxley plants an epitaph on all unbridled doctrines of progressive evolution.

> So long as [man] remains liable to error, intellectual or moral; so long as he is compelled to be perpetually on guard against the cosmic forces, whose ends are not his ends, without and within himself; so long as he is haunted by inexpugnable memories and hopeless aspirations; so long as the recognition of his intellectual limitations forces him to acknowledge his incapacity to penetrate the mystery of existence; the prospect of attaining untroubled happiness, or of a state which can, even remotely, deserve the title of perfection, appears to me as misleading an illusion as ever was dangled before the eyes of poor humanity. (118)

Apocalyptic in its balanced clauses, suspended syntax, and the tolling knell of its anaphora ("so long as," "so long as"), the passage recalls Huxley's 1888 essay entitled "The Struggle for Existence in Human Society." In that prophetic lecture, life upon the earth's surface is said to describe "a trajectory like that of a ball fired from a mortar; and the sinking half of that course is as much a part of the general process of evolution as the rising" (62). Huxley reminds Utopians that "the old Babylonians wisely symbolized Nature by their great goddess Istar, who combined the attributes of Aphrodite with those of Ares" (62). Sooner or later, Huxley warns, the terrible aspect of Istar, representing a reckless non-moral nature, will tear asunder the ethical fabric of every Atlantis or Utopia. The evolution of the globe will eventually enter "so far upon its downward course that the cosmic process [will resume] its sway; and, once more, the State of Nature [will prevail] over the surface of our planet" (118). Qualifying his bleak prediction that very few species now living "will transmit progeny of any kind to a far distant futurity," Charles Darwin concludes *The Origin of Species* by blithely assuring the reader that "as natural selection works solely by and for the good of each being, all corporeal and mental endowments will tend to progress towards perfection" (2000, 231). Despite such touching optimism, the great shock that Huxley (if not Darwin himself) administers to the Victorian psyche is, not the idea that man descends from the apes, but that evolution is random. Variations are accidental, and change is arbitrary. Progressive evolution is a fiction and has to be exorcised like any other obsolete belief.

Whereas Lear's god, like Job's, is all-powerful but cruel, Tennyson's Arthur believes we are children of a "lesser god" ("The Passing of Arthur," line 14), benign but not all-powerful. Just as the book of Job betrays a faith that bad things never happen to good people, so *King Lear* systematically disappoints every hope or expectation nourished on behalf of Cordelia and her father. Lear's protest that "I am a man more sinned against than sinning" is so Job-like that sometimes we mistake it for a quotation from the Bible. Though Edgar asserts "the gods are just" (5.3.171), subsequent events betray his faith more calamitously than anyone could have foreseen. The most bewildered Victorian response to Edgar's speech comes from John Ruskin, who cites misplaced faith in God's justice as evidence of profound uncertainty in Shakespeare himself.

In his beautiful lecture "The Mystery of Life and Its Arts," Ruskin is astonished that the greatest poets—Dante, Milton, Homer, and Shakespeare—should all appear confounded and undone by what Tennyson in "To Virgil" calls the "doubtful doom of human kind." An ambiguity at the heart of life is disclosed in their most imaginative visions. Ruskin thinks the fall of Satan and the other angels in *Paradise Lost* is unbelievable to Milton himself, who degrades and spoils the whole episode by borrowing from Hesiod's *Theogony* an account of the war of the younger gods against the Titans. Dante's vision in *The Divine Comedy* Ruskin finds even more untenable. It is a dream filled "with idle puppets of . . . a scholastic imagination," a dream "in which every grotesque type or phantasm of heathen tradition is renewed and adorned" (Ruskin, 1938, 974). He also believes "there is no sadder image of human fate" than the *Iliad,* where Achilles, for the sake of a dead friend, "gives up his kingdom, his country, and his life—casts alike the innocent and guilty, with himself, into one gulf of slaughter, and dies at last by the hand of the basest of his adversaries" (975). Ruskin thinks Shakespeare, though as disillusioned as Homer, is more inconsolable, because he lacks Homer's faith in the presence of any just and helpful gods. When Edgar says, "the gods are just, and of our pleasant vices, / Make instruments to plague us" (5.3.170–71), he is affirming a causal connection between what good people do and what happens to them. But Shakespeare's play, like the book of Job, totally betrays and discredits Edgar's faith. Ruskin concludes that Shakespeare differs from Homer "chiefly in this—that he recognizes, for deliverance, no gods nigh at hand; and that, by petty chance—by momentary folly—by broken message—by fool's tyranny—or traitor's snare, the strongest and most righteous are brought to their ruin, and perish without word of hope" (975).

Coming from Ruskin, a great admirer of Shakespeare in his youth, these words of shock and disillusion seem wrenched out of him against his will. In despair and bitterness Ruskin broods on such "petty chances" as the changing of the foils in *Hamlet;* the "momentary folly" of forgetting the execution order in *King Lear;* the tragic miscarriage of information in *Romeo and Juliet;* the tyranny of Leontes's jealousy in *The Winter's Tale;* and the treacherous Iago's "snare" in *Othello.* Disenchantment with Shakespeare is best explained, I think, by Francis O'Gorman, who associates "the limits of Shakespeare's teaching" with the instruction Ruskin received from his father (2003, 212). Of Ruskin senior, a Shakespeare devotee, the author of *Praeterita* said he "would have sacrificed his life for his son, and yet forced his son to sacrifice his life to him, and sacrifice it in vain" (*Praeterita* 18.xxviii). O'Gorman thinks that Ruskin came to discern a disturbing ambiguity in Shakespeare: his "texts could mean conflicting things." "Ruskin's nervousness about Shakespeare's 'inconceivable' mind in the 1880s marked a moment when an important early assumption about the relation between a cherished author and his texts was visibly under pressure" (214).

Just as the death of Shakespeare's only son seems to have darkened "the mystery of life and its arts" in the great tragedies, so disappointment seems to have darkened Ruskin's own vision. For the ten best years of his life, Ruskin tried to promote Turner's art and convince the world of Turner's supremacy among English painters since Reynolds. Finally, after years of effort, the

Trustees of the National Gallery commissioned Ruskin to prepare three hundred examples of Turner's drawings for exhibition at Kensington. "At Kensington they were, and are, placed for exhibition; but they are not exhibited, for the room in which they hang is always empty" (Ruskin, 1938, 970). The shock of an exhibition's not exhibiting anything jars the ear and disappoints every hope and expectation. Instead of an abiding presence, we face only an abiding absence, like a gift or a grace out of season. "This," confides Ruskin, "was the first mystery of life to me." But like the tolling of a bell, graver mysteries are to follow. Why are patrons of the arts always so stuffed with apathy? Ruskin is thrown off balance by a blindness that "stands in the way of every perception, every virtue": "We were all plunged in a languid dream—our hearts fat, and our eyes heavy, and our ears closed, lest the inspiration of hand or voice should reach us—lest we should see with our eyes, and understand with our hearts, and be healed" (972). All would be well if only by turning on the hinge of his hopefully poised chiasmus, Ruskin could open sealed hearts, lighten heavy eyes, and transform a diseased sensibility into a sane and fresh appreciation of the arts.

If Nature is our goddess, then she presides over the same hollowed-out rituals of dead innocence as the Fool in *King Lear,* as Thersites in *Troilus and Cressida,* and as Tennyson's Dagonet and Tristram in "The Last Tournament." The most resounding Victorian indictment of Edmund's goddess is J. S. Mill's essay "Nature," which addresses the mystery raised by Job and *King Lear:* why dreadful calamities overtake innocent people. Some dark truths that Mill had suppressed in his *Autobiography* come close to the surface of this posthumously published essay. In his memoir Mill had made no reference to his brother's suicide, his parents' objection to his marriage, or the ill health of his wife. But in "Nature," rewritten at a time when both Mill and his wife were dangerously ill, the prospect of death gives special force to a ruthless anatomy of nature's horrors.

> Nature impales men, breaks them as if on the wheel, casts them to be devoured by wild beasts, burns them to death, crushes them with stones like the first christian martyr, starves them with hunger, freezes them with cold, poisons them by the quick or slow venom of her exhalations, and has hundreds of other hideous deaths in reserve, such as the ingenious cruelty of a Nabis or a Domitian never surpassed. All this, Nature does with the most supercilious disregard both of mercy and of justice, emptying her shafts upon the best and noblest indifferently with the meanest and worst. (Mill, 1938, 737)

As a convert to the utility of poetry, Mill writes in this passage with felicity and passion. Indeed, he lashes out with a fury and eloquence more typical of Swift than of such self-controlled advocates of rationalism as his mentors, Bentham and James Mill. Spilling over ten lines of print, the balance of the prose breaks down. The torrent of verbs, which Mill makes more relentless by dropping connectives ("impales," "breaks," "casts," "burns," "crushes," "starves," "poisons"), levels the "best and noblest," "the meanest and worst" alike. Mill is just as critical of the Stoic precept "naturam sequi" as he is of Bentham's brand of Utilitarianism, which is to ethics what democracy is to politics. If quantity rather than quality is the preferred criterion, Bentham is surely right to insist that pushpin is as good as poetry. But then Utilitarianism suffers from the same disadvantage as democracy: it merely counts the votes instead of weighing them.

Assailed by the jeers of his wise fool, Lear is consumed with rage that he, a man more sinned against than sinning, should have to bite the dust. But his rage is compassionate, for it is expressed on behalf of all "poor, naked wretches, wheresoe'er [they] are." Equally distressed, Mill tries to salvage God's goodness at the expense of his power. Though we may admire, like Kant, the grand immensity of nature, we can never truly admire, Mill insists, her amoral economy or her refusal to turn "one step from her path to avoid trampling us into destruction" (737). Out of nowhere comes the brutal assault. Cancer strikes. A blind Fury slits a daughter's thin-spun life. Like a hurricane or tornado, the leveling verbs leave nothing standing in their wake. They evoke only a panic-stricken sense of nature's cruelty and indifference.

Trying to solve the mystery that baffles Job and Lear, which is the mystery of why terrible things happen to good people, Mill believes it is inconceivable that an omnipotent, sentient God would create a world as cruel as this one. He concludes God intended man to amend nature, not imitate it. For if nature knows nothing of Isabella's chastity in *Measure for Measure,* it knows nothing of Portia's mercy or justice either. When Edmund embraces Nature as his goddess, he is enslaving himself to a capricious tyrant. A just God is never to be confused with such a despot, for in the strict sense of the term he is not omnipotent at all. Helpless to subdue or tame a hurricane that "destroys the hopes of a season," God allows "a flight of locusts" to desolate "a district" or a "trifling chemical change in an edible root" to starve "a million of people" (738). Mill concludes that "not even on the most distorted and contracted theory of good which ever was framed by religious or philosophical fanaticism, can the government of Nature be made to resemble the work of a being at once good and omnipotent" (741). For Mill, as for Hume, "Epicurus's questions are yet unanswered. Is [God] willing to prevent evil, but not able? then he is impotent. Is he able, but not willing? then is he malevolent. Is he both able and willing? whence then is evil?" (Hume, quoted in Ayer and O'Grady, 1992, 204). Woody Allen gives the conundrum a twist when he quips that if God is omnipotent but not evil, he is surely a notorious underachiever. Alternatively, if God never directly causes our misfortunes, then he is good but not omnipotent, like the "lesser god" of Tennyson's "The Passing of Arthur" (line 14), or perhaps like the "divinity that shapes our ends" in *Hamlet.*

6

A Choral Mind Trap

HARDY AND THE HOMILISTS

ONE OF THE MOST HARROWING YET POIGNANT SCENES IN VICTOrian fiction is Angel Clare's symbolic entombment of his bride on their wedding night in Thomas Hardy's novel *Tess of the d'Urbervilles.* Though Tess's bolting upright in the Abbot's tomb reenacts the climactic moment in *Romeo and Juliet* when the drugged Juliet awakens in the crypt, the words Angel pronounces over the woman he wraps in a shroud then carries in his arms resonate most powerfully with the ending of *King Lear.* Angel's "Dead, dead, dead" is an echo of Lear's words "Howl, howl, howl" as the old king, carrying Cordelia in his arms, plunges the audience into what one critic calls "the most terrifying five minutes in literature" (Booth, 1983, 11). What ought to be a "smooth ceremony of conclusion" turns into a betrayal of ends that is cosmically disturbing.

> *Kent.* Is this the promis'd end?
> *Edgar.* Or image of that horror?
> *Albany.* Fall, and cease!
> (*King Lear* 5.3.263–64)

We are preparing to leave the theater, waiting for the play to end happily, as in all earlier versions of the story, when events begin to roll on interminably, crushing every hope and expectation of happiness we have nurtured on Lear's behalf.

We want Lear and Cordelia, as we want Angel and Tess, to be whole. Instead, the play, like the novel, gives us a broken whole. Each work sets up expectations that it systematically disappoints. When Albany, for example, the man of virtue and authority, seems about to distribute rewards at the end of the play by using a formal couplet to signal a return to order, the audience reasonably anticipates a just and happy outcome.

All friends shall taste
The wages of their virtue, and all foes
The cup of their deservings [bitter woes].
(5.3.301–5)

But alas, interrupted by a spectacle too calamitous for words, Albany sees Lear carrying in the body of the dead Cordelia. Breaking off from the expected couplet, Albany can offer the audience only a shattered fragment. And yet the ruined couplet's promise of order, even when replaced by two anguished deictics ("O see, see!"), attests, as one critic says, "to an orderliness in the play as play that persists even in defeat" (Booth, 1983, 27).

Though not the most ghostly of Shakespeare's tragedies, *King Lear* is the spookiest, the darkest and most ghastly, because the black king on its chessboard can be identified with no single character in the play. Gloucester comes closest to identifying this black king or sinister power when he says "As flies to wanton boys, are we to th' gods, / They kill us for their sport" (4.1.38–39). But who can decisively challenge and overthrow the gods? Since the ghosts of King Hamlet and Banquo help vanquish the villains Claudius and Macbeth, the tragedies in which they appear, though more ghostly than *King Lear,* are also less ghastly or spooky. The diffuse power of evil in Shakespeare's darkest tragedy is to the villainy of Claudius or Macbeth what J. R. R. Tolkien's ring-wraiths and Sauron, Dark Lord or Mordor, are to a debased wizard like Merlin in Tennyson's *Idylls of the King.*

If we are never quite prepared for Angel's repudiation of his bride, it is for the same reason that an audience is never quite prepared for the ending of *King Lear.* Vestiges of design remain intact even after all design seems shattered. In Hardy's novel we are less dismayed by a bridegroom's symbolically burying his bride on their wedding night than by the way he does it. Instead of carrying Tess across the threshold of their future home, Angel takes his bride in his arms, carries her out of the house, and lays her in a tomb. It is not just Tess we are grieving for. We are grieving for our own vulnerability, and the vulnerability of Angel. Pushing beyond their own assigned limits, the rituals roll across and efface the boundaries separating weddings from funerals, life from death, joy from despair. Thin partitions divide one ritual from the other. Both weddings and funerals use words to do or perform something. "With this ring I thee wed," "we commit this body to the ground." Angel's pronouncing Tess to be dead *makes* her die. His bride is not dead in her heart until he says she is. In presiding over a funeral, Angel is trying to wake from a nightmare that has prevented the consummation of his marriage. The trauma may diminish if Angel can conduct a burial in which he is both the chief mourner and the chief celebrant.

Just as Shakespeare's play puts upon the rack both the audience and King Lear, so Hardy's novel tests the endurance, not only of Tess, but also of Hardy's narrator and his readers. We are as shocked by Tess's symbolical burial as we are by Cordelia's death because each work of art raises hopes that it then betrays. As Angel approaches Tess, dressed only in his shirt, her heart fills with desire. Her bridegroom even speaks the words of endearment she is eager to hear. But as Browning's lover says in "By the Fireside," which the narrator quotes two chapters earlier, "the little less, and what worlds away!" (197). The groom who should possess his bride and consummate their marriage is sleepwalking and speaking in a voice indescribably sad. Instead of making love to her in their bed, he lays her out on a tomb. Hardy observes in his poem "Hap" that "Crass Casualty" and "dicing Time . . . had as readily strewn / Blisses about [their] pilgrimage as pain" (lines ll-14). The scene would be less harrowing if funeral and marriage rites were less grotesquely commingled. As in *King Lear,* which deceives the audience by signaling a happy ending, we feel this outcome should have been different. Anticipating the consummation of a marriage, we are offered death in its place.

Angel compares Tess to Lear when he admits she is a victim "more sinned against than sinning" (194). But her most Shakespearean moment comes when she rises from the tomb to support the exhausted sleepwalker, whom she helps back to the house. Cast in the role of a guardian spirit escorting Angel to heaven, Tess reenacts the most moving moment in *King Lear,* when the old father in his brief reunion with his daughter after her return from France mistakes Cordelia for an angel. Unforced and brief, the scene is the most touching in the play.

> You do me wrong to take me out o' th' grave.
> Thou art a soul in bliss; . . .
> You are a spirit, I know. Where did you die?
> (*King Lear* 4.7.45–46, 49)

The more brutal side of *Lear,* recalled in Hardy's later allusion to the gods' killing men for their sport (330), is eased and lightened in this scene by one of the most ethereal and life-giving moments in nineteenth-century fiction. In the return to the house, the roles of bride and groom are reversed. The rite of Angel's bearing Tess out of the house is balanced by the rite of Tess's carrying Angel back. The love she is not allowed to show in life is preserved in the solicitude of a spirit who takes Angel out of the grave, as Cordelia takes her father.

Adrian Poole believes that Angel's carrying his bride in his sleep raises fears of Tess's being drowned like the innocent Ophelia. "Angel Clare is the character in [Hardy's] fiction most frequently associated with Hamlet, and there are points at which his relations with Tess are darkly shadowed by Hamlet's with Ophelia, especially in the extraordinary scene in which Angel carries her in his sleep down to the stream, as if to drown her" (2004, 151). This may be so. But surely the overriding impression left in a reader's mind by the scene in which Angel carries Tess to the stream is Lear's bearing Cordelia in his arms after she dies. Tess's later discovery of Angel lying beside her on the Abbot's tomb also stunningly reenacts Juliet's coming to life in the crypt only to find Romeo lifeless beside her.

When Angel wakes in the morning, he struggles in vain to remember what has happened during the night. The simile "deep as annihilation," which the narrator applies to Angel's sleep, is a shocking one. It has the force of one of Wordsworth's similes: "Heavy as frost, and deep almost as life" ("Ode: Intimations of Immortality," line 129). Is sleep "deep as annihilation" because, in banishing pain, it has retained no trace of the woman whom the sleepwalker called "sweet," "good," and "true" the night before? The puzzling equation of sleep with annihilation may mean that in his nocturnal walk Angel has buried Tess figuratively and that nothing can be more annihilating than her death. No playgoer ever forgets the two words that migrate most menacingly through *King Lear:* "nothing" and its cognate "never." "Nothing will come of nothing" finds its echoing wail in Lear's fivefold repetition of "never." These negatives operate as exhaust pumps leaving a vacuum in their wake. A comparable emptiness is left at the center of Tess's world when she discovers that the words of endearment Angel speaks to her in his sleepwalking—"sweet," "good," and "true"—are as tenuous and vagrant as a dream. If so, Angel has exorcised a monster at the inadmissible price of stripping away the warm and breathing beauty of a creature his heart found delightful. Tess can only conclude that love is a chimera. Its only trace in Angel's memory is a vapor trail that has faded like Prospero's dream and left not a rack behind.

From Andrew Lang to R. G. Collingwood, critics of *Tess of the d'Urbervilles* have consistently and passionately condemned Hardy for using his fiction as a pulpit from which to deliver blasphemous homilies. But Hardy's critics forget that it is typical of tragedy that the gods should be stupider and more malignant than the humans they oppress. Using measured ironies and balanced tones to refute the charge, Hardy sets out in his novel's fifth and later editions to defend himself against Lang's attack. "I can assert against this great critic," Hardy rallies, "that to exclaim illogically against the gods, singular or plural, is not such an original sin of mine as he seems to imagine. True, it may have some local originality; though if Shakespeare were an authority on history, which perhaps he is not, I could show that the sin was introduced into Wessex as early as the Heptarchy itself. Says Glo'ster in *Lear,* otherwise Ina, king of that country: 'As flies to wanton boys are we to the gods; / They kill us for their sport'" (Hardy, 1965, 3).

How justified is Hardy in claiming Gloucester's comment in *King Lear* as a precedent for his novel's arraignment of "the President of the Immortals" in its final paragraph? It is true that at rare moments in Shakespeare's plays we do overhear the playwright speaking in unison with a character. If such a voice sometimes offends, it is not because it is blasphemous, but because we feel Shakespeare has allowed a mask to slip and is intoning for a moment through a puppet. Words more in character for the playwright than the speaker set choral mind traps for the playgoer. Shakespeare sets such a trap in Henry V's stirring exhortation to his troops before the battle of Agincourt. The political propaganda of the dying John of Gaunt and the pedantic Polonius's homily to his son set similar traps. No playgoer objects to the use of a chorus at the beginning of *Romeo and Juliet,* where the playwright sacrifices surprise and forgoes suspense by rehearsing the tale of two star-crossed lovers. Like Coleridge, Shakespeare prefers a sense of fulfilled expectation—"God said let there be light, and there was *light*"—to a sudden shock effect: "and there *was* light." The disappearance of a chorus after the play's second act suggests, however, that its use is unnecessary. Its reappearance as Time in *The Winter's Tale* is a self-consciously antique and quaint device. Of a piece with the preposterously contrived appearance of Wall in *A Midsummer Night's Dream,* Time's choral commentary is allowed to expire as a graceful joke (*The Winter's Tale* 4.2.30–32).

To dispel the impression that he is using choral commentary as a mind trap, Shakespeare sometimes disguises it as a soliloquy. Such is the oblique choral view that Shakespeare takes of Macbeth's will to murder. As Macbeth sees the imaginary dagger and reaches out to grasp it, he draws his actual dagger and sees the other blood-stained weapon as his own will soon become. "This double vision is characteristic of Macbeth," one critic observes, "and makes the choral type of soliloquy especially appropriate on his lips; he both is, and sees, Macbeth. In the remainder of the . . . episode he seems actually disembodied, a spirit watching its own body—a cadaver, withered murderer, moving upon its prey like a ghost" (Harbage, 1963, 381).

Less successful are the choral passages where a rhapsodic Shakespeare can be heard talking through an elderly Capulet or Montague. When Romeo's father speaks of the East beginning "to draw / The shady curtains from Aurora's bed" (1.1.42–43), we hear, not a prosaic old Montague, but a lyrical

Shakespeare, the poet of his recently composed sonnets, talking through a mask. Only in the balcony scene, when Romeo calls the light the East and Juliet the sun, does the dramatic action catch up with the bridal metaphors of the play. The best comment on such choral mind traps comes from Coleridge, who complains that "the poet is not . . . entirely blended with the dramatist" in the early scenes of this play. Speaking of the love "lusty young men feel" when April treads on winter's limping heel, Capulet displays a "high and active" fancy. But Coleridge associates such fancy with Shakespeare the poet rather than with Shakespeare the playwright (Coleridge, 1930, 2, 137). Such lapses into ventriloquism can also be detected in Browning, who passes awkwardly in "Fra Lippo Lippi" from the exalted tragedy of "Christ's sad face on the cross" (line 156) to the black humor of the murderer's crossing himself in the sanctuary while shaking a fist at his victim's father. The lofty sentiment of the bracketed passage is more in character for a saintly Fra Angelico than for an earthly Masaccio. It is more appropriate to Browning, the Christian apologist, than to the sensual monk who speaks the monologue.

Actors who play the parts of Lear and Cordelia have little to look forward to at the end of the tragedy. Unlike the dying Hamlet or Othello, they have few words to speak. Once she is arrested, Tess, too, is subdued and too dazed for speech: "'It is as it should be,' she murmured. 'Angel, I am almost glad—yes, glad! This happiness could not have lasted. It was too much. I have had enough'" (328). Since Tess is too stunned to defend herself, Hardy's narrator feels impelled to indict the offender, "the President of the Immortals," on her behalf. But what we hear is a far cry from the controlled irony or reasoned attack of a prosecutor in a law court.

> "Justice" was done, and the President of the Immortals, in Aeschylean phrase, had ended his sport with Tess. And the d'Urberville knights and dames slept on in their tombs unknowing. The two speechless gazers bent themselves down to the earth, as if in prayer, and remained thus a long time, absolutely motionless; the flag continued to wave silently. As soon as they had strength they arose, joined hands again, and went on. (330)

These final sentences replace the wit and learned sarcasm of an angry jurist with the stupor and stays against confusion of a narrator who sounds more like a baffled witness than a prosecutor, and who is too shaken, too traumatized by tragedy, to organize ideas logically. What we hear instead is the strain of a mind under stress, trying desperately to attain some "calm of mind, all passion spent."

The speaker dwells for a moment on the distanced feudal spectacle of the d'Urberville knights and dames who, as apostles of higher ignorance, rest unknowing on their ancient tombs. He then passes on to the speechless gazers, Liza-Lu and Angel, bent down to earth as if in prayer. Ending not with an arraignment but with a ritual of wordless supplication, the narrator uses paratactic syntax and a sequence of biblical "ands" to achieve a simplicity oracular in its effect: "And [they] slept on in their tombs," "and remained thus a long time," "joined hands again, and went on." From the motionless observers the coda moves on to the silently waving flag and to a reenactment of the last scene in *Paradise Lost,* as Adam and Eve, hand in hand, take their solitary way out of Eden. I can think of nothing less shrill or polemical than these concluding lines, or less like the rant R. G. Collingwood objects to in his notorious attack upon the novel's concluding paragaraph.[1]

Hardy has carefully prepared a reader for his novel's extraordinary coda. In *Fiction and Repetition: Seven English Novels,* J. Hillis Miller devotes an entire chapter to the narrator's intrusive commentary after Tess's seduction or possible rape (1992, 116–46). Just as the blur, density, and non sequitur quality of the narrator's comments after the seduction betray instability and trauma, so in the novel's last paragraph mental agitation momentarily transfers itself from Angel and Liza-Lu to Hardy's narrator. In an effort to explain what cannot be explained, the narrator, like the reader, grasps at incongruities. It is best to remain in uncertainties, Hardy seems to be saying, without irritably searching for answers that do not exist.

As a spokesman for higher ignorance, Angel Clare appropriately prepares for these uncertainties by taking refuge in a Temple of the Winds, an edifice with no obvious interior to protect him. As a fitting temple for a sphinx without a secret, a mere façade of mystery, this enigmatic Temple is to Coleridge's eolian harp what Hardy's darkling thrush is to Shelley's skylark. Played upon by the wind, this ghostly edifice is not a lyre swept into melody by the breeze, but a gigantic one-stringed harp capable of emitting only an unsubtle monotone. And so in this temple of a curiously withdrawing deity, it is appropriate that when Tess asks if their love for each other will survive her death, Angel merely kisses her but does not speak. Again she asks, and he remains silent. Like Lear, Angel learns (perhaps too late) that "love is the last and secret name of all the virtues" (Murdoch, 1970, 81). But to the critical question at the critical time he can give no answer. Even the landscape turns taciturn, as if creation itself bears witness to the justness of Angel's silence and to the logic of some vast and inscrutable theology of reserve.

If anyone is ranting at the end of Hardy's novel, it is not Hardy but a dramatic character, his narrator, who momentarily loses his peace of mind before recovering it gradually in the rest of the paragraph. Such indeed is the line of reasoning Collingwood himself adopts when explaining how a dramatic writer "may rant in character" (1938, 123). As Collingwood justly observes, "It is not the author who is ranting, but the unbalanced character he depicts; the emotion the author is expressing is the emotion with which he contemplates that character; or rather, the emotion he has towards that secret and disowned part of himself for which the character stands" (124). Ironically, Collingwood's claim that the last paragraph of Hardy's novel rings false because it is rant is best refuted by Collingwood himself.

Having cogently defended "ranting in character," it seems incredible that Collingwood should then accuse Shakespeare of creating haranguing ciphers in whom "he takes no interest at all, but [whom] he uses simply as pegs on which to hang what the public wants, like Henry V" (124). The greatest English king of the fifteenth century is admittedly no Hamlet. But neither is he the mere mouthpiece Collingwood implies. Swinburne claims Shakespeare "was too national to be provincial" (1918, 113), and favorably compares his patriotic verse to Tennyson's. Though Henry V may fall into a choral mind trap when he rallies his troops before the battle of Agincourt, Collingwood should not expect a pep talk to troops to hold the same absorbing interest for Shakespeare as Hamlet's meditation on death or as the inward insurrections of a Brutus or Macbeth. I am at a loss to explain why so intelligent a commentator as Collingwood should fall into so obvious a mind trap himself.

I agree with Francis Sparshott that "of all writers on art who are not artists," Collingwood "is almost the only writer on the subject whom artists will always take seriously" (1982, 368). *The Principles of Art* is "the one essential book of aesthetics" because it displays "a passionate concern with the centrality and seriousness of art," and because it recognizes the kind of risky wager any critic and artist must be willing to take" (368). I assume Collingwood is taking just such a risk when he attacks the concluding paragraph of Hardy's novel as rant. Just when Collingwood seems most secure in his judgment, having praised Hardy with insight and skill, he reveals that his knowledge as a philosopher of art is of no use to him as a critic. In risking what seems at first a safe judgment, Collingwood reveals a total incomprehension of the use to which a gifted novelist like Hardy may put a narrator who is as dramatic in his own right as Alec d'Urberville, as Angel Clare, or as Gloucester in *King Lear*.

⁂

So far I have been defending Hardy from charges made against him. But to say he never substitutes homily for drama or rhetoric for art would be as disingenuous as to attack him indiscriminately. In a few poems of cosmic inquisition Hardy proves just as fallible as other Victorians. In one choral mind trap, "God's Education," we hear Hardy the homilist lecturing through a mask. He sounds less like a poet than an irascible schoolmaster rapping the knuckles of a wayward pupil.

> I asked: "Why do you serve her so?
> Do you, for some glad day,
> Hoard these her sweets—?" He said, "O no,
> They charm not me; I bid Time throw
> Them carelessly away."
>
> Said I: "We call that cruelty—
> We, your poor mortal kind."
> He mused. "The thought is new to me.
> Forsooth, though I men's master be,
> Theirs is the teaching mind!"
>
> (lines 11–20)

The conventional wisdom is that God educates man through suffering. But "the teaching mind" of Hardy's homilist turns the tables on God by daring to instruct the Teacher. Changing "God's Education" from a subjective to an objective genitive, Hardy substitutes for biblical theology the ancient evolutionary theology of Aeschylus, who instructs Zeus in a higher moral law, and of later Greek tragedians like Euripides, who in lines that express "the spectacle of life passing into religious emotion" (Whitehead, 1933, 277) puzzles over the nature of God in the act of praying to him: "Zeus, whether thou are Compulsion of Nature or Intelligence of Mankind, to thee I prayed" (*Trojan Women,* 886–87).

Hardy's full look at the worst is the opposite of hope, which is "the virtue of the past, the eternal sense that the next time we'll do better" (Frye, 2004, 88). Though Tennyson shares much of Hardy's despair, it is balanced in *In Memoriam* by faith, a projection of hope into the future. Even when Hardy's cosmic inquisitions deviate into simple unbelief, as in "God-Forgotten" and "Unknowing," which read like versified footnotes to Herbert Spencer's agnostic treatise "The Unknowable," the lilt or simple monotony of the lines may still be used to comment obliquely on the homilist's own lack of depth. What is said trippingly or buoyantly can be beguilingly at odds with how it is said. It is as if the homilist who has fallen into a choral mind trap knows that his pessimistic profundity is not really profound. Hardy the apostate offends less in this regard than Swinburne, the intoxicated atheist, who in hymning the virtues of pagan fortitude and faith (his most congenial themes) uses the oracles of Apollo to pervert Greek sentiment.

If Shakespeare is the wayward spirit Hardy claims he is, maintaining "a sway / Not fore-desired, in tracks unchosen and unchecked" ("To Shakespeare after Three Hundred Years," lines 11–12), then a poet who imitates Shakespeare must curb a temptation to lecture or bully his readers. To this end Hardy tries to forgo the role of homilist or sage, preferring the sway of an "all-uncared effect," like a vagrant wind.

> Bright baffling Soul, least capturable of themes,
> Thou, who display'dst a life of commonplace,
> Leaving no intimate word or personal trace
> Of high design outside the artistry
>   Of thy penned dreams,
> Still shalt remain at heart unread eternally.
>
> Through human orbits thy discourse to-day,
> Despite thy formal pilgrimage, throbs on
> In harmonies that cow Oblivion,
> And, like the wind, with all-uncared effect
>   Maintain a sway
> Not fore-desired, in tracks unchosen and unchecked.
>   ("To Shakespeare after Three Hundred Years,"
>   lines 1–12)

Like Shakespeare, the poet with the most to reveal but often the least to say, Hardy appears to have removed some "intimate word or personal trace" from his elegy "At Castle Boterel." The poem achieves a measure of Shakespearean abandon and caprice by making explicit the disparity between the possible meaninglessness of something once said—a mere piece of nonsense perhaps—and the emotional truth of the words we are not allowed to hear. At the same time, the symmetrically sculpted stanzas balance any transport of wayward surmise by carrying over from one stanza to the next a sense of repose, simplicity, and extraordinary restraint.

> What we did as we climbed, and what we talked of
>   Matters not much, nor to what it led,—
> Something that life will not be balked of
> Without rude reason till hope is dead,
>   And feeling fled.
> It filled but a minute. But was there ever
>   A time of such quality, since or before,
> In that hill's story?
>   (lines 11–18)

As in Browning's poem "By the Fireside," it is important that the actual conversation not be heard. Even when Hardy speaks, his words look two ways at once. Is the hill the recorder, like the primeval rocks in the next stanza? Or is Hardy chronicling *his* story of the hill? In either case, as Hardy bids farewell to the young Emma's "phantom figure" (line 28), it is hard to tell who is more benighted, the poet or the ghost.

In his poem "Rain on a Grave," Hardy replaces the discourtesy of death with a more attractive picture of a daisy-covered mound.

> Soon will be growing
> Green blades from her mound,
> And daisies be showing
> Like stars on the ground,
> Till she form part of them—
> Ay—the sweet heart of them,
> Loved beyond measure
> With a child's pleasure
> All her life round.
>
> (lines 28–36)

Nature has a kind of lover's quarrel with the woman. They mend their differences only when she consents to become, not just a portion of the star-like daisies springing from their mound, but also "the sweet heart of them" (line 33). Hardy redeems platitude by coaxing words into poetry without bullying them. The possibility of being ravaged or violated in the privacy of an erotically secluded place is the elegy's unspeakable (and unspoken) under-thought. As in Wordsworth's Lucy poems—or Hardy's own *Tess of the d'Urbervilles*—the girl's death will not bear talking about. Instead, the touch of horror that resides in the very softness and pleasure of the trap is offset by the boisterously innocent pleasure that the child delights in. In an overflow of feminine rhymes and a resurgence of a buoyant dance-like rhythm, the girl's pleasure sounds quite at odds with the grimness of what the lines imply. Bright and baffling, and uncapturable in words, there is something at the heart of such a lyric that, like Shakespeare's artistry of "penned dreams," remains, as Hardy says, eternally "unread" ("To Shakespeare," lines 4–6).

One of Hardy's best lyrics, "During Wind and Rain," is also his most Shakespearean. As Hardy says of Shakespeare, the poem cultivates an "all-uncared effect," "like the wind" ("To Shakespeare," line 10). And yet far from "cowing Oblivion," the ravages of Ovid's "tempus edax," the great devourer and destroyer of dreams, secure oblivion its final triumph.

> They sing their dearest songs—
> He, she, all of them—yea,
> Treble and tenor and bass,

And one to play;
With the candles mooning each face. . . .
Ah, no; the years O!
How the sick leaves reel down in throngs!

They clear the creeping moss—
Elders and juniors—aye,
Making the pathways near
And the gardens gay;
And they build a shady seat. . . .
Ah, no! the years, the years;
See, the white storm-birds wing across!

They are blithely breakfasting all—
Men and maidens—yea,
Under the summer tree,
With a glimpse of the bay,
While pet fowl come to the knee. . . .
Ah, no; the years O!
And the rotten rose is ript from the wall.

They change to a high new house,
He, she, all of them—aye,
Clocks and carpets and chairs
On the lawn all day,
And brightest things that are theirs. . . .
Ah, no; the years, the years;
Down their carved names the rain-drop ploughs.
("During Wind and Rain")

"For the rain it raineth everyday" appears in the Fool's song in *King Lear* as well as in Feste's song in *Twelfth Night.* But it is Feste's song one mainly hears, with its boisterous refrain, "hey, ho, the wind and the rain," and its beautiful sadness of acceptance, tempered in Hardy's case by a revulsion verging on sickness or nausea.

As Feste says of the duped Malvolio, "the whirligig of time brings in his revenges." The most humiliating of these revenges in Feste's song is the lost innocence of the "little boy," the failed potency of the young man, the lost wisdom of age, which sedates its fall with drink. Most panoramic is the final stanza, which runs all times together.

A great while ago the world begun,
With hey, ho, the wind and the rain,

> But that's all one, our play is done,
> And we'll strive to please you every day.
> (*Twelfth Night* 5.1.414–17)

The playwright's wisdom is not immortal: it is not immune to time's revenges. But like God's creation of the world "a great while ago," it is a light to order chaos and a power by which to live.

It is fashionable to call Hardy a Victorian novelist and a modern poet. But in each capacity Hardy exhibits a sensibility that is both Victorian and modern. Erik Gray reminds us that Hardy "always considered himself a Victorian poet; moreover, most of the poems look back to the early 1870s, and the belatedness of their composition is central to their meaning" (2010, 286). Though Hardy is an heir of Wordsworth and a contemporary of Tennyson, he is also, it must be acknowledged, a founder of what Donald Davie calls a twentieth-century tradition of British "liberal" poetry. Davie deftly points to Hardy's "human skill" in this poem, which is more than a triumph of "technical virtuosity." The concluding line of the third stanza, "And the rotten rose is ript from the wall," substitutes two anapests for the normal iambs. "Though symmetry is maintained," as Davie says, "between that stanza and the first two, it is so masked by the rhythmical variation that, instead of checking back to register how this stanza reproduces the earlier ones, we are propelled forward to see what will happen in the last." As in Feste's song, "the feeling flows into each stanza, brims and three times pours into the next" (Davie, 1972, 60).

In Hardy's masterpiece it is not just the simple cycle of change that kills. It is the wrenching sadness and sense of waste that afflicts the poet like an attack of headache or nausea. The gentility of everyone he once loved and the courtliness of everyone he was close to seem hollowed out and vain. The last lines in each stanza echo Dagonet's song in Tennyson's idyll "The Last Tournament": "and the wan day / Went glooming down in wet and weariness" (lines 214–15). But in Hardy's stanzas, Dagonet's "death-dumb autumn-dripping gloom" (line 750) is absorbed into a garden poetry of festive celebration familiar to readers of Tennyson's *Maud*. In Hardy's "high new house" one hears an echo of Maud's "high Hall-garden" and of its dreadful counterpoint, the hollow behind the little wood, whose "red-ribbed ledges" encroach on the garden and its hall. The symmetrical grammar and phonetically paired lines of Hardy's lyric, like the poem's gay gardens and neat pathways, are touchingly at odds with the eerie, reverberating, reproachful lament that passes like a suppressed wail down each stanza's tremor of open vowels. In a disillusioned but more tranquil mood, Tennyson's lotos-eaters say "all things are taken from us, and become / Portions and parcels of the dreadful past" (lines 46–47). Hardy's refrain is comparably disenchanted but less restrained. Mounting to a surge of revulsion in each of the harshly stressed and alliterating final lines, his refrain is by turns plaintive, haunting, and verging on nausea.

In the last stanza, for the first time in the lyric, the rhymes in the opening and closing lines are faintly dissonant. "Ploughs" is slanted away from its rhyme word "house." Heard in one tone, the refrain "Ah, no; the years O!" is a deserved reversion of decadence to decay and annihilation; heard in another tone, it is a heartbreaking dramatization of the breaking points of the human voice: "Ah, no, the years, the years." Torn between primitive exultation and a cry of pain, the speaker finds his emotional attachment to the dear dead people is strongest when he is about to look at their carved names on the grave and take leave of them for a final time. As in Feste's song in *Twelfth Night,* which he is left alone on the stage to sing, the poise of the festivity and blithe breakfasting, though under assault, is never lost. What keeps out the wind and the rain is the poet's art.

When Hardy writes "Good-bye is not worth while" ("Without Ceremony," line 15) or "the sweet heart of them" ("Rain on a Grave," line 33), he is asking a reader "to conspire" in what Richard Poirier calls "a sympathetic understanding of domestic and social clichés" (1977, 152). But that is not the only demand Hardy makes. "During Wind and Rain" also asks the reader to conspire with Hardy in an understanding of literary allusions to Shakespeare and Tennyson. As Poirier says of Frost, Hardy "asks us to be *both* kinds of readers; and his unique difficulty is in the demand that we be common and literary all at once" (152).

7

Wisdom and Wit

LEAR'S FOOL TO DAGONET

A WISE FOOL LIKE SHAKESPEARE'S TOUCHSTONE OR FESTE HAS less in common with Tennyson's fool Dagonet in "The Last Tournament" than with the witty ironist who narrates Trollope's novel *Barchester Towers.* He also resembles the bemused Fool staring at his face in a mirror in the frontispiece illustration of Thackeray's *Vanity Fair,* who portrays an important side of the narrator's own character. As for the disillusioned Dagonet, he combines the cynicism and jeering of Shakespeare's Thersites with the wit and wisdom of the Fool in *King Lear.* Dagonet's songs are jovially exuberant. But like Thersites's jests in *Troilus and Cressida,* they are also strident and jeering.

> I have wallowed, I have washed—the world
> Is flesh and shadow—I have had my day.
> The dirty nurse, Experience, in her kind
> Hath fouled me—an I wallowed, then I washed.
> ("The Last Tournament," lines 315–18)

Words in love with their own sound assume a mercenary, venal quality. Reducing everything to his own level, Dagonet the Fool has no weapon but his tongue. His language is lethal, and feeds on itself as greedily as the ever-present lechery and lust that abound in *Troilus and Cressida,* the play "The Last Tournament" most resembles.

As Oscar Wilde observes, "One may hate the villains of Shakespeare, but one cannot help loving his fools" (1986, 130). The Fool in *King Lear* is an isolated, lonely figure. Unlike Thersites, who is a cynical choral commentator, or Feste, who is a master of ceremonies left alone on stage to sing the final song in

Twelfth Night, Lear's Fool has the stage pulled from under him in the third act. Like Dagonet in "The Last Tournament," who calls Arthur the "king of fools," the Fool harps on one persistent note: the king's irretrievable folly in dividing his kingdom and banishing the one daughter who truly loves him. Barbed enough to sting, his thrusts are also generalized enough to be proverbs. "Truth's a dog must to kennel; he must be whipped out, when the Lady Brach may stand by th' fire and stink" (*King Lear* 1.4.124–26). The king who whips his Fool and drives him from court is sending truth to his kennel and being more churlish than a dog. An Elizabethan word for she-hounds, both canine and human, "Brach" is the Fool's term of reproach for Goneril and Regan, who must be spurned like curs before they wound their master.

During the storm scenes the Fool's artless prose and snatches of song function as recitative for Lear's great arias. In the play's early scenes the Fool's barbs are lost upon the king. But later in the play Lear fully understands the Fool, who sounds more dazed than the king. As the Fool's mind begins to wander, his prophecy about the future of Albion incongruously mingles dystopian pictures of priests who "are more in word than matter" with genuinely utopian visions (3.2.81, 86). During the scene in which Lear's mock court metes out utopian justice in fantasy, immediately before Cornwall's kangaroo court imposes much harsher "justice" in fact, the king addresses the fool as a "sapient sir." But the Fool sounds bewitched and unhinged now. He sings of leaky boats and of the madness of trusting "the tameness of a wolf, a horse's health, a boy's love, or a whore's oath" (3.6.18–19, 26). Inhabiting a world of absurd charm and fantasy, a topsy-turvy world where Lear will "go to supper in the morning" and the Fool "to bed at noon" (3.6.82–83), the Fool opposes the sanity of clowning to the madness of court intrigue and politics. With this last inversion of values, the Fool drops from the play. It is the last we see or hear of him.

Some critics think Shakespeare was merely careless about the Fool, or decided to reduce the play's overloaded cast. I think it more probable that the Fool has served his function and has nothing more to teach the king. The actor who played the Fool may also have played Cordelia, and as someone too good for the world, the Fool, like Cordelia, goes in the only way he can: out of it. In the early scenes the Fool as effectively criticizes Lear's anger and folly as Feste criticizes unnatural behavior in *Twelfth Night.* When Lear is driven out of his court into the storm, the Fool loses the stage on which he might have performed as an official censor or master of ceremonies. The Fool's fate is best summed up by John Bayley. "Made to play his part on the stage of the court, the Fool shrivels into a wretched little human being on the soaking heath and in the teeth-chattering chill of the hovel. . . . The Fool does his best to rally in the mock-trial scene, but his part is a passive one. All for him is cheerless, dark, and deadly; and his final comment, while failing to rise to the situation, gives his sense of the upside-down world through which he is being hurried" (Bayley, 1981, 61–62).

In a song in which he strains to cheer himself up, the Fool tries to adjust to a harsh world of wind and rain.

> He that has and a little tiny wit,
>   With, heigh-ho, the wind and the rain,
> Must make content with his fortunes fit
>   Though the rain it raineth every day.
>
> (*King Lear* 3.2.74–77)

The same refrain occurs in Feste's song in *Twelfth Night.* Though the scourges of wind and rain in Shakespeare are heard again in Hardy's lyric, "During Wind and Rain," the Fool's most important influence on Victorian poetry is Dagonet's song in "The Last Tournament," where Tennyson's fool calls Arthur "the king of fools" for believing he can make figs out of thistles.

>   "Lo, fool," he said, "ye talk
> Fool's treason; is the King thy brother fool?"
> Then little Dagonet clapt his hands and shrill'd:
> "Ay, ay, my brother fool, the king of fools!
> Conceits himself as God that he can make
> Figs out of thistles, silk from bristles, milk
> From burning spurge, honey from hornet-combs,
> And men from beasts—Long live the king of fools!"
>
> ("The Last Tournament," lines 351–58)

The Fool thinks King Lear is a fool for holding a love auction and dividing his kingdom between two heartless daughters. According to Dagonet, Arthur is equally foolish for building Camelot out of music and for thinking beasts are angels. In trying to be better than the world, Arthur is already on the threshold of immorality. "If 'Christianity' is to mean the taking the Gospels as our rule of life," F. H. Bradley says, "then we none of us are Christians and, no matter what we say, we all know we ought not to be" (quoted in Ayer and O'Grady, 1992, 67). Just as Browning's Abt Vogler yearns to create out of three sounds not a fourth sound but a star, so Arthur is a foiled Ovid, trying to turn thistles into figs and bristles into silk. We know the star Dagonet calls "the harp of Arthur up in Heaven" is a star neither he nor Tristram will ever see. But the true fool may be Tristram, who thinks the Beatitudes are a blueprint for a paradise of fools and the Sermon on the Mount only a formula for tyranny.

Arthur is the Octavius Caesar of *Idylls of the King.* He has sacrificed his personality to his reputation as the perfect knight. Just as Octavius has spread himself too widely over a vast empire, so Arthur, despite his many virtues, strikes us as cold and distant. Empathizing with everyone, he has nothing left over, no love for himself or his queen.

If one model for Dagonet is the Fool in *King Lear,* the jeering commentary of Thersites is Tennyson's main model for Tristram, who keeps decrying the decadent ethic of "The Last Tournament." Coleridge calls Thersites "a *Lear* of the satirical drama, a *Lear* . . . without its soul-searching flashes" and "ear-cleaving thunder-claps" (1930, 1, 108–9). His typical soliloquy is a vituperative swearing song. It has as much in common with the leering jests of Tristram in "The Last Tournament" as with the raucous lilt of Browning's delinquent monk in "Soliloquy of the Spanish Cloister." To rail at oneself in a void, as Browning's Caliban rails at Prospero, may be a mark of savagery or primordial intelligence. But in Thersites's case it is also a sign of critically amused detachment and wit.

> How now, Thersites! What, lost in the labyrinth
> of thy fury! Shall the elephant Ajax carry it thus?
> He beats me, and I rail at him. O, worthy satis-
> faction! Would it were otherwise; that I could
> beat him, whilst he rail'd at me. 'S foot.
> (*Troilus and Cressida* 2.3.1–5)

The audience of his own acting, Thersites is both inside and outside the love and war games. He is a more intelligent Caliban, a comic rationalist for whom the Trojan War is a comedy or farce, and whose only vestige of heroic enterprise is raillery. A victim of the damaging chiasmus, Thersites finds that his reversals wound *him* more than his adversaries. "*He* beats *me,* and *I* rail at *him.* O, worthy satisfaction! Would it were otherwise; that *I* could beat *him,* whilst *he* rail'd at *me*" (italics mine). As a substitute for violence, the verbal abuse of cursing may be preferable to physical beating. But it seems to have no greater end in view than Sisyphus's pushing his stone up the hill only to have it roll down again. In Thersites's soliloquy, the disproportion between the massive effort expended and the puny result achieved compromises everyone. Ajax has brute strength, and Achilles the skill of a rare engineer. But they use massive irons to extricate a mere fly from the web spun by the spider Paris. Though delicate art is required, they use bludgeons. It is as if Jupiter himself were to forfeit his power as king of the gods and Mercury "lose all the serpentine craft of [his] caduceus."

For Thersites as for Caliban, the mind is its own place. But whereas Caliban finds refuge in lyric vision and reverie, in his surmise that "heavens had opened," Thersites's great refuge is his belittling wit, which leaves a perplexed Achilles no vestige of dignity.

> *Achilles.* My mind is troubled, like a fountain stirred;
> And I myself see not the bottom of it.
> [*Exeunt Achilles and Patroclus*]
> *Thersites.* Would the fountain of your mind were clear again, that I might water an ass at it! I had rather be a tick in a sheep than such a valiant ignorance.
> [*Exit*]
>
> (4.1.311–16)

Instead of abetting Achilles in his self-satisfied reflection that a profound thinker can never fathom the depths of his own mind, Thersites discerns in Achilles's profound-sounding thought only the quintessence of ignorance, a valiant stupidity. Unlike Homer, whose compassion includes the victor Achilles, Shakespeare follows Virgil in slandering such Greek compatriots as Ajax, Menelaus, and even Achilles, while ennobling Hector.

Worse than Actaeon's transformation into a stag is Thersites's reversion to so low and primordial a form of life as Menelaus, in whom "too much blood" predominates over "too little brain." "To be a dog, a mule, a cat, a fitchew, a toad, a lizard, an owl, a puttock, or a herring without a roe, I would not care; but to be Menelaus! I would conspire against destiny" (5.1.66–69). There is as much alliterative venom as wit in Thersites's Ovidian fantasies. Menelaus may begin as a bull like Jupiter when abducting Europa. But instead of abducting anyone, it is his own wife who is kidnapped. This mock-epic Jupiter swiftly declines from a bull into the hybrid offspring of an ox and an ass. Though Cressida's lament that the "error" of her "eye" directs her "mind" is as strong a proof of guilt as the admission "My mind is now turn'd whore" (5.2.114), Troilus fears that in "publishing a truth" about Cressida's duplicity he would also be lying about "a credence in [his] heart," a hope "so obstinately strong" that it refutes the testimony of what he sees and hears. Will Troilus "swagger himself" out "of his "own eyes," Thersites asks in disbelief (5.2.136)?

The cynic's last soliloquy is a prophecy that not until "the sun borrows" from the fickle moon will Diomedes, who is all mouth and no performance, learn to keep his word (5.2.101–2). As choral commentator, Thersites's function is to reduce Troilus's faith in Cressida to the bleakest atheism. Coleridge calls Thersites "the Caliban of demagogues." He is "the admirable portrait of intellectual power deserted by all grace, all moral principle; . . . just wise enough to detect the weak head, and fool enough to provoke the armed fist of his betters" (1930, 1, 111). If Thersites's cynicism is the rage of Caliban at seeing his face in the mirror, Troilus's disillusion is the despair of the theist who looks into the mirror of nature and finds reflected there no image of a Creator. At a loss to "read the riddle of Shakespeare's design in the procreation" of *Troilus and Cressida,* Swinburne judges it a "mysterious and magnificent monster of a play" (1918, 199).

Significant rage, like Lear's, is not only the record of a preexisting emotion: it is also deepened and refined in the act of being expressed. By contrast, Posthumus's rage in *Cymbeline* takes place in a void: it has no efficient cause and no end or conclusion to which it might reasonably proceed. Before succumbing to headstrong jealousy, Posthumus has been a dull but faithful husband. Now he is suddenly intemperate and vicious. Ripped from a dying mother's womb and the only survivor of his family, Posthumus harbors a grudge against the mechanics of procreation and the genesis of life itself. "We are all bastards," he proclaims, because all wives are unfaithful. Since women must be "half-workers" in the process, his mind is at war with the very instruments of conception, which requires the minting of counterfeit coins. The tool of such counterfeiting belongs to a "full-acorned boar," whom the mother dallies with, pretends to resist, then shamelessly embraces.

Posthumus secures a shock effect by repeating the phrase "the woman's part in me" (*Cymbeline* 2.5.20, 22). We are accustomed to think that "the woman's part" is a man's compassion and forbearance. But Diana's metamorphosis into the lusty playmate of a boar turns "the woman's part" into sexual license and aggression. In Posthumus's soliloquy the needle sticks in the groove of a single grating pronoun: "Lust and rank thoughts, *hers, hers;* revenges, *hers*" (2.5.24, my italics). Women are constant in nothing, not even in their vice. As each defect starts to divide like an amoeba, Posthumus uses incisive caesural pauses to punctuate each renewed indictment. When a vice is only a minute old, women will exchange it for one less than half as old. The worst revenge Posthumus can wish on women is that they should have their will, which is a desire to outdo his own imbalance and urge to destroy.

Comparable rancor corrodes *Timon of Athens.* If there is more prosecution than harangue in Lear's arias, which are inquisitions on a cosmic scale, there is more harangue than prosecution in Timon's soliloquies. The wit and satire of the Fool's recitatives help carry the weight of Lear's towering arias. But Timon's arias have no Fool to support them. Even in turning blasphemy into a heroic enterprise, Timon's arias suffer from a monotony of repetition that the sustained recitatives of the Fool in *King Lear* manage to avoid. As a result Timon has less in common with the lofty Lear than with Tamburlaine, a Marlovian cartoon. Inspired by Thersites's vituperative rhetoric, Timon's localized curse on the Athenians expands at the end of his first soliloquy into a universal hate, a withering denunciation of all mankind.

> hear me, you good gods all,—
> Th' Athenians both within and out that wall!
> And grant, as Timon grows, his hate may grow
> To the whole race of mankind, high and low!
> Amen.
>
> (*Timon of Athens* 4.1.37–41)

Like Shakespeare's Ulysses, Timon uses a long-delayed predicate to consign to a chaos of "confounding contraries" the expansive invocations and word lists of an epic satirist.

> Piety, and fear,
> Religion to the gods, peace, justice, truth,
> Domestic awe, night-rest, and neighborhood,
> Instruction, manners, mysteries, and trades,
> Degrees, observances, customs, and laws,
> Decline to your confounding contraries,
> And [let] confusion live!
>
> (4.1.15–21)

Promoting the maiming verbs "creep" and "cripple" to the head of blank verse lines, he even uses two trochaic feet to kick down his victims and lame them.

> Thou cold sciatica,
> Cripple our senators, that their limbs may halt
> As lamely as their manners! Lust and liberty
> Creep in the minds and marrows of our youth,
>
> (4.1.23–26)

Like Thersites, Timon is a rhetorician rather than a poet, a chorus rather than a person. His audience is the universe, and his prayer a malediction.

In his satire on Bulwer-Lytton, "The New Timon, and the Poets," Tennyson contrasts the rage and rancor of Shakespeare's Timon with the pettiness of Lytton, the dandy and aesthete, a would-be Alexander Pope and Beau Brummel.

> What profits now to understand
> The merits of a spotless shirt—
> A dapper boot—a little hand—
> If half the little soul is dirt?
>
> (lines 33–36)

The animus and wit come to a focus in "the little soul" of dirt, which recalls Pope's portrait of Sporus in *The Epistle to Dr. Arbuthnot:* "Yet let me flap this Bug with gilded wings, / This painted Child of Dirt that stinks and stings" (lines 309–10). By portraying the critic of "School-Miss Alfred" as an effeminate dandy, Tennyson deftly hoists Bulwer-Lytton with his own petard. As Lytton evolves from a lion shaking a mane of curl-papers, to a subaltern, to a rouged and dapper dandy and a bandbox, the satire becomes "in a definable sense Shakespearean." As Reuben Brower says of Pope's Sporus, "Dramatic speech brings a character to life through continuously evolving metaphors, 'modified,' as Coleridge would say, 'by a predominant passion,' the revulsion from physical and moral ambiguity" (1959, 298).

Equal in intensity to Timon's venom are the torrents of denunciation unleashed by Count Guido in *The Ring and the Book.* If we are intoxicated by Guido's heady rhetoric, regardless of what it exaggerates and defiles, then we ought to find even more to admire in Shakespeare's Iago or Milton's Satan. Park Honan has shown that the more lurid Guido's wolf images become, the more they disclose to his judges that his animal nature has no connection with his professed ideal nature (1961, 307–9). We may be deafened by Guido's thunder claps and blinded by the lightning bolts of his rhetoric, which discharge a volley of dazzling blasphemies: "Be holy still, / And stupid ever" (*The Ring and the Book* 11.2077–78). But torn between piety and atheism, deference to church authority and the rankest heresy, Guido suffers from a type of verbal schizophrenia that calls into question his mental balance and sanity. An act is commendable or criminal, he argues, depending on whether the defendant labels it murder or sacrifice. If he had tried to persuade the ecclesiastical court that he was sacrificing Pompilia to "the Unknown God" or "the Genius of the Vatician" (11.2029–30), Guido believes he would have been exonerated. Even if he had urged such a preposterous motive as doctrinal concern about the heretical upbringing of his son, he believes the judges would have acquitted him.

Just as resourceful as Browning's Caliban or Shakespeare's Prospero in heaping vituperative abuse upon their victims is the precocious young Tennyson of "The Devil and the Lady." As the Prospero of this verse drama, Tennyson's Magus threatens the Devil in the same abusive terms as Shakespeare's Prospero threatens Caliban. Just as Shakespeare's magician vows to "rend an oak, / And peg [Caliban] in its knotty entrails" until he has "howled away twenty winters" (*The Tempest* 1.2.294–96), so Tennyson's Magus vows to imprison the Devil within the stump of a felled tree. He will "rive yon Mighty Cedar-Tree / Sheer from its topmost windiest branch unto / The lowest fang o' the root," then quash his victim's "bunching body" as "flat / As [a] spider" inside the "cleft stem" of its trunk ("The Devil and the Lady," 3.2.39–41, 44–45, 43).

Unlike Shakespeare's inspired blasphemers, Timon of Athens and Lear, Swinburne is a failed Baudelaire whose curses are assaults of sound only.

Fame flutters in front of pretension
    Whose flagstaff is flagrantly fine:
And it cannot be needful to mention
    That such beyond question is mine.
Some singers indulging in curses,
    Though sinful, have splendidly sinned:
But my would-be maleficent verses
    Are nothing but wind.
        ("Poeta Loquitur," lines 57–64)

In their mad surrender to the alliterative impulse, these satirical verses mock Swinburne as a poet out of Bedlam, whose "gospel is wind" (line 48). A decadent armchair Prospero, Swinburne is also a magician who, like Browning's Setebos, makes "soap of the sea" (line 40) by raising storms indiscriminately.

The Shakespeare who shapes the wit and wisdom of Tennyson is not the "Shakespeare bland and mild" whom Tennyson describes in "The Palace of Art" (line 134). As Isobel Armstrong says, "The art of the Palace . . . plunders indiscriminately in spite of its purity" (1993, 79). In sharp contrast to the poet as a "luxury commodity" is the poet as prophet or seer, a bard who dominates *King Lear* and *Troilus and Cressida.* This vatic bard also casts his shadow over *Idylls of the King,* where disillusion as deep as that of Timon, Posthumus, and Troilus is concentrated in three of that work's darkest idylls: "Pelleas and Ettarre," "Balin and Balan," and "The Last Tournament."

I showed in chapter 4 how Hamlet, in the spirit of the Psalmist, asks what man is that God should be mindful of him. As in Pope's great surge of prophecy in *An Essay on Man* (2:15–18), a human bcing, in Hamlet's estimation, is both angel and dust, created half to rise and half to fall. Though the spectacle of running up and down a scale of marveling is moving and deeply felt, its power is the result of a panoramic, largely external point of view. Like Pope, Hamlet fences off any generous participation in experiences he both extols and deplores. He is too detached, too listless and weary, to embrace imaginatively the glory he beholds: "Man delights not me,—no, nor woman neither." There is pathos, indeed, in Hamlet's very distancing of pathos.

In striking contrast to this speculatively aloof Hamlet is Shakespeare's viscerally engaged Troilus, who has less in common with the Psalmist than with Browning's inarticulate savage as he initiates his stammer from the swamp in "Caliban upon Setebos." When Cressida betrays him, Troilus's blood congeals. The ungrammatical fragment "This she?" is all he can bring his numbed tongue and constricted throat to say. As his pulse speeds up, Troilus's heart bursts open in a volley of plaintive pleas and hypotheses: "if beauty have a soul," "if souls guide vows," "if vows are sanctimony." His repeated denial of what he sees—"This is not she"—is experienced as a sort of pain in the chest and a congestion of the lungs. Troilus's shocked recognition of his mistress's betrayal afflicts him like a headache or a wound. His faith in Cressida is "so obstinately strong" that it contradicts the evidence of what he sees and hears. If one believes in the essential sanity of faith, to negate these senses, he reasons, "has no taste of madness," since the only alternative is insanity and chaos, an untuning of the spheres.

> This she? no, this is Diomed's Cressida.
> If beauty have a soul, this is not she.
> If souls guide vows, if vows are sanctimony,
> If sanctimony be the gods' delight,
> If there be rule in unity itself,
> This is not she. O madness of discourse,
> That cause sets up against thyself,
> [Bi-fold] authority, where reason can revolt
> Without perdition, and loss assume all reason
> Without revolt: this is, and is not, Cressid . . .
> Cressid is mine, tied with the bonds of heaven.
> Instance, O instance! Strong as heaven itself;
> The bonds of heaven are slipp'd, dissolv'd, and loos'd.
> (*Troilus and Cressida* 5.2.137–56)

Enfolding beauty in souls, souls in vows, vows in sanctimony, Troilus launches into a daring sorites, a chain argument in the form of abridged syllogisms. But instead of ascribing to the first link in the chain, "beauty," what he ascribes to the last, as in a traditional sorites, Troilus breaks off the chain. "God's delight" is not repeated in the phrases that follow. Sorites is to logic what the great chain of being, the *scala naturae,* is to Renaissance cosmology. Heaven's bonds ought to reach down to sanctify and endorse Cressida's vows to Troilus. But sunder one rung in the ladder and the whole chain falls apart. When the bonds are "slipped, dissolved, and loosed," as Troilus says, "things fall apart." As in Yeats's "The Second Coming," "the center cannot hold; / Mere anarchy is loosed upon the world" (lines 3–4). If *a* is true, its opposite, *b,* must be false. "If there be rule in unity itself, / This is not she" (*Troilus and Cressida* 5.2.141–42). If such opposites cannot both be true, then their defiance of the law of contradiction evokes only "madness of discourse." Troilus meditates on the mysteries of identity: of two in one; or (in this case) of one split into two. His assault of puzzled wit in response to the apparent disunity and fragmentation of his world is rivaled in Shakespeare's canon only by the riddling paradoxes of identity and division in *The Phoenix and the Turtle.* Though a wrenching antinomy for Troilus and a luminous paradox for Hamlet, man's divided nature—his dubious glory as the angelic ape—is an indecent joke for Pandarus and a mere platitude on the lips of the cynical Thersites and Dagonet.

Like Milton's blind Fury, Atropos, who "slits the thin-spun life" with her "abhorred shears" ("Lycidas," lines 75–76), Shakespeare and Tennyson use thin cramped spondees—"thrilling regions of thick-ribbed ice" (*Measure for Measure*); "the blue fly sung" ("Mariana")—to convey the torment of the disenchanted moment. Comparable to *Troilus and Cressida* in its lived experience of torture and wan disillusion is Tennyson's painfully sensual idyll "Pelleas and Ettarre." When Pelleas discovers the faithless Ettarre asleep beside Gawain, his belief in Camelot's vows and ceremonies unravels as inexorably as Troilus's faith in Cressida. Most like Troilus's revulsion in its empathic in-feeling is the sexual loathing Pelleas feels as he crushes "the saddle with his thighs," clenches "his hands," and "maddens himself with moans": "The beauty of her flesh abashed the boy, / As though it were the beauty of her soul" (lines 450–51, 74–75). As in *Othello,* there is no way we can inhabit the courtly lover's mind—with its imagination of innocence, romance, and beauty—at the same time we are trapped inside the agony of a sexual dupe and cynic. As a courtly lover like Troilus, Pelleas has been exalting love while Ettarre has been peddling sex. A remarkable achievement of the idyll is that, far from negating any kinship with Pelleas, the poem broadens and intensifies a reader's intimacy with him as disillusion deepens and he is bestialized and degraded. In a ghastly metamorphosis, the knight who has suffered hallucinations of snakes is himself transformed into a serpent, the definitive emblem of sexual temptation and jealousy. In the moral deformity of Pelleas's trying to forget he is a man by coupling with wolves, the reader is invited to contemplate a terrible potentiality of all thwarted longing and desire.

Just as Troilus refuses to accept Cressida's betrayal in Shakespeare's play, so the more proof Balin has of Guinevere's infidelity in Tennyson's idyll, the more desperately he affirms her innocence: "Queen? subject? but I see not what I see. / Damsel and lover? Hear not what I hear" ("Balin and Balan," lines 276–77). A medieval version of *Troilus and Cressida,* "Balin and Balan" features a hero just as self-deceived as Troilus. *A Midsummer Night's Dream* proclaims the essential sanity of the lunatic, the lover, and the poet, and the madness of merely commonplace minds. *Troilus and Cressida* and "Balin and Balan" explore the dark counter-truth of that axiom. Mocked by Thersites for his incredulity, Troilus lives in an unreal paradise. He is as grossly deceived by Cressida as Camelot is by its two-faced queen.

We are as close to Balin as we are to Troilus, wanting to believe, and yet as alienated from his own refusals to understand as Thersites is from Troilus. In Tennyson, as in Shakespeare, we are asked to inhabit both the idealist's mind—with its imagination of romance and innocence—and the mind of the cynic. What is a coarse commonplace to Thersites is a tragedy to Troilus. Like *Macbeth,* Shakespeare's shortest play, which has almost no beginning and no middle, *Idylls of the King* is all ending, a prolonged descent into madness and disillusion. But there is no Macbeth in Tennyson's idylls. Arthur has his godlike moments, and Lancelot at times acts like a devil. But despite Guinevere's attempt to unite the two men in her mind, there is no single character in the poem who, in full command of Macbeth's towering moral imagination, also totally surrenders that faculty to demonic possession.

Tennyson mirrors Balin's mental imbalance in the structural asymmetry between the few lines in which he reacts in horror to his discovery of Guinevere's infidelity and the many lines in which he irrationally defends her. Like Troilus's response to Cressida's betrayal, Balin's willed refusal to "see . . . what [he] see[s]" (line 276) fragments the poetry, splitting it into questions: "Queen? Subject?" (276); "Damsel and lover?" (277). Just as Troilus desperately affirms his faith in Cressida by denying what he sees (*Troilus and Cressida* 5.2.141–42), so Balin refuses to zoom in on the scene, taking refuge instead in indefinite pronouns and articles: "the things before me" (279); "a churl, a clown" (281). Only when Balin starts to grind his teeth and yell like an animal does he replace his fractured questions and anguished pronouns with his first use of Guinevere's proper name. Through the haze of total madness comes his one lucid reference to Lancelot and the queen.

If betrayal and disillusion are the burden of Thersites's choral comments in *Troilus and Cressida,* decadence and decay are the subject of Tristram's song in "The Last Tournament." Giddy in its display of a weightless emotional vigor, the song executes dazzling turns upon a few repeated words.

> New leaf, new life—the days of frost are o'er:
> New life, new love, to suit the newer day:
> New loves are sweet as those that went before:
> Free love—free field—we love but while we may.
> (lines 278–81)

The sorites builds on the scaffold of what seems at first a logical progression. From "new leaf" it moves to "new life," and from "new life" to "new love." Assisted by alliteration, it then passes from "free love" to "free field," and to the dissolution of every bond tying love to anything more durable than the specious present. Isolt is later sick at heart when she realizes that her love for Tristram has no saving growth or future prospect.

Like the fool Dagonet, Tristram turns verbal cartwheels, beguiled as much by the alliterating sound of "leaf," "life," and "love" as by their meaning. In decomposing the unity of language to give separate excitement to each individual sound and word, his rhetoric proves at least as debased as the hollowed-out rituals of the Tournament of the Dead Innocence. As T. S. Eliot says of Swinburne, his poetry is more decadent in language than subject matter. One sign of this decadence is Tennyson's habit of giving special prominence to the similes, and of decomposing the similes to give prominence to the sound or resonance of an individual word. He beautifully evokes the great waves breaking upon the coast, "Whitening for half a league," and then thinning themselves "Far over sands marbled with moon and cloud, / From less and less to nothing" (lines 464–66). But since Tennyson uses the slow dissipation of the waves to describe something ugly and bathetic, the heavy-headed fall of a drunken knight, which happens suddenly and in an instant, the irrelevant splendor and lovely diminuendo of the lines seem merely decadent. Again, the simile of the mountain in midsummer snows, when all the purple slopes of flowers "Pass under white, till the warm hour returns" (line 230), does nothing to dignify the tawdry revels. The similes work the other way around, producing an effect that is jarring and dissonant.

At the beginning of "The Last Tournament," Dagonet is still in control, using his witty home truths to welcome Arthur as a "brother fool," "the king of fools" (lines 352, 358). He has the same function as the little novice in "Guinevere," who in prattling to the queen about betrayed bridegrooms almost kills Guinevere "with her innocent talk" (line 212). More penetrating than the novice, Dagonet is a master of the same wit and wisdom that Lear's Fool displays until driven from the court and forced to take refuge from the storm. But after Mark murders Tristram and the ceremony of innocence is drowned, Dagonet's stage disappears from under him.

> about his feet
> A voice clung sobbing till he questioned it,
> "What art thou?" and the voice about his feet
> Sent up an answer, sobbing, "I am thy fool,
> And I shall never make thee smile again."
> (lines 752–56)

Unable to play his part upon the court stage, Dagonet is pushed out into the "death-dumb autumn-dripping gloom" (line 750), where he sets up an oddly reproachful wail, like a waif. Failing to rise to the crisis, he is as out of his depth as the Fool is in *King Lear* when upstaged by Kent's remark that Tom o' Bedlam has no daughters (*King Lear* 3.4.67).

Often Tennyson's most transparent allusions to Shakespeare are not his most penetrating or pervasive. It is evident that Tennyson's fool Dagonet is a medieval version of the Fool in *King Lear*. But closer to the biting, embittered, vituperative tone of both Dagonet and Tristram are the jeering commentaries of Shakespeare's Timon and Thersites, which readers often overlook. Similar ironies are at work in Tennyson's "Mariana," which is clearly indebted to Shakespeare for more than just a title and an epigraph, but whose allusions are less straightforward than we tend to assume. When pressed by the Duke in *Measure for Measure* to identify herself, Mariana proves to be a model of anonymity and reserve. She refuses to remove her veil until her husband tells her to. And in her negative replies to the Duke's questions, she proves just as withholding as Cordelia.

> *Duke.* What, are you married?
> *Mariana.* No, my lord.
> *Duke.* Are you a maid?
> *Mariana.* No, my lord.
> *Duke.* A widow, then?
> *Mariana.* Neither, my lord.
> *Duke.* Why, you are nothing then: neither maid,
> widow, nor wife?
> (*Measure for Measure* 5.1.71–77)

In Tennyson's monologue this maid who comes to know her husband carnally, without his knowing it, inhabits a world of comparable equivocation.

Tennyson's most telling omission is the story's ending as dramatized in Shakespeare, which the epigraph from *Measure for Measure* glances at without interpreting. As a result of the Duke's intervention, Mariana does indeed wed Angelo and enjoy a happy marriage. But her situation is precarious. It depends on powers almost as magical and providential as those exercised by Prospero in *The Tempest.* Do these powers extend to the world where Tennyson's Mariana actually lives? As Christopher Ricks says, "Here the poem abruptly deepens its mystery" (1972, 49). If we are to take the epigraph from Shakespeare as more than "mere mood-setting and window-dressing," then we have to acknowledge its equivocal import. It is "optimistic and a cause for hope, in that Mariana is *not* to pine forever . . . ; pessimistic, in that the world of *Measure for Measure* is patently not the real vulnerable world, whereas the world of 'Mariana' may be" (Ricks, 1972, 49, 50). The refrain of Tennyson's Mariana ("I would that I were dead") accords well enough with

Angelo's request for "sequent death" in *Measure for Measure* (5.1.378). But as Eric Griffiths observes, "the poets have put" the lives of Mariana and Angelo "so far apart they themselves cannot hear each other speak" (2009, 159). What seems at first a straightforward allusion to Shakespeare turns out to be ambiguous and obscure. As Griffiths warns, "There were many people in the way between Tennyson and Shakespeare, and the chatter from this crowd was such that Tennyson had to listen hard to catch what Shakespeare was saying" (2009, 136).

8

The End of Illusion

CHILDE ROLAND AND CALIBAN

FLORIO'S TRANSLATION OF MONTAIGNE'S *ESSAYS,* ONE OF THE FEW books we know Shakespeare read, is a manual of wise skepticism and learned ignorance. Its informed or higher ignorance is not to be mistaken for the natural ignorance of a simpleton like Shakespeare's Justice Shallow. Nor is it to be confused with those quick-witted souls in *Middlemarch* who walk about "well wadded with stupidity" for fear of dying "of the roar than lies on the other side of silence" (1956, 144). Unlike simple ignorance or voluntary ignorance, a learned ignorance is the property of a skeptic like Montaigne, who wants to mark a limit to what he can know so that any edifice of learning he does manage to build will be solidly based.

Like Hamlet, whose speculative wonder and acknowledgment of mystery make him wiser than most men, Montaigne is diffident about the range of what he knows. "I have no authority to exact belief, nor do I desire it," he announces (1958, 52). Attacking uncritical deference to the authority of Aristotle, Montaigne favors Socratic learning, the kind of question-and-answer schema found in Falstaff's catechism on honor. It pleases him as much to doubt as to know, he tells us. "Aristotle's principles must no more be principles with him than those of the Stoics and Epicureans. Let their various opinions be put before him; he will choose between them if he can; if not, he will remain in doubt. Only fools are certain and immovable" (56).

We can apply James Carse's categories of ordinary, voluntary, and willful ignorance to Shakespeare. Though more learned than Ben Jonson seems to think, Shakespeare, with his small Latin and less Greek, has an *ordinary* ignorance of the classical learning of a Renaissance humanist like Roger Ascham. He also assumes a *voluntary* ignorance of medieval warfare by allowing anachronisms to enter his history plays. In Samuel Johnson's words, "Shakespeare never has any care to preserve the manners of the time. Pistols were not known in the age of [Henry IV]," but were introduced "about the author's time" and "used by the Scots" (1908, 115–16). Othello has a *willful* ignorance of Desdemona's innocence; and Brutus seems to have a willful ignorance of his motive in killing Caesar. Higher or learned ignorance is another matter. A legacy of Montaigne and the skeptics, it complicates Shakespeare's view of the honors won in war, of fate versus freedom, and of the great mysteries of death and the afterlife.

If we are looking for a powerful rendering of higher ignorance in literature, we have only to turn to Job and *King Lear.* There is a way things are, these works assure us. But the only people who think they know what they are, are fools like the false comforters, who think bad things never happen to good people, or playgoers who look forward to a happy ending in *King Lear.* The same can be said of "Childe Roland to the Dark Tower Came," in which victory and defeat are hard to tell apart. Shortly before writing "Childe Roland," which came upon him "as a kind of dream," Browning saw a performance of *King Lear* that moved him deeply. Friends recall how "his face grew gradually paler, till at last tears, of which he seemed unconscious, ran down his cheeks" (Griffin and Minchin, 1912, 286). The poem acknowledges Shakespeare's influence in its title, which quotes Edgar in his role as the madman, Poor Tom, in *King Lear.*

> "Childe Rowland to the dark tower came;
> His word was still, 'Fie, foh, and fum,
>   I smell the blood of a British man.'"
> (3.4.187–89)

Like Shakespeare and Montaigne, Browning's speaker is a knight, not of faith, but of higher ignorance and doubt. Yet his impulse to disbelieve everything, to accuse the hoary cripple of lying "in every word," also misleads him. The cripple does point the traveler to the right road to the tower. Though this candidate for knighthood is caught in a trap, it is partly a rhyme trap of his own invention.

> My first thought was, he lied in every word,
>   That hoary cripple, with malicious eye
>   Askance to watch the working of his lie
> On mine, and mouth scarce able to afford
> Suppression of the glee, that pursed and scored
>   Its edge, at one more victim thereby.
> ("Childe Roland," lines 1–6)

By placing two framing rhymes (*ab, ab*) around a reversed rhyme pair at the center (*ba*), the speaker snares himself in his own net. Indeed, it is as easy for him to fall into a trap as it is for Lear to be deceived by the bids he receives at the love auction, or for Gloucester to be hoodwinked by Edmund.

Recording with a pathetic exactitude the cry uttered by a water-rat, as it shrieks out like a babe (line 126), Childe Roland is also anxiously precise about the chopped heads of the thistle-stalk. He even parodies traditional theodicy by inferring a "brute" has been set loose, "Pashing . . . life out, with a brute's intent" (line 72). A victim of the paranoia that often accompanies feelings of displacement and loss, Childe Roland irrationally protests that the cripple who tells the truth is hateful and lies. Even Roland's query seems pointless. If "all agree" that the "ominous tract" into which Roland turns "hides the Dark Tower" (lines 14–15), why does Roland ask? And if the cripple tells the truth, why invest him with a "skull-like laugh" or with a crutch to write his victim's gravestone inscription?

Shuttling back and forth between observation and surmise, the speaker uses run-on lines to avoid any premature sense of arriving at an end.

Yet acquiescingly
I did turn as pointed: neither pride
Nor hope rekindling at the end descried,
So much as gladness that some end might be.
(lines 15–18)

Coming before the end of a line, even the repeated word "end" defers closure. It leaves the traveler hovering over two meanings of "end." Is he about to reach a finish line or about to arrive at some final cause or goal? In *King Lear,* Kent ineffectually interrupts the king's agony by asking, "Is this the promised end?" (5.3.264). In Browning's poem, whose desperate end games are inspired by *King Lear,* one of the few appearances of "end" at the end of a line describes the man about to die, who "feels begin and end / The tears" of those grieving for him (lines 26–27). Afraid to disappoint them, the dying man is embarrassed that his life should creep on, like the protracted simile that crosses the break between stanzas 5 and 6, refusing to end when everyone expects it to. Just as Donne extracts wry humor from the drama of delayed deaths in "A Valediction Forbidding Mourning," so Browning uses run-ons to mock and thwart the rituals of conventional leave taking. Renouncing the hope of succeeding in his quest—"Just to fail as they, seemed best" (line 41), and striving to be the end of a line that refuses to end, Roland imitates the end game in *King Lear,* a play that refuses to end when it should.

Never scrupulously externalized, the setting of "Childe Roland" is an interior landscape, like the "Unreal City" of T. S. Eliot's "The Waste Land." The nightmare quality is evident in the way the knight finds himself alone on a ghastly plain of weeds and stunted grass. A "blind horse" suddenly materializes out of nowhere, then just as mysteriously vanishes. It may surprise a reader to recall that Roland never actually sees the water-rats or the savage strife between "toads" in a "poisoned tank" and "cats" in a "cage." At the sacrifice of vividness, Browning keeps inserting "like" and "so": "The fight must *so* have seemed," "*like* two bulls," "*like* giants at a hunting" (my italics). The cautious use of simile reminds a reader that the terrors are only hypothetical and not externally real. The sudden appearance of "the little river" and the abruptness with which "the plain" merges into "mountains" have the indeterminacy of a dream. If design governs at all in such a place, it must be the brute design of a wild beast or "estray," an untamed, dispossessed creature, sponsored by neither god nor man, that chops off the heads of thistles and bends their stalks. Eager to watch the sport, the dying sun shoots "one grim / Red leer" through an atmosphere charged with bleeding color. "One stiff blind horse" (line 76), made rigid by the triple stresses, is even said to see with its obtruding bones, which are all "a-stare" and fleshless.

The catachresis of seeing with one's bones recalls Lear's attempt to sweeten his imagination by joking about Gloucester's blindness. Lear may dismiss as madness Gloucester's oxymoron of "seeing feelingly." But there is wise folly in his advice that "a man may see how the world goes with no eyes" (*King Lear* 4.6.153). The catachresis of looking "with thine ears," as Childe Roland's horse stares with his bones, can teach the blind man all he need know. If Gloucester were to get glass eyes, he could pretend to see things he does not, like a dishonest politician.

As in Lear's arias on filial ingratitude, the pride of great ones, and man's inhumanity to man, a deep distress humanizes Browning's knight. Like Lear on the heath, Roland finds his flashes of insight flicker less fitfully as the landscape grows bleaker and his despair deepens. His experience on the darkling plain intensifies his fellow feeling and widens the range of his compassion. Even his communion with animals qualifies an initial repugnance. When the wounded "water-rat" shrieks piteously like a babe, Browning expects us to recall the "mad" Edgar's fantasy of swallowing "the old rat and the ditch-dog" (3.4.137). Like Roland, Lear acknowledges his affinity with animals—"Man's life is cheap as beast's" (2.4.270)—and even imagines his dogs to be his faithless daughters, Goneril and Regan: "The little dogs and all, / Tray, Blanch, and Sweetheart—see, they bark at me" (3.6.65–66).

In a "time-out" or moment to reflect, Childe Roland hopes that the inward eye of memory can summon up more bracing visions. But his experiment fails when the downward spiral of rhymes, which descend from "gold" and "fold" to "cold," participates in Cuthbert's precipitate fall from grace. As the sentence lengths contract, the disappearance of run-on lines cribs in the speaker. On his "darkening path" he hears no sound and sees "no sight as far as eye could strain" (lines 104–5). As a victim of giants who stalk their game, Roland identifies only with subhuman forms of life: with the "black eddy" that spumes with "wrath," with the alder" that kneels "down over it," and with the suicidal throng of "willows" that fling themselves "headlong in a fit / Of mute despair." In stanza 21, the deferral for four lines of a principal clause suspends the speaker over a void. He has a horror of stepping on the cheek of a dead man or of thrusting his spear through his hair or beard. The worst terror he saves for the last line. In a surge of revulsion, Roland feels a squeamish distaste for having speared a rodent that cries out like a babe.

The knight can think of no sequence of events that quite explains the devastation everywhere. What clash of armies could leave in their wake a battlefield so savagely trampled and padded "to a plash"? Like toads in a tank of poison or cats in a red-hot cage, the contending armies must have been penned in or trapped, despite their having "all the plain to choose" from (lines 130–34). The more Roland speculates about some "mad brewage set to work their brains," or some contest between Christian and Jewish galley-slaves staged by a Turk for his amusement, the more off-key his conjectures sound. Since "no footprint" leads "to that horrid mews" and "none out of it" (lines 135–36), his conclusion that the wheel or brake must be a machine from the devil's armory, designed to "reel men's bodies out like silk," is a tortured fantasy, exquisitely refined, but implausible as an explanation of what he sees. We find comparable passages in *King Lear,* where, as one critic says,

> everybody knows that when Gloucester exclaims
>
> > As flies to wanton boys are we to the Gods
> > They kill us for their sport
>
> he is saying something obviously appropriate to his experience. . . . He is not touching a central core of tragedy, voicing a discovery the play wants to "leave" with us. (Bayley, 1981, 23)

Many of Roland's comments about shrieking water-rats and sadistic Turks seem "equally inappropriate, equally on a wrong note" (23).

As one form of blankness gives way to another, Childe Roland experiences the kind of cognitive overload Kant associates with the mathematical sublime. Roland's "drive" toward what Neil Hertz calls "the end of the line" (2003, 3) leaves him dazed and stunned. But finally, in the "wide wing dragon-penned" of a friend of Apollyon, the Devil of the Apocalypse, he is ready to encounter—in a noun framed by two expansive adjectives—a Miltonic sublimity.

At the thought
A great black bird, Apollyon's bosom-friend,
Sailed past, nor beat his wide wing dragon-penned
That brushed my cap—perchance the guide I sought.

(lines 159–62)

Launched on a receding series of black shapes and voids—"naught in the distance," "evening," "naught" ahead"—Roland in his dark "night of fear" is ready at last for an oracle, for some disclosure or prophecy of his end.

John Bayley reminds us that "much has been written about the meaning" of "Childe Roland" and "its deliberate mysteriousness, but its allegory is clear enough. The Dark Tower is the end of strenuous illusion; it is the mere thing in itself. Browning wrote the poem in Paris, after the difficulties of his marriage had begun to reveal themselves. Now the reality had begun: the thing itself was there" (1981, 44). Most readers will assent to the comment on disillusion. But the poem is too indeterminate to be an allegory, and I think Bayley underestimates the degree to which Roland on his wasteland is King Lear on his heath, responding to his companions as neither heroes nor traitors but as fully human beings. An allegory is unpopular with some critics, because it limits their freedom to interpret. *The Divine Comedy* not only creates a world; it also interprets and comments on it. The opposite of allegorical, the genius of "Childe Roland" and *King Lear* is existential, not moral or theological. Whereas *The Divine Comedy* seals off the dome of its edifice, Shakespeare and Browning cultivate a generous and open hospitality to many gods and beliefs.

Lear's arias during the storm are operatic soliloquies, cosmic in scope, in which the king is not so much addressing the Fool as talking past him. The blows that level Lear are not just natural assaults of wind, fire, and rain. Though two powerful metonymies, the storm's gross, full belly and the king's venerable head, concentrate the conflict, Lear is primarily a victim of filial ingratitude and age. The blows that fall with greatest force are the spondees that reduce him to an "infirm, weak, and despised old man" (3.3.20), a tattered coat upon a stick, whose greatest affinity is with the infirm and the poor. Urging Kent and the fool to precede him into the hovel, Lear kneels down like a child at bedtime to pray, not for himself, but for all "Poor naked wretches, wheresoe'er you are" (3.4.28). At the height of the storm, Lear commands pomp to

Take physic, . . .
Expose thyself to feel what wretches feel,
That thou mayst shake the superflux to them,
And show the heavens more just.

(3.4.33–36)

When Edgar's appearance as Tom o' Bedlam triggers Lear's madness, the voice that speaks out of the whirlwind of his mind soars and towers like God's voice in Job. As one critic says, his insanity yields "a kind of super-sanity" (Harbage, 1983, 418). Northrop Frye suggests "Lear's madness is what our sanity would be if it weren't under such heavy sedation all the time" (1986, 119–20). "Tossing about like bits of wreckage," fragments of wisdom and a consuming rage for truth are thrown out like lifelines to the dispossessed and poor.

> Did'st thou give all to thy daughters,
> and art thou come to this?
>
> (3.4.49–50)

> Is man no more than this? Consider
> him well. Thou ow'st the worm no silk, the beast
> no hide, the sheep no wool, the cat no perfume.
> . . . .
> Thou
> art the thing itself; unaccommodated man is no
> more but such a poor, bare forked animal as thou art.
>
> (3.4.107–13)

Gestured at but not named, man's humiliations and indignities defy description. Like Hamlet's "paragon of animals," who is also "the quintessence of dust," Lear's "unaccommodated man," "a poor, bare, forked animal," is now as far below the worm, the beast, the sheep, and the cat, as he was once proudly above them. When Lear is sane, his behavior is absurd. In the mad scenes, his rage for order is blindingly clear.

In *Alice in Wonderland,* the Mad Hatter says, "How you get there is where you'll arrive." Our destination depends on the journey that we take. Childe Roland does not have to journey to the Dark Tower to make his discovery. The Tower is his own wisdom in the only form it can take: a recognition that wherever he goes, there he is, and there he will end. "History is now and England," as Eliot says. Experience itself is the Dark Tower: with a destiny but no destination, the knight knows his journey's end, however distant, is here and now. As Robert Langbaum remarks, "Browning's poem is about a quest of which we do not know the purpose or whether in the end the knight succeeds or fails. It is the whole point of the poem that there is nothing more precise to be known, that the poem is about sheer questing—the experience not the situation" (1957, 192). Just when the fool in his heart says there is no god, behold, there he is, right on Childe Roland's heath. Like the god in *King Lear,* he is a hunting giant, "chin upon hand," watching his game at bay and waiting to kill it for his sport. "Now stab and end the creature—to the heft!" ("Childe Roland," line 192).

The voice that speaks out of the whirlwind of Lear's mind is the same voice Childe Roland hears on the heath. John Bayley says that for Lear "the reality of Cordelia is itself the Dark Tower. But he neither knows it for what it is nor is he capable of accepting it" (1981, 44). Did Browning know, or want to know, the meaning of what he had written? At first a heartless dummy who says nothing, Cordelia is the higher angel of her father's nature, whose death will be the end of all illusion. When Roland hears a trap shut and fears his end is at hand, he suddenly realizes he has reached his end in another sense: there before him stands the Dark Tower. In achieving his destiny he also arrives at his destination and death. If all victories are victories of imagination, then so are all defeats. There is nothing good or bad but thinking makes it so. Roland's celebration of his arrival at the tower in the final line is a choral moment, the only time in the poem when the words of *King Lear* and the speaker converge. When Childe Roland at last sees the tower, he is looking at the world as Lear comes to see it as one of God's spies after his reunion with Cordelia; or as Browning's Lazarus sees it, under the aspect of eternity. And no man can do that and live.

If the most enigmatic Victorian poem inspired by *King Lear* is Browning's "Childe Roland," Hopkins's sonnet "No worst, there is none" is surely the most harrowing. When the wheel of fortune turns, people at the bottom usually expect to move up. An exception is *King Lear,* where each turn of the wheel drops everyone another notch lower. Like earlier versions of Lear's story, all other plays by Shakespeare that feature a fool end happily. Samuel Johnson was so unnerved by Cordelia's death that he could not endure to sit through the last scene of the play. As Stephen Booth observes, we are shocked by downward turns of fortune's wheel in *King Lear,* not because of "*what* happens," but because of "*when* and *where* it happens" (1983, 6). When Lear enters in the last scene with the dead Cordelia in his arms, Shakespeare has already met the three criteria Aristotle prescribes for a tragedy: he has presented an action that is serious, complete, and of a certain magnitude. No one expects to see Aristotle's categories ignored. But that is precisely what Shakespeare does. Instead of allowing the audience to isolate, limit, and understand what has happened, Shakespeare "continues that action beyond the limits of the one category that no audience can expect to see challenged." As Booth says, "Shakespeare presents the culminating events of his *story* after his *play* is over" (1983, 11).

Both the audience of *King Lear* and the characters in the play have to endure the most wrenching turn of fortune's wheel. Just before he sees his blinded father led in by an old man, Edgar seeks refuge in the consolation of the desperately wretched and unhappy. The wheel has reached its lowest point, he reflects, and nothing can be worse than what he has had to endure up to now.

> To be worst,
> The lowest and most dejected thing of fortune,
> Stands still in esperance, lives not in fear.
> The lamentable change is from the best;
> The worst returns to laughter.
>
> (4.1.2–6)

The audience feels momentarily as secure as Edgar. It welcomes the "unsubstantial air" that Edgar embraces, confident at least that "the wretch that thou hast blown unto the worst / Owes nothing to thy blasts" (4.1.8–9).

What a shock, then, when the wheel drops another notch lower, and we see old Gloucester brought in blind. Though the audience has recently witnessed the blinding, it has momentarily erased the horror from its mind. It feels as unprepared and defenseless as Edgar.

> *Edgar.* [aside] O gods! Who is't can say "I am the worst"?
> I am worse than e'er I was.
> *Old Man.* 'Tis poor mad Tom.
> *Edgar.* [aside] And worse I may yet be. The worst is not
> So long as we can say "This is the worst."
>
> (4.1.25–28)

Abashed to be deceived by his own specious moralizing about the turn of fortune's wheel to a low point or ebb, Edgar now admits that it is impossible ever to reach the limits of what his mind—or the mind of Shakespeare's audience—may have to endure.

Watching *King Lear* is like viewing hell from Satan's point of view in *Paradise Lost.* Since each descent to a lower depth stands to its preceding depth as hell does to heaven, Milton's mindscape of hell includes within itself an image of each new hell to which Satan is falling, and within that image another image, in an endless regress of descents.

> Which way I flie is Hell; myself am Hell;
> And in the lowest deep a lower deep
> Still threatening to devour me opens wide,
> To which the Hell I suffer seems a Heav'n.
>
> (*Paradise Lost* 4.75–78)

Few passages better describe the mental anguish of Edgar in *King Lear,* who feels unprotected and vulnerable, never knowing what calamity awaits him next. "Come, let's away to prison," Lear says to Cordelia, "and take upon's the mystery of things." But Lear's appeal contains illusion within illusion. "Perhaps," as Iris Murdoch says, "there is no mystery and no God, only pain and utter loss and helpless senseless death" (1992, 119). "The play," she suggests, "has a double ending, a soft tragic end in 'calm of mind, all passion spent,' followed by another end in screams and howling. It could be called, from a traditional point of view an unChristian play, raising to the highest level Shakespeare's reticent attitude to Christianity" (1992, 119).

The boldest explorer of mindscapes in Victorian poetry is G. M. Hopkins, who recoils from the terror of falling off mountains in "No worst, there is none," a sonnet that echoes Edgar's words in *King Lear.* No sooner does Hopkins, the climber of mindscapes, plunge to a new depth of despair than he realizes there is always another depth, another lower level, to plunge to.

> No worst, there is none. Pitched past pitch of grief
> More pangs will, schooled at fore pangs, wilder wring.
> Comforter, where, where is your comforting?
> (lines 1–3)

Hopkins's sonnet seems written out of the whirlwind of a mind that has just read Job or *King Lear.* Pitched (in the sense of "hurled" or "thrown") past the sharpest note on the scale of torture and discord, the sufferer knows that the pain he has already suffered is merely a foretaste of a sharper dissonance to come. Before starting to subside, the pangs that wring his heart and the discords that ring in his ears will "wilder wring" (both as a squeezing or twisting, as in the wringing of a chicken's neck, and as the excruciating ringing of tinnitus in the inner ear). The solace that in line 3 enfolds the comforted in the embrace of a chiasmus—"Comforter, where, where is your comforting?"—is withheld from the speaker. Possessed by demons, the sufferer can give voice only to "a chief woe, a world-sorrow." His cries "heave, herds-long," and materialize as a maddened flock of Gadarene swine.

> Mary, mother of us, where is your relief?
> My cries heave, herds-long; huddle in a main, a chief
> Woe, world-sorrow; on an age-old anvil wince and
> sing—
> Then lull, then leave off. Fury had shrieked "No lin-
> gering! Let me be fell: force I must be brief."
> (lines 4–8)

Huddling together in a strung-out line of alliterating stresses, the blows that assault the speaker suddenly disperse in the momentary relief afforded by the less tortured music of a "lulling" and "leaving off." After the leveling stresses of "Woe, world-sorrow" and "age-old anvil wince" (line 6), the break at the end of line 7 splits in two the "lingering" of the Fury, which continues to hover tremulously over the line and word break before moving on to the last two syllables. The fractured noun softens the Fury's blow and validates its vow to be "brief" by making its announcement in two brief principal clauses: "Let me be fell: force I must be brief."

In his rapid sketching of mindscapes, no Victorian more resembles Shakespeare than Hopkins. By what telegraphy, we may ask, does the poet of "No worst, there is none" pass from the terror of a mountain climber, clinging to a cliff face, to the refuge sought by a wretch like Lear, shivering on a heath at the height of a storm? And by what succession of images does he then manage to wrest from the whirlwind of a mind as tormented as Job's the consolation of the coda? In line 12 we see "Here!" but also hear "Hear." Heed wisdom. Listen to the oracle. If the risks of such swift and elliptical explorations of a mindscape are great, then so are the rewards.

> O the mind, mind has mountains; cliffs of fall
> Frightful, sheer, no-man-fathomed. Hold them cheap
> May who ne'er hung there. Nor does long our small
> Durance deal with that steep or deep. Here! Creep,
> Wretch, under a comfort serves in a whirlwind: all
> Life death does end and each day dies with sleep.
> (lines 9–14)

In isolation, the lowly creeping of a wretch and the high suspension of a mountain climber, swaying perilously over a ravine, would seem to cancel each other out. But the swiftness of Hopkins's language leaves a reader little time to ponder or unfold the images. Hopkins's stress is not on visual impressions but on rapidly sketched, partially elided auditory impressions linked together by a series of echoes: first by the shorthand of "fall," "small," and "all," and then by a chain of both internal and terminal rhymes—"cheap," "steep," "deep," "creep," and "sleep." The most daring and abrupt transition, from the terror of the lofty and sublime to the comfort of the everyday and ordinary, is also the simplest and most moving.

In *King Lear,* Shakespeare takes care to remind a listener that the cliff graphically described by Edgar is a visionary cliff only. "Hark! do you hear the sea?" he asks his father, only to tell him a few lines later that "the murmuring surge of the sea" cannot be heard from a promontory as lofty as the one they are standing on. Edgar's lapse of memory is Shakespeare's way of saying that Gloucester and his son are not literally standing where Edgar says they are. It is also his way of anticipating and confirming Hopkins's insight that the mind's "cliffs of fall" are steeper and more terrifying than the plunge from any physical precipice we might imagine.

Hopkins distills the sheer, no-man-fathomed quality of the mind's mountains in two fearful metonymies: their "steep or deep" (line 12). If we climb up the mind's cliff-face, it towers high above us and seems precipitous and steep. If we fall over the edge, the chasm into which we plunge is unfathomable and deep. To attenuate the horror of what is "steep or deep," Hopkins cannot resist providing a third rhyme in the chain: "Here! creep," he urges. "If comfort has escaped you earlier, take comfort, wretch, in this truism: all / Life death does end and each day dies with sleep." But what if Hopkins's nightmares are just as tortured as his waking experience? What if Hamlet is right, and after death we fly to horrors that we know not of? Even the minimal consolation Hopkins finds in death after life and in sleep after toil fails to reassure him. It is too reminiscent of Edgar's specious reasoning in *King Lear.* Just as Edgar's idea of reaching the worst, and so of living in hope instead of fear, proves illusory, so the lifeline Hopkins throws out to his wretch in the storm will not do even as a platitude, much less as the wisdom Job expects to hear when God speaks to him from the whirlwind.[1]

It is fitting that the character in Shakespeare whom Browning displays the greatest virtuosity in imitating is Caliban, the savage who initiates his monologue as a stammer from the mud but who later rises to a summit of prophetic and poetic vision. Though Oscar Wilde maintains that Shakespeare sings with myriad lips while Browning stammers through a thousand masks, Caliban is one of the few characters in Shakespeare who stammers as well as sings. G. B. Shaw quips that Browning is a quite undramatic poet: his savage Caliban combines the theology of an evangelical churchman with the introspective powers of a Hamlet. But to accept Shaw's argument is to conclude that Shakespeare's Caliban is also undramatic, for his savage in *The Tempest* combines traits that are no less grotesque. Indeed, so entranced is Shakespeare's savage by musical voices and the hum of a thousand "twangling instruments" that when he wakes after dreaming of clouds opening and of riches ready to drop, he cries to dream again. Just as Ariel is no ineffectual angel, but an efficient executor of Prospero's commands, so Caliban is no slavish brute, but a drudge with the soul of a lyric poet.

Such incongruities are part of Caliban's charm, and can be found in Shakespeare's most probable source, Montaigne's essay on cannibals. Just as primitive as *The Tempest*'s Caliban and just as stirred by aesthetic impulses, Montaigne's cannibals are accomplished composers of war and love songs, much impressed by the beauty of snakes, whose exquisite markings they extol in their poems. These cannibals have also perfected the art of taunting their enemies. Since the cannibals' ancestors have feasted off the enemy's ancestors, their captors should realize that in eating the captured cannibals they are also feeding off the substance of their forefathers' limbs. "A shaft of wit that by no means savors of barbarism," Montaigne adds with a glint of irony (1958, 117). Indeed, all Montaigne's remarks about cannibals look two ways at once. Both witty and primitive like Shakespeare's Caliban, his savages are as exalted and moved by beauty as they are debased by inhuman impulses.

In his first speech in *The Tempest,* Caliban uses the edgy, asyndetic style we have come to associate with Browning. He drops conjunctions, stresses each noun of a triad ("bogs, fens, flats"), and crowds together three alliterating verbs in a row: "pinch," "fright me," "pitch me i' the' mire."

> All the infections that the sun sucks up
> From bogs, fens, flats, on Prosper fall and make him
> By inchmeal a disease! His spirits hear me,
> And yet I needs must curse. But they'll nor pinch,
> Fright me with urchin-shows, pitch me i' th' mire,
> Nor lead me, like a firebrand, in the dark
> Out of my way, unless he bid 'em;
>
> (2.2.1–7)

Though Caliban is afraid of the spirits Prospero uses as his spies, he also turns the tables on Prospero by using imperatives of godlike command to curse him. Like a vengeful god, he orders infections to fall on his master and transform him by inches into an ulcerous sore. Drawing upon both features of Shakespeare's portrayal, Browning subjects Caliban to the passive tortures of a victim, but also invests him with a rebellious god's power to blaspheme and destroy. When Caliban feels humbled and powerless, he refers to himself in the third person: when he swells with power like a god, he reverts to the first-person pronoun: "Would not I smash it with my foot? So He" ("Caliban upon Setebos," line 126).

Caliban's fear in *The Tempest* that the magician's spies will hear and punish him anticipates the fear of Browning's Caliban that a raven has reported his blasphemies to Setebos and that the angry god is now sending forth a storm to destroy him.

> What, what? A curtain o'er the world at once!
> Crickets stop hissing; not a bird—or, yes,
> There scuds His raven that has told Him all!

> It was fool's play, this prattling! Ha! The wind
> Shoulders the pillared dust, death's house o' the move,
> And fast invading fires begin! White blaze—
> A tree's head snaps—and there, there, there, there,
> there,
> His thunder follows! Fool to gibe at him!
> Lo! 'Lieth flat and loveth Setebos!
> ("Caliban upon Setebos," lines 284–92)

The blunt sarcasm of the delinquent's gibe that the decrepit god "may doze, doze, as good as die" (line 283) receives its rebuff sooner than expected. "Pillared dust" shouldered by the wind of a tornado or hurricane advances on Caliban like a house of death. As he watches the beheading of the trees and counts off the thunder rolls, five successive deictics reduce the stunned victim to a stammer: "A tree's head snaps—and there, there, there, there, there, / His thunder follows!" (lines 90–91). Six caesuras in a single line impart a savage chop to the phrases. They convey the desperation of a frightened slave whose god may be placable, but whose only rule for pleasing god is that there is no rule.

The only comparable Shakespearean use of "there" occurs in the storm scene in *King Lear,* where the "mad" Edgar uses the word four times to denote the omnipresence of the fiend.

> Bless thee from whirlwinds, star-blasting, and taking! Do poor Tom some charity, whom the foul fiend vexes. There could I have him now—and there—and there again—and there! (*King Lear* 3.4.62–64)

Caliban's repetition of "there" not only echoes the reverberating thunder rolls he counts off in the storm. It also echoes Edgar's "mad" music in *King Lear,* whose frantic repetitions—"There could I have him now—and there—and there again—and there!"—mark the appearance and disappearance of a fiend. They also express Edgar's diffused dismay, his baffled sense that he cannot name or localize his fears. As Stephen Greenblatt explains, "Repeated words of this kind are drained of whatever meaning they may have started with; they become instead placeholders for silent thinking" (2004, 281). The most rending use of an indefinite placeholder comes a few lines earlier in the play. "Hast thou given all to thy two daughters, and art thou come to this?" (*King Lear* 3.4.48–49). Norman Maclean says, "There is one big word within this speech—the one right word, the one word that is not a touching-up of another word which could itself have remained without the notice of aftertimes. The right word is also in the right place; it is the last word, 'this'" (1952, 614).

Though Caliban, the prophet of millennial disaster in Browning's monologue, gets his apocalypse sooner than expected, the storm sent by Setebos may partly objectify a prior guilt. It is possible, however, that Setebos and the ravens have nothing to do with invading fires and beheaded trees. In Caliban's first speech Shakespeare plants a similar suspicion about Prospero's vengeful motives, which Browning, I think, wants readers to recall.

> For every trifle are they set upon me;
> Sometime like apes that mow and chatter at me,
> And after bite me; then like hedgehogs which
> Lie tumbling in my barefoot way and mount
> Their pricks at my footfall; sometimes am I
> All wound with adders, who with cloven tongues
> Do hiss me into madness.
>
> (*The Tempest* 2.2.8–14)

Since Caliban, in one critic's words, "has been the object of so much romantic solicitude, it might be wholesome to consider whether his pangs are really inflicted by Prospero's sprites; perhaps he is just too stupid to steer clear of bogs and briers, or to pick spots clear of porcupines as he sets down his clumsy feet" (Harbage, 1963, 471).

Browning's idea that Caliban is a precocious savage, sensitive to beauty and capable of breathtaking speculation, owes most to the passage in Shakespeare where Caliban longs for the enchantment of sleep-inducing music. When Caliban wakes after long and soothing sleep, voices urge him to dream again of clouds opening and of riches ready to descend.

> Be not afeard. The isle is full of noises,
> Sounds and sweet airs that give delight and hurt not.
> Sometimes a thousand twangling instruments
> Will hum about mine ears; and sometime voices
> That, if I then had wak'd after long sleep,
> Will make me sleep again; and then, in dreaming,
> The clouds methought would open and show riches
> Ready to drop upon me, that, when I wak'd,
> I cried to dream again.
>
> (3.2.144–52)

The unspoken Hippocratic oath of the prophet-poet is "to follow the god to the open Delphi which [he carries] within himself" (Steiner, 2003, 17). As in Caliban's dream, a heaven must open. It must drop its riches upon an elect soul, a master spirit like Ovid's Protagoras or even Caliban, who is then moved to set "obsession on its way," sharing his "touches of grace and hope" with every responsive listener (18–19).

The best comment on the transport of a vision that has power to touch the soul and move it to wonder comes from Reuben Brower. After observing how "the clumsy humor of Caliban" soothes "the fears of Stephano and Trinculo," Brower adds that "immediately following come impressions of inexhaustible riches, both of musical sounds and visual beauties. There are feelings of magic and of the mystery of sleep, of intense sensuous delight, and of a childlike love of a dream-world" (1951, 213–14). I know of no passage in literature that better supports Sir Thomas Browne's claim that "we term sleep a death, and yet it is waking that kills us, and destroys those spirits that are the house of life" (1967, 85). "It is not a melancholy conceit," says Browne, in a passage recalling Prospero's vision, "to think that we are all asleep in this world, and that the conceits of this life are as mere dreams to those of the next, as the phantasms of night, to the conceits of the day" (84). Caliban's repetition of the phrases "make me sleep again" and "cried to dream again" creates an illusion of receding dreamscapes. By instilling a longing for that "slumber of the body" which is a "waking of the soul" (84), such marveling recursive effects also abet and help inspire the adventurous speculative flights of Browning's Caliban, who posits a God beyond God, the Quiet over Setebos who made him.

In his last speech, Shakespeare's Caliban tells Prospero that he will "be wise hereafter, / And seek for grace" (*The Tempest* 5.1.294–95). Instead of worshiping a drunkard like Stephano, he will look for gods less fallible and strange. This speech, more than any other, helps explain why Browning substitutes for Shakespeare's aesthetically sensitive savage the precocious theologian of "Caliban upon Setebos," who sues for his own form of grace. If Setebos is God, then God is not good; if the Quiet is God, then God is not God. Since either Setebos or the Quiet is divine, God cannot be good and omnipotent at the same time. "'Saith He is terrible: watch His feats in proof!" 200). As shrewd in his criticism of causal logic as Lear on the heath, Caliban realizes there is no necessary connection between goodness and prosperity. Often, a devastated Job is left crushed on the dust heap.

The hierarchy of gods implied in the child's question "Who made God?" has appealed to many thinkers besides Caliban. In *Varieties of Religious Experience,* William James suggests that the world comprises many gods, of different degrees of inclusiveness. Setebos is the god of Caliban's mother, and the idea of the god's power comes to Caliban from two sources: from the violence of nature and from Prospero's will to be lord of the isle and tyrant. At the same time the logic of perfection drives Caliban to convert his own bondage to necessity, accident, and brute compulsion into that embodiment of freedom, design, and persuasive agency he identifies with the Quiet, "the something over Setebos / That made Him" (lines 129–30). In the "Quiet" Caliban seals off the dome of the edifice and completes his masterpiece, his

Summa of "natural theology in the island," the phrase Browning used as the subtitle of his monologue. The Quiet is not the loving Father addressed by Christians in their prayers. As the God beyond God, It has most in common with F. H. Bradley's Absolute, which is too detached and austere to be "personal," "moral," "beautiful or true" (1893, 472). As for Setebos, he remains the ferocious old despot of Johannes Agricola's theology, the tyrant who gloats over the torments of the damned, and whose will exhausts the freakishness of arbitrary caprice. The only escape from this abyss of horror is the sedation offered by the Quiet, the dozing off and slow decline of the tyrant god, or the gradual decay of Christian theology itself.

Rejecting Karshish's belief in a god of both love and power, Caliban anticipates Thomas Hardy's hope that, just as man in the course of the ages has evolved a mind, so God may eventually develop, at man's insistence, a consciousness and moral sense. The idea of the Quiet, who remains the symbol of this possibility, may seem extravagant. But it finds a counterpart in Shelley's Demogorgon, Byron's Arimanes, and even (in the last century) in Paul Tillich's God beyond God. Just as Joseph Butler, the author of *Analogy of Religion,* finds a corresponding anomaly in nature for every anomaly in revealed religion, so Caliban—a kind of Butler in reverse—finds a corresponding contradiction in religion for every contradiction in the order of nature. Creating the world out of hate instead of love, and using the island and its inhabitants to remedy defects in himself, Caliban's god is a grotesque parody of the god described by Bishop Butler. For if the analogies between revealed religion and natural theology are valid, then (as Caliban also shows) any contradiction in either area of inquiry has two foreseeable consequences. A thinker is free to accept both natural theology and revealed religion, as Butler intends. Or he is equally free to reject them both, as Jeremy Bentham decided to do.

As Caliban turns into a vengeful David Hume, he teaches lesser forms of life that causality is one of natural philosophy's obsolete fictions. It is a mere psychological feeling, not a logical necessity.

> "So must he do henceforth and always."—Ay?
> Would teach the reasoning couple what "must" means!
> 'Doth as he likes, or wherefore Lord? So He.
> ("Caliban upon Setebos," lines 238–40)

Like Hume, Caliban walks a tightrope over the abyss of a causeless world. Though a vortex of swirling sense impressions keeps churning below, Caliban avoids vertigo by never looking down. Like the mistaking of a drunkard for god in *The Tempest,* the attempt of Browning's savage to identify God with a principle of arbitrary caprice falls as far below a reasonable understanding of deity as the sublime god of the psalmist rises loftily above it.

"Caliban upon Setebos" is as stunning an image of human tragedy as Shakespeare's Lear alone on the heath, or as Tennyson's picture of man the cosmic accident, a lonely and self-blinded Oedipus stumbling on stairs that slope through darkness in *In Memoriam* (55.15–16). Like the monster who initiates his monologue as a stammer from the mud ("'Will sprawl, now that the heat of day is best / Flat on his belly in the pit's much mire" [lines 1–2]), Browning gives the impression of stepping out of a Slough of Despond to cheer himself up with boisterous swearing songs. But what will lift his spirits when his puppets stop talking and he has to return to the swamp? Like Lear and the souls in Dante's purgatory, who willingly remain in the refining fire, Browning identifies with the indignities and defeats that overtake Childe Roland. But no refinement through fire seems able to console him. Browning the agnostic feels bitterly the Psalmist's wry words used as the epigraph for "Caliban upon Setebos": "Thou thoughtest that I was altogether such a one as thyself" (Psalm 50:21). The alternative to idolatry is Nicholas of Cusa's "learned ignorance" or *docta ignorantia,* the skepticism and restrained response to religion found in Montaigne's *Essays* and Shakespeare's greatest tragedy. Both proudly knowing and doubting everything, Browning is as thirsty for knowledge but as badly shaken as his paragon of monsters, the ignorant yet precocious Caliban. If the Quiet, a cold and remote god beyond god, exists, Browning like Caliban finds this deity too deficient in indignant compassion, too indifferent to the world's cruelties, to be worthy of his worship.

Unlike most Victorian scholars, I have always felt that Browning, the gregarious extrovert and optimist, is more tortured at the center of his faith than Tennyson, the brooding introvert. Despite Browning's exuberance and bravado, his chilling "Epilogue" to *Ferishtah's Fancies* acknowledges deep distrust and doubt.

> Only, at heart's utmost joy and triumph, terror
> Sudden turns the blood to ice: a chill wind disencharms
> All the late enchantment! What if all be error—
> If the halo irised round my head were, Love, thine arms?
>
> (lines 26–29)

Unlike Virgil, Browning and Shakespeare find there is no sybil or prophet they can trust to tell their future. An English Montaigne, Shakespeare is a skeptic, an oracle of higher ignorance. As another such apostle, Browning knows that, like Childe Roland's love for his lost comrades and peers, the adventurers of old, his own love for Elizabeth, "half angel and half bird, / And all a wonder and a wild desire" (*The Ring and the Book* 1.1391–92), is quickened by the void into which she is drawn down as a ghost. Just as Caliban's worship culminates in the unknown God beyond God he calls the Quiet, so Browning realizes that the person he is closest to in life can be understood and loved best in the space of his unknowing. If evil has its depths, then good must have its heights. But what if the Parthenon, the temple on the hill, has lost its deity? Without the Palladium, in what virgin moonlight can the soul now dwell? What if the wise goddess, like the good Cordelia, is only a dummy, as impossible to apprehend or conceive as the "Quiet"? Turning Browning's "blood to ice" is his fear that his angelic bird is an enchantment, his halo an illusion, and the dark tower a mere emptiness or ruin.

PART IV

GRACE & DEATH

9

A Toil of Grace

CLEOPATRA AND HER HEIRS

IN *ANTONY AND CLEOPATRA,* OCTAVIUS CAESAR SPEAKS ELOQUENTLY of the beauty he was cold to when Cleopatra lived but which kindles the poet in him when she dies. He says the poisoned queen so resembles a sleeping temptress that he would not be surprised if even in death she snared another victim.

> he looks like sleep,
> As she would catch another Antony
> In her strong toil of grace.
>
> (5.2.349–51)

While a tranquilizing simile ("she looks like sleep") relaxes the mind, a seductive comparison ("as she would catch") turns grace, an attribute of God and kings, into a sexual trap. At the same moment, however, an expansive metaphor—"toil of grace"—enlarges and transforms Antony and his queen. It transports them to a world of love and empire, a world of ennobling imagination, where no taint of scandal or reductive simile can diminish their grandeur. Shakespeare's "toil of grace," T. S. Eliot explains, "is expansive rather than intensive; its purpose is to *add* to what you see (either on the stage or in your imagination) a reminder of that fascination of Cleopatra which shaped her history and that of the world, and of that fascination being so strong that it prevails even in death" (Eliot, 1932, "Dante," 244).

Speaking of the "seemly violence" that "contracts [Shakespeare's] language," Frank Kermode observes that, though "grace can be justly thought of as a trap," Shakespeare suddenly moves "the sexual game with Antony . . . out of the reach of common metaphor." Though Kermode offers more insight when mistaken than most critics when right, he is wrong to assert that Eliot "still favors . . . passages from Dante because they have what he argues to be a 'rational necessity' that is lacking in Shakespeare" (2010, 16). On the contrary, after contrasting Shakespeare's expanding metaphor of the "toil of grace" with Dante's diminutive simile of the crowds in hell, who sharpen their vision "like an old tailor peering at the eye of his needle," Dante's champion surprises us by saying that the two figures he has just compared are in fact incomparable. "Between men who could make such inventions as these there can be no question of greater or less" ("Dante," 244).

Rosemond Tuve thinks that in this instance T. S. Eliot has loaded the dice against Shakespeare by comparing Dante's simile not only with another simile but also with a metaphor. There is no trope in Dante's use of the tailor, "none of what rhetorical theory calls 'translatio'—the actual wresting of signification so that each word means something it does not ordinarily say." By contrast, "Shakespeare's *strong toil* is [just] such a *translatio;* it operates immediately to furnish many meanings—which are possible, not compulsory, suggested, not stated, uncountable, not limited. . . . No wonder, then, that, as Eliot remarks, Dante's image is more translatable than Shakespeare's. Shakespeare's is already a *translation*" (Tuve, 1947, 100, 107). A metaphor like "toil of grace" opens a window on a vaster, more expansive world than Dante's simile of the "old tailor" scrutinizing his needle. Is Cleopatra's "toil of grace" a sexual snare? Or is it the web of an enchantress? It is hard to decide whether Shakespeare is referring to a sleeping siren or a goddess. "Grace" covers a wide spectrum of meanings in Renaissance culture. It could apply to anything from a gift, from the cultivated taste and polish of Castiglione's courtier, to the grace of God himself.

The difference between Cleopatra's first appearance to Antony on her barge and her dying words is the difference between what Harold Goddard calls an "immense tapestry or historical picture" and "an apocalypse" (1951, 590). In the first scene Cleopatra is "the earthly Venus, enveloped in incense," identified with each of the five senses and four elements. In the last scene she speaks simply as a woman, fondly addressing her "husband," her "baby," and her "nurse." "It is her Last Judgment on all Caesars," Goddard says, "hers and Shakespeare's—the revenge of poetry, which is the politics of heaven, on empire" (590). I used to think it was out of character for Octavius, the cold politician, to pay Cleopatra her finest tribute. But what better way of dramatizing Cleopatra's power to enchant men than by showing how she seduces in death even the one male detractor she outwits most spectacularly in life? "Gazing down, as if entranced, this man who had been cold to her and to her beauty while she lived, utters the most beautiful words ever spoken of her." As Goddard says, "She catches him in her strong toil of grace. She leads him in her triumph!" (591).

Shakespeare is a concrete, never prudish writer. Early in *Antony and Cleo-*

patra, Philo's bluff candor spares no detail of his great captain's sensual enslavement to his gypsy captor.

> Nay, but this dotage of our general's
> O'erflows the measure. Those his goodly eyes
> That o'er the files and musters of the war
> Have glow'd like plated Mars, now bend, now turn
> The office and devotion of their view
> Upon a tawny front. His captain's heart,
> Which in the scuffles of great fights hath burst
> The buckles of his breast, reneges all temper
> And is become the bellows and the fan
> To cool a gypsy's lust.
>
> (1.1.1–10)

More in evidence than any "toil of grace" is the toil of their strenuously physical love making. Antony's sexual prowess brings his gypsy to a crisis of heat. Then the fan of his panting and heavy breathing cools off his mistress's lust until each is ready for another round of sex. For the frank, angry Philo "the triple pillar of the world," the great Antony, is turned into "a strumpet's fool." But as far as Antony is concerned, Rome can melt in Tiber "and the wide arch of the empire fall." His space is here in Egypt, where "the nobleness of life" is to embrace Cleopatra. Philo criticizes his friend for allowing his dotage to overflow all measure. But the same can be said of Antony's bounty, which like the flooding of the river Nile overflows the bounds of common generosity and brings happiness to a people and prosperity to an empire. The double perspective, first of Philo and then of Antony, allows us to see the toil for what it is, both an infatuation and an ennoblement.

The enchantments of the temptress become more palpable in the great speech by Enobarbus describing Cleopatra's appearance in a barge. It is not only Antony who is caught in her toil of grace. Brought to life by diffused personification, each of the four elements and five senses proves just as amorous as Antony.

> The barge she sat in, like a burnished throne
> Burn'd on the water. The poop was beaten gold;
> Purple the sails, and so perfumed that
> The winds were lovesick with them; the oars were
>   silver,
> Which to the tune of flutes kept stroke, and made
> The water which they beat to follow faster,
> As amorous of their strokes. For her own person,
> It beggar'd all description. She did lie

In her pavilion, cloth-of-gold of tissue,
O'erpicturing that Venus where we see
The fancy outwork nature. On each side her
Stood pretty dimpl'd boys, like smiling Cupids,
With divers-colour'd fans, whose wind did seem
To glow the delicate cheeks which they did cool,
And what they undid did.

(2.2.196–210)

To enhance Cleopatra's grace, Enobarbus shows how she ravishes the senses. Her gold pavilion exceeds the visual splendor of Apelles's painting of Venus rising from the sea. The tune of the flutes keeping time to the oarsmen's strokes appeals to the ear; the perfumes that emanate from the purple sails and the poop entice the winds; and the fans that alternately heat up and cool the queen's cheeks have strong tactile appeal. When Antony is invited to supper a moment later, he is too lovesick to eat. He feasts with his eyes only. Like the five senses, each of the four elements—earth, fire, water, air—plays its appointed role. The air is as lovesick for Cleopatra as the water, which is said to be in love with her barge's strokes. So glittering and burnished is her throne that, in a leisurely crossing of the first break between lines, it is said to burn on the water. Antony himself is stranded on the land or earth; while the air, the fourth element, seems about to desert the marketplace to gaze on Cleopatra. Only in the last lines, where the bellows-like action of the fans recalls Philo's earlier description of cooling a gypsy's lust, does Cleopatra's grace become primarily sensual, a self-defeating snare like Penelope's web that undoes what it does, or unravels what it weaves.

In a display of technical virtuosity rare in Victorian criticism, Robert Louis Stevenson contentiously asserts that the appeal of Cleopatra's "purple" sails has nothing to do with their color. What appeals to Shakespeare is the intricacy of a sound pattern. The cluster of consonants in "the barge she sat in" recurs in the phrases "burnished throne" and "burnt on the water." The move from B to P in "burnt" and "poop" is adroitly duplicated in the move from P to F in "pur" and "fumed": "and so perfumed that / The winds were love-sick with them." "Indeed," Stevenson concludes, "the whole passage is a monument of curious ingenuity," including the subsidiary S, L, and W pattern in the sequence "sat," "sails" "so," "waters," "winds," "were," "love-sick" and "with" (Stevenson, 1938, 1509).

The most sustained Victorian allusion to Cleopatra's celebrated appearance on her barge verges on parody. It occurs in Tennyson's play *Queen Mary* (3.2), when Cardinal Pole, who under different circumstances might have been Mary's consort, describes his return to England on the river Thames in an inadvertently mock-heroic allusion to Cleopatra's first appearance to Antony on the river Cydnus (Tennyson, 1908, 8:89–90). Pole tries to make Philip a Spanish Antony and Mary an English Cleopatra. He even adds a strain of religious allusion: "Lo, now you are enclosed with boards of cedar / Our little sister of the Song of Songs!" But the cedar boards are too suggestive of a coffin to rival the grandeur of Antony's love for Cleopatra or even the lover's exotic apostrophe to the cedar of Lebanon tree in Tennyson's *Maud.* Instead of enthroning Mary or her consort Philip on the royal barge, the conceited Pole enthrones himself. The strain of egotism is never absent. It is as if Shakespeare's Cleopatra were to praise herself, instead of allowing Enobarbus to do it for her. Even "that long low minster," the dismal church where Mary and Philip were married, is depressed in memory by the dragging spondees and harsh successive stresses of Pole's description, which lengthens out its gloom.

Queen Mary filters the exotic play of Shakespeare's colors through a sieve of chaste silver-white impressions.

> We had your royal barge, and that same chair
> Or rather throne of purple, on the deck.
> Our silver cross sparkled before the prow,
> The ripples twinkled at their diamond-dance,
> The boats that followed were as glowing-gay
> As regal gardens; and your flocks of swans,
> As fair and white as angels; and your shores
> Wore in mine eyes the green of Paradise.
> My foreign friends, who dreamed us blanketed
> In ever-closing fog, were much amazed
> To find as fair a sun as might have flashed
> Upon their lake at Garda, fire the Thames;
> Our voyage by sea was all but miracle;
> And here the river flowing from the sea,
> Not toward it (for they thought not of our tides),
> Seemed as a happy miracle to make glide—
> In quiet—home your banished countryman.
> (3.2.4–20)

The waves are no longer amorous of the barge, but twinkle in a diamond dance that imitates the sparkling of the silver cross before the prow. The river that flows away from the sea, in apparent defiance of natural law, is no miracle but simply an everyday occurrence, the rising of the tide. Though the sun burns the Thames, as Cleopatra's burnished throne burns the water, Pole tells Mary that his foreign friends still associate England with a dismal northern setting, where "ever-closing fog" blankets the green of Paradise under a snow-like pall. Unlike Shakespeare's lovers, who in the last two acts of *Antony and Cleopatra* rise to a pinnacle of grandeur and "blaze their trail across the mind of humanity for all time," Pole lacks even the "grace to be dissatisfied" with Tennyson's fanatical and jaded version of Shakespeare's queen (Murdoch, 2009, 133).

Though Tennyson called *Maud* his "little *Hamlet,*" his story of a star-crossed lover who kills the brother of the woman he loves owes more to *Romeo and Juliet* than to *Hamlet.* When love first descends on Romeo, it blasts love's witty versifier into a new dimension.

> O, she doth teach the torches to burn bright!
> It seems she hangs upon the cheek of night
> Like a rich jewel in an Ethiop's ear—
> Beauty too rich for use, for earth too dear!
> (*Romeo and Juliet* 1.5.46–49)

"O," he says, in open-mouthed amazement, before slowly compressing his lips in an outburst of alliterative appreciation and wonder. Like a rich jewel suspended in the ear of night, Juliet is said to be "too rich for use, for earth too dear." Already she hangs upon the cheek of night as she will hang upon the foul air and darkness of a crypt. Just as the talking flowers perform a miniature ballet for the lover in *Maud,* so in the sonnet Romeo and Juliet exchange at the ball, the two lovers, like partners in a dance, take three steps back for every one step forward. Earlier in Shakespeare's play Romeo has talked like a Petrarchan sonneteer. Now at the ball, he wholly naturalizes the convention by framing his love with an English sonnet, Shakespeare's equivalent of a heart-shaped Valentine. Though Juliet allows Romeo to kiss her, the courtesy is still as exquisitely formal as the tact with which they share a couplet and split the sonnet's final line.

Though Tennyson's lover in *Maud* is at pains to dissociate himself from the coquettish wiles of a modern Cleopatra, he is as surely ensnared by Maud as Romeo is by Juliet and as Antony is by his Egyptian queen.

> What if with her sunny hair,
> And smile as sunny as cold,
> She meant to weave me a snare
> Of some coquettish deceit,
> Cleopatra-like as of old
> To entangle me when we met,

To have her lion roll in a silken net
And fawn at a victor's feet.

(*Maud* 1.212–19)

The lover is caught in a toil just as unyielding as the resilient "silken net" in which Cleopatra's lion rolls and fawns at its victor's feet. Felt most strongly when denied by her lover, Maud's force waxes and wanes like growing and fading sheets of auroral light.

Passionless, pale, cold face, star-sweet on a gloom
profound;
Womanlike, taking revenge too deep for a transient
wrong
Done but in thought to your beauty, and ever as pale
as before
Growing and fading and growing upon me without a
sound,
Luminous, gemlike, ghostlike, deathlike, half the night
long
Growing and fading and growing, till I could bear it
no more,
But arose, and all by myself in my own dark garden
ground,
Listening now to the tide in his broad-flung ship-
wrecking roar,
Now to the scream of a maddened beach dragged
down by the wave
Walked in a wintry wind by a ghastly glimmer, and
found
The shining daffodil dead, and Orion low in his grave.

(1.91–101)

Ghostly impressions of a "wintry wind," fitfully illuminated by glimmers of white light, detach Maud from the Edenic grove of weird opulence and perfumed warmth in which the lover finds himself. The recurrence of the same words and sounds, especially long arcs of adjectives of about the same size and shape—"passionless, pale, cold face" (91), "Luminous, gemlike, ghostlike, deathlike" (95), "broad-flung shipwrecking roar" (98)—sustains a sense of the circling flow of Maud's beauty, "growing and fading and growing . . . without a sound." The chain of epithets, made relentless by the repeated suffix ("gemlike, ghostlike, deathlike" [95]), also enforces the pulsating glow, as the ghastly glimmer of her "passionless, pale, cold face" continues to fluctuate in space like a long-distance film shot. From the sinuous horror of a maddened beach scream, which explodes like a bullet in the brain, there bursts a flame of frail beauty and expiring glory. We are not to imagine the lover hearing the roar of the sea, then looking at the shining flower before gazing forlornly at the sinking star. The effect Tennyson creates is more surreal. We receive instead, in a single mounting impression, something like "seabeach-madness, wintry-gleam, daffodil-star-death."

Tennyson recounts with pride the letter of the asylum doctor who assures him that his representation of madness in *Maud* is the most faithful since Shakespeare. "The doctor was an excellent literary critic," Dwight Culler quips, "for Tennyson's representation of madness is not only the best since Shakespeare—it is right out of Shakespeare" (1977, 207). Tennyson masters Shakespeare's trick of "having his madman speak home truths in a slightly crazed and translucent way" (207). In his lunacy the speaker in *Maud* combines the crazed pathos of Ophelia with the rage of the mad King Lear and the confused lucidity of Lady Macbeth in her deranged sleepwalking speech. Comparable to the mad Ophelia's use of phrases that apply both to Hamlet and to her father is the lover's use of phrases that apply both to his beloved's murdered brother and to the lover's own father in the madhouse scenes in *Maud*. Though the speaker thinks he is dead, he still longs for death, as Tithonus does; and his longing is endlessly thwarted. Now the thoughts move forward in rushes, and the speaker's voice keeps lapsing into rhyming fits of hysteria—fits that shape themselves into chainlike fragments: "Driving, hurrying, marrying, burying" (2.250) and multiple rhymes:

> For I thought the dead had peace but it is not so;
> . . . .
> But up and down and to and fro,
> Ever about me the dead men go.
>
> (2.253, 255–56)

Like Lady Macbeth's sleepwalking speech, the culminating nightmare recalls and confuses earlier events. If the details were simply to multiply in random disorder, according to principles of simple association, the poem would be condemned to sensual chaos or elemental raving. The pit that brings to mind the father's suicide would merge into pictures of social injustice, which would prompt denunciation by the hero, and so on. To control the flow, Tennyson borrows Shakespeare's device of using a couplet to signal closure at the end of a dramatic scene or a sonnet. In part 1 each block contains at least one passionate lyric followed by a reflective passage; and Tennyson marks each unit off either with couplets signaling closure, as in Shakespeare (1.8.312–13;

1.10.396–97; 1.13.487–88), or else with quatrains, which have the same resolving function as couplets (1.1.73–76; 1.16.567–70).

In the discourse of mad people, the first parts of speech Shakespeare removes are the prepositions and conjunctions. Lacking any connective tissue, the sleepwalking speech of Lady Macbeth is an acoustic chamber of remembered horrors. A diseased mind is constrained to amplify and echo past events endlessly. The opposite is true of the distemper of language that afflicts Mr. Candy, a victim of aphasia in Wilkie Collins's novel *The Moonstone.* If Lady Macbeth says nothing about everything, Candy says everything about nothing. His mind adheres like glue to a connective web of prepositions and conjunctions. But like an umbilical cord without its fetus or a feeding tube without a mouth, he has lost the power to name. He retains the grimace of a Cheshire cat after the rest of its face has faded. Maud's lover suffers a similar fate when the "passionless, pale, cold face" of the woman he loves dissolves into the "growing and fading and growing" of a ghastly auroral light he is powerless to tame or subdue.

At first Maud's lover simply confuses the time references, blurring details of the father's suicide and the brother's death. Recalling and confusing earlier events, he relives the sleepwalking speech of Lady Macbeth. But as the lover blends images of red and white, sweet scent and lips, which he had used earlier for both Maud and her brother (1.452), he begins to sound less like Lady Macbeth than a transformed King Lear. Northrop Frye says, "Eros doesn't care about convention or originality" (2000, 594). At first the lover sounds like a lunatic on a good a trip. He keeps as many images copulating as possible. But moved by the distress of other people, the lover soon discovers he can no longer keep his feelings separate for a different reason. Though the hallucinatory vision of roses as blood adds to the horror and confusion, it also dramatizes an exchange between love and hatred, vengeance and compassion. The hero begins to replace his taunts against Maud's father, "that gray old wolf," whom he blames for his father's suicide, with a finer, more searching irony: "For what will the old man say / When he comes to the second corpse in the pit?" (2.325–26). Instead of denouncing the "wolf's malignity," the speaker feels sorry for the old man, as Achilles is moved to pity when the grieving Priam pleads for release of his son's body.

Christopher Ricks has noticed that "Shakespeare, who needs and wants the words *lie, lies,* and *lying* hundreds of times in his work, has only three times the punless form *lied*" (1987, 377). Alive with the erotic potential of "lie," "lain," and "die," which often look multiple ways at once, *Maud* transfers the most explicitly erotic use of "die" from the bed of lilies on which Maud has "lain" (1.161) to the "daffodil sky," where "the planet of Love," Venus, is about "To faint in the light of the sun she loves, / To faint in his light, and to die" (1.861). Even if he had "lain for a century dead," in the horizontal posture of a corpse, Maud's lover says his dust would still be alive with an erotic pulse: it "would hear her and beat" (1.920–21). Like Shakespeare, Tennyson attests to the truth of Ricks's remark that the "marked paucity of suggestive rhyming for truth, which lends it a lonely dignity and integrity, contrasts sharply with the manifest and manifold rhymes which crowd upon or from *lie*" (1987, 376). When Maud's brother gives the speaker "the lie" (2.16), it is presumably because he charges the lover of "lying" with his sister. But later, when the lover remembers how the brother "lay dying there" (2.306), he uses an anti-pun to fend off both the sexual and the mendacious meanings of "lie." Only near the end of *Maud,* in the poem's rhyme of "lie" with "die," does Tennyson revive the use of "lie" as a subversive pun.

> Not that gray old wolf, for he came not back
> From the wilderness, full of wolves, where he used
> to lie;
> He has gathered the bones for his o'ergrown whelp
> to crack—
> Crack them now for yourself, and howl, and die.
> (2.291–94)

These powerful lines align the two fathers with the howling Lear, for whom there are no bones of comfort left to crack.

Maud's lover wants to forgive his enemy if he can. The reversal represents that shocked condition, that turning point in *Maud,* when love casts out fear and changes terror into awe. There is a gentle lucidity in the hero's thoughts, as there is in Lear's thoughts when he pities all "Poor naked wretches, wheresoe'er you are" (*King Lear* 3.4.28). His descent into madness is now propelled by an ascending leap from hate to love and by a new and unexpected power to pity. When Maud appears to the lover in a last flash of beauty, "like a silent lightning under the stars" (3.9), her shadow no longer pursues and torments him. The speaker is in control of the terror, no longer its victim. As if resentful of his own credulity in believing madness more real than sanity, despair more real than hope, the lover reverts passionately to the volatile beauty of "lightning under the stars," beyond earth altogether, and to the great love visions that transformed him earlier in the poem. Having experienced mainly the boredom and the horror, he now knows something of the glory as well.

Less overpowering and intimidating than the Maud who binds her lover with strong surges of eccentric force is the Maud who operates as an agent of grace. Seldom has a conceit been so marvelously expanded as the lover's sustained apostrophe to a cedar of Lebanon tree.

> O, art thou sighing for Lebanon
> In the long breeze that steams to thy delicious East,
> Sighing for Lebanon,
> Dark cedar, though thy limbs have here increased,
> Upon a pastoral slope as fair,
> And looking to the South, and fed
> With honeyed rain and delicate air,
> And haunted by the starry head
> Of her whose gentle will has changed my fate,
> And made my life a perfumed altar-flame;
> And over whom thy darkness must have spread
> With such delight as theirs of old, thy great
> Forefathers of the thornless garden, there
> Shadowing the snow-limbed Eve from whom she
> came.
>
> (1.613–26)

The lover's conceit of the branch-charmed tree combines Shakespeare's power of active association through rapidly sketched metaphor with an empathic in-feeling and suffused sympathy. So integral are the "delicate air" (1.619), the streaming breezes (614), and the "starry head" (620) to a woman, a landscape, and a biblical idea, that without any straining for effect the lover can link a chain of grand renewals in his simple address to a tree. The adornment of his passion in the gorgeous language of the Song of Songs is what Shakespeare in *Antony and Cleopatra* calls the "ostentation" of love, an opulent celebration of eros and empire.

As Walter Jackson Bate says of Keats's style, Tennyson perfects "an idiom that at its best approximates that of Shakespeare. The combination, at least, is rare since Shakespeare" (1960, 352). As Bate explains, the truly distinctive quality of Shakespeare and Keats is "less the substitution than it is the substantiation of one sense by another in order to give, as it were, additional dimension and depth" (1960, 345). Like Keats's "branched thoughts, new grown" in his "Ode to Psyche" (line 52), the "merry play" of the erotic stars, as they move "in and out" among the swaying limbs (*Maud* 1.629), displays an organically felt participation in the disparate objects that are joined. This kinesthetic gift is weaker in metaphysical poetry than in either Shakespeare or Tennyson. The stars' "merry play" introduces a stroke of broad parody across the solemnity of Adam's and Eve's creation in the "thornless garden" (1.625).

But instead of burning only as "Cold fires" (1.637), the stars also form a bridal crown for Maud, who is both Eve and Mary, the second Eve, the virgin of the *hortus conclusus* in the Song of Songs. This transformed Maud catches her lover in as strong a toil of grace as Cordelia catches Lear. She offers Tennyson's angry young man what Juliet offers Romeo and Cleopatra offers Antony: all the heart can wish.

Marshall McLuhan takes Tennyson and the Pre-Raphaelite poets to task for failing to create the kind of interior landscape found in the Symbolist poetry of Rimbaud and Baudelaire. In criticizing McLuhan for suggesting that all landscape poetry aspires to the condition of an interior landscape or geography of the soul, A. S. Byatt rightly praises as a valuable alternative the poetry of sensation perfected in *Maud* and extolled in Hallam's review of Tennyson's *Poems* of 1842. For Hallam, as Byatt explains, "the landscape is not interior, but *exterior* and valued because it is therefore less likely to lead to introspection and inertia than is reflective thought." In *Maud,* the landscapes are "setting for emotions, rather than substitutes. In fact, Tennyson uses them as both, . . . which is part of [the poem's] complexity" (1969, 78–79). Byatt neglects to mention, however, that in parts of *In Memoriam* (in the "Dark house" elegy of section 7, for example), Tennyson also fashions interior landscapes of the kind McLuhan thinks the Victorians were incapable of creating. It took a critic like T. S. Eliot, a great admirer of Laforgue and Rimbaud, to recognize the worth of what Tennyson had achieved in the interior landscapes of *In Memoriam,* if not in the more sensuous, exterior landscapes of *Maud.*[1]

In the last two sections of this chapter, I examine moments in Shakespeare, Christina Rossetti, and Tennyson when the lofty scaffolding comes down and we descend to the simplicity of Othello's "It is the cause, it is the cause, my soul," Macbeth's "She should have died hereafter," or Tennyson's "He is not here." T. S. Eliot says that "by looking innocently at the [simple] surface" of such words, "we are most likely to come to the depths, to the abyss of sorrow" (1932, 337). From the high style of speech and manner found in *Antony and Cleopatra* and the great tragedies, Shakespeare drops into the old Lear's simple and ingenuous appeal to Cordelia, "Come let's away to prison," which combines the sprightliness of a dance with the lightness of a dream. Coming after what John Gielgud calls "the big noble scaffolding which supports them," the extreme simplicity of Lady Macbeth's rueful words, "All the perfumes of Arabia will not sweeten this little hand," or of Lear's supplication, "Pray you undo this button," can be "infinitely touching" (1991, 51). Equally moving is Hopkins's simple prayer, "O thou lord of life, send my roots rain," and Christina Rossetti's protest: "You took my heart in your hand / . . . Then set it down, / . . . As you set it down it broke" ("Twice," lines 9, 12, 17). Reversing Shakespeare's protest against the defenseless simplicity of love in sonnet 64—"Time will come and take my love away" (line 12)—is Tennyson's assertion of love's power to endure in *In Memoriam:* "I cannot think the thing farewell" (123.12), he stammers out in a barely articulate statement of what he feels.

"Great simplicity," as T. S. Eliot says, "represents one of the most arduous conquests of the human spirit: the triumph of feeling and thought over the natural sin of language" (1932, "George Herbert," 361). Shakespeare's most poetic lines—"There's providence in the fall of a sparrow" or "Ripeness is all"—are often his simplest; and some of his most moving speeches are questions: "Hast thou given all to thy two daughters, / And art thou come to this?" (*King Lear* 3.4.48–49). "Some dimension, some significance, goes out of a speech," Norman Maclean argues, "if it is not a question but a declaration. . . . Gone is some of the immediacy of the moment, too big at its occurrence to be believed or recorded as fact. To a degree, then, pity and fear are made out of grammar." Maclean concludes that much of Shakespeare's art consists of "little brush strokes," especially "when what is being composed is 'the seemingly simple'" (1952, 614). "And after many a summer dies the swan" is a line of such seeming simplicity. Tennyson appears to have come upon it by chance. Like Shakespeare's "ripeness is all" or "the readiness is all," the words fall upon the ear with a grace and ease of movement that preclude lament. They seem as natural and effortless as breathing.

Though Shakespeare may lack "the severe and scrupulous self-restraint" of the ancients (Arnold, 1965, 603), to most modern readers his ability to sound grand without being inflated, to see an object as it actually is without sounding commonplace or ignoble, achieves that rare combination of the elevated and the simple which Arnold associates with Homer. While Tennyson "dawdles with the painted shell of the universe," and Clough tries "to *solve*" it, Shakespeare, like Arnold's Homer, "sees his object and conveys it to us immediately" (1896, 30). Adapting a striking phrase of Coleridge, Arnold says "the mist of alien modes of thinking, speaking, and feeling . . . 'defecates to pure transparency,' and disappears" (1896, 11) in Homer's best verse. No book on the Victorian poets and Shakespeare can hope to rival Arnold's lectures on translating Homer. As Douglas Bush says, Arnold's "gives one, as only rare books do, a real sense of enriched faculties and critical growth, and that sense is only confirmed by rereading" (1971, 89). As the greatest Victorian literary critic, Arnold has an advantage over Ruskin, the age's greatest art critic, simply because Arnold's criticism exists "in the same medium (language) as the art that it explores and esteems." As Christopher Ricks has noted, "This can give to literary criticism a delicacy and an inwardness that are harder to achieve" in criticism of the visual arts or music (2004, 7). Without trying to emulate Arnold, we can use his distinction between natural and artificial simplicity to distinguish the achievement of Shakespeare and Christina Rossetti from the achievement of Milton and Tennyson. Though Rossetti's "Give me the lowest place" is an example of natural simplicity, Tennyson's "Far on the ringing plains of windy Troy" is an example of *simplesse* or artificial simplicity. As Arnold says, Tennyson "distils his thought before he will part with it" (1896, 163).

One sign that Arnold has thoroughly appropriated Shakespeare as well as Homer, recasting Shakespeare in his own stoic mold, is his persistent misquotation of him. Ricks has noticed that in Hamlet's line "To grunt and sweat under a weary life," Arnold substitutes "weary load" for "weary life" (Ricks, 1987, 409). But even in subtracting from the imaginative life of Shakespeare's line, Arnold makes Hamlet's burden more oppressive. It takes more stoic resolve and grit to bear it.[2] Like Ruskin's "naturalist ideal," a "grand style" has to avoid what is "tumid," "artificial," and "literary." But neither can it be "commonplace" or wanting in "nobility." Such a combination of the lofty and the simple, of the grand and the plain, might seem impossible to attain. But "Homer has done it." Echoing Arnold, we might add that Shakespeare, too, is "precisely the incomparable poet he is, because he has done it" (1896, 30).

For a poet of profound simplicity, who unlike Cleopatra or Maud is never conscious of snaring Antony or an angry young lover in a toil of grace, or in a web of any kind, we must turn to the greatest and most sibylline of the Pre-Raphaelite poets, Christina Rossetti. Her persona is at times as disarming, ingenuous, and plain-spoken as Cordelia's. Facing huge personal tragedy like that of Shakespeare, whose only son was dead, Lear yearns to make the heavens more just. All that confronts Christina Rossetti is silence: the terrible silence of God. Minute by minute and hour by hour, she asks the question: Why? In Rossetti's words, "your silence breaks my heart." Like John Donne, Hopkins is too extravagant and conceited a poet to understand the artless art of a Cordelia or Christina Rossetti. In two of her lyrics Rossetti dons the mask of Lady Macbeth; and in *Goblin Market* she refines the good cheer and whimsy of a passage from *A Midsummer Night's Dream* (3.2.208–12). But as Antony Harrison observes, "References to Shakespeare and Milton are . . . extremely unusual in her writing" (1993, 131). Unlike Tennyson, whose verse is saturated with allusions to Shakespeare, Christina Rossetti is Shakespearean, not in the range of her references to the poet, but in her style and sensibility.

Lady Macbeth's rueful cry that "all the perfumes of Arabia will not sweeten this little hand" (*Macbeth* 5.1.51–53) provides Rossetti with the title of her early poem "Will these hands never be clean?" Twenty years later she returns to Lady Macbeth's lament in the ballad "Cannot Sweeten." What crimes has Rossetti's speaker committed that her hands should be black as ink and her feet as red as wine? Has she killed her parents or slain her siblings? No, the crimes of this Lady Macbeth are at once less spectacular and more damning. In a parody of the Eucharist, the banquet she fed on was her lover's body and the wine she drank was his blood.

> He loved me because he loved me,
> Not for grace or beauty I had;
> He loved me because he loved me;
> For his loving me I was glad.
> ("Cannot Sweeten," lines 17–20)

The love he proffered her was as simple and devoid of guile as the love Rossetti offers her heartless lover in the poem "Twice." True love is causeless. It is as simple as the wrenching tautology "He loved me because he loved me." And in rejecting love for no reason, except to play with love or disdain it, the speaker has turned her hands black, her feet red, and her heart a dark shade of scarlet.

In "A bruised reed shall he not break," Rossetti is as exacting in her honesty as Cordelia, who refuses to heave her heart into her mouth when commanded to say how much she loves her father. Surely, Christ says, you will not pray against my will to accept, if not your love of me, then at least your will to love. "Alas, I cannot will," she says (line 8). If you cannot will, Christ then assures her, I shall at least receive and accept "the inner and unseen longings" of your soul. It is enough that you should merely wish to love. Alas, "I cannot wish," she says (line 16). In each successive stanza the soul is able to do less and less. Nothing, we fear, will come of nothing. Only in the third and last stanza of the poem does the reply "I do not deprecate" (line 24) signal a change. It is her first faint hint of affirmation in disguise.

To deprecate is to pray earnestly against something. But to negate that negative prayer is already to prepare for a reversal of the soul's will-less state. Though no active willing may be possible, Rossetti can at least anticipate the first stirring of affective life. The last stanza of the poem abandons confession for divine prophecy. Instead of urging Rossetti to will or wish something, Christ resolves to do something on her behalf.

> What, neither choose nor wish to choose? and yet
> I still must strive to win thee and constrain:
> For thee I hung upon the cross in pain,
> How then can I forget?

If thou as yet dost neither love, nor hate,
Nor choose, nor wish,—resign thyself, be still
Till I infuse love, hatred, longing, will.—
I do not deprecate.
(lines 17–24)

We think that Christ will appeal to the soul's memory of the Crucifixion as a way of restoring the poet's love. He will chastise her by asking, How can *you* forget? But that is not what He says. Rather, if Christ was crucified for this will-less (though not unwilling) soul, the question to be asked is, How can *I* forget? Over the expected platitude, Rossetti has inscribed her own censorship of platitude. On behalf of the poet's bruised and damaged soul, Christ has already suffered too much to forget that suffering now. Nor does he presume to criticize or minimize her anguish, for he has known the same anguish himself.

Everything depends on the power of contraction. The final line is the most contracted, for here the utterance of both speakers—Christ and the soul—is gathered into a single concentrated phrase. Indeed, for the first time in the poem, Christ and the soul are able to speak in unison. The last line, "I do not deprecate," is equally in character for either speaker. To protest that one does not deprecate or plead earnestly against something is the most restrained way of saying one prays for it. Though readers are shocked, I think, to find "hatred" included in the catalogue of affective states Christ chooses to "infuse"—love, hatred, longing, will—it is part of Rossetti's honesty that she should make Christ the author of her own persisting hatred of himself.

"All poetry is difficult," as T. S. Eliot says, "almost impossible to write; and one of the great permanent causes of error in writing poetry is the difficulty of distinguishing between what one really feels and what one would like to feel" (1932, "George Herbert," 361). In her lyric about bruised and broken hearts, Rossetti is trying to find in life's most minimal offerings something residual that will suffice. In examining the renunciations of a soul that has perhaps renounced too much, Rossetti contracts language to the vanishing point. But even as the refrains decline from the modest to the minimal, Rossetti shows how the last trace of a false refuge can be relinquished and abandoned. Though her exacting honesty makes her exhaustion harrowing, it is part of her greatness as a poet that she can replace a querulous rhetorical voice with a quavering prophetic one: a voice that, despite its simplicity, leaves the soul defenseless and in a quiver.

Like *King Lear* and Hopkins's sonnet "No worst, there is none," Christina Rossetti's poem "The Lowest Place" is an exercise in humility and an experiment in how low one can go.

Give me the lowest place: not that I dare
    Ask for that lowest place, but Thou hast died
That I might live and share
    Thy glory by Thy side.

(lines 1–4)

The poem is a series of self-corrections. Even in asking to live and share Christ's glory, she is repeating the error for which Christ reproaches the sons of Zebedee when they ask to sit at his right side. "You will drink of my cup, but to sit at my right hand and at my left is not mine to grant, but it is for those for whom it has been prepared by my Father" (Matthew 20:23). No sooner has the poet asked for the lowest place than she says she dare not ask for it. Accordingly, the poet corrects herself for a third time by starting her poem over again in the second stanza.

Give me the lowest place: or if for me
    That lowest place too high, make one more low
Where I may sit and see
    My God and love Thee so.

(lines 5–8)

In the first six lines the superlative adjective "lowest" has crept too close to the head of a line. To amend such presumption, Rossetti now places the word "low" at the end of the line, where both she and the adjective belong. If the lowest place is still too high for her, and the superlative form of "low" still comes too close to the head of a line, she is prepared to demote the superlative degree of "low" to the comparative degree, "more low," and place it at the end. The only appropriate place for Rossetti is the one commended in the Gospel of Luke, where the marriage guest is told to sit in the lowest place "so that when the host comes he may say to you, 'Friend, go up higher'" (Luke 14:9–10).

While Goneril and Regan are outbidding each other in the auction for their father's love, Cordelia refuses to place a bid at all. Love is not an auction, nor is it a contest for gaining glory at the right hand of God. Neither Christina Rossetti nor Cordelia understands the nature of a love contest or a bid for affection. It is no wonder Rossetti thought highly enough of "The Lowest Place" to make it the concluding poem in *The Prince's Progress* and that her brother should choose it as her gravestone memorial.

Like Shakespeare and Ovid, Tennyson is a master of transitional states. Whether subsiding in grief in the lines to Dufferin or mounting to subdued elation in "Tithonus" and "To Virgil," his best poetry wavers between glory and despair. Just as Cleopatra and Maud cast as strong a toil of grace in death as in life, so Tennyson both celebrates and mourns the buried sun as a "glory done."

> Sad Hesper o'er the buried sun
> And ready, thou, to die with him,
> Thou watchest all things ever dim
> And dimmer, and a glory done.
> (*In Memoriam* 121.1–4)

Northrop Frye coins the term "outscape," a variant of Hopkins's "inscape," to describe the haiku's "convention of pure projected detachment, in which an image, a situation, or a mood is observed with all the imaginative energy thrown outward to it and away from the poet" (1957, 297). Section 121 of *In Memoriam* turns a mindscape into just such an outscape by projecting fleeting affinities of hope and despair in the poet's mind onto Hesper and the sun. Is Tennyson using "o'er" as a spatial preposition? Is the star Hesper literally shining over or above the sun? Or does the preposition "o'er" hark back to the adjective "sad"? Is the sadness of the star a result of the sun's burial? Elision allows for double meaning. Is Tennyson omitting the verb "grow" before the dimming sun, or is he turning "dim" into a verb, as when Othello speaks of "putting out" or "dimming" a light?

Hopkins, a reluctant admirer of Tennyson, who dismissed *Idylls of the King* as medieval charades, declared of these lines' calligraphy of farewell, "The maturest judgment will never be fooled out of saying that this is divine, terribly beautiful" (1938, 72). In its flickering hesitation, wavering in emphasis between "a *glory* done" and a "glory *done,*" Tennyson's sculpting of ruin is as beautifully detached as a haiku and just as impersonal. Victorian beauticians may now be out of favor. But Tennyson's artifice, like Shakespeare's, will always have a future, for in lines of such difficult simplicity it is the artifice of eternity.

Shakespeare celebrates an equally bold transition in *The Winter's Tale.*

> Still, methinks,
> There is an air comes from her. What fine chisel
> Could ever yet cut breath?
> (5.3.77–79)

The best comment on the lines in which Hermione's statue moves and comes to life is Frank Kermode's. "However fine the workman, statues cannot be made to breathe, but we nevertheless experience the marvelous intermediate phase when stone is magically refined to breath and the revelation of Hermione's living presence, another greater miracle, will follow" (2010, 16).

The statue's coming to life is not something we are asked to "believe in," like the resurrection of a dead god. It is our necessary angel, our supreme fiction. Northrop Frye reminds us that "in Ovid most of the 'metamorphoses' are changes downward, from some kind of personal or human being into a natural object, a tree, a bird, or a star. But there can also be metamorphosis upward" (1986, 170). Bottom says he will have Peter Quince write a ballad of his dream, which "shall be called Bottom's Dream, because it hath no bottom." There is something bottomless or unfathomable about the weaver's dream of the beautiful Titania and her love for his asinine face. Bottom's announcement of his dream is usually greeted with roars of laughter. "Laughter there should be," Harold Goddard concedes, "but laughter shot through with a beauty and pathos close to tears. Only an actor of genius could do justice to it" (1951, 80). When Falstaff dies, he babbles about green fields and flowers, of going into "Arthur's bosom" and of talking with the Whore of Babylon. Like Bottom's dream, which mangles the words of St. Paul, the absurdity of turning mortal grossness into spirit is part of its power. As Geoffrey Hartman says, "In Shakespeare the visionary babble remains vision *and* babble. The mistake, the lapse, is part of the essence: the word takes its revenge on the Word" (1980, 89). Like Falstaff's vision and Bottom's dream, the magic of *The Tempest* and the marvel of cutting breath from stone in *The Winter's Tale* are wonderful beyond description. They offer new possibilities of reviving spirit and redeeming matter that Shakespeare has the genius to imagine and the generosity to share with grateful and astonished readers.

10

Off the Edge

END GAMES AND ELEGY

Like Shakespeare's Claudio, Hamlet fears death may be a sleep disturbed by nightmares worse than he can possibly imagine. Since Victorian Anglicans and Dissenters do not believe in purgatory, and since few believe in hell, they seldom share Shakespeare's fear that death may bring in its wake Claudio's infinity of torments. On the contrary, Tennyson's Lucretius, Arnold's Empedocles, and Browning's Cleon are all more afraid that when they've spun their "last thread," they "shall perish on the shore" (Donne, "A Hymne to God the Father," lines 13–14). Many Victorians feared that death would simply annihilate them. Their "sin of fear" was a terror of going off the edge, of confronting the void, of facing mere nothingness as such. This is the "furnace-fear" raging in Larkin's poem "Aubade," the horror of experiencing "no sight, no sound, / No touch or taste or smell, nothing to think with, / Nothing to love or link with, / The anaesthetic from which none come round" (lines 27–30).

Shakespeare's most appalling imagination of death—one of the most graphic in literature—appears in Claudio's speech in *Measure for Measure*. We possess the speech by memory almost as soon as we hear it.

> Ay, but to die, and go we know not where;
> To lie in cold obstruction and to rot;
> This sensible warm motion to become
> A kneaded clod, and the delighted spirit
> To bathe in fiery floods, or to reside
> In thrilling regions of thick-ribbed ice;
> To be imprison'd in the viewless winds,
> And blown with restless violence round about
> The pendent world; or to be—worse than worst—
> Of those that lawless and incertain thought

Imagine howling, —'tis too horrible!
The weariest and most loathed worldly life
That age, ache, penury, and imprisonment
Can lay on nature is a paradise
To what we fear of death.

(3.1.118–32)

A run of internal rhymes in the haunting opening line sets up eddies of lament and a swirl of surmises: "Ay, but to die," "and go, we know." When "kneaded" like rotting dough into a "clod," the body's "sensible warm motion" confronts only "cold obstruction." Even if its "delighted spirit" manages to survive, it will be subjected to one of two tortures: it will be either "bathed" in "fiery floods" or numbed slowly, then frozen into ice. In their Dantesque power to appall, Claudio's horrific portrayal of life after death makes anything Hamlet or Milton has to say on the subject sound tame and restrained by comparison.

To be tossed and blown on the winds is not to be liberated like a bird, but to be imprisoned. It is to suffer the "restless violence" that hurricane victims know. Instead of taking a spacious view of the world suspended below it like a pendant, such as a space traveler might enjoy, the dead soul that is hurtled through space will be the victim of a "viewless" wind blowing blindly through a void. Sir Thomas Browne says he is "not so much afraid of death, as ashamed thereof; 'tis the very disgrace and ignominy of our natures, that in a moment can so disfigure us that our nearest friends, Wife, and Children, stand afraid and start at us. The Birds and Beasts of the field that before in a natural fear obeyed us, forgetting all allegiance, begin to prey upon us. This very conceit hath in a tempest disposed and left me willing to be swallowed up in the abyss of waters; wherein I had perished unseen, unpitied" (Browne, 1967, 48). Graphic to the limits of endurance, Claudio goes even further than Browne. He asks us to imagine the worst howling of the insane, the worst lawless and uncertain thoughts of the mentally deranged. And then he wants us to imagine, if possible, something more horrifying. "Worse than worst" is all Claudio can say. Compared with a train of posthumous horrors, made to accelerate till it runs off the track, the worst trials in this life are a refuge and repose. No worst, there is none.

Surprisingly, despite the horror of becoming a morsel for worms, the beautiful sound of the line "The weariest and most loathed worldly life" momentarily soothes the soul and eases its pain like a narcotic. But just as its beguiling euphony starts to belie the terror of what Claudio is saying, he is jolted out of his fool's paradise by the worst of life's ardors, which are allowed to fall like hammer blows in the next line: "That age, ache, penury, and imprisonment / Can lay on nature." A series of harsh, leveling spondees, separated by caesuras, remind Claudio that, though the horrors we have to endure now are unrelenting, they are still a paradise to what we fear of death.

Warburton associates Claudio's fear of dying with the "impious wish" of Maecenas in the 101st epistle of Seneca. But *not* to live in the present, with full knowledge of what can degrade the spirit as well as uplift it, strikes Coleridge as the greater blasphemy. Construing Claudio's meditation on death as "a heroic resolve rather than an impious wish," Coleridge praises Claudio for defending the privilege to exist, "to be a mind, a will." Such exaltation of the self is "a perpetual religion, an inalienable acknowledgment of God" (1930, 1, 114–15). The true atheist is Arnold's Empedocles, who longs for annihilation when he finds intolerable the endurance of the mind, "the master part of him," a faculty that combines the majesty of a sovereign with the cruelty of an overbearing tyrant or despot (*Empedocles on Etna* 2.345–48).

Abandoned by his friends, Timon of Athens takes an actor's delight in dramatizing his death as the ultimate betrayal and desertion. "Come not to me again," he intones in valediction. The self-dramatizing misanthrope seizes every chance to render a sense of outrage and disbelief that, once he has been absorbed into "the beached verge of the salt flood, / Who once a day with his embossed froth / The turbulent surge shall cover" (*Timon of Athens* 5.1.215–17), the world will go tranquilly on without him. Only by assimilating himself to the ebb and flow of the tides can Timon attenuate the shock and try to reconcile the inner personal view of death with the outer Stoic one.

Oddly enough, news of Lady Macbeth's death fails to move Macbeth, for like her husband she experiences a death of the spirit before she dies physically. His only answer to the words "The Queen, my lord, is dead" is "She should have died hereafter, / There would have been a time for such a word." Harley Granville-Barker says this "is one of Shakespeare's most daring strokes because it is an effect of *omission.* She has been his very 'outward soul': she is dead, and he can feel nothing" (1960, 81). The pitiful decline and senseless muttering of Lady Macbeth's sleepwalking speech are her true end; after that the death of her body means nothing. The husband whose life has "fallen into the sere, the yellow leaf" has squandered a master spirit upon a poor player's part. Reduced to a walking shadow, he finds his life's story has become a "tale / Told by an idiot, full of sound and fury, / Signifying nothing." Dead before he dies, Macbeth's dissolution is exceeded only by the appalling breakdown of his deranged and suicidal wife.

Lady Macbeth's last words are one of the few truly sublime portrayals of madness in literature. For the root of her anguish lies too deep for speech, even for the bare, simple, desolating words that struggle to express the misery she endures. The difference between Ophelia's mad games and Lady Macbeth's is that "Ophelia's total insanity has effaced or greatly weakened the emotional force of the ideas, whereas to Lady Macbeth each new image or perception comes laden with anguish" (A. C. Bradley, 1957, 337). The best comment on Lady Macbeth's last words, which express a despair and anguish so sublimely bleak that it breaks her will and shatters her mind, comes from Bradley. "The soaring pride and power of Lady Macbeth's first speeches return on our memory," he says, "and the change is felt with a breathless awe. . . . For the moment . . . all the language of poetry—even of Macbeth's poetry—seems to be touched with unreality, and these brief toneless sentences seem the only voice of truth" (337). Denied the dignity of poetry, Lady Macbeth's last words anticipate the last words of Tennyson's Rizpah. Though Rizpah is apparently overheard by a deathbed attendant, we nervously wonder if her monologue is not also a soliloquy, what Richard Poirier calls "an expression of mad loneliness searching through an interior monologue for a listener" (1977, 113).

Death disfigures the last words of Cleopatra and Hotspur, who end their lives abruptly in mid-sentence. This proves especially wrenching in the case of Hotspur, whose voluble speech spills over horizons instead of closing on a boundary. Launched on a sorites whose expansive form belies its contracting content, Hotspur builds a causeway to another world.

> But thought's the slave of life, and life time's fool,
> And time, that takes survey of all the world,
> Must have a stop. O, I could prophesy,
> But that the earthy and cold hand of death
> Lies on my tongue. No, Percy, thou art dust,
> And food for—
>
> (*1 Henry IV* 5.4.81–86)

Since a kingdom is too small and bounded a sphere for his spirit to inhabit, it seems in character that time should have a stop for Hotspur before he can look over the horizon of the last sentence he speaks.

Though highly ceremonial and staged, Cleopatra's last words are also human in the fullest sense. As she takes the asp to her breast, as she might take and suckle a child, Cleopatra hears Antony calling, and she says, "Husband, I come!" (5.2.290). The lovers, once close rather than intimate, are truly together now for the first time.

> As sweet as balm, as soft as air, as gentle,—
> O Antony! —Nay; I will take thee too;
> [*Applying another asp to her arm.*]
> What should I stay—
>
> (5.2.314–16)

Without loss of dignity or a fine sense of occasion, Cleopatra behaves more like a child than a queen, and before she can finish her last sentence she falls asleep. We see her at the end, not as an enchantress or a wily serpent of the Nile, but as a mother who asks, in the simplest human way, "Dost thou not see my baby at my breast that sucks the nurse asleep?" (5.2.312–13).

Though Antony's botched suicide is undeniably grotesque, Shakespeare's only comic deaths occur in *A Midsummer Night's Dream,* where the double suicide of Pyramus and Thisbe parodies the fate of Romeo and Juliet. When Pyramus stabs himself over the dead Thisbe, he utters the immortal words

> Now am I dead,
> Now am I fled;
> My soul is in the sky.
> Tongue, lose thy light;
> Moon, take thy flight. [*Exit Moonshine.*]
> Now die, die, die, die, die.
>
> (5.1.306–11)

The lilt of the tripping lines is lighthearted, not sad. The literal withdrawal of the actor Moonshine when told to take flight is charming but absurd. We have only to compare the fivefold repetition of the verb "die" with Lear's repeated "never" to appreciate the difference between a repetition that is comically nonprogressive and one that adds tragically to the incremental force of each word it repeats.

The apostrophes to the Fates, the tongue, and the sword that Thisbe intones over the body of Pyramus are just as diverting.

> O Sisters Three
> Come, come to me,
> With hands as pale as milk;
> Lay them in gore,
> Since you have shore
> With shears his thread of silk.
> Tongue, not a word!
> Come, trusty sword;
> Come, blade, my breast imbrue!
>
> (5.1.343–51)

Straining to be poetical, Thisbe gets tangled in her own conceit. We know what she wants to say. But her search for rhyme words—"shore" to go with "gore" and "silk" with "milk"—traps her, not in a toil of grace, but in a tissue of refined and exquisite nonsense. The double suicides are potentially funny. The actress's dying speech—"And farewell, friends; / Thus Thisbe ends, /

Adieu, adieu, adieu" (5.1.352–54)—is not only repetitious in itself. It also repeats what Pyramus has just said.

To maintain the tragic impact of the double suicides in *Romeo and Juliet,* Shakespeare gives Juliet almost nothing to say when she wakes in the crypt to find Romeo dead beside her. There is no need for Juliet to give voice to a horror that Shakespeare has artfully removed to an earlier scene in the play. On that occasion Juliet's gruesomely prophetic imagination of dying strangled in the tomb is almost as graphic as Claudio's meditation on death in *Measure for Measure.*

> O, if I wake, shall I not be distraught,
> Environed with all these hideous fears,
> And madly play with my foregathers' joints,
> And pluck the mangled Tybalt from his shroud,
> And, in this rage, with some great kinsman's bone
> As with a club dash out my desp'rate brains?
> (4.3.50–55)

If Shakespeare had allowed Juliet to speak again in this vein at the end of the play, her repetition of Romeo's shocked reactions to her own supposed death might have resembled too closely Pyramus's comically nonprogressive repetitions in *A Midsummer Night's Dream.*

What is hardest for Hamlet to grasp in his famous "To be nor not to be" soliloquy is the idea that someday his consciousness will black out forever: subjective time will come to an end for him. When he says later there is providence in the fall of a sparrow, he is grasping death objectively, and so can face it with the detached calm of a stoic: "the readiness is all." But the internal view of death is not like that. To look to the future is generally to expect something. But if death closes all, there is nothing as such to expect. This is why Hamlet cannot fully believe that his inner life will be finished, and why he decides to bear with ills he now endures instead of flying to others he cannot remotely imagine or conceive.

Though Hamlet is more restrained than Claudio, he dwells longer on the weary weight of

> The oppressor's wrong, the proud man's contumely,
> The pangs of dispriz'd love, the law's delay,
> The insolence of office, and the spurns
> That patient merit of the unworthy takes.
> (3.1.71–74)

These burdens bear down and oppress the mind in six successive clauses. But it is better, Hamlet reasons, to bear oppression, grunting and sweating "under a weary life," than to face the horrors of death, "The undiscovered country from whose bourn / No traveler returns" (3.1.79–80). Hamlet's great fear is that death may not be the end of life after all, but only an entry into a world more horrible. To die or even sleep would be a consummation. But what if sleep brings dreams, and dreams turn into nightmares, worse than even Claudio imagines? Hamlet's inability to think of a time when he will experience neither pain nor pleasure, nor any sensation whatever, leads him to an even stranger conclusion: if death is only the termination of consciousness, Hamlet may be incapable of dying at all. As a suicide victim in danger of flying to worse ills, Hamlet may be consumed by as cruel an immortality as Tennyson's Tithonus, a victim of immortal age who is powerless to shake off an infinity of torments.

Inquiring and probative, Hamlet thinks, tests, and qualifies his ideas with the aid of metaphor. Will conscience make a coward of him, or will he be brave enough "to take arms against a sea of troubles, / And by opposing end them?" (3.1.59–60). Samuel Johnson calls death "kind Nature's signal of retreat." But Hamlet reverses the metaphor by identifying voluntary death, not with a military retreat, but with a call to arms. Using metaphor to clarify his thinking, Hamlet tacitly acknowledges the futility of opposing anything so protean and vast as a sea. To take arms against a sea is as pointless as whipping a fog or fighting a quagmire. And yet the alternative is too desolating. Not to fight at all is to submit to "the heart-ache and the thousand natural shocks / That flesh is heir to" (3.1.62–63). The beheaded trochees in "heart-ache," "thousand," and "natural" fall with the force of an executioner's axe. The hypermetric line in which these words appear also seems to protract the tortures endlessly.

Unfortunately, worse tortures, including "the dread of something after death," await a suicide victim. The philosopher Max Black affirms that "a prohibition against [the use of metaphor] would be a willful and harmful restriction upon powers of inquiry" (1962, 47). But it is also touch-and-go with Shakespeare's metaphors. However seductive and alluring the battle metaphor may be, it is a two-edged sword. The metaphor of shuffling off his "mortal coil" is too suggestive of a snake shedding its skin to ennoble Hamlet. Suicide may be the coward's way, not the courageous response of a Hotspur or Prince Hal.

Though no metaphor can prove the value of life, no metonymy can disprove it either. As Tennyson shows in "The Two Voices" and "The Ancient Sage," "proof" by metaphor or "disproof" by metonymy plays only a limited role in the conduct of life. Unlike Arnold's dour Empedocles, Hamlet develops his ideas with a passion and energy that show he has no intention of committing suicide. As one critic says, "Men do not hang themselves in obedience to the conclusion of a syllogism or a Q E D; and it would be a very naïve theatergoer who believed Hamlet would have killed himself if he had found fewer arguments against it" (Priestley, 1973, 169).

Shakespearean in its gravity and range of vision, the powerful meditation on death of Browning's Cleon anticipates with dread the day when he, the proud pagan, "the feeling, thinking, acting man, / The man who loved his life so over-much," shall lie asleep in his urn ("Cleon," lines 321–23). Acutely self-aware, Cleon is less able than even the introspective Hamlet to wrap his mind around the idea that "there will be a last day, a last hour, a last minute of consciousness, and that will be it. Off the edge." As Thomas Nagel explains, there is "something that can be called the expectation of nothingness, and though the mind tends to veer away from it, it is an unmistakable experience, always startling, often frightening, and very different from the familiar recognition that your life will go on for only a limited period of time. . . . It is the prospect of nothingness itself, not the prospect that the world will go on after I cease to exist, that has to be understood" (1986, 225–26).

Cleon's view of death would be less annihilating if he could believe, like St. Paul, in "Some future state revealed to us by Zeus, / Unlimited in capability / For joy, as this is in desire for joy" (lines 325–27).[1] But as one critic says, "The New Testament lacks an Epistle to the Athenians. . . . Paul could explain to Romans that Christianity was the fulfillment of the law, and to Corinthians that it was the fulfillment of love. But he was unable to explain to the Athenians [and to philosophers like Cleon] that it was the fulfillment of intelligence also" (Frye, 2004, 99–100). Though Cleon concedes that Paul must be literate, since he composes epistles, the patrician Greek is still too disdainful to consult in person a barbarian Jew whose only scholarly adherents are slaves. Instead, in gathering from the mere hearsay of a bystander that "their doctrine could be held by no sane man" (line 353), Cleon, the pagan rationalist, uses an irrational method of proving Christians are irrational.

In replying to his patron Protus's inquiry about how a cultivated Greek should face death, Cleon is less than encouraging. The oxymorons of despair—breadth of vision is desolation and "Most progress is most failure" (line 272)—create an abyss that is deeper for man than for the animals. Because his soul is "fastened to a dying animal," man climbs higher than the rest of creation "just to perish there" (line 236). Though God has made death invisible, we know it is there, and boldly question our destiny but receive no answer. This is why death is more agonizing for us than the animals. To create in man a thirst for knowledge he can never attain seems either a refinement of malicious irony, worthy of the God of Browning's Caliban, or else a promise of fulfillment. But if of fulfillment, "where is the sign?" Man succeeds that he may "use but a man's joy / While he sees God's" (lines 261–62).

Cleon's horror of death proceeds from his alarming insight that, in Yeats's phrase, "bodily decrepitude is wisdom." When young, man is ignorant; when old, he cannot experience. The crucial moments in his life are over just as he begins to understand them. Cleon expresses this distressing discovery most poignantly in his lament that he can transcend the world only by abstracting from its sensuous immediacy. A great poet depicts an immediacy he can never experience or share.

> Because in my great epos I display
> How divers men young, strong, fair, wise, can act—
> Is this as though I acted? If I paint,
> Carve the young Phoebus, am I therefore young?
> (lines 285–88)

The realization that the celebration of the "rower . . . with the molded muscles . . . all a-ripple on his back" (294, 299) must be an elegy on Cleon's own failing powers produces a faltering of the voice. The aging Cleon can write about love but not make it; he can pontificate about kingship but never rule. The immortality that rewards the artist is figurative immortality—fame—rather than literal. If Sappho and Aeschylus "survive" absolutely, and not merely vicariously, "let them come and take / Thy slave in my despite, drink from thy cup, / Speak in my place" (306–8). As the philosopher's soul grows more acute, "intensified / By power and insight," the "heavy years increase— / The horror quickening still from year to year" (311–12, 314–15). Like William James, who felt that in old age he was just becoming fit to live, Cleon fears "the consummation," when he "shall know most, . . . yet least enjoy" (315–16). This is hardly what Hamlet means by a "consummation," an outcome or an end "devoutly to be wished." Cleon passes instead from an old man's frenzy ("I, I the feeling, thinking, acting man") to an ineffably pathetic contemplation of his own annihilation. All that will remain of Cleon, "the man who loved his life so over-much," are a few ashes in an urn (321–22).

Like the beasts of the earth, people will be subjected by nature, Kant believes, "to all the evils of want, disease, and untimely death." "So it will be," he warns, "until one wide grave engulfs them (honest or not, it makes no difference), and throws them back—who were able to believe themselves the final purpose of creation—into the abyss of the purposeless chaos from which they were drawn" (2005, 227). An agnostic theist, Kant denies we can ever understand or know a transcendent God as we know and understand the laws of chemistry and physics. We cannot even *know* if such a God exists. But from this bleak conclusion Kant wrests an unforeseen inference. For he is equally insistent that "that man is morally *unbelieving* who does not accept that which, though *impossible* to know, is *morally* necessary to suppose" (xxii). To preserve our sanity, we are impelled to embrace as an incomprehensible certainty what

Kant calls "the regulative truth"—or what Wallace Stevens would call "the supreme fiction"—of a god who is good but veiled, moral if not all-powerful. Agnosticism keeps the mind supple and elastic. Kant's critical philosophy is to the mind what yoga is to the body. Hamlet, like Clough's Claude and Browning's Cleon, is an intellectual athlete. He lends credence to Pascal's aphorism that "denying, believing, and doubting are to men what running is to horses."

George Meredith's powerful elegy "The Day of the Daughter of Hades" captures the soul of defiant, indignant grieving both in the anguish of the beautiful maid Skiegeneia, who is allowed only a day of life on earth, and in the outrage of her thwarted lover, Callistes.

> So she stood awhile
> In the gloom of the terror afield,
> And the silence about her smile
> Said more than of tongue is revealed.
> I have breathed; I have gazed; I have been:
> It said: and not joylessly shone
> The remembrance of light through the screen
> Of a face that seemed shadow and stone.
>
> (10.13–20)

Stricken by loss, Callistes yearns to clasp the maid to his side and launch against the gods a revolt more sacrilegious than any mortal ever launched against "High Olympus." But as the youth shakes her frame, her warm and breathing flesh turns to ice in his hands.

Few evocations of death are more appalling than Meredith's fiercely nuanced account of "the terrible Charioteer," Darkness, "the God of implacable brow," who raged

> Through the wave like a boar of the wilds
> From the hunters and hounds disengaged,
> And a name shouted hoarsely: his child's.
>
> (10.38–40)

Meredith's view of death is a view from nowhere, for it is hard to say who is most bereft. Does Demeter grieve less than Persephone? Is the bride of darkness less stricken than her consort or his daughter, who is allowed to spend only a single day on earth? As for Callistes, the bereaved lover, he is left half crazed and witless, like Browning's Lazarus in "An Epistle of Karshish," or like Actaeon, who is devoured by hounds for gazing on the naked beauty of Diana. Though Callistes never prized Demeter, our Lady of Gifts, as much as he prized "her issue in darkness," even though she was only "tears to him," he oddly enough never wept for her. Instead, he merely "wasted within." In his frenzy to be reunited with Hades's lost daughter, Callistes keeps calling and calling for her. But sadly and mysteriously, in following "where never was track," he also travels an unmapped path. Like that undiscovered country from whose bourn no traveler returns, it is a path everyone has to travel alone.

Matthew Arnold, an admirer of Marcus Aurelius and Spinoza, is the most stoic of the great Victorians. The Stoic's wisdom is to passively accept and even will the fate he cannot otherwise control: "A God, a God their severance ruled! / And bade betwixt their shores to be / The unplumbed, salt, estranging sea" ("To Marguerite—Continued," lines 22–24). But what if a Stoic is fated to be weak instead of strong? Or what if his fate is to be aggressive in opposing fate instead of resigned in accepting it? It may not be in a Stoic's nature to be stoical. The Antony who falls in love with Cleopatra cannot remake himself as Octavius, however hard he may try. The Stoic response to fate is best expressed by Brutus, who is free to avoid the fate of a captive "bound to Rome," though not free to determine what the future holds.

> Why, then, lead on. O, that a man might know
> The end of this day's business ere it come!
> But it sufficeth that the day will end,
> And then the end is known. Come, ho, away!
> (*Julius Caesar* 5.1.123–26)

A Stoic may want to know in advance the outcome of a battle. But if the prediction favors his cause, it removes his chance to be a stoic. If it is unfavorable, then it is harder to behave stoically.

The Stoic's favored trope is tautology. Brutus has a habit of circling endlessly around his end, as if trying to defer an outcome by giving tone and color to echoes of "farewell" and "for ever," words that would otherwise sound flat or hollow.

> Therefore our everlasting farewell take.
> For ever, and for ever, farewell, Cassius!
> (5.1.116–17)

Though Antony calls Brutus the noblest of the Roman conspirators, he is more stoic in feeling than in deed, and often acts impetuously. Brutus says he owes more tears to the dead Cassius than "you will see me pay" (5.3.102). Though he swears "I shall find time, Cassius, I shall find time" (5.3.103), he is more saddened than grieved by his friend's death. We, too, are sad we cannot "find time" to grieve more for a man who is moved to sententious reflection rather than to grief when someone close to him dies. When Cassius hears that Brutus's wife is dead, he blurts out impulsively, "How 'scaped I killing when I crossed you so? / O insupportable and touching loss" (4.3.150–51). All Brutus can bring himself to say is, "No man bears sorrow better. Portia is dead" (4.3.147).

Though Julius Caesar mocks the superstitious fears of the soothsayers and his wife, Calpurnia, everyone in Shakespeare's audience knows that his self-sufficiency is misplaced. His stoic distrust of prophecy and his contempt for oracles verge on atheism.

> Cowards die many times before their deaths;
> The valiant never taste of death but once.
> Of all the wonders that I yet have heard
> It seems to me most strange that men should fear,
> Seeing that death, a necessary end,
> Will come when it will come.
>
> (2.1.32–37)

The terse tautology "come when it will come" marks the stoic's bleak acceptance of fate. It is the signature of a fatalist, someone who, according to Plutarch, believes that sudden death, or "death unlooked for," is the best kind. "Caesar's speeches are dramatically perfect," as John Bayley says, because "they are those of a man who is marked out for sacrifice, whose tone and speeches proclaim the fact while he himself is necessarily unaware of it" (1981, 131).

The Victorian poets, like Shakespeare, contrast beautiful deaths with gruesome ones, and deaths that are merely ceremonial with ones that are also touching or pathetic. The charm of the brothers' song in *Cymbeline* comes less from biblical wisdom, from Koheleth's sense that there is a time and season for everything, than from the rite of an exorcist or the spell of a magician like Prospero.

> Fear no more the heat o' the sun,
>   Nor the furious winter's rages;
> Thou thy worldly task hast done,
>   Home art gone, and ta'en thy wages.
> Golden lads and girls all must,
>   As chimney sweepers, come to dust.
>
> (*Cymbeline* 4.3.258–63)

Imogen has earned a reward. But if the wages of sin is death, then her wages seem undeserved, since of all Shakespeare's heroines she and Cordelia are the most virtuous. "Home art gone" promises domestic comfort. But this home is as desolate and unhomely as the Temple of the Winds in *Tess of the d'Urbervilles.* It is a place where chimney sweepers and lads and lasses of fair and shining promise come to common dust in the end.

In the last stanza of the brothers' song, a rite of exorcism is beautifully in progress. As Jonathan Crewe observes, the mourners' sister "is gently transferred to [a] posthumous refuge, allowing the living to exorcise their fears . . . , relinquish further responsibility, and move on. The final couplet, now departing from the vanitas commonplaces of all the previous stanza-endings, produces an effect of powerful closure" (2010, 521–22).

> No exorciser harm thee!
> Nor no witchcraft charm thee!
> Ghost unlaid forbear thee!
> Nothing ill come near thee!
> Quiet consummation have,
> And renowned be thy grave.
>
> (4.3.276–81)

Macbeth says "all our yesterdays have lighted fools the way to dusty death." But now, over death's reductive dust, four echoing "thees" cast a fond and lingering spell of feminine rhymes—"harm thee," "charm thee," "forbear thee," "near thee"—which momentarily suspend death's power.

The lament for "golden lads and girls" in *Cymbeline* finds a late-Victorian counterpart in A. E. Housman's lament for "golden friends" and "lightfoot lads" in *A Shropshire Lad.* In the poet's "rue-laden" heart, Dinah Brook also hears "a more distant echo" of "Ophelia's rue, given to Gertrude before she drowns in the brook" (2009, 53).

> With rue my heart is laden
> For golden friends I had,
> For many a rose-lipt maiden
> And many a lightfoot lad.
> By brooks too broad for leaping
> The lightfoot boys are laid;
> The rose-lipt girls are sleeping
> In fields where roses fade.
>
> (*A Shropshire Lad* 54.1–8)

For the lovemaking of lightfoot lads and rose-lipped maidens, Housman gently substitutes other ways of being "laid." As magical as the spell Imogen's brothers cast over their dead sister are the laying of the golden lads by brooks, the laying of the sleeping girls in fields, and the laying of the poet's own heart with rue.

Erik Gray finely notes that "the mortality rate in Housman's English Arcadia is much higher than in most pastoral poetry. Whenever love or strong desire comes to disturb the lads of Shropshire, almost inevitably death follows quickly behind" (2010, 285). Just as affecting as Housman's elegy for "golden friends" and "lightfoot lads" is the wintry metamorphosis he creates for Dick in his elegy "The night is freezing fast."

> The night is freezing fast,
> To-morrow comes December;
> And winterfalls of old
> Are with me from the past;
> And chiefly I remember
> How Dick would hate the cold.
>
> Fall, winter, fall; for he,
> Prompt hand and headpiece clever,
> Has woven a winter robe,
> And made of earth and sea
> His overcoat for ever,
> And wears the turning globe.
> (*Last Poems,* poem 20)

A wearer and weaver of worlds, Dick uses his "prompt hand" and "headpiece clever"—a strong, designing mind—to enter our space, envelop it, and finally take it over. There are no strong breaks between the three syntactic units of stanza 2. Instead, by replacing the expected punctuation mark at the end of line 10 with a graceful enjambment, the verb "made" is allowed to await its surprising conclusion in "overcoat," its grammatical object. Like an apocalypse that abolishes time, the ending overtakes and subsumes its beginning. The major break in stanza 2 coincides with the semicolon after "fall." The rest of the stanza expands into a spacious sequence of principal clauses detailing the stages of Dick's wintry metamorphosis.

Edgar's pronouncement that "ripeness is all" comes close to expressing Shakespeare's belief that a man may hope to die as a season like autumn comes to pass. When the sun sets and the tide is out, our leaving should be a consummation, a spending of our powers without remainder, not what Gloucester calls a mere "rotting" away of what is overly ripe and decayed. To say that "the fruit is ripening on the tree" or that "there is nothing new under the sun" is to make a statement about knowledge. By contrast, "ripeness is all" is a statement about how we experience time. Does it devour us, as Ovid thinks? Or as we move in rhythm with the seasons, can we learn to accept and even commend "whatever is begotten, born, and dies"?

The chill that falls across the "happy Autumn-fields" in Tennyson's lyric "Tears, idle tears" comes from an austerity of mind not far removed from Edgar's when he says "ripeness is all." The pastoral oxymorons of inner weather—"So sad, so fresh" (line 10), "So sad, so strange" (15)—prepare for the later accommodations of death and life, of everything included in the present moment and of everything beyond it in space or time. The speaker is moved by a double sense of cosmic setting and human littleness. If he is awed by the vastness of "the underworld" (7), he is also stirred, like Virgil and Pope, by an exquisite sense of the beauty in microcosms, by the charm of the "first beam glittering on a sail" (6) or "the earliest pipe of half-awakened birds" (12). In the Persephone-like return of "all we love below the verge" (9), the poet also discovers that the elusive present can be grasped, only fitfully, in unstable relation to dissolving forms, to remembered kisses after death and to things "that are no more."

The words "ripeness is all" appear to have haunted Tennyson during the last hours of his life. The day before he died he asked his son Hallam for *Lear, Cymbeline,* and *Troilus and Cressida,* "three plays that he loved dearly" (1897, 2:425). At the hour of his death, he opened his copy of Shakespeare to the lines in *Cymbeline,*

> Hang there like fruit, my soul,
> Till the tree die,

"which," according to Hallam, "he always called among the tenderest lines in Shakespeare" (2:427–28). As Christopher Decker explains, "It is natural, simply, for fruit to ripen, fall, and cease long before the tree itself perishes. To 'hang there like fruit' until 'the tree die' is to do something very unlike fruit, something very unnatural" (2003, 2:146). Instead of the tree's outlasting the fruit, withering into a gaunt old age, the fruit is exhorted to ripen in pace with the tree. To die at the moment the fruit is ripe and ready to fall is to expend all one's resources without remainder.

In Swinburne's "The Garden of Proserpine," lotos has turned to hashish: over-ripeness is all. The phrase "ripeness is all" more aptly describes Tennyson's lotos-eaters, who aspire to the condition of "the full-juiced apple" which, "waxing over-mellow, / Drops in a silent autumn-night" ("The Lotos-Eaters," lines 33–35). The phrase applies as well to Tennyson's "Tithonus," where there is as much natural rightness in the cycle of "earth in earth" as in Keats's ode to autumn: "Man comes and tills the field and lies beneath, / And after many a summer dies the swan" (lines 3–4). Tithonus wants to model his passing into easeful death upon Keats's ceasing upon the midnight with no pain. But in the two linked but contrasting cycles of "morn by morn" and "earth in earth," Tennyson has joined, in eternal paradox, the cold beauty of Aurora and the fragile web of a love that, despite Tithonus's resolve to forget the goddess, he never quite manages to break or dissolve.

⁂

When Shakespeare's Antony and Cleopatra die, they do so onstage, in public. Hanging in the balance is the fate of empires. Equally ceremonial is the passing of Tennyson's Arthur in *Idylls of the King.*

> Thereat once more he moved about, and clomb
> Even to the highest he could climb, and saw,
> Straining his eyes beneath an arch of hand,
> Or thought he saw, the speck that bare the King,
> Down that long water opening on the deep
> Somewhere far off, pass on and on, and go
> From less to less and vanish into light.
> And the new sun rose bringing the new year.
> ("The Passing of Arthur," lines 462–69)

Summoning up Aeneas's vision of the dim form of Dido glimpsed through the shadows the Virgilian underworld, "as early in the month one sees, or thinks he has seen, the moon rise amid clouds" (*Aeneid* 6.454), Tennyson also reinvents Milton's use of the same passage in *Paradise Lost.* In a diminishing epic simile, Milton reduces the conclave of demons to elves seen at midnight:

> Or Faerie Elves,
> Whose midnight Revels, by a Forrest side
> Or Fountain some belated Peasant sees,
> Or dreams he sees.
> (*Paradise Lost* 1.777–84)

Like Milton, Tennyson uses the phrases "saw, . . . / Or thought he saw" to diminish the size of an object that is becoming too small to see. The insistent coupling of "clomb" and "climb," "saw" and "saw," the passing "on and on" then going from "less to less" before vanishing, capture the drama of Bedivere's striving to see as he strains "his eyes beneath an arch of hand."

The king's gradual diminution, as he passes from less to less before dissolving, is also inspired, I believe, by the same passage in *Cymbeline* that Cowden Clark said moved Keats to tears (Ricks, 1983, 213). As Posthumus departs, Imogen says she watched her husband disappear until

> the diminution
> Of space had pointed him sharp as my needle;
> Nay followed him till he had melted from

The smallness of a gnat to air; and then
Have turned mine eyes and wept.

(1.3.18–22)

Neither spellbound like Aeneas nor enchanted like Milton's peasant in *Paradise Lost,* Tennyson's Bedivere, like Imogen, is intently scrutinizing, staring harder and harder at a shrinking object. As Arthur, gathered into glory, fades from sight, the final line, like the alexandrine at the end of a Spenserian stanza, signals closure by increasing the number of accents from five to six. But qualifying the terminal features of night, autumn, passing on and on, and vanishing, there remain two events not found in Tennyson's sources: the rising of the sun and the advent of another year.

As ceremonial as the deaths of Antony and Cleopatra, and as highly ritualized as the passing of Arthur, is the passage of the dying Ophelia down a river. Poignantly described by Gertrude, Ophelia's death is the expiry of a nature spirit. While Ophelia is weaving fantastic garlands and hanging them on a willow tree, a limb breaks off and carries her down onto the stream below. Caroling plaintive songs like a sea nymph, Ophelia floats on the stream until "her garments, heavy with their drink," pull her from "her melodious lay" to "muddy death" (*Hamlet* 4.7.182–84). The snatches of old tunes that Ophelia chants recall the ballads she sings when deranged by her father's death. Gertrude commends Ophelia's "good beauties," and there is certainly no guile in the girl who can endure Hamlet's tasteless jibes with restraint. Though revealing in her breakdown that she flinches from Hamlet's indecent innuendoes, Ophelia herself is vulnerably innocent and dignified. Shakespeare carefully discriminates between the insanity of the ferociously ambitious, guilt-ridden Lady Macbeth, who chills our blood, and the insanity of the gentle Ophelia, whose madness comes from undeserved pain and bereavement. The nightmare of Lady Macbeth's sleepwalking speech is to the plaintive lucidity of the dying Ophelia what a dance of death is to a grace note.

Whereas Hamlet merely feigns madness, its true victim is Ophelia, whose mind is unhinged when Hamlet kills her father and coarsely jokes with her in public. The disjointed words of Ophelia's first song could apply to either Hamlet or Polonius.

"How should I your true love know
From another one?
By his cockle hat and staff,
And his sandal shoon."

(4.5.23–26)

Deserted by the prince she loves, she also mourns his murder of her father, who is

> dead and gone, lady,
> He is dead and gone;
> At his head a grass-green turf
> At his heels a stone.
>
> (4.5.29–31)

Funeral rites abound, but as temporal and spatial connections fall away, the precise occasion and cause of the mourning are hard to identify. Is Ophelia grieving for Polonius or for the death of Hamlet's love? Though the stingy daughter of a baker may have been turned into an owl, Ophelia has done nothing to discourage her lover. Why should her owlish solemnity be purchased at the price of heartbreak and grieving?

> Well, God 'ild you! They say the owl was a baker's
> daughter. Lord, we know what we are, but know
> not what we may be. God be at your table!
>
> (4.5.41–44)

However unhinged Ophelia may be by Polonius's death, her proffering of herself as a Valentine at her lover's window tells us more about her frustrated love for Hamlet than about grief she feels for her father. In her fantasy of betrayed love, Ophelia sings snatches of a ballad about a faithless lover who swears cynically that he would have married his mistress, as promised, if she had not had sex with him first. Since there is no evidence that Hamlet, apart from his ill-considered jests before the court, has treated Ophelia dishonorably, there is more crazed fantasy than fact in her flights of ribald song. But Shakespeare balances any hint of coarseness in Ophelia by having her stoically opt for patience, even though she "cannot choose but weep" to think of her father's being laid to rest in cold ground. Her appeal for justice—"My brother shall know of it"—is qualified by her courtesy to Gertrude and gratitude for her "good counsel." She is less a foiled avenger like Hamlet than a fairy princess, a deranged Cinderella, calling for her coach and bidding sweet adieus to ladies of the court.

When Laertes returns, Ophelia repeats her mad performance before her broken-hearted brother. Her mournful song about her father's beard "as white as snow" is the madness of the bereaved: "Go to thy death-bed; / He will never come again" (4.5.193–94). But her derangement is also the madness of the lovelorn, who complains of "the false steward, that stole his master's daughter" (4.5.172–73).

Several Pre-Raphaelite painters, including Tennyson's friend John Everett Millais, associate the poet's Lady of Shalott with Ophelia. By the end of the

Victorian age, no fewer than fifty works of art had been based on Tennyson's poem, and though he "seemed resigned to the illustrations of his friend . . . Millais," Tennyson was "suspicious of the unlicensed additions evident in the work of Hunt and Rossetti" (Kooistra, 2002, 401). When Millais died in 1896, Arthur Symons praised him, not as the artist of *Bubbles,* a vapid painting of a curly-haired boy, but as the artist of early Pre-Raphaelite works like *The Lady of Shalott* and *Ophelia,* for which he is best remembered today.

Just as Ophelia is described as a "creature native and indued" to the element of "water," so the Lady of Shalott is a kind of water spirit, singing her last song as she passes down the river in her boat. Like Ophelia's fall into the brook on a broken willow branch, the Lady's entry into the river is associated with a boat she finds floating beneath a willow tree. As in "The Lotos-Eaters," the frequent use of feminine rhymes blurs and softens the line-endings.

> In the stormy east-wind straining,
> The pale yellow woods were waning,
> The broad stream in his banks complaining,
> Heavily the low sky raining
>   Over towered Camelot;
> Down she came and found a boat
> Beneath a willow left afloat,
> And round about the prow she wrote
>   *The Lady of Shalott.*
>
> (lines 118–26)

Even though the sexual loathing Gertrude incites in her son is a direct cause of Ophelia's death, she pays Ophelia a beautiful elegiac tribute. Lancelot, too, though the unsuspecting cause of the Lady of Shalott's death, is the only bystander to praise her. When over the dead maid, enchantingly at peace in her own English barge, Lancelot intones the words "God in his mercy lend her grace" (line 170), it is hard not to hear an echo of Octavius's tribute to the dead Cleopatra: "she looks like sleep, / As she would catch another Antony / In her strong toil of grace" (*Antony and Cleopatra* 5.2.349–51).

In the poem's revised version, the strict separation of Sir Lancelot's bright, bejeweled world from the wan shadows of the Lady's world inside the tower gives dramatic force to their final, fatal commingling. Originally the mirror was an incidental feature of the Lady's surroundings, no more important than the tinkling sheep bell. In the 1842 version the compression of substance amounts to a fact of form. The mirror now moves to the head of a stanza, and a long, colorful procession of churls and abbots is reflected from its surface. Caught in Lancelot's strong toil of grace, the Lady of Shalott weaves a web that is three times removed from the world it portrays. Her image of Lancelot reflects what she sees in a mirror, and that image reflects the knight's reflection in a second mirror, the river (lines 105–6). In the poem's final 1842 version, the strict separation of private and public worlds in the first three parts seems destined to will, in a destructive commingling of these worlds in the fourth part, the suicidal completion of a fated design. The Lady's cry "The curse is come upon me" (line 116) echoes the shriek of Blake's Thel. The shriek is that of "the disappearing ghost or the uprooted mandrake," as Northrop Frye observes of Blake's heroine; "and her tragedy," unlike Ophelia's, "could be anything from a miscarriage to a lost vision" (1947, 233).

Though Gertrude's beautiful elegy for Ophelia is a shaping presence in "The Lady of Shalott," remembrance of her elegy appears to embarrass Tennyson when he alludes to it indirectly in "A Dirge."

> There with fantastic garlands did she come,
> Of crow-flowers, nettles, daisies, and long purples,
> That liberal shepherds give a grosser name,
> But our cold maids do dead men's fingers call them.
>
> (*Hamlet* 4.7.168–71)

The fastidious young Tennyson finds Gertrude's reference to "long purples" coarse. He wants to suppress the fact that maids call orchids "dead men's fingers" and that "liberal shepherds" give to "dead men's fingers" the "grosser name" of "orchis," which in Greek means "testicle." And so in the 1842 revision of "A Dirge," Tennyson removes the quotation marks around the flowers' names.

> Round thee blow, self-pleached deep,
> Bramble roses, faint and pale,
> And "long purples" of the dale.
>
> (lines 29–31)

In his lyric "Adeline," "the language wherewith Spring / Letters cowslips on the hill" alludes creatively to the "crimson drops / I' the bottom of a cowslip" from *Cymbeline*. But as Christopher Ricks prods us to recall, what are the "crimson drops" compared to?

> On her left breast
> A mole cinque-spotted, like the crimson drops
> I' the bottom of a cowslip.
>
> (*Cymbeline* 2.2.37–39)

"Tennyson was surely right not to spell it out," Ricks concludes. "Unfortunately, in most of [his] early love poems he did not spell it in" either (1972, 53).

Minor matters of sexual delicacy and taste pale in importance, however, beside the homosexual love Shakespeare portrays in his sonnets, which "are not only an important source" for *In Memoriam* but also "its most important analogue" (Ricks, 1972, 214). Henry Hallam's destruction of his son's letters to Tennyson is an irreparable loss to scholarship. His disservice to learning has made it harder to understand the depth, nature, and power of love in the greatest elegy written in Victorian Britain.

Next to Tennyson, the Victorian poet with the most Shakespearean sense of the transience and hence the seriousness of beauty is Edward FitzGerald. His translation of *Rubaiyat of Omar Khayyam* combines the gusto of a drinking song with the depleted energy of Tennyson's hedonist in "The Vision of Sin." It also turns a medieval Book of Hours into a book of moments. For the cycle of devotional poems in John Keble's *The Christian Year,* FitzGerald substitutes a chain of discrete epigrams on beauty and death.

The last line of stanza 24 echoes the last words of the melancholy Jacques's discourse on the stages of man in *As You Like It:* "Sans teeth, sans eyes, sans taste, sans everything" (2.7.166).

> Ah, make the most of what we yet may spend,
> Before we too into the Dust descend;
> Dust into Dust, and under Dust to lie
> Sans Wine, sans Song, sans Singer, and—sans End!
> (stanza 24)

Whereas Jacques, like Aristotle, thinks death is the end, Fitzgerald imagines a process of decay that goes on forever: "Sans Singer, and—sans End!" In the one-way transit of ashes to ashes, dust to dust, FitzGerald traces the same swift passage as the familiar words of the burial service. He also echoes Macbeth's disillusioned thought that all our yesterdays have lighted fools the way to "dusty death."

Just as Tennyson's skeptic in "The Ancient Sage" is appalled to reflect that his beloved's dust is greening in the rose tree's leaf and her blood is reddening in its bloom, so FitzGerald is shocked to think that in treading on "the tender green" of a reviving plant he is walking on an herb that a "once lovely Lip" had nourished.

> And this reviving Herb whose tender Green
> Fledges the River-Lip on which we lean—
> Ah, lean upon it lightly! for who knows
> From what once lovely Lip it springs unseen!
> (stanza 20)

FitzGerald uses two stark metonymies—the "Lip" of "the River and the "once lovely Lip" of the beloved—to ensure that reviving herbs and greening earth will not bewitch the mind unduly. Rhymed couplets sound more "poetic" than blank verse, and blank verse sounds more "poetic" than prose. Shakespeare makes use of this fact when he deploys the blank verse of the players' speech in the second act of *Hamlet* against a ground of prose, and the rhyming couplets of their speech in act 3 against a ground of blank verse. Tennyson uses a similar device in "The Ancient Sage," where the blank verse of the seer becomes the discursive ground against which the lyric snatches of the skeptic's rhyming tetrameter and trimeter lines is made to sound "poetic."

> O rose-tree planted in my grief,
> And growing on her tomb,
> Her dust is greening in your leaf,
> Her blood is in your bloom.
> O slender lily waving there,
> And laughing back the light,
> In vain you tell me "Earth is fair"
> When all is dark as night.
>
> (lines 163–70)

Haunted by the chime of mutability that is heard sounding and resounding in Shakespeare's sonnets, FitzGerald is as obsessed as Hamlet with the mystery of death, the undiscovered country from whose bourn no traveler returns.

> Strange, is it not? that of the myriads who
> Before us pass'd the door of Darkness through,
> Not one returns to tell us of the Road,
> Which to discover we must travel too.
>
> (stanza 64)

Like Carlyle's ghost, which emerges from the inane, hastes stormfully across the astonished earth, then plunges again into the inane, the soul's flight is as fitful and swift as the flight of the bird that passes in and out of the mead hall in Venerable Bede's great parable.

> What, without asking, hither hurried *Whence*?
> And, without asking, *Whither* hurried hence!
> Oh, many a Cup of this forbidden Wine
> Must drown the memory of that insolence!
>
> (stanza 30)

Oblivion drowns our knowledge of where we come from and where we are going. It takes even stronger wine to "drown the memory" of fate's decree that Hamlet's inquiry about an "undiscovered country" should receive no answer. Who is more "insolent," FitzGerald asks: the proud questioner who would eat from the tree of knowledge, or the proud god who refuses his interrogator the courtesy of a reply?

Few of Shakespeare's sonnets are at once more beautiful and ruinous than the seventy-third, "That time of year thou mayst in me behold." The first quatrain allows us to feel intensely what an aging, palsied speaker may have to endure as he hovers over each caesural pause, tremulous with indecision: "When yellow leaves, or none, or few, do hang" (line 12). In a progressive shrinkage of time and space, the sonnet compares death, first to autumn, the last of the seasons, then to the setting of the sun, the last event in a day, and finally to the fading glow of an ember in a fire that is dying on a hearth.

> That time of year thou mayst in me behold
> When yellow leaves, or none, or few, do hang
> Upon those boughs which shake against the cold,
> Bare ruined choirs, where late the sweet birds sang.
> In me thou seest the twilight of such day
> As after sunset fadeth in the west,
> Which by and by black night doth take away,
> Death's second self that seals up all in rest.
> In me thou seest the glowing of such fire
> That on the ashes of his youth doth lie,
> As the death-bed whereon it much expire,
> Consumed with that which it was nourished by.
> This thou perceiv'st, which makes thy love more
> strong,
> To love that well which thou must leave ere long.

Successive "flash-overs" in the sonnet allow us to fluctuate between subdued elation and grief. As in Wittgenstein's rabbit-duck figure, we first see one image and then another. For an instant there flashes before the eye the ribbed vaulting of a tree divested of its leaves. Next we glimpse the chancel of a ruined Gothic cathedral, where choristers once sang at heaven's gate. The second quatrain anticipates the gutted glory of Tennyson's lyric in *In Memoriam,* "Sad Hesper o'er the buried sun." Do we behold a "glory *done*" or a "*glory* done?" Most equivocal are the next four lines. Do they confront us with the spectacle of ash collapsing on a funeral pyre? Or do we witness in a glowing ember the combustion of a world in one small grate, as if its work had finished in that flare? The fire that stirs about the poet may glow more intensely as he ages. But even as it seems to make his beauty over again, like the "eternal lines" in which the fair youth grows "to time" in sonnet 18, any triumph of beauty over time is tempered by the lines time carves into the fairest face. The sculptor confers on each type of line—the lines etched by age and the lines of Shakespeare's sonnet—a grace of fluctuation, a beauty of transition. Expiry can be viewed either as the extinction of a flame or as a consummation devoutly to be wished. As life that nourished a flame is consumed at last by the fire it fed, it uses up all its resources without remainder. Harold Bloom reminds us that the root meaning of the verb "to ruin" is "rushing to a collapse." In both the "ruined choirs" and the collapsing fire, "Shakespearean *ruin,* whether as verb or substantive, has an aura: the splendor of Lear in his madness or of Antony in his fall" (Bloom, 2011, 79).

Commenting on the third quatrain of Shakespeare's sonnet, Winifred Nowottny concedes that her "mind baulks at the difficulty of youth as a death-bed . . . , yet leaps at the resolving image of ashes . . . and grasps for a concept of continuous process in which consuming and nourishing are one" (1962, 171–72). Something similar occurs, she believes, at the end of Arnold's "Sohrab and Rustum," where a sudden leap to meaning depends on the contrast of the sluggish river with "the bright speed" it once possessed as a stream in its "mountain cradle" (lines 886–87). Like the last quatrain of Shakespeare's sonnet, "the shock-impact of the quasi-synaesthetic image, 'bright speed,'" "the permanence of the 'high 'mountain-cradle,'" and the suggestion that "the river has identity as a human being," all "project a symbol, at once consolatory and elegiac, of human destiny" (1962, 171).

No less beautiful or ruinous than the coda of "Sohrab and Rustum" or the third quatrain of Shakespeare's seventy-third sonnet is the death of hope, life, and ambition contemplated by Browning's painter Andrea del Sarto in his exquisite "twilight-piece." The monologue captures the spirit of Shakespeare's seventy-third sonnet by rising in hope and ebbing in despair, fluctuating in wavelike motions between beauty and disenchantment, loveliness and death. As in the first two quatrains of Shakespeare's sonnet, the passing of Andrea's youth and hope, the diminution of his early promise as a painter, the decline of the year and the day, all work together to modify Andrea's perception of "A common grayness silver[ing] everything."

> You smile? why, there's my picture ready made,
> There's what we painters call our harmony!
> A common grayness silvers everything,—
> All in a twilight, you and I alike
> —You, at the point of your first pride in me
> (That's gone you know),—but I, at every point;
> My youth, my hope, my art, being all toned down
> To yonder sober pleasant Fiesole.

> There's the bell clinking from the chapel-top;
> That length of convent-wall across the way
> Holds the trees safer, huddled more inside;
> That last monk leaves the garden; days decrease,
> And autumn grows, autumn in everything.
>
> (lines 33–45)

Out of dissimilar impressions of refuge and fear, seclusion and death, which reach the eye through a strange veil of sight, Andrea creates "what we painters call our harmony" (line 34). Like the starkly etched austerity of Shakespeare's leafless choir stalls, Andrea's peculiar atmosphere of mixed gray-and-silver lights is a palpable illusion to be touched and seen on the dark air. As the trees within the convent wall seem to huddle more inside for warmth and safety, the garden empties of monks as the days empty of light. In a progressive shrinking of clauses, each successive emptying takes up less and less space: "That last monk leaves the garden; days decrease." Only in the last line do clauses once again begin to cast a wider net as the chill expands, and "autumn grows, autumn in everything."

Just as Shakespeare's seventy-third sonnet alliterates "love," "leave," and "long" (line 14), so Hopkins in "Spring and Fall: To a Young Child" makes Goldengrove's unleafing as "unleaving"—as abiding in memory—as the fallen leaves that keep their green in *In Memoriam.* Though time hurries the present from us and narrows the span of the future, it also keeps the past in store for us by holding open the door of memory. In Hopkins, as in Tennyson, "the days that are no more" are overlaid, not lost. Hopkins discloses not only the abyss in things but also the tears. He has less affinity with Shakespeare's "backward and abysm of time" or Ovid's "tempus edax rerum" than with Tennyson's "passion of the past" and Virgil's "sunt lacrimae rerum." Though the leaves have fallen, the words themselves descend with as much natural grace and ease of movement as a season might hope to pass or a man to die. Like Tennyson's buried sun or Shakespeare's bare ruined choirs, whose glory is both consecrated and gutted, Hopkins's Goldengrove is both unleafing and unleaving. It is a place of divested beauty, a leafless vault. But like anything we love and lose, it has a future in the memory of those elegiac poets who have the will to revalue their past and the genius to commemorate it.

For Shakespeare and the Victorians, a stage-tragedy death makes an impact; but a real death like Cordelia's induces a tremor. It affects us as our own. George Eliot offers a fine account of this important difference in *Middlemarch.* "When the commonplace 'We must all die' transforms itself suddenly into the acute consciousness, 'I must die—and soon,' then death grapples us, and his fingers are cruel" (bk. 4, chap. 42). In *The Thread of Life,* Richard Wollheim makes a similar distinction between an "impact and a tremor." The terrible news of a friend's sudden death makes an "impact." News that I have terminal cancer, provided it is accepted and believed, induces a "tremor." As Wollheim says, "The tremor is a part of our natural sensibility, and we may think of it as a sensible index of self-concern" (1984, 237).

The Victorian poet who best dramatizes the difference between a staged and a real death is Tennyson, who occasionally steps out of a picture space or passes through a frame. In his monologue "Tiresias," for instance, the ritual of sacrifice solemnly enjoined by the prophet is ceremonial and staged. "One far-shining fire" on "one far height" (line 177) makes the appropriate dramatic impact. But only in the postscript to Edward FitzGerald, the friend to whom he was to send "Tiresias" as a birthday gift but who has died in the interval, does Tennyson truly touch anyone. One might have thought that the coda of "Tiresias," which rings throughout with the finality of death, had fully exhausted its subject. But in his postscript Tennyson questions the adequacy of the poem's lofty coda. As a shrewd critic, his friend FitzGerald would probably have recommended "a less diffuse and opulent end" ("To E. FitzGerald," line 60). Indeed, when the "tolling" of his friend's "funeral bell" suddenly breaks in upon the "Pagan Paradise" of a highly staged and ceremonial poem, Tennyson realizes that FitzGerald's death has provided a fitter ending than his own. By speaking not simply of his own futile march toward the grave, but of "*Our* living out" (line 80) and "*our* poor . . . dawn" (line 77; my italics), Tennyson revives the piercing truth of Donne: "Ask not for whom the bell tolls; it tolls for thee." The poet has made FitzGerald's death our own.

A staged death like Ophelia's or the Lady of Shalott's makes a strong ritualized impact. The silent, almost unnoticed passing of Tennyson's son Lionel in the verse epistle to Dufferin induces a strong shock or tremor. Death intrudes from outside the epistolary convention: it seems harshly at odds with the social convention of writing a letter of thanks to the dead son's hosts in India. The terrible finality of the seeming afterthought—"and he wrote no more" (line 36)—is so understated that we are in danger of missing it. A life seems to expire in the time it takes to pause for breath between the quotation from Lionel's letter and the father's heartbroken comment on it.

> But ere he left your fatal shore,
> And lay on that funereal boat,
> Dying, "Unspeakable," he wrote
> "Their kindness," and he wrote no more.
> ("To the Marquis of Dufferin and Ava," lines 33–36)

Death's uncivil intrusion in this poem is discourteous. Like an uninvited guest, it blunders into a graceful verse epistle, a father's letter of thanks to his son's hosts, where it has no right to be. And yet this unspeakable breach of courtesy is beautifully repaired by Tennyson's own decorum, which gives Lionel's words about Dufferin's unspeakable kindness to him a heartbreaking turn. As the brevity of the last clause ("and he wrote no more") turns the brevity of a letter into a brevity that is for ever, Tennyson, like his son, falters in his capacity to find words.

Continued vocalization may induce a state of stupor in which Ida's "Ask me no more" also means "Ask me once more," and in which "the days that are no more" are inseparable from memories of a sail that "sinks with all we love below the verge." Used as a mantra, the phrase "no more" moved Tennyson deeply. Often it induced in him a trancelike state. I associate the phrase with the last words I spoke to my daughter Alyssa on a visit to a hospice in a distant part of northern Canada three weeks before she died. I asked, "May I call you on the phone? I love to hear your voice." "You're not good on the phone," she replied. "Write instead." With instinctive courtesy, she asked at once if I "was OK with that." Though hurt by her request, I know why she made it. Realizing our loss was "unspeakable," she chose to speak "no more." Behind her unspoken "speak no more" I heard and keep hearing the haunting "wrote no more" of the lines to Dufferin.

A response to the magic repose of Arthur's passing out to sea is totally at odds with the shock of seeing Lionel pass down into it. The first is a ceremonial, staged death, as ritualized as the death of Ophelia or Desdemona. The second is a real death, which seems to stop the letter writer in his tracks. As Tennyson forces himself to watch his son's coffin fall and flash in the Red Sea, he all but welcomes the horror of a real death, preferring it to the remote rites of a death "I have not seen" and "one drear sound I have not heard" (lines 39–40). Though the sentiment of the sage—"I may meet him soon" (line 48)—is more assured and controlled than the bereaved father's grief, the expression of anguish is more precise and irreplaceable. We do not believe in Arthur's stage-tragedy death as he passes out to sea, and so we have leisure to grieve over it. But we are shocked by Lionel's death because, as Tennyson imagines the burial at sea, the horror of that distant event seems unspeakably real. Nothing can mute its shock because, like Cordelia's death, nothing has quite prepared for it. No ceremony can ritually absorb a real death or make it less desolating.

Nietzsche believes that "we have already grown beyond whatever we have words for. In all talking there lies a grain of contempt. Speech, it seems, was devised only for the average, medium, communicable. The speaker has already *vulgarized* himself by speaking" (Nietzsche, 1968, 82–83). When Lear demands to know how much Cordelia loves him, she is silent. What can she say?

Cordelia. Nothing, my lord.
Lear. Nothing?
Cordelia. Nothing.
Lear. Nothing will come of nothing. Speak again.
(1.1.87–90)

The pauses in these lines are probably much longer than any of the four speeches we actually hear. How long Cordelia and Lear are silent depends on the nerve of the actors. But their silence is at the very core of Shakespeare's art. Christopher Ricks associates Perdita's "communicative blush" in *The Winter's Tale*—"For this / I'll blush you thanks" (4.4.593–94)—with Tennyson's silent "blushing" of the lover's "happy news" in *Maud* (1984, 186–87).

Pass and blush the news
    Over glowing ships;
Over blowing seas,
    Over seas at rest,
Pass the happy news,
    Blush it through the West.
(*Maud* 1.581–86)

When words fail, all that can speak in their place is a voiceless blush.

Frank Kermode reminds us "that the soliloquy, brought to perfection in Hamlet, is speech in silence, the speech of silence." Shakespeare "discovers that "silence itself could be eloquent. When nothing is said, . . . silence speaks" (Kermode, 2000, 11–12). A Shakespearean soliloquy is silent-speaking, because it voices thoughts that normally only a dramatic character, the soliloquist, could hear. A Victorian monologue is silent-speaking, because only in the silent theater of a reader's mind do its words receive a voice. Victorian poets and Shakespeare are also silent-speaking in a third sense: consuming a world in one small word, their language often consists of one part speech to three parts silence. Words are too often a substitute for loss. Iris Murdoch, one of Shakespeare's shrewdest commentators, says "we are here close to the metaphysical enigma of tragic art, and indeed, by extension, of all art and discourse. As soon as you talk about it you lose the object" (1992, 125). When we speak too consolingly of the dead, we may no longer be speaking of a real loss but of a love like Goneril's or Regan's that has died in the heart.

Classical mourners like Ulysses, Tithonus, and the great earth-mother in "Demeter and Persephone" are grandiloquent actors and skilled performers. The grieving father of the lines to Dufferin is the opposite of eloquent: he can barely stammer out what he feels. The difference between Demeter's coda and the father's halting words in the verse epistle to Dufferin is the difference between the impact that a rhetorician like Mark Antony makes in his funeral oration and the shock wave or tremor induced by a private grief like Lear's. Demeter's prophecy is audible as public enactment: it has much in common with the ceremonial performance of the dying Antony or Cleopatra. By contrast, Tennyson's letter to his friend is confidential and restrained. Like Cordelia's death, the father's loss of his son cannot be talked about: it is too unique and irreplaceable—too real, in a sense—for words.[2]

11

The Hills Are Shadows

TIME THE DEVOURER

SHAKESPEARE, THE MOST OVIDIAN OF POETS, ENJOYED SPECIAL prominence in the age of evolution, the age of Darwin and Lyell, who studied changes wrought in biology and the earth's history by time the devourer, the subject of Shakespeare's most moving sonnets. Honing Ockham's razor, Darwin used it to dispense with design and submerge the world in a maelstrom of accidental variation and random flux. Any study of Shakespeare's influence on the poetics and intellectual milieu of the Victorians raises the ghost of Ovid's *tempus edax.* With childlike simplicity Shakespeare protests, "Time will come and take my love away" (sonnet 64, line 12). Time the devourer is the subject of Protagoras's chilling prophecy in the fifteenth book of Ovid's *Metamorphoses.* Like filial ingratitude or the mouth that tears the hand for lifting food to it, Ovid's Muse is self-devouring. In the end it eats itself up because its hunger is insatiable. Prophets of time's power to level and destroy, Shakespeare and Ovid, Tennyson and T. H. Huxley all attest to the terrible divinity of Krishna, who announces in words made famous by Robert Oppenheimer: "I am come as Time, the waster of the peoples, / Ready for that hour that ripens to their ruin."

As a sculptor of ruin in Shakespeare's sonnets, *tempus edax* is a leveler, not because it devours everything, but because (as the greatest Victorian metaphysician tells us) "time is so far from enduring the test of criticism, that at a touch it falls apart and proclaims itself illusory" (Bradley, 1893, 183). As Augustine said, everyone understands time until asked to explain, then no one can say what it is. Imaged in vast expanses of geological time, "the iniquity of oblivion blindly scatters her poppy," Sir Thomas Browne says, "and deals with the memory of men without distinction to merit of perpetuity" (1967, 282). No alms for oblivion can moderate or tame the powerful undertow of Ovid's Muse, time the devourer. To counter its terrible beauty, Shakespeare and his Victorian heirs try to grapple with the monster before it wastes their generations and sweeps them from the stage. Ovid is to Shakespeare what Lyell is to Tennyson: a Muse of mutability. Ovid and Lyell strand each poet "on the shore / Of that wide world" where Keats stands "alone," brooding on oblivion, till his dream of "Love and Fame to nothingness" does "sink" ("When I Have Fears," lines 12–14). The Victorian poet's fear of oblivion is the center of a much larger anxiety about metamorphosis shared by Shakespeare and Ovid, who realize that "the question *ubi sunt* may turn up in snow or flowers long before it's realized to be death" (Frye, 2004, 13).

In *The Tempest,* Prospero's "dark backward and abysm of time" (1.2.50) turns a menacing backside to Miranda's mind whenever she tries to open channels to her past. Like Tennyson, she experiences an inexpressible yearning for the long ago and done. But as time slowly erodes her earliest memories, they become portions and parcels of "the dreadful past." The "passion of the past," an indefinable regret and yearning for things that are no more, is expressed most eloquently in Tennyson's Virgilian lyric "Tears, Idle Tears," where the chill that falls across the "happy Autumn-fields" is not far removed from the chill that descends on Tithonus when Aurora bathes him coldly in her deathly but enticing rosy shadows.

When Tennyson asks, "Is this the end? Is this the end?" in *In Memoriam,* an elegy that took seventeen years to complete, his echo of Kent's ineffectual interruption of Lear's protracted agony, "Is this the promised end?," is less an appropriation of Shakespeare than an example of Shakespeare's taking possession of *him.* We may say of such lines what T. S. Eliot says of the "Dark house" elegy in *In Memoriam:* they give us the shudder. As Hopkins says of Wordsworth's "Ode: Intimations of Immortality," the soul has been in a quiver, like a vibrating string, trembling between dread and subdued elation, ever since.

There are few apocalypses in Victorian poetry and fiction, and few in Shakespeare. Tennyson's monologues end at the penultimate moment, not at the moment their speakers anticipate and expect. When Kent asks about a promised end in *King Lear,* Edgar speaks only of "an image of that horror." As in *In Memoriam* and many of Tennyson's monologues, everything in *King Lear* "tends toward a conclusion that," as Frank Kermode observes, "does not occur; even personal death, for Lear, is terribly delayed. Beyond the apparent worst there is a worse suffering, and when the end comes it is not only more appalling than anyone expected, but a mere image of that horror, not the thing itself" (1966, 82). Like Shakespeare, the Victorian poets and novelists live in a post-apocalyptic world: "no end, there is none." The poet of *In Memoriam* and the great elegiac monologues—"Ulysses," "Tithonus," "Demeter and Persephone"—meditates at length on death. But like Lear and Cordelia, he lives in "an age too late for apocalypse, too critical for prophecy" (Kermode, 1966, 88).

When Tennyson turns to prophecy in section 123 of *In Memoriam,* it is not to disclose any apocalyptic end to time and the world but to offer his own vision of endless change. He uses Lyell's *Principles of Geology,* not as a template to process data for a new theory of evolution, as Darwin does, but as an oracle of science to give authority to an ancient prophecy of Protagoras in Ovid's *Metamorphoses.* "I have seen what once was solid earth now changed into sea," says Ovid's prophet, "and lands created out of what was once ocean" (Ovid, 1955, 341).

> Vidi ego quod fuerat quondam solidissima tellus
> esse fretum, vidi factas ex aequore terras.
> (*Metamorphoses* 15.262–63)

Such interchange of land and sea is the subject of section 123 of *In Memoriam,* a time-lapse photograph of the earth extending over billions of years. Carved by time, mountains that once were seas loom up as vast sculptures in Lyell's scientific archive of the earth. Reflecting the influence of several sonnets by Shakespeare, section 123 recalls another passage in the same fifteenth book of Ovid's poem. It is the prophecy predicting that "tempus edax rerum," time the devourer, "and the jealous years that pass" will "destroy all things, and nibbling them away, consume them gradually in a lingering death" (Ovid, 1955, 341).

> Tempus edax rerum, tuque invidiosa vetustas,
> omnia destruitis vitiataque dentibus aevi
> paulatim lenta consumitis omnia morte!
> (*Metamorphoses* 15.234–36)

Writing in *In Memoriam* as the scribe of the new geology, Tennyson demonizes random force as the will of a mindless harpy, a female demon like the sibyl with raving mouth" in Heraclitus, who utters "solemn, unadorned, unlovely words" that sound and echo for "a thousand years."

> From scarped cliff and quarried stone
> She cries, "A thousand types are gone;
> I care for nothing, all shall go. . . ."
> (*In Memoriam* 56.21–24)

Though Tennyson tries to subdue mutability in the first of his two "little metaphysical pieces," "Nothing Will Die" and "All Things Will Die," we should not make his vision of geological end games and change less radical than it is. He crosses Ariel's song from *The Tempest* with Lyell's prediction of a great "Geological winter."

'Tis the world's winter;
Autumn and summer
Are gone long ago;
Earth is dry to the centre,
But spring, a new comer,
A spring rich and strange,
Shall make the winds blow.
("Nothing Will Die," lines 17–23)

As Isobel Armstrong explains, "The simple, carefree song is a versification of new geological theory. In a later letter Tennyson refers punningly to the great 'Geological winter' proposed by Charles Lyell in the first volume of his *Principles of Geology.* It seems that he knew of these speculations before Lyell's book appeared in 1830" (1993, 57). Recalling Shelley's chorus from Hellas, "The world's great age begins anew, / The golden years return" (lines 1–2), Tennyson draws on Ariel's "sea change, rich and strange," to advance his own vision of a constantly changing world devoid of any divine origin or final cause.

Armstrong believes that "Ariel's song haunts" the early Victorians, "suggesting a confidence in transformation even when Tennyson subjects his own enquiries to critique. . . . We should remember that *The Tempest* is an ambiguous reference at this time. It is available to both conservative and radical readings" (1993, 58). Alarmed by Tennyson's "deep-fermenting tempest," the conservative critic John Wilson ("Christopher North") angrily attacks Tennyson's *Poems* of 1830 in his infamous 1832 review article in *Blackwood's Magazine.* What strikes North as radical in Tennyson's adaptation of *The Tempest* is his geological conclusion that "the world was never made. . . . Nothing was born" (lines 30, 36). For a world made by God, in which the Son was begotten by the Father, the young agnostic substitutes as a scientific alternative the unbegotten world of Charles Lyell and his new geology. To some Victorians such a world must have seemed as "unsponsored, free," and as stranded in space and time, as Wallace Stevens's "old chaos of the sun / Or old dependency of day and night, / Or island solitude" in "Sunday Morning" (8.5–7).

In the first quatrain of Shakespeare's sixtieth sonnet, taken directly from Ovid, the hypermetric first line retards the waves' motion, moderating the leveling force of the opening trochaic feet.

Like as the waves make towards the pebbled shore,
So do our minutes hasten to their end,

> Each changing place with that which goes before,
> In sequent toil all forwards do contend.
> (sonnet 60, lines 1–4)

Though the pace accelerates in the second line, the exchange of minute with minute, and of wave with wave, is as patterned and orderly as the exchange of partners in a dance.

More disturbing is the second quatrain, which substitutes for a predictably contentious pattern of "sequent toil" the cycle of slow ascent followed by sudden decline that the Renaissance associates with Lydgate's view of tragedy in *The Fall of Princes*.

> Nativity, once in the main of light,
> Crawls to maturity, wherewith being crowned,
> Crooked eclipses 'gainst his glory fight,
> And Time that gave doth now his gift confound.
> (sonnet 60, lines 5–8)

As J. W. Lever notes, in this quatrain "the Ovidian figure *editus in lucem* is combined with the English phrase 'the watery main' from [sonnet] LXIV to produce a dynamic new metaphor, 'the main of light'" (Lever, 1956, 253). Appareled in celestial light, the earth once possessed the glory and the freshness of a dream. Though lofty Latin words—"nativity" and "maturity"—impede the pace by loading weight on the monosyllabic "main of light" and "crawls," nativity crawls to maturity faster than we think. "Maturity" is reached, not at the end of the line in which nativity is said to inch forward, but before a medial six-syllable caesura: "Nativity, once in the main of light, / Crawls to maturity." Jamming together two stressed alliterating words, "crowned" and "crooked," Shakespeare uses the zenith as a hinge or pivot. Coronation launches an immediate counter-movement of reversal and decline. For even as the conjunction of "crowned" and "crooked" conjures the shade of a later monarch, Richard Crookback, who fights against the glory of his nephew princes by murdering them in the tower, the crowned king is deposed as swiftly as Richard II.

As the sea of light becomes a solar eclipse, the promise of "glory" in "gave" and "gift" is countered by the ascent and sudden fall of a second alliterating group: "crawls," "crowned," "crooked," and "confound." Anticipating Wordsworth while harking back to the passage on time the devourer in Ovid, the quatrain dramatizes time's increasing malignity. Where is it now, the glory and the dream? The best comment on the sinister grouping of sounds comes from Helen Vendler. "The apogee and eclipse," she observes, "occur at the very same moment in the immediate affronting of *crowned* by *crooked,* and of *gift* by *confound.* In this model, existential change is unnatural (eclipse, not sunset), involuntary, and destructive; it is ascribed to an agent, Time, who is at first generous (gave) and, at the end, malign (confound)" (1997, 284).

Time's blows in the third quatrain are swifter and more insidious. From the neutral verb "transfix" it passes at once to the subtly malign "delve" and finally to the voracious and remorseless "feed." From a mere assault on youth the attack proceeds to the destruction of physical beauty and an assault on man's most godlike attributes, his noble reason and angelic apprehension. Since these qualities, according to Hamlet, make man the beauty of the world and the paragon of animals, their destruction is the most brutal and devastating.

> Time doth transfix the flourish set on youth,
> And delves the parallels in beauty's brow,
> Feeds on the rarities of nature's truth,
> And nothing stands but for his scythe to mow.
> And yet to times in hope my verse shall stand
> Praising thy worth, despite his cruel hand.
> (sonnet 60, lines 9–14)

To magnify the daring and aggression of time's assault, Shakespeare moves each successive action word forward until in "Feeds" the final transitive verb is positioned to launch its attack directly from the head of a line. Youth, beauty, and rarest qualities of mind and feeling are all equally subject to *tempus edax.* "Nothing stands" before time's hungry "scythe," whose savagery is caught in the toil of two defective rhymes—"brow" and "mow." But "standing" firmly on its metrical feet, redressing what is frail and vulnerable in the first use of "stands," Shakespeare's tribute to his friend remains steadfast and secure.

Like Shakespeare's sixtieth sonnet, a few lyrics in *In Memoriam* have visionary openings at their center. In the "Dark house" elegy the music is Tennysonian, but the sentiment is defiantly anti-Romantic and urban. The poet inhabits a city of dreadful night. Yet even as he creeps like a "guilty thing" toward the door of the dead friend's house, a hunger for revelation seizes him. "He is not here," a voice announces. Who is speaking? For a split second the words of the angel to Mary Magdalene can be heard. What are we reading, a New Testament Gospel or a preview of Eliot's *The Waste Land*? As the "noise of life begins again," "the drizzling rain" and "blank day" dismally reassert themselves. But the lyric's baldness—its stark clarity of anguish and loss—is balanced by a visionary impulse to move in and through "the symbolist hole in the middle."

I borrow the phrase "symbolist hole" from Seamus Heaney, who uses it to describe a similar opening at the center of Shakespeare's sixtieth sonnet. "Nativity, once in the main of light, / Crawls to maturity" (sonnet 60, lines

5–6). Heaney thinks "something visionary happens" in these lines. "'Nativity,' an abstract noun housed in a wavering body of sound, sets up a warning tremor just before the mind's eye gets dazzled by 'the main of light,' and for a split second we are in the world of the *Paradiso.*" Heaney concedes that "the rest of the poem lives melodiously in a world of discourse." But what assimilates it to *In Memoriam* is that single "unpredictable strike into the realm of pure being" which "marks the sonnet with [an] extravagant genius" unique to Shakespeare (2002, 145).

Wherever it sounds and resounds, Pythagoras's oracle in Ovid strikes a melancholy chord of mutability. We hear it in Henry IV's reflection that "the revolution of the times / Make[s] mountains level, and the continent, / Weary of solid firmness, melt[s] itself / Into the sea!" (*2 Henry IV* 3.1.46–49). Sad mortality is heard as both chord and discord in Spenser's cantos of mutability and in Shelley's lyric on the same theme: "Man's yesterday may ne'er be like his morrow, / Nought may endure but Mutability" ("Mutability," lines 15–16). Shakespeare strikes the chord again in sonnet 64, where the triple stresses of "Time's fell hand" deface the "rich proud cost" of "outworn buried age," spondaic units that seem at first just as formidable. Shakespeare confronts a reader with two equally matched metrical adversaries.

When I have seen by Time's fell hand defaced
The rich proud cost of outworn buried age,
When sometime lofty towers I see down razed,
And brass eternal slave to mortal rage;
When I have seen the hungry ocean gain
Advantage on the kingdom of the shore,
And the firm soil win of the wat'ry main,
Increasing store with loss, and loss with store;
When I have seen such interchange of state,
Or state itself compounded to decay,
Ruin hath taught me thus to ruminate;
That Time will come and take my love away.
  This thought is as a death which cannot choose
  But weep to have that which it fears to lose.
(sonnet 64)

The first four lines execute a graceful chiasmus. An act of majestic ravaging precedes the glory of what is ravaged. Then the lofty towers are leveled and the brass is enslaved to mortal rage. The *abba* pattern persists in the second quatrain, where first the ocean gains on the shore and then the shore on the watery main. The culminating chiasmus, "increasing store with loss, and loss with store" (line 8) at first presents a puzzle. How can loss increase anything, or abundance constitute a loss? The apparent paradox is explained if we consider first the ocean's increase at the expense of the shore and then the land's increase at the expense of the sea. If we take a detached enough view, there are no losers or winners in the exchange. From far enough out on his eighth sphere, Chaucer's Troilus can afford to laugh. Sad mortality is a comedy to those who see its end games from afar, but a tragedy to those close enough in to hear its discords and be shaken by its shock waves and tremors.

When everything, then, is in a state of reversible equilibrium, is there any cause for alarm? What is lost today will be won again tomorrow. Even the turn on "state" in the concluding quatrain seems to confirm a reassuring pattern of reversal and exchange. Unfortunately, the change from a "state" or condition of matter to the decay or entropy of a whole "state," a nation or empire, is not as reversible as we may think. "Ruin" or loss can no longer be recuperated in the large Latin verb "ruminate." For the containing power of chiasmus Shakespeare substitutes a progression that is heartbreakingly linear. The prophecy that "Time will come and take my love away" is moving in its alarm and defenseless simplicity. The monosyllables are affecting and creep up on us like death. Time is a destroyer and devourer of dreams. We are in love and love what vanishes. What more is there to say?

In the first line of sonnet 65, not even the leveling blows of harsh iambic stresses, where each accented syllable coincides with a long quantity and a strong caesural break, have power to "oversway" the force of "sad mortality." If the rages of earth and sea are impotent, surely a fragile, flower-like beauty has even less hope of dominating anything.

> Since brass, nor stone, nor earth, nor boundless sea,
> But sad mortality o'ersways their power,
> How with this rage shall beauty hold a plea,
> Whose action is no stronger than a flower?
> O how shall summer's honey breath hold out
> Against the wreckful siege of batt'ring days,
> When rocks impregnable are not so stout,
> Nor gates of steel so strong, but Time decays?
> (sonnet 65, lines 1–8)

Tenuous but defiant, how, we might ask, can the three successive stresses of summer's honey "breath hold out" against the formidable alignment of stresses and long vowels in time's "wrackful siege of batt'ring days"? Though paired metrically, the two antagonists seem woefully mismatched.

The two four-line rhetorical questions of the octave, whose answer the poet shrinks from giving, prompt the sestet's "fearful meditation." Afraid of the answer he must give, he stops short at the seventh-syllable caesura, hesitant to proceed with his inquiries. When Shakespeare summons the courage to go on, his questions accelerate in intensity and tempo. From the leisurely four-line questions of the octave, the questions now contract in length from the line-and-a-half question at the head of the sestet to two one-line, panic-stricken questions, made urgent by anaphora.

> O fearful meditation: Where, alack,
> Shall Time's best jewel from Time's chest lie hid?
> Or what strong hand can hold his swift foot back,
> Or who his spoil of beauty can forbid?
> (sonnet 65, lines 9–12)

Paired off as adversaries, beauty and time now fight a metrical war. The triple stresses of "Time's best jewel" battle the oblivion in "Time's chest . . . hid." Time not only ravages or "spoils" beauty but claims it as its spoil.

As a poet's bible of end games and change, Ovid's *Metamorphoses* is as seminal a source book for Shakespeare as Charles Lyell's *Principles of Geology* is for Tennyson. Lyell's influence is nowhere more evident than in section 123 of *In Memoriam,* where the transformation of hills into shadows and solid lands into mist extends over billions of years.

> There rolls the deep where grew the tree.
> O earth, what changes hast thou seen!
> There where the long street roars, hath been
> The stillness of the central sea.
>
> The hills are shadows, and they flow
> From form to form, and nothing stands;
> They melt like mist, the solid lands,
> Like clouds they shape themselves and go.
>
> But in my spirit will I dwell,
> And dream my dream, and hold it true;
> For though my lips may breathe adieu,
> I cannot think the thing farewell.

We knows from his son's *Memoir* that Tennyson read Lyell's *Principles of Geology* in 1837. One scholar, E. B. Mattes, compares the lines just quoted, not with Ovid or Shakespeare, but with the spectacle of change recorded at the end of the first volume of Lyell's treatise: "Many flourishing inland towns, and a still greater number of ports, now stand where the sea rolled its waves" (cited in Ricks, 1969, 973). As Tennyson registers these geological truths, allowing the echo of "there" in "where" and of "rolls" in "roars" to reverberate across space and time, land and sea dissolve before his eyes.

The poet makes his vision compelling by alternating predictably between images of motion and fluidity—"There rolls the deep" (1); "they flow / From form to form" (5–6)—and solid stable images: "where grew the tree" (1); "where the long street roars" (3). Despite the regularity, each time an example of change is cited there is a slight adjustment of the fluid and stable elements. The noise of the rolling deep, the unstable element in the first example (1), is transferred to "the long street," the solid element in the second example (3–4); and the fluid sea becomes silent (4). In addition, the second example ends with the image of the sea that introduces the first example, clamping the illustrations into a chiasmic vise: *abba*. The exchange of elements that accompanies the recurrence of logical and syntactical patterns reaches a minor climax in the third example of change (5–8), where the most fluid and solid elements are paradoxically identified: "The hills are shadows" (5); "They melt like mist, the solid lands" (7). To reinforce the paradox, Tennyson introduces strong caesural pauses and allows the phrase "solid lands" to sound like a knell in two spectral variants that mock its durability and feed off its substance: "they melt"; "they shape themselves and go."

The great spectacle of transmutation foreseen by Ovid, Shakespeare, and Charles Lyell reaches a climax in the short, rigid clauses of the central stanza. The imposition of the stern parataxis—"and they flow," "and nothing stands"—on the yielding lyric similes—"like mist," "like clouds"—establishes a momentary pathos. But the absolute parity of all the forms, of the moving and the motionless, of the gentle and the remorseless, amounts to a sudden collapse in beauty and interest. Alan Sinfield notes that "the solid lands," instead of coming first, are "completely engulfed by images of insubstantiality; and 'go' is made starkly to end the sentence and the stanza so that the solid lands seem to slide suddenly away into an indefinite void" (1971, 84). The pageant threatens to end in terrifying absurdity, leaving the mind of a dispossessed spectator blank and indifferent.

As in Ovid and Shakespeare, the reduction of creation to a nameless "thing," at once spectral and physical, is harrowing. But "thing" refers, not primarily to the eye's outward vision of dissolving worlds, but to the "I's" inward journey, to the privacy of its "dream." By converting the most tenuous element, the dream of love, into the most solid and enduring element, "the thing," the soul can show how the more solitary it becomes, the more aware it is of its power to create a world that survives. Like George Herbert's "seasoned timber" in the poem "Virtue," which "though the whole world turn to coal, / Then chiefly lives" (lines 14–16), the self-conscious mind, despite its apparent fragility, is durable as "rock" (*In Memoriam* 131.3). As "living will that shalt endure" (131.1), the soul will outlast even the wreck of nature, "When all that seems shall suffer shock" (131.2), and the whole inanimate creation will flow through the void into nothingness. There is still a resistance in the soul—and a power in memory to recreate its world—that save.

Like Wordsworth, who believes that heaven lies about us in our infancy,[1] the mourner in *In Memoriam* yearns to go back to an earlier time when Hallam was still alive. He is much less attracted, I think, by the prospect of moving on to some "far-off divine event" at the end of the poem. In *In Memoriam,* to remember is to be. Tennyson cannot fully value the Somersby garden until he writes about it as a place now uncared for but fully alive for the first time in his fond and loving memory of it. His "passion of the past" bears an intolerable weight of nostalgia. As John Bayley says, for poets like Tennyson and Wordsworth "to remember and to write was to create their lives, and their sense of living things. The actual experience was nothing beside it, a mere blur always on the move, always disappearing" (1999, 264). By contrast, Shakespeare's world is less a remembrance of things past than an original creation. Only in his sonnets does Shakespeare, like the Victorian poets, make beautiful lyrics out of the destruction wrought by *tempus edax.* One does not think of Shakespeare's creating Prospero's vision of a dissolving world after the event. For Shakespeare the prophecies of Prospero and Ovid *are* the event.

I used to think that "dream my dream" (123.10) was Tennyson's private joke. Instead of being unnerved by a fear of mutability, the poet refuses to be undone by the deathly sublimities foreseen by Ovid's Protagoras and scientifically established by Robert Chambers and Charles Lyell. "Dreaming his dream" and "holding it true," Tennyson seems at first to be embracing the narcissism of cognates. If so, we may discern a flicker of irony in the phrase "dream my dream," as he strives to stave off his terror of the isolating illusion to which "dream" consigns him. I think now, however, that there is a more compelling way of reading the lines: Tennyson cannot "think" Hallam's love and soul "farewell," not because it is too devastating to do so, but because it is logically impossible. For there is as much magic in the web that binds the dreamer to his dream as there is in the web that unites the tree in the garden to the perceiver of that tree. According to Tennyson's friend J. F. Ferrier, a Victorian George Berkeley, the resilient strength of the web ensures that what God has joined together no man can sunder. Let Tennyson beware: he must not rush in where angels fear to tread. Nor should he admit impediment to the marriage of true minds to nature, however hard scientists like Darwin or theologians like Bishop Wilberforce may try to divide the two partners or sanction their divorce.

A revolution in thought can as effectively dismantle a scaffold of theory as an insurrection can dismantle a grid of empire and power. We now prefer Copernicus to Ptolemy and Newton to Aristotle because we believe, like Ockham, that a simple explanation is preferable to a complex one. Clarity and economy of description help explain the replacement of the Ptolemaic universe by the Copernican; the phlogiston theory of Priestley by Lavoisier's theory of oxygen gas; and the replacement of Newton's theory of absolute positions and absolute motions by Einstein's theory of relativity. A philosophical idealist as well as an empirical Ockham, who excises Locke's material substance as a mere chimera or fiction, Berkeley insists that the qualities we perceive inhere, not in matter, but in spirit. In his dialogue with Hylas, Berkeley's Philonous vanquishes his opponent by combining a common sense theory of knowledge with a theory of being that is immaterial and ghostly. A sprightly, quixotic thinker, who writes with wit, irony, and intellectual finesse, Berkeley shows that it is just as impossible to sunder ourselves from the world we have been joined and married to in a wedding dance of spirits as it for God to sunder the world from his perception of it. Since Berkeley's world continues to exist because God keeps watching it, then "it's a good thing," as one critic quips, "that [in the Psalmist's words] God neither sleeps nor slumbers" (Frye, 2004, 84).

By using a lens or a properly placed mirror to make a ghostly subject visible, an observer can confer existence on that subject, just as Berkeley's God can sustain a ghostly world by perceiving it. In *Richard II,* the mirror that reflects the sorrowing king's image prompts him to consider how a grieving eye can compose multiple fractured images into a unified image, one that is single and whole. Infected with a kind of viral malignancy, the king's reflection in the glass splits apart into as many fragments as the "substance of a grief" with "twenty shadows." "For sorrow's eye," as Bushy explains,

> Divides one thing entire to many objects,
> Like perspectives, which rightly gaz'd upon
> Show nothing but confusion, eye'd awry
> Distinguish form;
>
> (2.2.17–20)

Only when viewed "awry" from the proper oblique angle can the confusion of images resolve into momentary clarity of vision like a sight gag, a familiar feature of perspective illusionism in baroque art. Otherwise, the eye is lost in a maze of sorrows, mirroring only images of images that compose themselves into a ghostly illusion, something neither abiding nor discernible. Richard's world then has less in common with the medieval universe that sanctifies kingship than with the phantom world David Hume compares to "a kind of theatre, where several perceptions successively make their appearance; pass, re-pass, glide away, and mingle in an infinite variety of postures and sensations" (1888, 253).

In *Julius Caesar,* Cassius spies on truth from a distance. He circles round and round his meaning, as if he wanted Brutus to apprehend the truth obliquely, en passant, like an inconspicuous pawn on a chessboard poised to surprise and take the king.

> *Cassius.* Tell me, good Brutus, can you see your face?
> *Brutus.* No, Cassius; for the eye sees not itself
> But by reflection, by some other things.
> *Cassius.* 'Tis just,
> And it is very much lamented, Brutus,
> That you have no such mirrors as will turn
> Your hidden worthiness into your eye,
> That you might see your shadow.
> (1.2.51–58)

Unable to behold itself, the eye must see itself reflected in a mirror or in the face of some observer. In trying to recruit Brutus as a fellow conspirator, Cassius is offering to serve as just such a mirror. Unless he allows Cassius to show him his shadow or reflection, Brutus will not know his own interior thoughts as well as Cassius knows them. Playing skillfully upon multiple meanings of "shadow"—the mirror, the image reflected in a mirror, and a shady region of the mind—Cassio tells Brutus that without the aid of his friend's mirror, his shadow self—the ghost behind his masks—will remain in eclipse, hidden even from himself. If, like an eye that cannot observe itself, we are ignorant of our own deepest motives, they must often seem as obscure or opaque as Hamlet's motives are to us or as Brutus's are to Brutus himself. Just as in the "lean and hungry look" of Cassius a subversive Brutus is invited to see reflected a shadow of his "hidden worthiness" (1.2.57), so in Hallam's lucidly veiled ghost a speculative Tennyson is tempted to see reflected an image that "half reveal[s] / And half conceal[s] the Soul within" (*In Memoriam* 5.3–4).[2]

As Frank Kermode has shown, Shakespeare returns to the image of the shadow and the hidden eye again and again (2000, 88–89). It is a favorite conceit of Richard II and of Achilles in *Troilus and Cressida,* who tells Ulysses that

> speculation turns not to itself,
> Till it hath travell'd and is mirror'd there
> Where it may see itself. This is not strange at all.
> (3.3.109–11)

In isolation, both the self and the world that mirrors that self are insubstantial ghosts. In Berkeley's famous phrase: "esse est percipi." To celebrate the marriage of the mind to nature in love and holy passion, Berkeley performs a wedding dance, a veritable waltz of ghosts. We exist and see ourselves only as we are seen and understood by other ghosts.

Any self-representative system, whether it be Josiah Royce's attempt to draw a map of the United States on a portion of that country's surface, or the self's attempt to represent its own annihilation, generates an infinite regress: there is no end to the process. For the map of Royce's cartographer must include in its representation that tiny portion of the country's surface on which his map is being drawn, and within that representation the even smaller surface on which he is drawing his map of that map, and so on. In a similar way, any effort of a self-conscious mind to conceive its own annihilation must posit (as the containing frame around the consciousness being annihilated) the annihilating consciousness itself. As soon as it tries to detach the annihilated self, another self springs up to frame the process. In his *Institutes of Metaphysics,* Ferrier uses just such an argument to prove we cannot in fact conceive our own death: we merely think we can. Try to detach our death from our consciousness of it, and its inconceivability becomes clear.

As soon as Tennyson thinks of an absent Hallam, that thought becomes part of his own mindscape. Every future "dream" or thought of that mindscape will include a "dream" of Hallam, and a dream of the mourner dreaming of Hallam, and so on. When the mourner dreams his dream, he is not merely using cognate forms. Rather, he is currently dreaming of an earlier dream: one of his many remembrances of Hallam. Dreaming that Hallam may be thinking of him "as in a pensive dream" (64.18), Tennyson anticipates *Through the Looking-Glass,* where the dozing Red King dreams about Alice, who is asleep and dreaming about the Red King. As one commentator notes, "In both dreams, each dreams of the other, forming a pair of infinite regresses" (Gardner, 1996, 3). Shakespeare's Prospero says that we are such stuff as dreams are made on. But if our dreams are one of the things we dream about, then whatever the world in its endless regress of dreams is searching for must be substantial somewhere. It is as inconceivable to think otherwise as to imagine an infinite universe in which our planet should have no double or twin.

In section 101 of *In Memoriam* (whose odd angle of vision, the remembrance of things no longer seen, catches the poet's eye), a garden "unwatched," "unloved," and "uncared for" also catches his breath.

> Unwatched, the garden bough shall sway,
> The tender blossoms flutter down,

Unloved, that beech will gather brown,
The maple burn itself away;

Unloved, the sun-flower, shining fair,
Ray round with flames her disk of seed,
And many a rose-carnation feed
With summer spice the humming air.
(lines 1–8)

Against the backdrop of Shakespeare's sonnets, which record the poet's memories, the oblivion wrought by time the devourer, and the glory of autumn as it burns away, Tennyson finds he can best remember the past by seeming to forget it.

Several prophecies in *The Tempest* sound Ovid's melancholy chime of mutability. As in the prophecy of Ovid's Protagoras in book 15 of his *Metamorphoses,* they foresee a day when the most solid things in nature will dissolve and melt away. Towers, temples, and palaces are lofty structures. They seem to require solid walls and basements to support them. We are therefore shocked to hear that their fabric is "baseless," a substance without foundation.

Our revels now are ended. These our actors,
As I foretold you, were all spirits and
Are melted into air, into thin air;
And, like the baseless fabric of this vision,
The cloud-capp'd towers, the gorgeous palaces,
The solemn temples, the great globe itself,
Yea, all which it inherit, shall dissolve,
And, like this insubstantial pageant faded,
Leave not a rack behind.
(*The Tempest* 4.1.148–56)

Prospero gives each noun its appropriate adjective. The towers are cloud-capped, the palaces gorgeous, the temples solemn, and even the globe itself, like Shakespeare's playhouse, is said to be great. We are more alarmed and shocked, then, when this parade of solid objects, spread across two and a half lines of stately verse, disappears suddenly in the short, three-syllable phrase "shall dissolve." As the pageant is swallowed up, vacuumed down a black hole, all that can be glimpsed in the cosmic void is an occasional rack or tattered wisp of fading cloud.

The spectacle might alarm us less if the substantial and dissolving elements were kept apart. But the pageant's two framing nouns, which ought to protect it like armor, make it vulnerable to outside attack. The stately Miltonic masque, "an insubstantial pageant faded," dissolves at once on both sides. When Prospero announces, "Our revels now are ended," a seventh-syllable caesura terminates the mask sooner than expected. To emphasize the ethereal quality of "air," Prospero also repeats the noun and reminds us how thin or tenuous it is: "melted into air, into thin air." Clouds are mentioned twice. "The cloud-capped towers" are simply lofty: they wear the heavens as a king might wear a crown. But a drifting cloud or "rack" is a mere wisp or remnant; it will soon fade and be lost forever. Such dissolution pales, however, before the ultimate dissolution, the disappearance of oneself. "We are such stuff / As dreams are made on, and our little life / Is rounded with a sleep" (4.2.156–58). Our life is not only terminated by sleep; we are encompassed or surrounded by it.

Tennyson concentrates his most Shakespearean, Prospero-like uses of "on" in stanzas 7 to 10 of section 95 of *In Memoriam.* Instead of saying "the silent-speaking words" broke the silence, he says they broke "strangely on the silence" (line 25). Inseparable from that "strangeness" is his intransitive use of "broke." Just as Wordsworth speaks of experiences "felt in the blood, and felt along the heart," challenging the assumption that the heart is only a pump, so Tennyson challenges the idea that silence is only a void. The silence that the words of the dead man's letters break upon is tangible, almost solid. It functions as a platform or a floor, something he can feel, touch, and even tread upon. Indeed, Tennyson veritably dances on the silence. He executes a glissade upon it before allowing it to shatter like glass.

Instead of dwelling in disbelief, as an atheist might inhabit a house of despair, Tennyson uses the preposition "on" (line 30) to skim or glide over the mere surface of his doubts. His strangest uses of "on" are the last two. Before claiming that his soul is wound in Hallam's and "whirled / About empyreal heights of thought," all Tennyson will say is that Hallam's "living soul was flashed on [his]" (line 36). Capturing only a flickering reflection of that flash, as in a mirror, the passive use of an intransitive verb leaves Tennyson on the mere edge of a mystery. The indefinite pronoun "this" allows Tennyson to distance himself even further: "The living soul was flashed on mine, / And mine in this was wound" (lines 36–37). Tennyson's last use of "on"—"And came on that which is, and caught / The deep pulsations of the world" (lines 40–41)—is his best, most chastening reminder that what he has merely chanced or stumbled on is something he can never fully penetrate or hope to understand. As Karen Weisman says of elegies in general, *In Memoriam* "pushes against the limits of our expressive resources precisely at the moment in which we confront our mortality, which is as much to say that it throws into relief the inefficacy of language precisely when we need it most" (2010, 1).

Bearing directly on the potency of Prospero's magic powers is the great passage on witchcraft, specter-work, and demonology in Thomas Carlyle's chapter "Natural Supernaturalism" in *Sartor Resartus.* Though Prospero is shaken by the shadow of conspiracy as surely as Luther is disturbed by visions of the devil, not all sorcery is black magic or madness. Why demean magic by calling it "Madness" or "Disease of the Nerves"?

> In every the wisest Soul lies a whole world of internal Madness, an authentic Demon-Empire; out of which, indeed, his world of Wisdom has been creatively built together, and now rests there, as on its dark foundations does a habitable, flowery Earth-rind. (Carlyle, 1970, 238)

Since the lover, the poet, and the lunatic are of imagination all compact, any world of wisdom that "has been creatively built together" will always perch perilously over dark foundations. Like any manufacture of cosmos out of chaos, poetry (and wisdom) master an "authentic Demon-Empire," an "infernal boiling-up" of a "Nether Chaotic Deep," whose transformation never ceases to astonish Shakespeare or move Carlyle to wonder.

A Victorian Prospero, quoting directly from both *Hamlet* and *The Tempest,* Carlyle substitutes for the prince of Denmark's adage "Conscience doth make cowards of us all" the axiom "Custom doth make dotards of us all" (1970, 237). As mere bastard morality, what Hegel calls *Sittlichkeit,* custom lies upon us with a weight "heavy as frost," as Wordsworth says, "And deep almost as life" ("Ode: Intimations of Immortality," lines 128–29). Familiarity with marvels blinds us to the truth that, in our stupefied state, we regard the most miraculous event as commonplace. Conflating time and space, Carlyle's astronomer beholds "all Herschel's Fifteen-thousand Suns per minute" (236), a unit that measures both sixty seconds of time and the sixtieth part of a degree on a compass. Are we to allow stupor in the presence of such marvels to decline into mere stupidity or custom? Should the charting of "some few computed centuries" or "measured square-miles" of the zodiac be allowed to dwindle into schoolroom arithmetic or into the calculus of some common land surveyor or geometer?

According to the prophet, our little life is rounded, not by Prospero's sleep, but by what Carlyle is bold enough to call "Eternity," a realm in which "minutes are as years and aeons" (242). Just as memory is a time-traveler's voyage to the past, so hope is his voyage to the future. The empirical Samuel

Johnson longed all his life to see a ghost, unaware he was a ghost himself. Carlyle's warrior and his war-horse tread the earth as if it were a solid foundation instead of a thin film spread over a seething nether deep. When the globe's fragile earth rind splits apart, all its storm troops will be swallowed up and lost, "sunk" forever beyond plummet's sounding. Echoing the famous valediction of Prospero, who vows to drown his book "deeper than did ever plummet sound," Carlyle says no plummet can measure the depth of the descent to oblivion of the warrior and his ghostly war-horse. The only element to endure as they plunge over the cliff edge of mystery is the repeating negative "A little while ago, they were *not;* a little while, and they are *not,* their very ashes are *not*" (243; italics mine).

All Carlyle is willing to affirm is that the stormy procession of life is from spirit to spirit, as in Plato's myths; from dream to dream, as in *The Tempest;* and from the darkness outside the mead hall back into darkness, as in the great parable of Venerable Bede: "We emerge from the Inane; haste stormfully across the astonished Earth; then plunge again into the Inane. Earth's mountains are leveled, and her seas filled up, in our passage" (243). As in section 123 of *In Memoriam,* the full pathos and terror of man's foothold in time comes from Ovid's and Lyell's sense that the earth itself is as unstable as man's stormy passage across it. Just as the scent of morning air summons the ghost of Hamlet's father to the underworld, so even Alexander the Great's military campaigns are specter-hunts, the coming and going of whole platoons of phantoms, in which ghosts battle ghosts.

Phantoms are shaped into bodies, then vanish into air, lost in the scouring oblivion of *tempus edax rerum,* which washes out all traces of the past. To have life, a ghost should possess the personality and creative resource of a magician like Prospero, through whom there runs an odd strain of Stoicism, as if he were a quixotic, mercurial version of the Roman emperor Marcus Aurelius, who holds in his *Meditations* that "all things of the body are as a river, and things of the soul as a dream and a vapor." "Finely compressed in 'baseless fabric,'" "the stuff' of dreams," as Reuben Brower observes, "is at once cloud-stuff (air) and cloth" (1951, 115). In calling our life the stuff of dreams, Prospero is not merely saying that "our little life" is as fragile as a dream. We are not only made *of* a dreamlike fabric. *Upon* the surface of that fabric, we construct such strange conjectures of origins and ends as make the angels weep. Driven by panic and fear, Prospero's great prophecy of dissolution seems out of all proportion to its immediate cause: a threat of revolt that leaves his "old brain" vexed. In the sleep that rounds out his little life, Prospero is seeking an anodyne. His prophecy rises unbidden, like an apocalypse, out of an infirm and troubled mind.

However subject we may be to dissolution, *The Tempest* keeps intimating that we are more than just passing phantoms or ghosts. We are also *embodied* spirits: living statues, Hermiones of matter molded into spirit, chiseled out of air. As Harold Goddard asks, "How else could things as frail as dreams have survived the tempest and chaos of material evolution? 'How with this rage shall beauty hold a plea / Whose action is no stronger than a flower?'" (1951, 678). When released by Prospero, Ariel does not use his freedom to fly away into a world of disembodied air. On the contrary, he continues to suck "where the bee sucks . . . / In a cowslip's bell." The marriage of spirit to nature is as indissoluble as Ferdinand's love for Miranda or as Romeo's for Juliet. Rightly to perceive the world is to see it through the eye of a loving intellect or awakened imagination.

In Prospero's second farewell speech, the absence of any strongly end-stopped lines allows his clauses to cascade majestically over the edge of a line or else halt prematurely at a mid-line break.

> Ye elves of hills, brooks, standing lakes, and groves,
> And ye that on the sands with printless foot
> Do chase the ebbing Neptune, and do fly him
> When he comes back; you demi-puppets that
> By moonshine do the green sour ringlets make,
> Whereof the ewe not bites; and you whose pastime
> Is to make the midnight mushrumps, that rejoice
> To hear the solemn curfew; by whose aid
> (Weak masters though ye be) I have bedimmed
> The noontide sun, call'd forth the mutinous winds,
> And 'twixt the green sea and the azured vault
> Set roaring war; to the dread rattling thunder
> Have I given fire and rifted Jove's stout oak
> With his own bolt.
>
> (5.1.33–46)

The oddest feature of the speech is its lack of a principal verb. Though the elves of the hills, the demi-puppets, and the spirits that wander earth at night are all impressively summoned, they are not exhorted to do anything. The imperatives of command are missing. It is as if Milton's Satan were to hold his council in hell and announce to the fallen angels that there is nothing to decide or do. Perhaps the old magician's mind has begun to wander. He may be so beguiled by his power to darken the sun, summon the winds, and cause the tides to rise in the past that he forgets what he wants to do now.

Though Prospero uses expansive run-on lines to celebrate his godlike acts of opening graves and calling forth mutinous winds, he announces in two brief, four-syllable clauses his decision to "abjure" his "rough magic" and "drown" his "book."

> But this rough magic
> I here abjure; and when I have required
> Some heavenly music (which even now I do)
> To work mine end upon their senses that
> This airy charm is for, I'll break my staff,
> Bury it certain fathoms in the earth,
> And deeper than did ever plummet sound
> I'll drown my book.
>
> (5.1, 50–57)

Since Prospero's splendid set piece is based on a speech of Ovid's Medea, a sorceress who is also an infanticide in *Metamorphoses* 7.197–209, we may well ask if his magic is a civilizing force or an agent of subversion. Though his incantations can induce a settled calm, they can also intoxicate and excite. The vision of art as both blasphemy and benediction, as both a parody of God's creative word and a power to order chaos, informs everything the magician says.

Because *The Tempest*'s epilogue harks back to two earlier leave-takings in the play, its farewell to the audience is a valediction more resonant and solemnly magical than Feste's beautifully sad farewell speech in *Twelfth Night.* The first speech to nest inside the epilogue is the great prophecy of dissolution in which Prospero both celebrates and takes leave of his revels. The second nesting speech is the one just quoted in which Prospero abjures his magic. Though art can be entertainment (as in Prospero's masque to divert the newlyweds) or magic (as in his performance of potent deeds), it can also be supplication for divine mercy or human forgiveness. Such is the art of prayer that Prospero associates with the theological language of his epilogue.

> Now I want
> Spirits to enforce, art to enchant;
> And my ending is despair
> Unless I be reliev'd by prayer,
> Which pierces so that it assaults
> Mercy itself and frees all faults.
> As you from crime would pardoned be,
> Let your indulgence set me free.
>
> (Epilogue, lines 13–20)

We should not minimize the audacity of Prospero's appeal. It is surely daring (if not blasphemous) to transfer to an approving and forgiving audience the power of absolution usually invested in a priest or God. As a magician who opened graves and raised storms, Prospero may have trespassed on God's powers. Since the defenseless Prospero, stripped of his magic, may fear divine disfavor, the audience's applause is associated with something immeasurably greater than approval of a play. It is prayer for the magician's release. "Forgive me my crimes," Prospero entreats the audience, "as you would have a merciful god free you from yours." His words endow the audience with more power than it anticipates. For just as Prospero himself has freed Ariel, so the audience, as a gracious and surrogate god, is now implored to free Prospero.

Even though Prospero has forsworn his magic, the tetrameter couplets of his prophetic epilogue are linked formally to the masques he has conjured. Has Prospero's art or his power to invoke spirits been a crime? Have his prophecies been subversive? In supplicating a higher power than art—mercy, forgiveness, and the "rarer action" that lies in "virtue than in vengeance," Prospero has been purifying rather than corrupting the consciousness of his audience. Since we wish Prospero and the greater magician who created him to prosper, the gentle breath of approval is a grace no playgoer is willing to withhold.

The most memorable Victorian sonnets on Shakespeare (by Browning, Hopkins, Swinburne, Meredith, and Arnold) all celebrate his godlike, Olympian qualities. But they also betray a thinly disguised "anxiety of influence." In his sonnet "The Names," Browning says that, unlike the biblical prophets who feared to profane God by naming him, nothing impedes fellow poets from pronouncing Shakespeare's name. Yet the same awe that led the prophets to contemplate God in silence pervades Browning's veneration of his great precursor. A belated immigrant into realms of thought once charted before him by Shakespeare, Browning recognizes that his own "finite" world proceeds from the antecedent "infinite" world of the poet who not only preceded but also in some sense "invented" him (lines 13–14).

Browning turns Shakespeare into the same Prospero-like magician summoned by Carlyle in "Natural Supernaturalism." Though Carlyle has more in common with Fichte and Nietzsche than with Paracelsus or Shakespeare, Browning and his wife continue to revere Carlyle as the Fourth Person of the Trinity. Like the musical genius who names "the ineffable Name" in "Abt Vogler," the Shakespeare Browning invokes is a great necromancer, another Prospero or Paracelsus, second in majesty only to the God who brooded over creation in Genesis, and who in Hebrew tradition—as Elohim or the tetragrammaton, YHVH—is too sublime to name.

> Shakespeare!—to such name's sounding, what
> succeeds

> Fitly as silence? Falter forth the spell,—
> Act follows words, the speaker knows full well,
> Nor tampers with its magic more than needs.
> Two names there are: That which the Hebrew reads
> With his soul only; if from lips it fell,
> Echo, back thundered by earth, heaven and hell,
> Would own "Thou didst create us!"
> ("The Names," lines 1–8)

As in God's creation through verbal fiat, "Let there be light, and there was light," so in Shakespeare "act follows word." Spellbound admirers of his art are silent in its presence. They dare not tamper with its power. Like the Nameless of the hundred Names in Tennyson's poem "The Ancient Sage," Shakespeare is a creator and sustainer of worlds. If his art is godlike—a majestic and daunting "invention of the human," as Harold Bloom believes, then a promised end or goal of all poets must be to make Shakespeare's works their worship and delight. As Pope says of Homer, they should read him by day and meditate by night.

A similar drama unfolds in Hopkins's unfinished sonnet on Shakespeare. The special prerogative of Hopkins, "this Jack, joke," is to make himself what Christ is, "immortal diamond." Miraculously, this feat has already been achieved by Shakespeare, whose spirit started "Upwards at once [to] win [its] aureoles" (line 8). Like Scotus, Hopkins believes an elect soul can leap at once to a univocal apprehension of God without painstakingly climbing a ladder of analogy. In the case of a master spirit like Shakespeare, it may be equally possible for Hopkins to be spared the effort of laboriously mounting a ladder of judicious critical evaluation. Just as no human soul can scan the scroll in which the book of life is written, so no critic is to be canvassed for votes by declaring for or against the greatness of Shakespeare. Yet strong and credible premonitions are entertained by Hopkins, who venerates Shakespeare and even translates into Greek and Latin songs from *The Merchant of Venice* and *The Tempest.* Though the heavens will not unveil themselves, there is much Hopkins "guesses" about Shakespeare or intuitively "knows."

Jumping the gap between the Last Judgment and death, Shakespeare has beaten Scotus at his own game. God's "dateless thought" has closed the gap between Doomsday and death, and assigned Shakespeare his proper home among the immortals.

> In the lodges of the perishable souls
> He has his portion. God, who stretched apart
> Doomsday and death—whose dateless thought must
> chart

All time at once and span the distant goals,
Sees what his place is; but for us the rolls
Are shut against the canvassing of art.
Something we guess or know; some spirits start
Upwards at once and win the aureoles.
("Shakspere")

Hopkins takes the phrase "dateless night," which Shakespeare applies to "death," and transfers it to "thought" instead. The long span of time separating death from Doomsday contracts in God's mind to nothing. It is not for God a distant goal at all. As a super-critic, a judge of art as well as souls, God has already assessed and confirmed Shakespeare's supremacy as a poet.[3]

In his sonnet on Shakespeare, Swinburne surfs his way to the far shore of tribute, where "Shakespeare's praise is this,—he can be praised by none."

Not if men's tongues and angels' all in one
Spake, might the word be said that might
speak Thee.
Streams, winds, woods, flowers, fields, moun-
tains, yea, the sea,
What power is in them all to praise the sun?
His praise is this,—he can be praised of none.
("William Shakespeare," lines 1–5)

If Swinburne is belated in his praise, it is not because Shakespeare ever surfed on a sea of words such as Swinburne braves. Nor is Swinburne thwarted because prior celebrants of Shakespeare have exhausted everything to be said on his behalf. Swinburne cannot praise Shakespeare as his subject deserves because, as Hopkins also ventures to suggest, the playwright inhabits an eternity as vast and dateless as "time's own period."

All joy, all glory, all sorrow, all strength, all mirth
Are his; without him, day were night on earth.
Time knows not his from time's own period.
All lutes, all harps, all viols, all flutes, all lyres
Fall dumb before him ere one string suspires.
All stars are angels; but the sun is God.
(lines 9–14)

The crowded name lists, a feature of the epic manner, evoke the grand commotion of *Paradise Lost.* But if Milton is an angelic spirit and a "star," only Shakespeare constitutes a sun. As a god or titan, an Apollo or Hyperion, Shakespeare's essence is just to exist. Like Aristotle's "Unmoved Mover," he "exults not to be worshipped" but "to be" (line 7).

The most Olympian and detached Victorian Shakespeare appears in Arnold's sonnet on the playwright, which makes "the heaven of heavens" Shakespeare's "dwelling-place," and which hides from "the foiled searching of mortality" the "cloudy border of his base" (lines 6–8). Anticipating and preempting the Stoic Arnold of "Resignation" and "Mycerinus," the Shakespeare of Arnold's sonnet is said to be "Self-schooled, self-scanned, self-honored, self-secure." Though other poets may submit to scrutiny, Arnold's Shakespeare refuses to consolidate the mental level on which most inquiry is conducted. Like Socrates, he answers questions by inviting better ones.

> Others abide our question. Thou art free.
> We ask and ask: Thou smilest and art still,
> Out-topping knowledge. For the loftiest hill
> That to the stars uncrowns his majesty,
> Planting his steadfast footsteps in the sea,
> Making the Heaven of Heavens his dwelling-place,
> Spares but the cloudy borders of his base
> To the foil'd searching of mortality:
> And thou, who didst the stars and sunbeams know,
> Self-school'd, self-scann'd, self-honor'd, self-secure,
> Didst walk on Earth unguess'd at. Better so!
> All pains the immortal spirit must endure,
> All weakness that impairs, all griefs that bow,
> Find their sole voice in that victorious brow.
>
> "Shakespeare"

Nina Auerbach calls Arnold's "nobly mountainous" Shakespeare "an inscrutable specter of nature whose smiling stillness" he "exalts into demi-divinity" (2003, 192). An Olympian god, Arnold's Shakespeare "out-tops knowledge," both because his personal life and beliefs elude the scrutiny of biographers and because by temperament he is a Proteus or ghost, a specter with the least to say but the most to disclose.

Like the Stoics, Shakespeare's impenetrable shade seeks a center of repose and calm, removed from all "weakness that impairs" and "griefs that bow." He is as still or silent as the stars and tranquil as the sea. But as we round the corner of line 2, we discover he is "still" as well in the adverbial sense of "always." "Still out-topping knowledge," he is constantly, invariably surpassing what we know about him. Though in his power to outdistance us Shakespeare is as lofty and abiding as the stars, he is also heroically anchored in an Emersonian reliance on the "self," a noun Arnold repeats four times in a single line. The only visible sign of the conflict discerned in Shakespeare by Keats—a fierce dispute between damnation and impassioned clay—is his blank facial expression. Only in the "victorious brow" of his portrait, which is mute and dumb, do the secrets of Shakespeare's heart and mind begin to approximate anything so unique or articulate as a voice.

One of the few Victorians to celebrate Shakespeare in English or Shakespearean rather than Italian sonnets is George Meredith. His two sonnets on Shakespeare celebrate England's greatest poet and playwright as a child of Mother Earth. He was not a cynic like Jacques, or a misanthrope like Thersites who jeered at "love deflowered." On the contrary, Shakespeare's loving intellect embraced both the wise wit of Rosalind, as she explored and refined her love for Orlando, and the genial wit of Falstaff, as he expressed his deep affection for Hal.

> Thy greatest knew thee, Mother Earth; unsoured
> He knew thy sons. He probed from hell to hell
> Of human passions, but of love deflowered
> His wisdom was not, for he knew thee well.
> Thence came the honeyed corner at his lips,
> The conquering smile wherein his spirit sails
> Calm as the God who the white sea-wave whips,
> Yet full of speech and intershifting tales,
> Close mirrors of us.
>
> ("The Spirit of Shakespeare," lines 1–9)

Though Shakespeare was as calm as the Stoic Olympian Arnold celebrates, Meredith's god knew how to come down from the mountain as well as ascend it. His genius was as wedded to nature as Aristotle's final and formal causes were inseparable from matter. Serene amid the storm, Meredith's Shakespeare was calm even when whipped by waves he conjured from the deep like Prospero.

With a soul as wide and comprehensive as the gaze of ten thousand cattle as they graze at pasture, Shakespeare's conquering smile is the smile of Mother Earth herself. Meredith is the great Victorian celebrant of Shakespeare's power to awaken "spiritual life in the animal man," to "redeem man" and "earth in all [their] materiality" (Goddard, 1951, 80). When philosophy is divorced from matter, when it becomes its adversary or alien instead of its soul, then Earth is left to fatten. Without soul the world languishes, and without vision it dies.

> thence thy songs, that winnow chaff
> From grain, bid sick Philosophy's last leaves
> Whirl, if they have no response—they enforced
> To fatten Earth when from her soul divorced.
>
> ("The Spirit of Shakespeare," lines 11–14)

The unnatural severance of vision from matter, of spirit from earth, sanctions an unnatural use of word order ("they enforced / to fatten"), which gives an appropriately awkward wrench or turn to the sonnet's last two lines. Though Meredith looks as deeply into the abyss as Hardy does, he extols in Mother Earth the same inspired sanity and robust sense of comedy he finds in Shakespeare.

The second of Meredith's two sonnets on Shakespeare claims that, instead of viewing "the beauteous face" of nature "in a cracked glass," the playwright anticipates and affirms Wordsworth's belief that nature is a nurse, a guide, a guardian of the heart, and soul of all our moral being. Not even in *King Lear* does Shakespeare endorse Tennyson's view that nature is a wicked stepmother, a "rigid harridan," "red in tooth and claw," who holds her wretched victims captive "till the end of time." The disenchantment of a Pessimist-Anticant like Thomas Carlyle or of a world-weary atheist like James Thomson, poet of "The City of Dreadful Night," would draw from Shakespeare only a wry grin or amused smile.

> How smiles he at a generation ranked
> In gloomy noddings over life! They pass.
> Not he to feed upon a breast unthanked,
> Or eye a beauteous face in a cracked glass.
> But he can spy that little twist of brain
> Which moved some weighty leader of the blind,
> Unwitting 't was the goad of personal pain,
> To view in curst eclipse our Mother's mind,
> And show us of some rigid harridan
> The wretched bondmen till the end of time.
> O lived the Master now to paint us Man,
> That little twist of brain would ring a chime
> Of whence it came and what it caused, to start
> Thunders of laughter, clearing air and heart.
> ("The Spirit of Shakespeare—Continued")

By what "twist of brain" could such anomalies as Hamlet's angelic paragon, the god who is also the quintessence of dust, produce such discords in the scale of being as an intellectual without love? Like the witty male students at the academy of Navarre, who are in love with words about love but not with love itself, only some perverse "twist of brain" could make man, the paragon of animals, play such fantastic tricks before high heaven as make the angels weep.

It is not for Meredith or anyone to say what distemper of heart or brain led Iago to destroy Othello. No one knows what led the bastard Edmund to eclipse the main of light, the sun of our beneficent mother, by preying upon humanity like some monster of the deep. Only some "goad of personal pain" could trick a cynic into saying one touch of fallen nature makes the whole world kin. Rather than explain the mystery of iniquity or deliver some prophecy of doom, Shakespeare, were he alive today, would celebrate the power of imagination to bring order out of chaos. Echoing the thunder of Falstaff's boisterous laugh or the wise wit of Rosalind, Shakespeare would exalt and extol the power of that "little twist of brain," the divine faculty in man, to mold earth's matter into its own shape, like stone in the hands of an accomplished sculptor.

12

Oracle Meets Wit

THE PROMISED END

LITERARY INFLUENCE IS NEVER A MATTER OF MERE QUOTATION. It also embraces more elusive elements of rhetoric and style. One unexpected discovery made in the course of this study is that Browning and Hopkins, the Victorian poets who sound most like Shakespeare, allude to him less often than do Tennyson and Clough. Few monologues are more Ovidian (and hence Shakespearean) in subject matter than Tennyson's "Tithonus," whose speaker in Greek myth suffers the indignity of being turned into a grasshopper. But the poem is full of sound effects and grammatical devices that are less typical of Shakespeare than of Keats and Milton. Aligning Browning and Hopkins with Shakespeare are two rhetorical tropes, asyndeton and hendiadys.

> Lust
> Is perjured, murderous, bloody, full of blame,
> Savage, extreme, rude, cruel, not to trust.
> (sonnet 129, lines 2–4)

Asyndeton, or the dropping of connectives, imparts a savage chop to Shakespeare's lines. Incisive caesural breaks compact a sense of riot and madness in the blood with a sense of pained and heavy breathing. Equally frenetic and terror-stricken are the lines in which Browning's Caliban, a vengeful David Hume, sheds connective words as fast as Hume sheds fictions of causal necessity.

> "So must he do henceforth and always."—Ay?
> Would teach the reasoning couple what "must" means!
> 'Doth as he likes, or wherefore Lord? So He.
> ("Caliban upon Setebos," lines 238–40)

Though Browning, like Shakespeare, retains many Latinate words, he "moves," as one critic says, "toward the native English monosyllable, which often makes his verse creak and grind with its knots of consonants: "Irks care the crop-full bird? Frets doubt the maw-crammed beast?" (De Vane, 1954, 478). Often Hopkins's style is equally contorted and elliptical.

> But how shall I . . . make me a room there:
> Reach me a . . . Fancy, come faster—
> Strike you the sight of it? look at it loom there,
> Thing that she . . . there then! the Master,
> *Ipse,* the only one, Christ, King, Head.
> ("The Wreck of the Deutschland," 28.1–5)

Language falters, halts, then stops altogether, reduced to fragments by a daring use of aposiopesis, the rhetorical art of breaking off in the middle of a sentence, as if from some deep reluctance or incapacity to proceed. Of this technique Shakespeare's Antony in the funeral oration from *Julius Caesar* is the undisputed master.

In his sonnet "Thou art indeed just, Lord," Hopkins shares Lear's distaste of procreation or breeding. The dropping of connectives, the rude alliteration, and the sharp caesural breaks are as harsh and intemperate as Shakespeare's.

> Wert thou my enemy, O thou my friend,
> How wouldst thou worse, I wonder, than thou dost
> Defeat, thwart me?
> (lines 5–7)

"The sots and thralls of lust" may thrive more than Hopkins. But what if they beget monsters by their breeding, who betray their progenitors, condemn them to death, or torture them like Edmund? Shakespeare views both childlessness and parenthood with terror. Lear experiences parenthood, the fathering of "Pelican Daughters," as nemesis. And Edgar tells his brother that "the dark and vicious place" where their father begot him cost Gloucester his eyes. But the terror of being childless is just as great. Without heirs, Macbeth's desire to be founder of a royal line will be thwarted. And in sonnet 16 Shakespeare's reproof of the youth who refuses to propagate his kind is as gently stern as it is witty and paradoxical: "To give away yourself keeps your self still." Equally oppressed by celibacy, Hopkins, "Time's eunuch," who builds not but strains, expresses dismay that he alone can breed no "work that wakes." In sonnet 13 Shakespeare chides the celibate youth: "You had a Father, let your Son say so." He would rather commit an Irish bull than thwart the purpose of a creator who built procreation into the dictionary definition of "father." Indeed, even Hopkins's God wouldn't be God unless he were Father to a Son. The rest of creation breeds and fathers-forth. Why should Hopkins alone, like the surly celibate in Shakespeare's sixteenth sonnet, refuse to procreate? As the sonnet approaches its close, however, the courteous and prophetic tones of a prayerful servant begin tempering and displacing the indignant pleas of a plaintiff in a law court. It is hard to exaggerate the difference in tone between the cold, distant "Lord" of justice in the plaintiff's opening arraignment and the gracious "Lord of life" who sends his "roots rain" in the hushed and awe-filled prayer of the closing line.

The trope that binds Shakespeare most securely to Browning and Hopkins is hendiadys, the figure of speech that splits an expression in two, and which means literally "one-through-two." The phrase "austerity and garb," a hendiadys Aufidius uses to describe Coriolanus, strikes a note of patrician aloofness and hauteur. Browning uses hendiadys to define similar qualities in his aristocratic Duke of Ferrara, who speaks of "the depth and passion" of his dead wife's "earnest glance." Instead of marveling at her "deep feeling," Browning's Duke uses hendiadys to give increased formality and Latinate elegance to her "pictured countenance." Like metaphor, hendiadys allows Browning to keep several meanings afloat. Does the duchess, with X-ray vision, see deeply into the Duke? Or does the glance reflect a depth of feeling in herself?

Shakespeare's most pervasive use of hendiadys occurs in *Hamlet,* where Frank Kermode detects "a sort of pathological intensification of the device" (2000, 102). To express contempt for the hedonist who merely sleeps and feeds, Hamlet uses a hendiadys, "his chief good and market of his time" (4.4.34), to equate the main duty and glory of life with the shameless sale and gluttonous consumption of food. At its most compulsive, hendiadys dominates the repetitious counsel of Polonius.

> And thus do we of wisdom and of reach,
> With windlasses and with assays of bias,
> By indirections find directions out;
> So by my former lecture and advice,
> Shall you, my son.
>
> (*Hamlet* 2.1.64–68)

In these lines the genuine hendiadys of "wisdom and of reach" (where "wise" modifies the act of reaching) turns into a mere double epithet, where a conjunction is used to join two words of identical or similar meaning: "windlasses" and "assays," for example, or "lecture and advice."

In his essay "Hendiadys and *Hamlet,*" George T. Wright alerts the reader to the disturbing unease and sense of terror these doublings may create. Kermode notes that Claudius uses a "sinister doublet" in his first conversation with Hamlet: "But now, my cousin Hamlet, and my son." This remark, Kermode says, "sums up in advance the evil doubling that is at the heart of the play and to which Hamlet, in his first line, replies with another punning doublet: 'A little more than kin, and less than kind' (64–65)" (Kermode, 2000, 103). Terrified that he may have to give evidence against himself, "even to the teeth and forehead of his faults," Claudius later uses hendiadys to give a grotesque twist, bordering on caricature, to his guilt. Unless we consider carefully Shakespeare's predilection for wrenched syntax and for such tricks of rhetoric and grammar as asyndeton and hendiadys, we shall be left with a highly distorted impression of his influence. It will be hard to understand why Tennyson, though more saturated with allusions to Shakespeare, is still a less Shakespearean poet than Hopkins or Browning. The Shakespeare who haunts the Victorians may be heard in Tennyson's allusion to *Hamlet:* "That hoard, and sleep, and feed, and know not me" ("Ulysses," line 5). But that allusion occurs, as we have seen, in a monologue whose blank verse sounds more like Milton's than Shakespeare's. We recover a more authentic Shakespeare in Hopkins's "No worst, there is none," a sonnet that not only alludes to *King Lear* but that also abounds in such Shakespearean habits of speech as wrenched syntax, ellipsis, and asyndeton.

The most Shakespearean attribute of the Victorian poets, however, is not their addiction to hendiadys or hyperbaton but their reticence, the classical restraint of their great monologues, and their sudden descent from grandeur to simplicity. *Maud,* for example, is the kind of poem that all festive love celebrations from the Song of Songs to Spenser's "Epithalamium" and Shakespeare's *Antony and Cleopatra* exist to express. But it also includes the simplicity of "I have led her home, my love, my only friend," which combines the lyric joy of "Go not, happy day" with the marveling ease of a psalm-like prayer. For the two-way, sometimes opposite kinds of vision that grow from the heart of Shakespeare's plays, few poets have a greater feel than the Tennyson who wrote "Ulysses" and the two Mariana monologues or than the Browning who wrote "Caliban upon Setebos" and "Childe Roland to the Dark Tower Came." Does the figure traced by "Childe Roland" have a center, like *The Winter's Tale* and *The Tempest,* with the result that Alpha is Omega and the end also a new beginning? Is it something Prospero might create? Or is Roland's pilgrimage, like Lear's, a tortuous maze that ends only in a mocking cul de sac?

To illustrate the "natural magic" of Shakespeare's first or lyric voice, Matthew Arnold cites Lorenzo's lines in *The Merchant of Venice.*

> The moon shines bright. In such a night as this,
> When the sweet wind did gently kiss the trees,
> And they did make no noise, in such a night

Troilus, methinks, mounted the Trojan walls—
 . . . in such a night
Did Thisbe fearfully o'ertip the dew—
 . . . in such a night
Stood Dido, with a willow in her hand,
Upon the wild sea-banks, and waved her love
To come again to Carthage.

(5.1.1–12)

Opening on a note of Greek radiance, "The moon shines bright," Lorenzo passes at once into a world of sweet winds and gently kissed trees, where nature proves as amorous as Troilus, Thisbe, and Dido. Like Wordsworth's beauteous evening, "calm and free," Lorenzo's noiseless night seems holy as a nun, "breathless with adoration." But what begins as a chaste love song ends "upon the wild sea-banks" with a gesture of farewell and a premonition of being stranded and betrayed. As Dido, willow in hand, waves "her love / To come again to Carthage," she foreshadows one of those lost souls in Virgil's underworld who stretch forth their hands in love of a farther shore.

Lorenzo's words can be heard behind Arnold's plea in "The Scholar-Gipsy," where more arresting than the expansive Miltonic simile comparing the scholar to a Tyrian trader is the concentrated Shakespearean simile comparing him to Dido. "Fly hence, our contact fear!" Arnold passionately exhorts the scholar:

Still fly, plunge deeper in the bowering wood!
 Averse, as Dido did with gesture stern
 From her false friend's approach in Hades turn,
Wave us away, and keep thy solitude!

("The Scholar-Gipsy," lines 207–10)

The great discourtesy of Dido, as she turns her back on her unfaithful lover, is caught in the suspended grammar. All the adjective "Averse" can cling to is the elided pronoun "thou," the subject of three imperatives: "fly," "Wave . . . away," and "keep thy solitude." Using wrenched syntax ("gesture stern") and the graceless stutter of "Dido" and "did," Arnold's simile captures the essential trauma and melancholy of Virgil's epic, whose most famous line speaks of tears. Just as melancholy is inseparable from the scholar's constant sacrifice of his ignoble present to a noble past, so, as Dido turns away from Aeneas in the underworld, many readers find themselves moved by the same element of sacrifice in Virgil. His compassion embraces not only losers like Dido and Turnus but also the victor, Aeneas, who has to sacrifice love for the future good of Rome. Behind Dido's contempt for Aeneas, the lover who deserted her, it is hard, I think, not to detect Arnold's own scorn of faithless philistines and sciolists, enemies of "sweetness and light" who oppose in principle any tradition of humane or liberal learning in their culture.

The creation of a third, dramatic voice in poetry is the special achievement of Shakespeare's plays. It is an achievement no Victorian poet can match. By trying to dramatize "action in character" rather than "character in action," Browning indulges a damaging impulse to concentrate on the complex psychology of one leading character instead of distributing his interest equally among several characters. If Browning is a dramatic poet, his "dramatic gifts are best exercised," as Eliot says, "outside of the theatre. . . . How many of us have read a play by Browning more than once; and, if we have read it more than once, was our motive the expectation of enjoyment? What personage, in a play by Browning, remains living in our mind?" (1961, "Three Voices," 102).

Unlike Browning, who is a master of the second rhetorical voice of poetry but not of Shakespeare's third dramatic voice, Tennyson enjoys limited distinction as a playwright. Instead of allowing only one or two imaginary persons to talk poetry on the stage, Tennyson writes plays like *Becket* and *Queen Mary,* which more evenly distribute the dramatic interest. Like his monologue "St. Simeon Stylites," these plays explore the psychology of martyrdom in Becket, in the Protestant martyrs put to death by Mary, and in Mary herself, who is martyr to a fanatical ideal. Since one seldom, if ever, beats Shakespeare at his own game of writing in the third, dramatic voice of poetry, or of having a soul comprehensive enough to identify with every character in a play, it may be prudent for a playwright to accept some rhetorical expedient or prophetic compromise. To give his audience the shudder that T. S. Eliot claims to get from *In Memoriam,* Tennyson introduces the choral commentary of Cardinal Pole: "Our altar is a mound of dead men's clay / Dug from the grave that yawns for us beyond" (1908, *Queen Mary* 5.2). To generate similar shock waves in *Murder in the Cathedral,* Eliot creates a chorus of Canterbury women, who pass from the horrors of assassination and death to the Last Judgment and then to a final "Emptiness, absence, separation from God" (1935, 77). Behind the visible agents of death, beyond the cramped thin spondees of "the white flat face of Death," and even behind the throne of Judgment itself, stands the great reflexive image of the Void, collapsing everything inside it like a black hole or burned-out star.

In "A Death in the Desert," Browning, the most speculative and metaphysically probing of the Victorian poets, reports the dying words of St. John, the most philosophical and cultured of the Gospel writers. Sounding as much like Plato as a biblical prophet, John is the metaphysician who tries to make sense of the first three Gospels by viewing them as a way of placing and timing an eternal mystery. Like the paradox of the Word within a word, unable to speak a word, the irony of the Word's entry into a world that fails to recognize it as its own creator is analogous to the world's denying that an obscure, underbred glover's son from Stratford could have created plays and sonnets of surpassing excellence and worth. If we cannot hold the elements together, living with the paradox or taming it, then we may find it detonating in our face like an explosive.

Just as the three Persons of the Trinity provide Browning with a paradigm of Power, Love, and Knowledge, which shapes his understanding of faculty psychology and God in *Paracelsus* and "Saul," so Ariel's exquisite songs function like Luke's canticles as the voice of the spirit; the loving and beloved Cordelia operates as a "soul in bliss"; and decrees like Lear's "Take physic, pomp; / Expose thyself to feel what wretches feel" (3.4.33–34), or "He that parts us shall bring a brand from heaven / And fire us hence like foxes" (5.2.22–23), take on the authority of a commanding legislator, a prophetic father or seer.

T. S. Eliot's first or lyric voice of poetry, which is a voice in a state of rapt communion, either with itself or someone else, can be heard in the songs of Ariel in *The Tempest.* "Full fathom five" is a magical song, spoken by a spirit of the air to Ferdinand. Eliot's second voice of poetry, the voice of persuasion, is heard most distinctly in Prospero's reminder that "the rarer action is / In virtue than in vengeance" (*The Tempest* 5.1.27–28); in Brabantio's advice to Othello: "Look to her, Moor, if thou hast eyes to see; / She has deceived her father, and may thee" (*Othello* 1.3.293–94); and in Kent's prophetic words to Lear: "See better, Lear, and let me still remain / The true blank of thine eye" (*King Lear* 1.1.158–59). Eliot's third voice of poetry, the dramatic, is preeminently Shakespeare's, the voice of the poet speaking through a dramatic character. We hear such a voice not only in his plays but also in his sonnets, which are less confessional lyrics than dramatic masks. As Stephen Greenblatt explains, "The sonnets are a cunning sequence of beautiful locked boxes to which there are no keys, an exquisitely constructed screen behind which it is virtually impossible to venture with any confidence" (2004, 249).

In Shakespeare, as in the Victorian poets, we occasionally overhear a voice more universal and disinterested than the playwright's voice or the voice of a dramatic character. This voice speaks to us out of the whirlwind of a mind possessed or inspired, and comes from the far side of rhetoric or applied persuasion: "Men must endure / Their going hence, even as their coming hither," for example, or "There is providence in the fall of sparrow." Just as lines from the "Dark house" elegy in *In Memoriam* give Eliot a shudder, so a fourth voice in Shakespeare leaves his soul in a quiver. Though Eliot never actually speaks of this voice, he comes close to identifying it when he writes in "The

Three Voices of Poetry," "And finally, there are the lines, in plays by one of the supreme poetic dramatists, in which we hear a more impersonal voice still than that of either the character or the author: 'Ripeness is all,' or 'Simply the thing I am / Shall make me live'" (1961, 110).

In an earlier study, *Origins of the Monologue: The Hidden God,* I tried to distinguish between the rhetorical voice of a Victorian monologue and the dramatic voice of a Shakespearean soliloquy. Tennyson's monologue "Ulysses" is a mask lyric. It uses the printed voice of Dante's and Homer's Greek hero as a thinly veiled disguise for Tennyson's own lyric reveries. A rhetorical rather than a lyric mask, Browning's monologue "Caliban upon Setebos" uses the printed voice of Shakespeare's precocious savage in *The Tempest* as a mouthpiece for ideas that combine the introspections of Hamlet with the theology of a Victorian Bishop Butler. By contrast, in Hamlet's own soliloquies we overhear rather than hear a dramatic character speaking. A prince of men, Hamlet thinks it an offense against the divinity that shapes his ends to limit the illumination of his godlike apprehensions in the domain of thought. But it is always Hamlet, not Shakespeare, whom we hear speaking. Like Houdini, Bilbo Baggins, or the god of the deists, the playwright has performed a disappearing act. Unlike the Victorian poets, who are always onstage or speaking through a mask, Shakespeare, a god of many masks, has magically withdrawn from his creation. As T. S. Eliot says, "If you seek for Shakespeare, you will find him only in the characters he has created; for the one thing in common between the characters is that no one but Shakespeare could have created them. The world of a great poetic dramatist is a world in which the creator is everywhere present, and everywhere hidden" (1961, "Three Voices," 112), an omnipresent but invisible god.

Shakespeare, in other words, never speaks through Hamlet in "To be, or not to be" or even through Prospero in "Our revels now are ended" in the same hortatory or deliberative way that Browning, the Christian apologist, speaks through the Arab physician Karshish, or through the Greek philosopher Cleon. At rare moments, however, we do hear the second, rhetorical voice of Victorian poetry turning into an oracular fourth voice, less polemical and more disinterested. Even in "An Epistle of Karshish," we can catch the voice of the poet behind the mask undergoing a sea-change. We hear it turning into that strange and ghostly fourth voice of poetry, more disinterested than coercive, which conveys "just that combination of intelligibility and remoteness" that T. S. Eliot finds in Shakespeare (1932, 241).

> The very God! Think Abib; dost thou think?
> So, the All-Great, were the All-Loving too—

> So, through the thunder comes a human voice
> Saying, "O heart I made, a heart beats here!"
> (lines 304–7)

Admittedly, neither the voice that speaks to Karshish through the thunder nor the comfort that Hopkins throws out to the wretch in the storm in "No worst, there is none" rises to the grandeur of the words that ignite Lear's rage for order or fuel Hamlet's tribute to the glory of man, the paragon of animals. But we should not expect every god on Olympus to be Zeus. Instead of waiting for an oracle, for a voice that speaks out of the whirlwind of Lear's mind at the height of the storm, we may prefer to attend to the "ghostlier demarcations, keener sounds"[1] of Ulysses's voice: "The long day wanes; the slow moon climbs; the deep / Moans round with many voices" (lines 55–56), or the ineffably sad epitaph planted on creation by Tennyson's Tithonus: "Man comes and tills the field and lies beneath / And after many a summer dies the swan" (lines 3–4).

Appreciative readers may also register the change in tone that transforms Bishop Blougram from a casuist of cunning artifice and tricky argument into an oracle of disinterested simplicity and power.

> Just when we are safest, there's a sunset-touch,
> A fancy from a flower-bell, someone's death,
> A chorus-ending from Euripides, —
> And that's enough for fifty hopes and fears
> As old and new at once as nature's self,
> To rap and knock and enter in our soul,
> Take hands and dance there, a fantastic ring,
> Round the ancient idol, on his base again, —
> The grand Perhaps!
> ("Bishop Blougram's Apology," lines 182–90)

Like Browning's "moment, one and infinite," such experiences, though fugitive and the opposite of everlasting, remind us that something can be eternal without lasting forever. Browning uses the fourth voice of poetry to turn his Bishop from a self-serving pragmatist into a prophet of tremulous insight and uncertain vision. For a moment, in the wavering voice coming through him, we overhear G. K. Chesterton's "voice of God, uttering his everlasting soliloquy" (1903, 172).[2]

❖ ❖ ❖

In three of the seven Victorian poets featured in this study—Tennyson, Arnold, and Clough—a reader hears mainly the first or lyrical voice of poetry, in which the poet speaks in his own person. Sometimes a reader hears a rhetorical or dramatic displacement of this voice. In the remaining four poets—Browning, Hopkins, Christina Rossetti, and Hardy—the voice we hear is mainly the second or rhetorical voice, breaking on occasion into the first lyric voice or into a fourth voice we might call ghostly or prophetic: a voice from the whirlwind, such as God uses when addressing Job. In Shakespeare, the great master of this fourth voice is Lear, the prophet, who is not to be confused with an imposter like Timon. Ariel is the genius of the first or lyric voice, and Polonius, the tedious imposer, the practitioner of a rhetorical voice. Absorbing and controlling all the other voices is Shakespeare himself, the great impersonator, the master of a third or dramatic voice in poetry.

The first or lyric voice of poetry—the voice of Lorenzo's *laus musicae* in *The Merchant of Venice* ("How sweet the moonlight sleeps upon the bank")—caresses the ear. We are more aware of meter striking across speech than of speech striking across meter. In the third or dramatic voice of poetry the reverse is true: "That it should come to this! / But two months dead! Nay, not so much, not two" (*Hamlet* 1.2.137–38). Only in the second or rhetorical voice of poetry, which is heard most distinctly in dramatic monologues and soliloquies, are the demands of drama, syntax, and meter all so deftly met that is hard to tell, in one critic's words, "whether speech is striking across meter or meter striking across speech" (Brower, 1963, 10). In "My Last Duchess," for instance, the rhyming couplets and iambs fall as if unplanned, without violence to conversational speech. But as the Duke pauses to admire his wife's portrait, he also uses the lofty syntax of Genesis ("Fra Pandolf's hands / Worked busily a day, and there she stands"; "Let there be light, and there was light") to assert the counter claim of vatic utterance or oracle. In Tennyson's Ulysses and his lotos-eaters, we hear the first and second, the lyrical and rhetorical voices, of Victorian poetry. These voices are more ghostly and antiphonal than the third dramatic voice of poetry, which we hear fully embodied in Shakespeare.

I use the adjective "vatic" or "prophetic" to refer not just to a fragment of wisdom but to any appearance of a simple but affecting fourth voice in poetry: "One touch of nature makes the whole world kin," for example, or "Ripeness is all." At such moments the voice we overhear is more impersonal and compelling than the voice of either the character who is speaking or the poet. Prospero's admonition that "the rarer action is / In virtue than in vengeance" affirms his sense of what it means to be human. But his utterance is oracular and gnomic, not dramatically motivated, since (as one critic observes) it "makes Prospero renounce a vengeance he has shown no prior sign of desiring" (Harbage, 1963, 480). John Bayley notices that *King Lear* "slips out of every area for which there is something appropriate and intelligible to be said" (1981, 23). When Gloucester says, "As flies to wanton boys are we to the Gods / They kill us for their sport," he is not using the second, rhetorical voice of poetry to express some "discovery the play wants to 'leave' with us" (Bayley, 1981, 23). On the contrary, such ghostly utterances, though powerful as prophecies, are dramatically out of place. As oracles rather than homilies, they are pronouncements about a comprehensive wrongness that is cosmically disturbing. They come to us from the far side of rhetoric as a prophetic fourth voice in poetry.

Behind many rhetorical voices lurks the ghost of a homily, and behind many lyrical voices the shadow of an oracle. When Browning's delinquent monk in "Fra Lippo Lippi" says he will "interpret God" to all of us, we are grateful he backs off. There is always a fear that a chorus or poetic epilogue may thinly veil an oracle. When a propagandist like John of Gaunt starts prophesying on his deathbed about the glory of England or Henry V at Agincourt starts talking like a patriot, an audience at once becomes wary. Such prophecies seem bribed or fraudulent, like the Greek oracle prophesying a Persian victory, which was paid for with Persian money. But to be distinguished from all such assaults on our intelligence or bids for our national allegiance are those towering lines in Shakespeare, oracles like "Ripeness is all," which are totally free of homiletic design or patriotic fervor. They shape our ends and touch the most sensitive readers at the deepest level.

Shakespeare is the opposite of a great rhetorician or teacher. Values come *through* but not *from* him. Overheard as a poet rather than heard as an orator, he is a prophet on whom Victorians may eavesdrop. If they trap his wisdom at all, it is usually in a parenthesis or aside, as an insight captured *en passant*. Even when Macbeth elaborates an idea in the manner of an orator, his progression of verbs—"minister," "pluck from," "raze out," "cleanse"—"comes from the native vigor of genius," as J. H. Newman observes (1959, 273). The "many-numbered period" into which Macbeth expands his query is also the achievement of a great poet.

> Canst thou not minister to a mind diseased,
> Pluck from the memory a rooted sorrow,
> Raze out the written troubles of the brain,
> And, with some sweet oblivious antidote,
> Cleanse the stuffed bosom of that perilous stuff
> Which weighs upon the heart?
>
> (*Macbeth* 5.3.40–45)

Though Newman admits Shakespeare could have used fewer words in this passage, he argues that Macbeth manages to fertilize his ideas, germinating them "into a multitude of details" that allow him to rejoice "in his own vigor and richness of resource" (Newman, 1959, 272–73). So soothing is the appeal of "some sweet oblivious antidote" that, despite the anguish of his wife's sickness unto death, which nothing can assuage, Macbeth's lament over "a mind diseased," "a rooted sorrow," and the "written troubles of the brain" turns a potential trap, a mere plaintive snare, into a toil of grace. Only in a pedant like Polonius does oratory become an opaque substitute for the lucid art of the poet. An orator replaces wisdom with charisma, which is Greek for "ham," a performer who overacts. Though not invariably stupid, orators and homilists hark to the sound of their own voice. Too easily satisfied with what they know, they are not truly interested in discovery. Polonius cannot bear to have his certainties disturbed, and so lectures Laertes as a pedant rather than as an attentive, caring father.

Like a lyrical voice, the voice that speaks out of the whirlwind of Lear's mind at the height of the storm is overheard rather than heard; and like a dramatic voice, it may speak in unison with a dramatic character. Unlike any of the other voices, however, it is also impersonal and fragmented, shored against our ruin. A voice like Wittgenstein's commands assent by sounding true. As a character of Iris Murdoch says, "A philosopher's thought suits you or it doesn't. It's only deep in that sense, like a novel" (1980, 2). Displaying a gift for vatic utterance, a godlike voice is notable for its gnomic authority and reserve. As we understand God's Word through his words, so we understand Shakespeare through the lyric, rhetorical, and dramatic tones of the characters who speak in his plays. But Shakespeare also uses oracles and aphorisms, the idioms of an enigmatic fourth voice of poetry, to ignite Lear's rage for order during the storm or to launch the wavering glory of Hamlet's tribute to man, the paragon who is also the quintessence of dust. The searing insights and towering hopes of this fourth voice can no longer be conveyed in the tones of conversational speech that dominate the three other voices of poetry. As Jonathan Bishop says, "Tone is less than Voice; but more can be expressed in tones than in any Voice we can yet hear" (1972, 233).

Shakespeare and his Victorian heirs impress us with their rhetoric and move us with their poetry. But there are also times when, as masters of simplicity, they touch us with their genius, snaring us in as strong a toil of grace as Cleopatra snares Antony. We take pleasure in beauty, but are moved to heights of bliss and sublimity by Hamlet's discourse on the paragon of animals, the god in exile who is also the quintessence of dust. Only by releasing Ovid's "deus in nobis," the god who stirs within each responsive listener, do poets of genius like Tennyson and Browning or prophetic critics like Arnold fulfill their mission. Prophets should be poets not grave diggers. They should lift the soul, not bury it. Timon's arias are mere harangues, whereas Lear's arias soar. Antony's funeral oration and Polonius's lecture to Laeretes may impress a listener. Macbeth's lament for a mind diseased may move us. But only the speculative wonder of a Hamlet or the descent to simplicity of a Lear or Cordelia can truly touch a reader.

The fourth voice of poetry is to the second voice what oracle is to homily. An oracle embraces and expresses the precept that a truth in art is one whose opposite is also true. A homilist, by contrast, too often sounds convinced that he alone is wise. The truth that Polonius cannot be false to anyone if he is true to himself turns to falsehood on his lips. For the wisdom he once possessed as a statesman has been lost in the homilist. Poetry never speaks the language of ideology or homily. Those are the province of "verse," not poetry. Like the witches' prophecies in *Macbeth,* an oracle says opposite things simultaneously. But in appearing to double its meanings, it may also empty them of content. An oracle may confront a reader with the truth of all great tragedies: there is a way things are, and only a fool thinks it is knowable or known. One of Shakespeare's shrewdest critics, Harold C. Goddard, says that "the oracle remains the type of the purest poetry. Oracles are *ambiguous* (a very different thing from *obscure*). They are uttered, as the world seems to be made, to tempt men to meet them halfway, to find in them one of at least two fatally different meanings. Life or death hangs on how they are taken. 'The Lord at Delphi,' says Heraclitus, 'neither speaks nor conceals, but gives a sign'" (Goddard, 1951, 11).

Oracles without interpretation are empty, and homilies without vision are blind. Like a treatise on mourning, a homily errs in a good cause. But it lacks the gravity of a grief or the weight of a vision. Perhaps this is another way of saying that the oracular fourth voice of poetry needs the second rhetorical voice, and vice versa. I had hoped to "go deeply" into the fourth voice of poetry, the subject of an earlier study, *Secrets of the Oracle.* But, as Northrop Frye discerns, "going deeply into a subject is not necessarily to go into it profoundly. Neither is its opposite necessarily being superficial." Since I want to explore all four voices of poetry, I have tried to maintain a sense of proportion. If you're building a fence," as Frye says, "you don't batter one post into the ground so far that it gets out of alignment with the other posts" (2004, 109).

The impulse to enlarge horizons while restraining anarchy is a focus of Ulysses's great speeches in *Troilus and Cressida.* Although he cautions the Greeks against the chaos precipitated by any failure to observe order and degree, Ulysses also challenges Achilles to abandon his tent for the adventure of man-to-man combat in the open field. Shakespeare finds more to extol in the spacious sweep of Hamlet's "god-like reason" and "large discourse, / Looking before and after," than in the crowded dactyls of "Bestial oblivion, or some craven scruple" (*Hamlet* 4.4.36–40). Tennyson, too, finds less to celebrate in the shrunken world of his lotos-eaters than in the ever-expanding world glimpsed by Ulysses through the arch.

> Yet all experience is an arch where through
> Gleams that untravelled world, whose margin fades
> For ever and for ever when I move.
>
> (lines 19–21)

Readers can literally see how the "fading margin" of that world coincides with a slight fading of the poem's right-hand margin on the printed page. Indeed, long vowels and assonances combine with the visual impact of the poem's "printed voice" to create an impression of spaciousness so vast that Matthew Arnold felt "these three lines by themselves take up nearly as much time as a whole book of the *Iliad*" (1896, 76).

In "Ulysses" we overhear, not only Hamlet's question "What is a man, / If his chief good and market of his time / Be but to sleep and feed?" (4.4.33–35), but also a less obvious reference to Ulysses in *Troilus and Cressida.* Hallam Tennyson records that his father admired Ulysses's simile of hanging out of fashion "like a rusty mail / In monumental mockery" (*Troilus and Cressida* 3.3.152–53). The comparison influences the indictment of rusting "unburnished" instead of shining "in use" (lines 22–23) in Tennyson's own "Ulysses," which also reverses Othello's injunction, "Keep up your bright swords, for the dew will rust them" (*Othello* 1.2.59). It is important for Ulysses to "shine in use," even though no weapon he now uses will be dewed with blood. The resilient quality of a well-tempered blade survives in his final shining metaphor of the mariners'

> One equal temper of heroic hearts,
> Made weak by time and fate, but strong in will
> To strive, to seek, to find, and not to yield.
>
> (lines 68–70)

To rust away unused is to waste to nothing, like a piece of machinery in a junkyard. To shine in use, by contrast, is to assert one's status as a life-affirming organism. As Tennyson's Ulysses understands, it is to assert, not his strength or capacity, but his will.

Yet countering the active, heroic allusions to *Troilus and Cressida* and *Hamlet* is a passive, subsurface cluster of words linking the horror of Ulysses's being washed down by the waves to Clarence's nightmare of drowning at the bottom of the sea in *Richard III.*

> *Clarence.* Methought, I had, and often did I *strive*
> *To yield* the ghost; but still the envious flood
> Kept in my soul, and would not let it forth

To seek the empty, vast, and wand'ring air;
But smother'd it within my panting bulk,
Which almost burst to belch it in the sea.
(1.4.36–41)

As Christopher Decker has argued (2009, 69), the italicized words that migrate in zigzag fashion through the maze of this passage create a powerful undertow just below the surface of Tennyson's tribute to the glory of Ulysses and his ghostly mariners. Shakespeare achieves a similar effect in *Henry V,* when he allows the image of a wrack of "sunless treasures," sunk "in the ooze and bottom of the sea" (1.2.164–65), to cast in doubt the glory of England's military campaign against France.

Though alive with allusions to Shakespeare, Tennyson's "Ulysses" combines elegiac and heroic styles that sound more Miltonic than Shakespearean. By throwing a great cantilever or arch over two worlds, the magnificent opening sentence of *Paradise Lost* joins the paradise lost by Adam to the paradise regained by his antitype Christ, the second Adam.

Of Man's First Disobedience, and the Fruit
Of that Forbidden Tree, whose mortal tast
Brought Death into the World, and all our woe,
With loss of Eden, till one greater Man
Restore us, and regain the blissful Seat,
Sing Heav'nly Muse . . .
(1.1–6)

Alliterative bonds between "Fruit" and "forbidden," "Disobedience" and "Death," Restore" and "regain," create a sequence of actions and an association of ideas that are as causally exact as they are expansively epic and heroic. The comparably spacious effect of Tennyson's line, "Far on the ringing plains of windy Troy" ("Ulysses," line 17) is created in part by Milton's device of separating out the elements that alliteration joins. "Ringing" is divided from "Troy" and assigned to "far" and "plains," while "windy," as it were, gives up "plains" and is assigned to "Troy." "Ringing plains" stands for the clamor of war, while "windy Troy" suggests the ruinous, windswept result of war instead of the city itself at its "ringing" zenith.

As heroic to Browning as Ulysses is to Tennyson or as the first and second Adam are to Milton is the gritty, life-denying pedant of "A Grammarian's Funeral," a constipated monster who has fed off books.

He settled *Hoti's* business—let it be!
Properly based *Oun*—

> Gave us the doctrine of the enclitic *De,*
> Dead from the waist down.
> (lines 129–32)

The grammarian has more of Holofernes in his veins than of Hamlet. But his "huge strength of intellectual muscle," as Wilde calls it, aligns him less with Shakespeare than with Ben Jonson. Who but Jonson could have combined such "concentrated realism with encyclopedic erudition" (Wilde, 1968, 30)?

> That low man goes on adding one to one,
> His hundred's soon hit;
> This high man, aiming at a million,
> Misses an unit.
> (lines 117–20)

Striving for infinity, the grammarian appears to achieve less than lesser men. Are we to applaud his contempt for quantitative assessment, or reject him as the ruin of a scholar mastered by monomania?

Unlike Yeats's scholars, who "cough in ink" and "think what other people think" ("The Scholars," lines 7, 9), or Browning's grammarian, who "decided not to Live but Know" (line 139), Tennyson's Ulysses decides to shake the dust of archives from his feet, and prove his truths by living them. Despite his allusions to Hamlet and Othello, he owes less to the Ulysses found in Shakespeare or Homer than to Dante's Ulysses. Not as obvious but more pervasive is the influence of Shakespeare's Ulysses on Tennyson's lotos-eaters, who are as indifferent to Ulysses's ringing, commanding voice in the first line of the poem as Achilles is to Ulysses's stirring exhortation to rejoin the fray in *Troilus and Cressida.* The most famous line in the speech of Shakespeare's Ulysses, "One touch of nature makes the whole world kin" (*Troilus and Cressida* 3.3.75), breaks down in context. We are all undone by the same enemy, Time, who is an ungrateful, hypocritical host. Welcome smiles but Farewell sighs, and we are no sooner pushed out the door than our host is embracing a new guest. Everyone is fooled by illusion and undone by time. If our envious and calumniating enemy annihilates everything of value, including the most shining reputation, why should Achilles stir? Not even the final touch of flattery, the reminder that Achilles's "glorious deeds" drove Mars himself to faction, succeeds in moving the great warrior. Who, then, is wiser: Achilles, who recognizes the vanity of fame and refuses to renew the battle in the plain; or Ulysses, who wants to refurbish armor that will rust tomorrow?

Shakespeare's Ulysses is also an unwitting agent of the anarchy he condemns. To shame Achilles into action, Ulysses decides to hold a lottery that selects Ajax instead of Achilles as the Greek hero who challenges Hector in single combat. As Harold Goddard says, "Imagine a believer in degree resorting to a lottery! No wonder it is to be a 'loaded' lottery" (1951, 400). If Achilles' fame has to be defended hour by hour, day by day, then, far from being stable or unwavering, it possesses at most the shimmering illusion of a mirage.

> Time hath, my lord, a wallet at his back,
> Wherein he doth keep alms for Oblivion.
> (*Troilus and Cressida* 3.3.145–46)

It is a justly famous, even great speech; but what does Ulysses mean? The plea of a personified time, begging for alms—"Alms, brother, alms, a great act or heroic deed from each of you"—is haunting but futile. If time's end product is oblivion—blackout and indifference—how can alms make any difference? No charitable deeds can glut or appease the hunger of oblivious enmity, a "great-sized monster of ingratitude." Ulysses is asking Achilles to perform an impossible task. For as Keats fears, a desire to be remembered is as futile as writing words on water. If "tempus edax" is as all-devouring as Ovid claims, then Oblivion can never benefit from any belated alms posterity is willing to stuff into its wallet. If it did benefit, it would lose the name Oblivion. How few will be "saved," Matthew Arnold laments, "in the sweep and pressure of time.... What a fate, if [one] could foresee it! To be an oracle for one generation, and then of little or no account for ever" (1964, 181). Time is a devious friar, a mendicant, who beggars everyone. Though a few immortals like Shakespeare will be saved, the great flood of history is sure to submerge the rest of us in the end.

In the odd-numbered Spenserian stanzas of their choric song, Tennyson's lotos-eaters, like Shakespeare's Achilles, reject Ulysses's challenge of ever climbing up the climbing wave. Ulysses's commanding, staccato voice, heard in the opening line, continues to sound and resound in lines recounting the struggle of "the ten years' war in Troy" ("The Lotos-Eaters," line 77). But in most of the song, Tennyson invents a counterpoint to Ulysses. He imagines what objection Shakespeare's Achilles might have made to the wisest of the Greek warriors. Like Achilles, the mariners are too disillusioned and exhausted to rejoin the struggle. They want to relax the will instead of brace it for action. The substitution of repeated words for rhymes in the poem's first four lines induces a state of trance or suspended animation.

> "Courage!" he said, and pointed to the land,
> "This mounting wave will roll us shoreward soon."
> In the afternoon they came unto a land
> In which it seemed always afternoon.
> (lines 1–4)

As John Hollander observes, "The choice of non-rhyme to evoke languor . . . is a master-stroke. . . . It is not only what Tennyson himself called the 'no rhyme' of *land* and *land* which sounded 'lazier,' but the added and interwoven repetition of *afternoon* as well, which conjures up the gentle imprisonment in one's own perceptions which helps define the narcotized state: a world in which all rhymes are repetitions" (1975, 132–33).

In the trembling, downward movement of the stream, Tennyson also uses sound to visualize tiny increments of change.

> And like a downward smoke, the slender stream
> Along the cliff to fall and pause and fall did seem.
> (lines 8–9)

The two extra syllables combine with the vertical pattern of falling and pausing to prolong the water's slow descent. The stream draws ever closer to the edge without actually appearing to fall. A similar effect is achieved in Tennyson's alexandrine—"the mild-eyed melancholy Lotos-eaters came" (line 27)—where the weak syllables that sag at the center represent a state of arrested motion.

Tennyson's fine attention to sound values in "The Lotos-Eaters" links his verse with relaxed uses of assonance, repetition, and internal rhymes in Shakespeare's *Richard II* and Spenser's *The Faerie Queene.*

> Sleepe after toyle, port after stormie seas,
> Ease after warre, death after life does greatly please.
> (*The Faerie Queene* 1.9.40)

Spenser's rhyming of "seas," "ease," and "please," which anticipates the languorous use of assonances and internal repetitions in "The Lotos-Eaters," points to a common element of meaning in two of the three rhymes. A similar effect recurs in *Richard II,* the Shakespearean play which W. B. C. Watkins finds "nearest to Spenser as well as Marlowe" (1950, 286).

> But whate'er I be
> Nor I nor any man that but man is
> With nothing shall be pleased, till he be eased
> With being nothing.
> (*Richard II* 5.5.38–41)

Though "Shakespeare makes Spenser's simple statement (ease does please) sharper and more causal (nothing doth please *till* ease)" (Watkins, 1950, 286), he shares with Spenser an interest in the use of individual sounds to produce a web of comparison and inference that is equally typical of Tennyson. In his lotos-eaters' choric song, which adapts Spenser's description of the "trickling streame" and "ever-drizzling raine" (*Faerie Queene* 1.1.41) that lull Morpheus to sleep, Tennyson writes in an appositional Spenserian style that defers the principal verbs and makes skillful use of indefinite caesuras. Even in the mariners' culminating resolve to seek rest after "labour in the deep mid-ocean" (line 172), we hear an enticing echo of the mermaids' appeal to Guyon and the palmer as they travel to the Bower of Bliss: "This is the Port of rest from troublous toyle" (*Faerie Queene* 2.12.32). The mariners' searching indictment of creation: "Why should we only toil, the roof and crown of things?" echoes Phaedria's appeal to Cymochles (*Faerie Queene* 2.6.17); and in the fourth strophe the easeful allure of death, which the mariners welcome as "the end of life" (line 86), repeats the casuistry of Spenser's Despair that "Death is the end of woes" (*Faerie Queene* 1.9.47), a seductive argument that also tempts Hamlet in his soliloquy "To be or not to be."

Like Epicurus in his garden, the Lady of Shalott in her tower, or the soul in its Palace of Art, Tennyson's lotos-eaters seek escape from the shocks and heartache of a world where death closes all. But like the stream that pauses tremulously at the brink, about to fall without actually falling, the lotos-eaters never quite achieve the paradise they seek. Odd as it may sound, in Ulysses's heroic counter voice, commending adventure and risk, we also hear the voice of death, blowing away what one observer calls "the boundaries of life" and establishing "a horizon in its place" (Carse, 1980, 462). Though Ulysses never reaches the "untraveled world whose margin fades / For ever and for ever" as he moves ("Ulysses," lines 20–21), until he moves toward that world by passing through the arch of experience, no horizon exists.

To sink into lotos-land is to sink into an eternity beneath time, not above it; into a bounded world of changelessness, not into a boundless world of endless change. Indeed the lotos-eaters' fate is hard to distinguish from the fate of the eternally old Tithonus, who, unable to die, is unable to live either. As Kierkegaard's Victor Eremita explains, the "unhappiest man" is the person who cannot die because he has lived outside all time's dimensions. "In one sense of the word he cannot die, for he has not really lived; in another sense he cannot love, for love is in the present, and he has no present, no future, and no past" (Kierkegaard, 1959, 1:224). Though George Eliot says every parting is an image of death, she neglects to add that, without death, we could never truly live. For to live in a bounded world untouched by death is to live like the lotos-eaters in a world without horizons. As James Carse explains, it is also "to lose the power of effective speech, because the conversation of the Epicureans in their garden and the scientists in their laboratory cannot have any intention of engaging history, altering the future of the conversants, without violating the very genius of their retrospective philosophies" (1980, 57).

So far I have concentrated on Ulysses's appeal to Achilles in *Troilus and*

Cressida. But equally famous and influential is Ulysses's speech on order. Without the push beyond existing boundaries, no progress is possible. Yet without the gradations of rank, which are the rungs on the ladder, the great chain of being, the *scala naturae,* would fall apart. Order would dissolve into an anarchy of sundered things in throngs. Though enamored of ever-receding horizons, Ulysses also champions fixed platforms and boundaries. As long as society respects degree and order, the blank verse remains ample and fluid. Coleridge goes so far as to call Shakespeare a "philosophical aristocrat." He delights "in those hereditary institutions which have a tendency to bind one age to another, as in that distinction of rank, of which, although few be in possession, all enjoy the advantage" (1930, 1, 176).

If hollowed-out rituals are the dead faith of the living, Ulysses's defense of "primogeniture and due of birth" is a defense of tradition, the living faith of the dead. As his word lists expand, each important item is preceded by a caesura that isolates and gives weight to every phrase and noun.

> How could communities
> Degrees in schools, and brotherhoods in cities,
> Peaceful commerce from dividable shores,
> The primogeniture and due of birth,
> Prerogative of age, crowns, sceptres, laurels,
> But by degree, stand in authentic place?
> (*Troilus and Cressida* 1.3.103–8)

As soon as degree is withdrawn, however, the string is untuned, and harsh leveling spondees replace the smooth iambs with a sorites that builds a causeway to hell.

> Then everything includes itself in power,
> Power into will, will into appetite,
> And appetite, a universal wolf,
> So doubly seconded with will and power,
> Must make perforce an universal prey,
> And last eat up himself.
> (1.3.119–24)

As a huge ouroboros, a snake with its tail in its mouth, society slowly eats up its body and devours its own mouth. A mouth-devouring mouth is worthy of an Escher drawing or of a torture befitting an act of cannibalism at the depth of Dante's hell. If such a perversion of nature does not wipe itself out altogether, like the vanishing Bilbo Baggins, it leaves behind a corpse too monstrous to picture. A comparably grotesque deformity litters the ruin of Lear's world: "Filial ingratitude, / Is it not as this mouth should tear this hand / For lifting food to't?" (*King Lear* 3.4.14–16).

Among the Victorians, both Tennyson and Hopkins share the fear of Shakespeare's Ulysses that a loss of secure resting places or platforms will produce blackout and death. Without the fixed intervals of a diatonic scale, Hopkins faces the bleak chromatic blending of his oracle "Spelt from Sibyl's Leaves." Insisting that "eternal form shall still divide / The eternal soul from all beside" in *In Memoriam* (47.6–7), Tennyson also resists any entry into a world where all cows are black. Even fields of light alarm him. If Hallam's spirit has to diffuse itself, it is important that before he fades away he has a chance to stand upon "some landing-place" and say audibly and forcefully, "Farewell! We lose ourselves in light" (47.5–16). If nature is only a spume that plays upon a ghostly paradigm of things, then the ascent of the soul is not, as T. S. Eliot thinks, a way up into plenitude, but an ascent into nothing. At the very least it is disappearance into a mist that Plato himself would think twice before penetrating.

What the Victorians value in Shakespeare is the sense of wonder, the horizon seen through and beyond the dome of belief. When Hector in *Troilus and Cressida* declares that value is as precious in itself as in the prizer, he is affirming that the good, the true, and the beautiful are Platonic universals presiding over a timeless world of essences. But his words pass over the heads of most Trojans. Charles Williams notices that Hector's "dispute of value is a real and intense dispute, yet it is abruptly abandoned—not so much by Hector as by Shakespeare making use of Hector. It is not there that [Shakespeare] must dwell, in the councils of the philosophers" (1936, 16–17).

Against the ugliness and poverty of his own age, Matthew Arnold values the beauty of medieval Christianity, when the sea of faith was "at the full." Shakespeare, too, values an age when not all the water in the rough rude sea could wash the balm off an anointed king. In *Richard II,* however, the doctrine of the divinity of kings is making a last-ditch stand as one of Arnold's "dead time's exploded dreams." Even when assuring his brethren that "value dwells not in particular will," Hector's defense of Platonic realism smacks too much of the smug homilist. It counters Paris's fumbling heresies with self-confident pieces of dogma. Like Shakespeare and the Victorians, few Trojans are concerned with "dateless realities lodged in some metaphysical heaven" (Collingwood, 1938, 325). Their real interest lies elsewhere: in "the only interior crisis worth talking about; . . . that in which every nerve of the body, every consciousness of the mind shrieks that something cannot be. Only it is. Cressida *cannot* be playing with Diomed. But she is. The Queen *cannot* have married Claudius. But she has. Desdemona *cannot* love Cassio. But she does.

Daughters *cannot* hate their father and benefactor. But they do" (Williams, 1936, 194).

The so-called debates in *Troilus and Cressida* are only group monologues. Ulysses and Hector argue, Achilles sulks, and Thersistes jeers, but nobody budges an inch. More moving and far rarer is the wisdom achieved by Lear, Tom of Bedlam, and Cordelia. Beyond coercion, they see into the life of things. If Cordelia is a "paradoxical, theatrically scarcely intelligible, character," it is because "like a Platonic Form, she is immobile" (Murdoch, 1992, 122). The concern of Shakespeare and his audience is not just with a Platonic Form but with a world in motion, with the conflicts and passions of their own place and time, including "the agony and strife of human hearts." Just as speaking of glory in the spirit of Hotspur and Hal seems a horrid impiety to Falstaff, so to Shakespeare the Platonic Hector in *Troilus and Cressida* sounds too angelically removed from life's cruelty and mercies to be credible. The power of *King Lear* is its "terrible concentration," not on some idea lodged in a Platonic heaven, but on a moment when Lear finds it hard to decide whether his daughter is alive or dead. As one critic says,

> This thing was Cordelia; she was alive, she is dead. . . . From the power of intellect and will, from the imaginative sweep of madness, Shakespeare brings Lear to this; to no moralizing or high thoughts, but just to
>
> She's gone for ever.
> I know when one is dead and when one lives;
> She's dead as earth. Lend me a looking-glass;
> If that her breath will mist or stain the stone,
> Why, then she lives.
>
> (Granville-Barker, 1936, 150)

A. C. Bradley thinks that Lear, at the very last, believes Cordelia lives, and dies of the joy of it. Harold Goddard goes further than Bradley. He thinks that Cordelia survives as a spirit, and that at the end of the play "King Lear and his child [are] lifted up into the realm of the gods" (1951, 556). Though unable to read *King Lear* in this way, I concede that for those with a different experience of life or the play it may be possible to contest the view that *King Lear* is one of "the darkest document[s] in the supreme poetry of the world" (Goddard, 1951, 557). Shakespeare's great theme is the soul's indecision as it sways between opposing possibilities and wavers between worlds.[3] In Montaigne's *Essays,* Shakespeare finds Renaissance Humanism starting to unravel. Its center of classical wisdom and Christian faith no longer holds. When skepticism erodes Hamlet's belief and anarchy is loosed upon Troilus and Lear, Ovid's *Metamorphoses,* a poet's bible of transformation and change, helps absorb the shock. Its myths come to Shakespeare's aid as a substitute scripture.

I could never understand T. S. Eliot's argument that Dante's love of Aristotle and Aquinas, better philosophers than Seneca and Montaigne, made Dante a poet who "understands deeper degrees of degradation and higher degrees of exaltation" than Shakespeare. "From the *Purgatorio* one learns that a straightforward philosophical statement can be great poetry; from the *Paradiso,* that more and more refined *states of beatitude* can be the material for great poetry" (1932, "Dante," 252). A metaphysician like Dante often conducts a serious affair of the understanding as if it were a free play of his imagination. Like Hamlet, Shakespeare prefers to conduct a free play of his imagination as it were a business of the understanding. A metaphysician by training, Eliot seems to think that behind every major poet stands a great philosopher or thinker.[4] But there is a danger that "people who enter into religious systems," as Dante and Eliot do, compromise "the integrity of the verbal universe" (Frye, 2001, 141). The domed worlds of Dante and Eliot are sealed off at the top. Only when an open dome turns a temple of the gods into an observatory can a watcher of the skies see a new planet swim into his ken through "this excellent canopy, the air." Readers who prefer Shakespeare to Dante want their Pantheon to have a hole in its roof. "The open top has something to do with the *als ob* basis of poetic truth" (Frye, 2001, 141).

The Victorian poets follow Shakespeare in substituting for Michelangelo's closed dome the unsealed dome of the Pantheon. When orthodox belief threatens to seal off the imaginative worlds of Hopkins and Christina Rossetti, the two most theological poets of the Victorian age, they replace holes in the dome with trap doors on each stair. In his free fall through space, there is no temporary resting place from which Hopkins, like Gloucester in *King Lear,* may not suddenly be pitched to new depths below: "No worst, there is none." Christina Rossetti creates her own vortex by asking for a place "more low" and by "praying always" for a world *after* all "befores" and "afters," in which Ovid's great devourer, time itself, will be devoured.

When Wordsworth and Coleridge extol the semi-divinity of the human mind, they are celebrating Kant's so-called Copernican revolution in philosophy. The Romantics affirm with Kant that, as the author of synthetic a priori propositions, every human being, by birth and by nature, is a poet, an artist, a fashioner of worlds. Experience is a kind of potluck supper or picnic. Though the eye and ear bring food to the table, the mind that organizes the banquet, that gives it spatial and temporal form, contributes at least as much as it takes in. Whereas the ghostly paradigms of Plato are merely prior to experience, and the booming, buzzing confusion of pure sense perception is slavishly dependent on experience, the mind for Kant is lord and sovereign over outward sense. Such sovereignty allows Wordsworth to proclaim the mind a thousand times more glorious than the earth, in beauty more exalted, as it is itself of quality and fabric more divine.

Kant's legacy to the Victorians is more troubled and disturbing. Demolishing all arguments for God's existence except the moral argument, Kant believes that, having no content in sensuous intuition, God can never be reached through any exercise of Pure Reason. As one philosopher observes, "so radical was Kant's thinking that we have still not caught up with it, nearly two hundred years after his death, just as most educated people still do not understand Einstein's Theory of Relativity, nearly a hundred years after its publication.... The fact is that Kant has destroyed traditional 'proofs' of the existence of God. Atheists, however, can take no comfort for this, for the same arguments demolish the intellectual foundations of atheism as well" (Magee, 1977, 156). Such Victorian heirs of Kant as Sir William Hamilton, H. L. Mansel, Arthur Hugh Clough, and T. H. Huxley all demonstrate how any attempt to understand a Being who is at once infinite, absolute, and a first cause generates antinomies that are incurably idolatrous because logically contradictory. The Romantic poets' glory of the world, the Hamlet who is angelic in apprehension and almost a god, becomes for his Victorian successors the great anomaly in creation. He is Tennyson's "monster," a "dream of discord"; Hopkins's "Jack, Joke, poor potsherd"; Clough's tortured agnostic, a mere damned "depth-hunter"; or, at best, Arnold's gipsy-child by the seashore, bewildered by glooms that, even as they enhance and glorify the earth, evoke the sadness of an exile "in an alien planet born."

As tortured at the center of his faith as Shakespeare's Troilus, Hopkins reflects the influence of David Hume. The great English skeptic was a favorite philosopher of J. H. Newman, the mentor who received Hopkins into the Roman church and gave him a teaching post at the Birmingham Oratory. Like Hume, Newman adopts an empirical theory of knowledge, according to which the mind works upon distinct religious impressions in the same way that it operates on discrete impressions of sense.

Acknowledging that neither sensory nor religious impressions can lead to knowledge of truth beyond these impressions themselves, Newman warns, "Let the Catholic dogmas, as such, be freely admitted to convey no true idea of Almighty God, but only an earthly one, gained from earthly figures, provided it be allowed, on the other hand, that the senses do not convey to us any true idea of matter, but only an idea commensurate with sensible impressions" (1880, 340). As one commentator says, "Here Newman brought his readers to the brink of a radical Humean skepticism, a cauldron of doubt and uncertainty that would produce the agnosticism of the next Victorian generation" (Turner, 2002, 504).

One legacy of such skepticism is the anarchy of sundered things in throngs that confronts Hopkins in his bleak testament "Spelt from Sibyl's Leaves," where all bonds are "slipped, dissolved, and loosed," as in *Troilus and Cressida.* Hopkins may have found a partial antidote to such atomism in his Oxford tutor, T. H. Green, who in his notes on Hume's *Treatise on Human Nature* attacks Hume's premise that a fact or datum can be experienced in isolation as a discrete impression of sense. Even where Hopkins speaks of "time's vast, womb-of-all, home-of-all, hearse-of-all night" ("Spelt from Sibyl's Leaves," line 2), he is assuming, like Green, that the thrice repeated "all" is a whole that precedes and unifies its component parts. The mind's awareness of successive elements—the hyphenated womb, home, and hearse—is never a mere succession as such. In apprehending Hopkins's "kingdom of daylight's dauphin, dapple-dawn-drawn Falcon" ("The Windhover," lines 2–3) instantaneously and as a whole, the mind is not allowed to sort out atomic impressions of dapple color, dazzling light, and aerial motion. Instead, as Green had argued, the mind receives in a single mounting impression a parataxis of highly charged sensations: a spacious riding-of-the-rolling-level-underneath-him-steady air. At the same time the discrete atoms of sense favored by Hume and Newman provide the fixed intervals or pitches of Hopkins's diatonic scale. Hopkins's fear of positivism is exceeded only by his horror of being absorbed into Hegel's Absolute, the night in which all cows are black. In what Scotus calls *haecceitas,* or the unique pitch or "thisness" of each item of ecstasy, Hopkins finds a bulwark against any invasion of the Absolute. Such an invasion is most overpowering in "Spelt from Sibyl's Leaves," where the blackout of annihilation is as great a threat as in Hopkins's Lear-like fall through space in his sonnet "No worst, there is none."

As a Passion play whose god has died or disappeared, *King Lear* ought to be unbearable. And for some it is. Samuel Johnson is not alone in feeling that Shakespeare has inflicted suffering on him personally. As Frank Kermode explains, "Cruelty is always a matter of a poet's calculation. . . . There is a cruelty in the writing [of *King Lear*] that echoes the cruelty of the story, a terrible calculatedness that puts one in mind of Cornwall's and Regan's. Suffering has to be protracted and intensified, as it were, without end" (2000, 197). Though Shakespeare harrows the heart and hurts the soul, for those who can endure the experience *King Lear* is the most sublime and Greek of his creations. Like a performance of a tragedy by Aeschylus or Sophocles, a performance of the play is less a popular entertainment than a spiritual happening or event. Any oracle the play unseals ruthlessly revokes the soft and magical consolations of traditional religion. As Iris Murdoch says of Dostoevsky's *The Possessed,* one has to experience "the puzzling dreadful enormity of the thing. One has to go down into the pit with [King Lear]—it's no use standing on the brink and peering" (2009, 222). The truest Victorian assessment comes from Swinburne, who combines a poet's eloquence with a skeptic's candor: "We have heard much and often from theologians of the light of revelation: and some such thing indeed we find in Aeschylus; but the darkness of revelation is here" (1918, 172).

Kent's disturbing query about endings in *King Lear*—"Is this the promised end?" (5.3.264)—raises the problem of knowing when something ends. In one critic's words, it is also "a variation on the problem of knowing *if* something ends and whether it will ever end" (Booth, 1983, 15). Both Shakespeare and Browning envisage ends that recede from view the more closely we approach them. Framed by the word "naught" at both the beginning and the end of a line, Childe Roland seems immobilized for a moment in a mind-trap or clamp.

> And just as far as ever from the end!
> Naught in the distance but the evening, naught
> To point my footstep further!
>
> (lines 157–59)

Though Roland complains of being "as far as ever from the end," an end has already crept up on him, since the word "end" appears for once at the end of a line.

Like Shakespeare, who could have ended *King Lear* with the reunion of Cordelia and her father, Tennyson extends his monologues beyond their natural boundaries and breaking points. At the end of "Mariana," the speaker is still pining for Angelo, without any hint of their eventual reunion in *Measure for Measure.* At the end of "St. Simeon Stylites," the monk is still yearning for death, without any final attainment of his martyrdom. Reading the monologue is like reading a farcical version of *King Lear.* We are waiting for a death that has been prepared "For ages and for ages" and that now seems overdue. Near the beginning Simeon prophesies

> my end draws nigh;
> I hope my end draws nigh.
>
> (lines 35–36)

But each time he repeats the word "end," it moves farther away from a line-ending on the printed page. Simeon stretches us out on the rack of his suffering by trying to end an action that, despite all effort to terminate it at "A quarter before twelve" (line 218), is still in progress when the monologue concludes.

the end! The end!
Surely the end! What's here? a shape, a shade,
A flash of light. Is that the angel there
That holds a crown?

(lines 198–201)

Christopher Decker observes that the "spectral presences from Shakespeare that haunt" the lines in which Simeon clutches for "the crown! the crown!" (lines 204–5) include the sighting of the ghost in *Hamlet* (1.1.145–47), Macbeth's vision of the dagger (2.1.33–35), and Gloucester's obsessive desire "to catch the English crown" in *3 Henry VI* 3.2.179. "Tennyson's allusions," as Decker says, "are like these apparitions, images of the dead or of desire, both here and gone, present and absent" (2009, 73–75), forever receding the closer we come to grasping them.

Like St. Simeon, Tithonus should find fulfillment in attaining immortality. Instead, he withers before our eyes into immortal old age. Even Lucretius lingers onstage too long. Instead of merging with the flaring atom-streams, ruining down the illimitable inane, he suffers the humiliation of being poisoned by a love philter. Unlike Homer's hero, Tennyson's Ulysses finds no fulfillment in a safe return to Ithaca. Instead, he must set off like Dante's Ulysses on a final suicide mission. As in *King Lear,* each monologue goes on after it should be over. We might risk a paradox and say that it is precisely because Tennyson's preoccupation with the enigma of postponed endings is so authentically Shakespearean that it ceases to be consciously modeled on Shakespeare. When in section 12 of *In Memoriam* Tennyson allows a drama to unfold relentlessly beyond its expected termination point, in an echo of Kent's ineffectual interruption of Lear's agony—"Is this the promised end?"—he is not appropriating Shakespeare: Shakespeare is taking possession of *him.*

Like *Love's Labor's Lost, Amours de Voyage* is a work of beginnings, with no middle and no end, in which the anticipated lovemaking and marriage never take place. *The Tempest,* by contrast, is all about ends or moments just before the end. Prospero has planned his valediction well in advance, and forthcoming weddings are celebrated before any extended courtship takes place. *In Memoriam* and many of Tennyson's monologues are poems about penultimate moments. As in *King Lear,* the promised end always manages to elude the speaker. In *Macbeth,* by contrast, the shortest of Shakespeare's plays, which has the "abrupt and steep simplicity" of an "epic tragedy" (Swinburne, 1918, 182), the end comes swiftly. Like Shakespeare's English chronicle plays, Browning's monologues consist mainly of middles. Plunging *in medias res,* they start rather than begin, finish rather than conclude. Like history itself, they unfold endlessly in an indeterminate middle ground. What is ever concluded or decisively established in a Browning monologue that there is anything to bring to a conclusion or terminate?

❖ ❖ ❖

One way to identify a prophetic fourth voice in poetry is to look for a place "where oracle meets wit" (Frye, 2000, 480). Oracles without wit are empty: too often they are choral mind traps or homilies. And wit without prophecy is blind: too often its oracles decline into mindless jokes and feeble puns. According to Thomas De Quincey, a literature of knowledge gives the reader a rudder to steer by, but only a literature of power provides the sail.

> Thou seëst all things, thou wilt see my grave;
> Thou wilt renew thy beauty morn by morn.
> ("Tithonus," lines 73–74)

These lines put the soul in motion. But their power is inseparable, I believe, from the restrained wit of the two lines that follow.

> I earth in earth forget these empty courts,
> And thee returning on thy silver wheels.
> (lines 75–76)

The coda moderates the goddess's triumph even as it dooms the speaker. While Aurora is renewing her beauty "morn by morn," her chief admirer resolves to wipe her from his mind altogether. Tithonus expresses the eternity of his beloved in limited meteorological terms, as an everlasting brevity, an eternal dawn. But the concluding lines temper Aurora's triumph by granting the goddess the most tenuous of sanctuaries in the mind of a worshipper about to forget her. Moreover, even as Tithonus pays his last meticulous courtesies to Aurora, returning daily on her silver wheels, he himself becomes the butt of a second muted joke. For Tennyson expects us to know that Tithonus will not end his life with as much relaxed dignity as he ends his beautifully composed monologue. He will turn ignominiously into a grasshopper instead.

Lamenting that "the Gods themselves cannot recall their gifts" (line 49), Tithonus recalls and reverses Pericles's complaint that, unlike the Gods, who "make us love [their] "goodly gifts, / And snatch them straight away," "we here below / Recall not what we give" (3.1.23–25). Playing upon two meanings of "recall"—"remember" and "revoke"—Tithonus remembers that what the Gods recalled or "took back" from Pericles, the life of his beloved wife, they refuse to take back from Tithonus, the gift—or curse—of immortal old age. As Eric Griffiths says, Tithonus "feels sure there cannot be misery loftier than his own, and partly for the reason that his suffering includes knowledge of what Pericles went through, and that there is worse," as Edgar came to realize in *King Lear.* Though "so dizzy a poignancy is exceptional in its literary refinement," Griffiths shows "it arises from ordinary processes of understanding what someone else says" (2009, 159).

When Edgar's appearance as Tom o' Bedlam triggers Lear's madness, the voice that speaks out of the whirlwind of his mind would be less exalted if its super-sanity were not also a place where oracle meets wit in the form of a sublime but wrenching joke.

Didst thou give all to thy daughters,
and art thou come to this?
(*King Lear* 3.4.49–50)

Gloucester's purse, Lear says, may be light. But the sockets, the case and purse of his eyes, are heavy, because what they carry, his blinded eyes, have no light in them. There is reason in Lear's madness and lucidity in his outrage. And he has the wit to sweeten his imagination with a joke.

Even Hamlet's stirring lines on the nobility of man would be less glorious without their self-criticism, less prophetic without their sly and glancing wit. Though Hamlet possesses his ignorance as if it were knowledge, he also sounds listless, enticed by neither man nor woman: "Man delights not me,—no, nor woman neither, though by your smiling you seem to say so" (2.2.321–22). Since neither angelic apprehension nor sex attracts him, in both the style of his prose and the deportment of his mind Hamlet is prepared to mock everything. His levity is the despair of self-distrust. A playful skepticism grounds lofty speculations about the beauty of the world, the paragon of animals, in jesting and wit.

If there is more solemnity than wit in Tennyson's pun on the leaves of Hallam's letters, which keep their green in *In Memoriam,* there is more labored wit than oracle in the pun on the "far-off interest of tears" which the elegist studiously extracts from three sources in Shakespeare: sonnet 31, lines 5–7; *Rape of Lucrece,* lines 1796–98; and *Richard III* 4.4.322–24 (Ricks, 1987, 1, 864–65). More affecting is the fusion of oracle with wit in the teasingly elliptical tenth section of the elegy, whose power is partly a result of the frugal tetrameter quatrains, which are as skeletal as a haiku and as prone to two-way meanings as a riddle. We are shocked to learn that a "dark freight" can be weightless. How can something heavy defy physics by shedding mass altogether?

Thou bring'st the sailor to his wife,
And traveled men from foreign lands;
And letters unto trembling hands;
And, thy dark freight, a vanished life.
(*In Memoriam* 10.5–8)

The "dark freight" of a "vanished life" alarms and unnerves the reader. It defeats the understanding, and is only half intelligible. As a fictional character explains in A. S. Byatt's novella "The Conjugial Angel," "The *weight* of the freight, so to speak, is the weight of absence, of what is vanished, a lost life. It is not what remains that is heavy, but what is not there" (1992, 235). Like the letter received by trembling hands, the lyric gives the soul a shudder that few passages in Victorian poetry or Shakespeare's plays manage to surpass.

The conjunction of oracle and wit is no less potent and unnerving in section 12 of *In Memoriam.* Without loss of inner seriousness, the mourner's high joking about ending a long poem that has barely begun coexists in costly but noble tension with a prophecy at the end of *King Lear.* What ought to be a "smooth ceremony of conclusion" in that play turns into a towering, cosmically disturbing oracle of Lear's fate.

> *Kent.* Is this the promis'd end?
> *Edgar.* Or image of that horror?
> *Albany.* Fall and cease!
> (5.3.263–64)

F. H. Bradley says that for the truth, he comes back always to the doctrine of Hegel, that "there is nothing behind the curtain other than that which is in front of it." Now, however, Shakespeare, the god of many masks, seems about to lift a veil by unsealing an apocryphon or books of secrets. The "symphonic ritual" of apocalypse does not merely describe events. As John Bayley observes, it also "takes them over" (1981, 10). An oracle of fate should foretell our end by unsealing a "fatum" or divine decree that has literally "been spoken" by the gods. But when the veil is rent and the book of secrets is unsealed, it is hard to say whether Lear's end will be felicity or despair. The play, I now think, is the exact opposite of a sacrament. In "sacrament," as one critic says, "something is brought to life: in sacrifice, which is tragedy, something is killed" (Frye, 2004, 18). Trying to interpret Shakespeare, I am consumed—often against my will—by the same fire that re-created Keats after reading *King Lear.* Against the ravages of *tempus edax,* destroyer of daughters, devourer of dreams, who has not cried out with Edgar: "World, world, O world! / But that thy strange mutations make us hate thee, / Life would not yield to age" (*King Lear* 4.1.10–12)? "Begetter of our deep eternal theme," Shakespeare explores the mind's steepest mountains and cliffs of fall. Even in casting out a rope-bridge, he leaves us swaying perilously over an abyss.

Aristotle says that tragedy should raise emotions of pity and fear which it then proceeds to purge. If Aristotle is right, then Henry James's novel *The Wings of the Dove* should be more cathartic than *King Lear.* For James purges his heroine's "unapproachable terror" of her end by viewing it through the appreciative but largely self-aggrandizing perspective of Mrs. Lowder, who turns death into an aesthetic object. "It was almost as if she herself enjoyed the perfection of the pathos; she sat there before the scene, as he [Merton Densher] couldn't help giving it out to her, very much as a stout citizen's wife might have sat during a play that made people cry, in the pit or the family circle. What most deeply stirred her was the way the poor girl must have wanted to live" (James, 1965, 414–15). In shocking contrast is our direct, unmediated experience of Cordelia's death in *King Lear.* Playgoers are encouraged to say what they feel about her death, not what Aristotle, a master critic, or Henry James, an accomplished novelist but failed dramatist, thinks they ought to say. Cordelia is a fugitive and gracious light, shy to illumine. When that light is put out, everyone from the playgoer in the theater to the scholar in his study feels her death is cruel and unfair. Cordelia's death is the end of illusion. She was the higher angel of her father's nature. When she dies, she takes her father's heart out of the world with her. We are in love, and love what vanishes. What more is there to say? Except that Cordelia was a beautiful person. And now she holds all who loved her, all who know love is the last and secret name of all the virtues, in a strong toil of grace.

Toward the end of his life, Northrop Frye said, "Whether I have any more books to write or not, I still want to consider the points of silence in religion: the silence of before being, expressed by the word creation; the silence of being after, expressed by the word apocalypse" (2000, 722). "Too late for apocalypse, too critical for prophecy," Tennyson finds himself wrestling in the twelfth section of *In Memoriam* with the silence of apocalypse, "the silence of being after." The oracle about a "promised end" is formulated as a question, and as a question about betrayed ends in a quatrain, a canto, and a poem that all refuse to end: "no end, there is none." With the coming of the burial ship, the drama of Hallam's life is formally concluded. But the great Victorian elegy continues to move on interminably. It rolls across and crushes the very framework of closure that helps the reader isolate and limit confusion or disorder in other elegies.

> And saying; "Comes he thus, my friend?
>   Is this the end of all my care?"
>   And circle moaning in the air:
> "Is this the end? Is this the end?"
>
> (*In Memoriam* 12.13–16)

Even the diction looks two ways at once. Is Hallam's death the goal or final cause of all the mourner's care? Or is it the end or termination of it? In neither *In Memoriam* nor *King Lear* does the promise of an afterlife put a comfortable frame around the life that has just ended. As Prospero binds Caliban and

Cleopatra snares Antony, so Shakespeare catches us today, as he caught the Victorians, in a "strong toil of grace." Concentrating on moments when order seems wholly lost, when they speak what they feel, not what they ought to say, Kent, Albany, and Edgar create such enigmatic but familiar lines as "Is this the promis'd end? / Or image of that horror? Fall, and cease" (5.3.263–64). The mourner in *In Memoriam* lightens the ritual by asking in plain, heartbroken words, "Is this the end? Is this the end?" When the "big noble scaffolding" comes down, his descent to simplicity, like Lear's prayer not to be mad, is affecting beyond measure.

Notes

Introduction

1. In Philip Larkin's elegy "An Arundel Tomb," the unobtrusive gesture of the knight's ungloved hand as it reaches out to touch the hand of the sculptured figure reposing by his side proclaims in all but words their only true and enduring blazon: "What will survive of us is love" (line 42). When two of my daughters died, I instinctively turned to Shakespeare and the Victorian poets, writers I knew or loved best, to ask what, if anything, survives of us. Does death close all, or is it a point of entry into "that deep dawn behind the tomb" evoked by Tennyson in *In Memoriam* 46.6? Is death a passport to Hamlet's undiscovered country, or just "the anaesthetic from which none come round" (Larkin, "Aubade," line 30)?

2. Quite distinct from such Shakespearean imitations as *The Princess* or "Caliban upon Setebos" are poems like *The Wreck of the Deutschland,* which is less an example of Hopkins's appropriating Shakespeare than of Shakespeare's taking possession of *him.* Tennyson, Hopkins, and Christina Rossetti develop styles of such breathtaking simplicity and power that we feel impelled to say: this is the kind of poetry that a song, a soliloquy, or a sonnet by Shakespeare was invented to express.

3. Unlike Browning's hero, the visionary Shelley, Shakespeare is so self-withholding that Browning wonders if he truly possessed a poet's soul at all. The speaker in *Aristophanes' Apology* calls Shakespeare an extraordinary word machine (line 5141). Reducing the poet's facility with words to a mere computing mechanism, Browning's Bishop Blougram suggests that after making enough money as a playwright, Shakespeare retired to a bourgeois life in Stratford, because his interest in his art was, in the end, only commercial. In Browning's poems "House" and "Shop," Shakespeare's true home is the Globe Theatre, which he operates as a production company. We like to think that Shakespeare's art, like God's grace, is part of the economy of gift. But Blougram believes Shakespeare, the Stratford burgher, showed more interest in the market value of his art than in any gift he might possess as a poet or a playwright. It is useful to remember that the word "talent," which now means "gift," once denoted a unit of money.

Ironically, Henry James says of Browning what Browning himself says of Shakespeare. James found it hard to believe that Browning, the man-about-town he met at dinner parties, possessed the acute psychological insight into minds and motives displayed in *The Ring and the Book* and a host of introspective lyrics and dramatic monologues. Browning was "no more like to Paracelsus than I to Hercules," James writes to William Dean Howells. He was "a great chatterer, but no Sordello at all" (quoted in Edel, 1985, 224). Similarly, how could Shakespeare, the burgher who retired from the theater to live in the finest house in Stratford, have written the immortal plays and sonnets? The man and his masks are too far apart. Only a spy like James, who preferred to eavesdrop on life from the sidelines, could have kept an incognito so perfectly in place as Shakespeare. In a little-known preface to *The Tempest,* written in 1907 for Sir Sidney Lee's edition of Shakespeare, James expresses his conviction that Shakespeare the man, the burgher of Stratford whom curious biographers still want to know and meet, never in fact existed. As Leon Edel puts it, "What existed was simply the Artist—'the monster and magician of a thousand masks'" (562). Like Browning, James insists that Shakespeare gives us the mere illusion of "meeting and touching the man." We meet the essential Shakespeare only in his art.

4. It is fitting that when Shakespeare, the most silent and self-effacing of playwrights, appears in *Hamlet,* it is as the ghost of Hamlet's father. Like Shakespeare's prince of Denmark and Browning's spiritual medium, Mr. Sludge, the Victorian poets are constantly trying to make contact with ghosts. Thomas Hardy is haunted by the ghost of his wife, Emma. And many of Browning's most famous monologues are séances at which the medium conjures up shades of historical personages like Andrea del Sarto and Fra Lippo Lippi or the ghosts of such fictional characters as Shakespeare's Childe Roland and Caliban. Like Dante's Ulysses, who is only a shade in hell, Tennyson's Ulysses is a specter among ghosts. According to Homer, Ulysses is the last survivor of the Trojan War. As the mind of Tennyson's hero begins to wander, drifting in reverie from one imagined auditor to another, his final injunction to the mariners, his comrades of old, may be only a bracing pep talk to ghosts. "Ulysses," then, is a mask lyric behind whose speaker we hear the voice of Tennyson and the ghosts of Hamlet, Othello, and Shakespeare's own Ulysses in *Troilus and Cressida,* who may be addressing only a cohort of ghosts.

1. Word and Love Games

1. As saturated with references to Shakespeare as the early correspondence of Tennyson, the love letters of Robert and Elizabeth Browning reveal a comparable infatuation with the playwright. In letters filled with amused, sometimes coded, often moving allusions to Shakespeare, the quotations the two lovers toss off come as naturally as breathing. In her first letter to Robert, Elizabeth invokes Lear's praise of Cordelia's "soft, / Gentle, and low" voice, "an excellent thing in woman" (5.3.273–74). In just such a voice, she says, she now begs Robert for a "sentence or two of general observation" on her faults as a poet (Browning, 1969, 1:5). When Robert responds that Elizabeth's verse is better than his own, she repeats Lear's words to Cordelia: "Pray do not mock me" (1:79). Since Shakespeare speaks in Browning's own idiom, in the voice of a dramatic poet, she fears that her quoting Hamlet or Lear to Robert is like quoting the New Testament to St. Paul. For Elizabeth to have lived in isolation at Wimpole Street without meeting Browning would be like dying without ever reading Shakespeare. The confession is touching and deeply felt (1:41). For his part, Robert says that even if he were to be "shut . . . in four walls of a room" with Elizabeth, he would still be as great "a lord of infinite space" as Hamlet (1:254).

> O God, I could be bounded in a nutshell and count
> myself a king of infinite
> space, were it not that I have bad dreams.
>
> (*Hamlet* 2.2.260–22)

Unlike Hamlet, however, or his own Andrea del Sarto, who is confined like a bat to the four walls that make his world, Browning himself, except in the sequence of four obscure poems called "Bad Dreams," is seldom stricken by remorse of conscience or shaken by nightmares.

2. To move us to wonder while achieving economies of form, Shakespeare and the Victorian poets often organize their ideas musically. T. S. Eliot has shown how there emerges from the opening scene in *Hamlet* "a kind of musical design" that checks and accelerates "the pulse of our emotions without our knowing it" (1961, "Poetry and Drama," 80–81). From "the short, brusque" exchange of the guards at the beginning, "the verse glides into a slower movement with the appearance of the courtiers Horatio and Marcellus" (79). In Marcellus's observation that during Advent "the bird of dawning singeth all night long," "there is a deliberate brief emergence of the poetic into consciousness" (81). But Horatio's answer, "So have I heard and do in part believe it," is the simplest possible response. His speech, Eliot says, could be spoken as either poetry or prose. When Horatio observes that "the morn, in russet mantle clad, / Walks o'er the dew of yon high eastern hill," he is speaking poetry that lifts the audience immediately to a higher plane. But to show how Horatio is still speaking the language of natural conversation, Shakespeare follows the lofty sentiment with a half line of utter simplicity—"Break we our watch up," which has the bluntness of a stage direction.

Just as Shakespeare musically organizes the first encounters with the ghost in *Hamlet,* so Tennyson uses a musical design to oppose and balance contending forces in *In Memoriam.* As in music, here the mourner experiences a kind of continuity in change. Because sections 34 to 37 simultaneously adhere to and remain separate from each other, like movements in a quartet or symphony, the mourner's fears can be clarified and resolved. Section 34 is one of the most desolating. If death is the end, then nature is merely rapacious, like the serpent whose jaws expand into a metaphor for earth and sky, luring man to "darkness." In section 35 the experience is still one of terror and loneliness. No longer exalted like Hamlet's "paragon of animals," man is now only a curious accident: a footnote to self-sustaining natural law. Both the substance and the spirit of section 36 follow from what precedes. But like a quartet's development of a theme in the sonata-allegro form, the need to hold each element in more than one context helps the mind enlarge its vision and assimilate its dread. At first the links are reinforced by the economic metaphor of line 4—"Of Him that made them current coin"—which answers the earlier question: "what profits it to put / An idle case?"(35.17–18). But now the watching eyes also perceive a design and final cause in nature. The beauty of the reef is muted and incidental. Tennyson subordinates it to the "loveliness of perfect deeds," a theological mystery "More strong than all poetic thought." He also ascribes the wildness to a creature beholding God's creation, whereas in section 34 he attributed it to God himself. The reader never knows how much meaning he can extract from these metaphors and when they will cease to yield. Like the transformations of a theme in music, they are very much alive. In the midst of death, they are like life itself.

2. The Trespass of Intimacy

1. Browning's art of conjuring historical ghosts needs a word of comment, since the comparison of the poet's art to necromancy, though foreshadowed in *The Tempest,* is unique to Browning, who asks in *The Ring and the Book* if the ghosts that abound in his poetry claim descent from the ghosts raised by Prospero or from Banquo's ghost. Do they rise from a grave or a ditch? This is another way of asking whether the Victorian poets practice white or black magic. Is their ghostly conjuring a grace-bearing act, a resurrection, or a malign

deed of sorcery? As a conjurer of historical and fictional personages, Browning may be a benign magician like Prospero and the biblical Elisha. Or he may be a black magician like Agrippa or Faust, a necromancer who in selling his soul to the devil consistently abuses his occult powers.

Whenever he raises the ghost of a historical personage (a Renaissance artist like Andrea del Sarto or a biblical hero like Saul), Browning is acting as the medium at a séance. He admits that "to raise a ghost" may seem satanic. One thinks of his zombie-like Lazarus in "An Epistle of Karshish," well suited after his resuscitation (perhaps by mesmerism) for a Victorian Chamber of Horrors. Browning the conjurer insists, however, that resuscitating a corpse need not be a form of Faust's black magic. It may be more like Prospero's conjuring in *The Tempest,* a form of white magic, or even a miracle of resurrection such as Elisha performs in 2 Kings 4:29–35.

> ". . . then write my name with Faust's!"
> Oh, Faust, why Faust? Was not Elisha once?—
> Who bade them lay his staff on a corpse-face.
>
> (*The Ring and the Book* 1.759–61)

Browning wants to resurrect his ghosts as Elisha revives the Shunammite's dead son. He has no desire to resuscitate them with the aid of magnetic fields or electric currents, as did the Austrian physician Mesmer.

2. Browning's earliest monologues explore states of immediate extroversion, where sensualists, hedonists, and artists in crime live in bondage to their senses. It is the stage of life Kierkegaard calls aesthetic, but which we might more accurately describe as "pleasure for pleasure's sake," a term F. H. Bradley uses in his influential *Ethical Studies* (1876). Performing in a highly theatrical Hollywood of spectacle and sensation are such actors as the strangler in "Porphyria's Lover," the priest in "The Confessional," who is a specialist in clerical cunning, and the court lady in "The Laboratory," who kills her rival with a costly, exquisitely colored poison. In "A Toccata of Galuppi's," the prototype of the masked revelers at the Venetian carnival is Don Juan, Kierkegaard's own example of the sensualist, who in the end is bored and defeated by his own hedonism.

Browning, I suspect, has the same relation to near contemporaries like F. H. Bradley and Kierkegaard as Shakespeare has to Edmund Spenser. Just as Spenser distinguishes among recreative, plaintive, and moral eclogues in *The Shepherd's Calendar,* so Shakespeare moves from the holiday world of his festive comedies, through the darker world of his problem plays, to the transforming vision of his great tragedies, *The Tempest,* and late romances like *The Winter's Tale.* Hal as reveler, Falstaff as inspired clown, Faulconbridge as disingenuous practitioner of expedience, seem all at first flat and two-dimensional. Yet one's identity is seldom synonymous with one's role as a masked reveler, a hypocrite, or a drinking companion at the Boar's Head Tavern. Like Don Juan, a mere hedonist soon gets bored. If every working day were a holiday, as Henry IV reminds his son, to sport would be as tedious as to work.

Falstaff is not just a reveler: he is also, as Harold Bloom says, the Socrates of Eastcheap. The spy who travels incognito in "How It Strikes a Contemporary" is not just an idler or a tramp; he is also a poet, an advisor to the king, and a chief legislator of the state. The beggar in "Imperante Augusto" is not just a Roman street person, a vagrant or a waif: he is also Caesar Augustus, the emperor himself. A spy assumes an incognito to hide his true identity. But just as Don Juan tires of his role, so the wise man or seer who travels incognito will eventually experience discomfort and guilt. He has betrayed his daemon or genius by pretending to be someone he is not. The true self may appear in a dream, a vision, or a reflective aside. Hal confides in a soliloquy that he will discard his mask as a playboy when he becomes king. Kent will remove his disguise as Tom o' Bedlam when he needs to rally Lear's spirits at their lowest ebb.

3. Oscar Wilde's impatience with Victorian moral attitudes toward art impairs his otherwise valuable comments on Shakespeare and Browning. Though Wilde is one of Browning's most discerning Victorian critics, like most aesthetes he has an imperfect sympathy with the dynamic, moral Browning, whose ideas are always evolving, always on the move. Wilde calls Browning "the most Shakespearean creature since Shakespeare (1968, 202). But he fails to see that, for Browning as for Kierkegaard, the moral life of a Socrates is constantly modifying or amending the defects of a sensualist like Don Juan, who like Guido or the Duke of Ferrara is defeated by boredom. Nor does Wilde seem to grasp how the sacrificial love of Caponsacchi and Pompilia might liberate from frustrating self-defeat a speaker like the thwarted Don Juan of "Two in the Campagna," who fails to clinch his argument for free love. Wilde also underestimates the range of Browning's ethical sympathies. To Wilde, "virtue and wickedness are . . . simply what the colors of his palette are to the painter." To Browning, however, the most ethically inquisitive and probing of the great Victorian poets, virtue and vice are never reducible to "the perfect use of an imperfect medium" (Wilde, 1968, 242, 230). Even if Browning took as much delight in creating Guido as Pompilia, the one remains as "morally horrible" as Iago and the other as "stainlessly pure" as Imogen. For the subtlest Victorian explorer of moral deception and casuistry, ethics is infinitely more fascinating, more complex and devious, than Wilde's idolatry of art allows.

4. The Angel of Dust

1. In his conversation with Rosencranatz and Guildenstern, Hamlet both outwits and appears to befriend these two birds of prey.

> *Guil.* My lord we were sent for.
> *Ham.* I will tell you why; so shall my anticipation prevent
> your discovery, [and] your secrecy to the King and Queen
> moult no feather.
>
> (*Hamlet* 2.2.303–6)

Since Hamlet is using "discovery" as both a subjective and an objective genitive (your discovery of my plot but also my discovery of yours), his readiness to talk is cunning in disguise. Are the spies on the point of discovering a sinister plot by Hamlet, or is he about to discover a conspiracy on his friends' part? Either his anticipation of what the friends want to discover will prevent their discovering anything, or else his anticipation of their spying will prevent the king's discovering that his plot has been exposed.

The shrewdest Victorian comment on Hamlet's college friends comes from Oscar Wilde, who observes that Rosencrantz and Guildenstern are "types fixed for all time. To censure them would show a lack of appreciation. They are merely out of their sphere: that is all" (1968, 161). In Wilde's view, these two ciphers serve only to isolate Hamlet's "high thoughts and high emotions." The prince assures them that, though they have molted feathers of secrecy to him, in the eyes of the powers that commissioned them none of their plumage has been lost. "What Ophelia herself could not understand" in Hamlet, Wilde reminds us, "was not to be realized by 'Guildenstern and gentle Rosencrantz,' nor by 'Rosencrantz and gentle Guildenstern'" (161). As John Stokes concludes, Hamlet becomes Wilde's favorite point of reference for what is secretive and obscure in Shakespeare, "replacing both Romeo and even the sexually ambiguous Rosalind because of his inscrutability" (2003, 190).

5. Thou, Nature, Art My Goddess

1. Other Victorian references to Polixenes's speech appear in John Skelton's article "What Are the Functions of the Artist?," a review essay of John Ruskin's *Modern Painters* in *Fraser's Magazine* 55 (June 1857): 631, and in Skelton's review of "Mr. Dallas, *The Gay Science*" in volume 74 of the same periodical (December 1866: 782). Similar ideas, without the supporting quotation from Shakespeare, appear in John Eagles, "The Natural in Art," *Blackwood's Magazine* 51 (April 1842): 435.

6. A Choral Mind Trap

1. The harshest judgment of Hardy's choral mind traps and homilies comes from R. G. Collingwood in his *Principles of Art.*

> Thomas Hardy, at the end of a fine and tragic novel in which he has magnificently expressed his sorrow and indignation for the suffering inflicted by callous sentimentalism on trusting innocence, soils everything by a last paragraph fastening his accusation upon 'the president of the immortals.' The note rings false, not because it is blasphemous (it offends no piety worthy of the name), but because it is rant. The case against God, so far as it exists, is complete already. The concluding paragraph adds nothing to it. All it does is to spoil the effect of the indictment by betraying a symptom of the emotion which the whole book has already expressed; as if a prosecuting counsel, at the end of his speech, spat in the prisoner's face. (1938, 123)

According to Collingwood, rant betrays unbalanced emotion. Its attempt to turn blasphemy into a heroic enterprise produces only the intemperate rhetoric of Shakespeare's Timon or Marlowe's Tamburlaine. If Hardy's novel were a play and its last paragraph a choral epilogue, Collingwood's charge would be unanswerable. But *Tess of the d'Urbervilles* is a Victorian novel, and its narrator is a fallible, human participant in a prose fiction, not the mouthpiece of a choral commentator. Like the wry, bemused narrator of *Barchester Towers,* or the elusive sage who narrates *Vanity Fair,* the narrator is as engaged and three-dimensional a character as Angel Clare. He is his heroine's apologist, readier to blame a malign god for her fate than Tess herself. He has, of course, affinities with Hardy, who subtitles his novel "a pure woman faithfully presented." But as a cosmic inquisitor who asks questions he cannot answer, and who is impelled to speak when silence is more appropriate, he should not be identified uncritically with the author.

8. The End of Illusion

1. The mastery of rapidly sketched metaphors and of a hurried elliptical style makes Hopkins's sonnet "No worst, there is none" one of the most Shakespearean Victorian productions, even though Hopkins was virtually unknown to the Victorians themselves. "Hidden transitions and rich gaps which later ages struggled to fill in" exemplify, as Philip Davis says, "what Shakespeare and his live thinking meant to the greatest Victorians" (2003, 89), to sages like Ruskin, Carlyle, George Eliot, and Newman. In the wrenched syntax and violent ellipses of Browning's poems, these Victorians also feel and admire the swift turns and swerves of thought they value in Shakespeare. In soliloquies by Hamlet, Lear, and Aufidius

in *Coriolanus,* who are among the subtlest and most rugged of Shakespeare's "Alpine mountaineers," what the Victorians experience, "even before [they] start to unpack the language, is its pace, its sudden turns and backtrackings, its metaphors flashing . . . and disappearing" before they can fully grasp what they mean (Kermode, 2000, 246).

9. A Toil of Grace

1. Shakespeare's influence on *Maud* is not just confined to scenes in the madhouse. There is something Shakespearean—or at least Elizabethan—in the gusto as well as the pathos of the lover's question: "O, why should Love, like men in drinking-songs, / Spice his fair banquet with the dust of death?" (*Maud* 1.653–54). Mingling with the taste of spice and the chorus of a drinking song is a sensation as grittily tactile as a temporal reversion of dust to dust and as visually fair and enticing as a banquet gazed upon in wonder.

2. Less satisfactory, surely, is Arnold's treatment of Shakespeare in his famous essay "The Study of Poetry," where the critic assumes that "short passages, even single lines" of poetry, can serve as "an infallible touchstone for detecting" greatness in poetry (1961, 312). The short excerpts he selects from Henry IV's "expostulation with sleep" and Hamlet's dying words to Horatio are meant to isolate the essence of Shakespeare's style. But what the rocking of the ship-boy's brains in the cradle of the sea has in common with Horatio's absenting himself "from felicity awhile," Arnold neglects to say. In this matter it seems safer to trust Samuel Johnson than Arnold. Anyone who tries to illustrate Shakespeare with selected touchstones, Johnson warns, "will succeed like the pedant in Hierocles, who, when he offered his house for sale, carried a brick in his pocket as a specimen" (quoted by Bate, 1975, 401). A poet of not one but many styles, Shakespeare has the abundance, variety, and complete competence T. S. Eliot associates with Tennyson, whose poems seem written by a corps of different craftsmen.

10. Off the Edge

1. The only major philosopher to support the claim that the soul survives the death of the body is Plato, whose theory of immortality appeals to some Christian apologists and mystics. The problem with immortality is that in eliminating death it also diminishes life. The idea of living forever is chilling. Who could tolerate living forever with the same people? G. K. Chesterton observes that "there are people who pray for eternal life who don't know what to do with themselves on a rainy Sunday." A terrible monotony attaches to any pleasure garden we could possibly inhabit. To deny death is to opt for a life without risk, where nothing is at stake. Under such conditions, James Carse maintains, "there could be no curiosity about a future in which anything could happen that one wishes to happen. . . . A person's character is shaped by tragedy, suspense, hope, regret, an occasional victory over improbable odds, and an occasional irreversible defeat—but in an indefinite existence all this would be meaningless. Where then is character? Where the person?" (1980, 30). In a similar vein Stanley Fish argues that "without the specter and period of death, there would be no urgency of accomplishment, no expectations to be realized or disappointed, no anxieties to be allayed. . . . It is the inevitability and shadow of death that provides life with a narrative arc, and provides moments in that narrative with a meaning" (2011, 154). And yet if Carse and Fish are right, why does the classical form of grief continue to engage in the anti-life struggle of holding onto the body in a direct battle with death?

No philosopher explores this question more honestly than Jean-Paul Sartre in his essay "My Death" in *Being and Nothingness.* Sartre insists that since we are not free to cease being free, we are not "free to die." But if death is a force that overtakes us anyway, however stubbornly we strive against it, is our Ulysses-like hunger for experience, like our need to be free, not also, in Sartre's desolating phrase, "a useless passion"? By snapping at our heels like a tireless hound, death robs us without warning of our flight toward freedom. If "death closes all," it cannot be an event that belongs to our future of ever-receding horizons, but to a past that binds and imprisons us and is in some sense already over.

2. I have never fully understood what E. M. Forster meant when he said "death destroys a man but the idea of death saves him." Does he mean that the prospect of an endless life with its infinity of torments is too painful to bear? Living forever, like Tithonus or the Sibyl, we might be less aware of the transience and hence the seriousness of beauty. In the absence of any end game, life might lack the power to recharge its batteries or "reboot" like a computer. Alternatively, since all philosophy, according to Socrates, is a meditation on death, Forster may be implying that without the mystery of death we would be less reflective, less tolerant of uncertainty, less receptive to second thoughts, and so less human in the end. Perhaps death has less in common with an end game in chess than with that force which drove Adam and Eve out of paradise, which propelled them through boundary after boundary, allowing them to experience dimensions of joy as well as loss.

11. The Hills Are Shadows

1. Wordsworth and Blake believe that childhood is a state or phase of imagination existence: when young, we think we are immortal. Though "shades of the prison-house" close upon the growing boy, "Not in utter nakedness, / But trailing clouds of glory do we come / From God, who is our home" (Wordsworth, "Ode: Intimations of Immortality," lines 62–65). The idea that knowledge is reminiscence, and that in a pre-natural state we all share a measure of angelic apprehension, originates in Plato. It is confirmed by Wordsworth's claim that "our birth is but a sleep and a forgetting" (line 58) and by Emerson's testimony that "in every work of genius we recognize our own thoughts; they come back to us with a certain alienated majesty" ("Self-Reliance," 1965, 556).

2. Like Shakespeare, the Victorians experiment with a variety of optical metaphors. Browning's Pope argues that light has to be refracted to be seen: under a vertical sun the exposed brain would be less certain to wither up and die at once than a mind confronted with God's blinding light. In "A Death in the Desert," St. John compares truth to a galaxy of distant stars. They can be seen only when reduced to tiny points on the reflector of a telescope. In *Middlemarch,* truth is seen at first as a mere array of scratches on the surface of a pier glass. Not until viewed in candlelight do these scratches assume a flattering illusion of concentric arrangement. A detailed account of optics as it bears on Victorian critical theory and poetic practice may be found in my essay "The Optical Metaphor: Victorian Poetics and the Theory of Knowledge," *Victorian Studies* 23 (1980): 293–324.

3. In his sonnet on Shakespeare, Hopkins's announcement of the playwright's semi-divinity turns him into a kind of literary John the Baptist. It is intriguing to speculate how far Victorian interpretations of Shakespeare, like nineteenth-century interpretations of Socrates and Plato, refine and parallel experiments in biblical hermeneutics and typology, especially in poems like Hopkins's "New Readings." Although conservative hermeneutical critics like John Keble and J. H. Newman teach the Victorian interpreter to be loyal to the text, the more liberal hermeneutical traditions of Browning, F. H. Bradley, and Friedrich Strauss instruct the interpreter not to be too loyal. Even in escaping from the limits of his own personality by losing himself in impersonal scholarship, the Browning who interprets

St. John's gospel in "A Death in the Desert" never forgets that the knowledge he brings to Scripture is not just knowledge of the kind he can look up in a commentary by the Church Fathers. It is knowledge of the interpreter himself. In insisting that, even in adhering to the letter of ancient Greek, Roman, and Hebrew texts, the good interpreter should resuscitate and inject new life into his source, Strauss and Browning are also following the precept and example of Shakespeare. For however closely Shakespeare may follow the chronicles of Plutarch and Holinshed, he also offers his own imaginative interpretation. As Harold Goddard says, Shakespeare's "Greeks and Romans, his Britons and Italians, all became, in one sense, Elizabethan Englishmen, and, in another, what for lack of a better term we can only call 'Universal Man'" (4). Shakespeare's Cadwal in *Cymbeline* does not merely act out a story, like his older brother Polydore. Cadwal, the more imaginative of the two interpreters (while not a sorcerer like Agrippa or Faust), is a miracle-worker in the tradition of Elisha, who reinvents stories and resurrects them. Though favored by Browning, Strauss, and F. H. Bradley in his *Presuppositions of Critical History,* the Cadwals are rejected by conservative Tractarian interpreters like Keble and J. H. Newman, the Polydores of Victorian hermeneutics. Yet Goddard is surely right to insist that "the men who have loved Shakespeare best and have kept him most alive have all been Cadwals," not Polydores (4).

12. Oracle Meets Wit

1. Wallace Stevens, "The Idea of Order at Key West," line 55.

2. One difficulty in assessing the influence of Shakespeare's language in any age is the abundance and variety of its styles, which all students of the subject, from A. C. Bradley to Frank Kermode, acknowledge. In his *Study of Shakespeare* (1879), Swinburne anticipates Bradley and Eliot by distinguishing between an early lyric and fantastic, a middle comic and historic, and a final tragic and romantic phase in Shakespeare's art. After *Hamlet,* Bradley says, "the pervading effect of beauty gives place to what may almost be called explosions of sublimity or pathos" (1957, 69). As Kant and Hegel explain, in sublime forms of art beautiful material forms dissolve or fade away so that an otherwise inexpressible spiritual content may make its presence felt. In Bradley's words, "The sense has rather to be discerned beyond the words than found in them" (69). Shakespeare's style "becomes grander, sometimes more swelling, even tumid. It is also more concentrated, rapid, varied, and, in construction, less regular, not seldom twisted or elliptical" (68).

In *Venus and Adonis* and *Love's Labour's Lost,* Shakespeare is still trying to move, as Eliot says, "from artificiality to simplicity, from stiffness to suppleness" (1961, "Music of Poetry," 29). But after discovering in *Antony and Cleopatra* how anything can be said with "naturalness and beauty," Shakespeare gradually moves away "from simplicity toward elaboration" in *Cymbeline, Coriolanus,* and *The Winter's Tale.* As if to extenuate Shakespeare's excesses when experimenting with complex syntax and ellipsis, Eliot concedes that "it is often true that only by going too far can we find out how far we can go." One has to be a very accomplished poet like Shakespeare or Hopkins "to justify such perilous adventures" and experiments with language (1961, 29–30). Victorian poets tend to sound most Shakespearean when they cultivate the associative power of his compressed metaphors, his active in-feeling and empathy, his ability to pass with ease from words that are simple and human to Caliban's vision of clouds opening and of riches dropping upon him.

3. The willingness of Shakespeare's speakers to correct or amend their first thoughts is a hallmark of that "antiphonal style" Geoffrey Hill praises in nineteenth-century writers like Newman and Pater, whose thought is marked by an "undertow of reluctance" (93). Shake-

speare's antiphonal style survives in the irresolute ebb and surge of Clough's hexameters in *Amours de Voyage,* which contains fragments of thought not wholly formed or worked out. Geoffrey Hill maintains that the most consistent nineteenth-century practitioners of this style are "Coleridge, in the prose works, and Hopkins; isolated, significant examples are to be found in Newman and T. H. Green" (1984, 94).

Listening to voices in poems that are musically organized like *In Memoriam* or in tragedies like *Hamlet, Romeo and Juliet,* and *King Lear,* we may begin to experience the effects Oscar Wilde describes in his extraordinary passage on music in *The Critic as Artist.* "It creates for one a past of which one has been ignorant, and fills one with a sense of sorrows that have been hidden from one's tears. I can fancy a man who had led a perfectly commonplace life, hearing by chance some curious piece of music, and suddenly discovering that his soul, without his being conscious of it, had passed through terrible experiences, and known fearful joys, or wild romantic loves, or great renunciations" (1968, 200). Yet qualifying Wilde's extravagant praise and Pater's dictum that all art aspires to the condition of music is Auden's wise observation that, whereas "music is immediate," and "goes on to become," "a verbal art like poetry is reflective; it stops to think" (quoted by Hoggart, 1999, 195). Those who value perplexed persistence and doubt and who cherish the challenge of an unresolved, antiphonal way of thinking will always rank literature above music.

4. The fact that Shakespeare is not Lucretius, Dante, or Milton, and does not explicitly embrace a system of thought or a creed, does not make him a lesser poet or thinker than Dante. As Richard Rorty argues, in any "philosophy without mirrors," which is the kind of philosophy he advocates, there is no longer a need for the imaginative proposals of poets or the logical arguments of philosophers to aspire to what Kant has called a truth of pure reason. Though Minerva's owl is no ascending lark, singing at heaven's gate, philosophers can still learn as much from the poets as Shakespeare learns from a speculative thinker like Montaigne. Truth may be an imagination that succeeds, an intuition that guesses some law of nature or the universe. But no one has ever confused Shakespeare with Galileo or Aquinas with Newton. Indeed, Rorty concludes that "the word *knowledge* would not seem worth fighting over were it not for the Kantian tradition that to be a philosopher is to have a 'theory of knowledge,' and the Platonic tradition that action not based on knowledge of the truth of propositions is irrational" (1979, 356).

Selected Bibliography

Although there are no definitive texts of Shakespeare, I have listed in the bibliography individual volumes in the New Oxford and Penguin editions whose variants I have consulted and whose commentary has increased my understanding of the plays. In other instances I have relied on the serviceable Cambridge edition of *The Complete Plays and Poems of William Shakespeare,* 1942, edited by William Allan Nelson and Charles Jarvis Hill (Cambridge, MA: Houghton Mifflin).

Albright, Daniel. 1986. *Tennyson: The Muses' Tug-of-War.* Charlottesville: University of Virginia Press.

Armstrong, Isobel. 1993. *Victorian Poetry: Poetry, Poetics and Politics.* New York: Routledge.

Arnold, Matthew. 1896. *On Translating Homer.* London: Smith, Elder.

———. 1932. *The Letters of Matthew Arnold to Arthur Hugh Clough.* Edited by H. F. Lowry. Oxford: Oxford University Press.

———. 1961. *On the Study of Celtic Literature.* 105–22. Reprinted in Robert L. Peters, *Victorians on Literature and Art.* Englewood Cliffs, NJ: Prentice-Hall.

———. 1964. *Matthew Arnold's Essays in Criticism: First and Second Series.* J. M. Dent: London.

———. 1965. *The Poems of Matthew Arnold.* Edited by Kenneth Allott. London: Longmans, Green.

Auden, W. H. 1976. *W. H. Auden: Collected Poems.* Edited by Edward Mendelson. New York: Random House.

Auerbach, Erich. 2003. *Mimesis: The Representation of Reality in Western Literature.* Princeton, NJ: Princeton University Press.

Auerbach, Nina. 1990. *Private Theatricals: The Lives of the Victorians.* Cambridge, MA: Harvard University Press.

———. 2003. "Perturbed Spirits: Victorian Actors and Immortality." In *Victorian Shakespeare,* 1:192–202. New York: Palgrave Macmillan.

Austen, Jane. 1971. *Emma.* Edited by David Lodge. London: Oxford University Press.

Ayer, A. J., and Jane O'Grady. 1992. *A Dictionary of Philosophical Quotations.* Blackwell: Oxford.

Ball, Patricia. 1974. *The Science of Aspects: The Changing Role of Fact in the Works of Coleridge, Ruskin, and Hopkins.* London: Athlone Press.

Barber, C. L. 1972. *Shakespeare's Festive Comedy: A Study of Dramatic Forms in Its Relation to Social Customs.* Princeton, NJ: Princeton University Press.

Bate, Walter Jackson. 1960. "Keats's Style: Evolution toward Qualities of Permanent Value." In *English Romantic Poets: Modern Essays in Criticism,* edited by M. H. Abrams, 340–53. New York: Oxford University Press.

———. 1975. *Samuel Johnson.* Washington, DC: Counterpoint.

Baxter, Charles. 2007. *The Art of Subtext: Beyond Plot.* St. Paul, MN: Graywolf Press.

Bayley, John. 1981. *Shakespeare and Tragedy.* London: Routledge and Kegan Paul.

———. 1999. *Elegy for Iris.* New York: Picador.

Berkeley, George. 1954. *Three Dialogues between Hylas and Philonous.* Edited by Colin M. Turbayne. Indianapolis: Bobbs-Merrill. Originally published in 1713.

Birch, Dinah. 2009. "Tennyson's Retrospective View." In *Tennyson among the Poets: Bicentenary Essays,* edited by Robert Douglas-Fairhurst and Seamus Perry, 37–56. Oxford: Oxford University Press.

Bishop, Jonathan. 1972. *Something Else.* New York: George Braziller.

Black, Max. 1962. *Models and Metaphors: Studies in Language and Philosophy.* Ithaca, NY: Cornell University Press.

Blackmur, R. P. 1954. *Language as Gesture.* New York: Columbia University Press.

———. 1980. *Henry Adams.* New York: Harcourt Brace Jovanovich.

Bloom, Harold. 1998. *Shakespeare and the Invention of the Human.* New York: Riverhead Books.

———. 2003. *Hamlet: Poem Unlimited.* New York: Riverhead Books.

———. 2011. *The Anatomy of Influence: Literature as a Way of Life.* New Haven, CT: Yale University Press.

Blunden, Edmund. 1936. "Shakespeare's Significances." In *Shakespeare Criticism, 1919–1935,* edited by Anne Ridler, 327–42. London: Oxford University Press.

Bok, Sissela. 1979. *Lying: Moral Choice in Public and Private Life.* New York: Vintage.

Booth, Stephen. 1974. "On the Value of *Hamlet.*" In *Literary Criticism: Idea and Art,* edited by W. K. Wimsatt, 284–310. Berkeley: University of California Press.

———. 1983. *King Lear, Macbeth, Indefinition, and Tragedy.* New Haven, CT: Yale University Press.

Borrow, George. 1902. *Lavengro: The Scholar, the Gypsy, the Priest.* London: Oxford University Press.

Bradley, A. C. 1957. *Shakespearean Tragedy.* London: Macmillan.

Bradley, F. H. 1876. *Ethical Studies.* Oxford: Clarendon Press. Reprinted 1970; London: Oxford University Press, edited by Richard Wollheim.

———. 1893. *Appearance and Reality: A Metaphysical Essay.* Oxford: Clarendon Press.

———. 1930. *Aphorisms.* Oxford: Clarendon Press, 1930.

Broadbent, John. 1972. *Paradise Lost: Introduction.* Cambridge: Cambridge University Press.

Brontë, Charlotte. 1957. *Villette.* London: J. M. Dent and Sons.

Brower, Reuben A. 1951. *The Fields of Light: An Experiment in Critical Reading.* New York: Oxford University Press.

———. 1959. *Alexander Pope: The Poetry of Allusion.* New York: Oxford University Press, 1959.

———. 1963. *The Poetry of Robert Frost: Constellations of Intention.* New York: Oxford University Press.

———. 1971. *Hero and Saint: Shakespeare and the Graeco-Roman Heroic Tradition.* New York: Oxford University Press.

Browne, Thomas. 1967. *The Prose of Sir Thomas Browne.* Edited by Norman J. Endicott. Garden City, NY: Doubleday.

Browning, Robert. 1969. *The Letters of Robert and Elizabeth Barrett Barrett, 1845–1846.* Edited by Elvan Kintner. 2 vols. Cambridge, MA: Harvard University Press.

———. 1981. *Robert Browning: The Poems.* Edited by John Pettigrew and Thomas J. Collins. 2 vols. New York: Penguin.

———. 2001. *The Ring and the Book.* Edited by Richard D. Altick and Thomas J. Collins. 2 vols. New York: Penguin.

Bryant, Mark. 1983. *Riddles Ancient and Modern.* New York: Peter Bedrick Books.

Buchanan, Robert. 1959. "The Fleshly School of Poetry: Mr. D. G. Rossetti." *Contemporary Review* (October 1871). Reprinted in *Victorian Poetry and Poetics,* edited by Walter E. Houghton and Robert G. Stange, 888–98. Boston: Houghton Mifflin.

Bush, Douglas. 1937. *Mythology and the Romantic Tradition in English Poetry.* Cambridge, MA: Harvard University Press.

———. 1943. "Tennyson's Ulysses and Hamlet." *Modern Language Review* 38: 38.

———. 1971. *Matthew Arnold: A Survey of His Poetry and Prose.* New York: Collier.

Byatt, A. S. 1969. "The Lyric Structure of Tennyson's *Maud.*" In *The Major Victorian Poets: Reconsiderations,* edited by Isobel Armstrong, 69–92. Lincoln: University of Nebraska Press.

———. 1992. "The Conjugial Angel." In *Angels and Insects: Two Novella.* New York: Random House.

Carlyle, Thomas. 1938. "The Hero as Poet. Dante; Shakespeare." Lecture 3 from *On Heroes, Hero-Worship, and the Heroic in History.* In *English Prose of the Victorian Era,* edited by C. F. Harrold and William D. Templeman, 182–96. New York: Oxford University Press.

———. 1970. *Sartor Resartus and Selected Prose.* New York: Holt, Rinehart and Winston.

Carse, James P. 1980. *Death and Existence: A Conceptual History of Human Mortality.* New York: John Wiley and Sons.

———. 2008. *The Religious Case against Belief.* New York: Penguin.

Chadwick, Owen. 1983. *Newman.* Oxford: Oxford University Press.

Chesterton, G. K. 1903. *Robert Browning.* London: Macmillan.

———. 1933. *St. Thomas Aquinas.* New York: Sheed and Ward.

———. 2005. "God the Rebel." In *Bread and Wine,* 165–67. Orbis Books: Maryknoll, N.Y.

Clemens, Wolfgang. 1964. *Shakespeare's Soliloquies.* Cambridge: Cambridge University Press.

Clough, Arthur Hugh. 1959. "Recent English Poetry." Originally published in *North American Review* 57 (July 1853). Reprinted in *Victorian Poetry and Poetics,* edited by Walter E. Houghton and G. Robert Stange, 395–403. Boston: Houghton Mifflin.

———. 1974. *The Poems of Arthur Hugh Clough.* Edited by F. L. Mulhauser. Oxford: Clarendon Press.

Coleridge, S. T. 1930. *Coleridge's Shakespeare Criticism.* Edited by T. M. Raysor. 2 vols. London: Constable.

———. 1969. *Coleridge on Shakespeare.* Edited by Terence Hawkes. New York: Penguin.

Collingwood, R. G. 1938. *The Principles of Art.* Oxford: Clarendon Press.

Collins, Wilkie. 1972. *The Moonstone.* London: Fontana.

Copleston, Frederick. 1965. *A History of Philosophy: Modern Philosophy Fichte to Hegel.* Vol. 7, pt. 1. Garden City, NY: Doubleday.

Crewe, Jonathan. 2010. "Elegy in English Drama, 1590–1640." In *The Oxford Handbook of the Elegy,* edited by Karen Weisman, 518–32. New York: Oxford University Press.

Culler, A. Dwight. 1968. "The Darwinian Revolution and Literary Form." In *The Art of Victorian Prose,* edited by George Levine and William Madden, 224–46. London: Oxford University Press.

———. 1977. *The Poetry of Tennyson.* New Haven, CT: Yale University Press.

Darwin, Charles. 2000. *Origin of Species.* In *Nineteenth Century Science: A Selection of Original Texts,* edited by A. S. Weber. Toronto: Broadview Press.

Davie, Donald. 1972. *Thomas Hardy and British Poetry.* New York: Oxford University Press.

Davis, Philip. 2003. "Implicit and Explicit Reason: George Eliot and Shakespeare." In *Victorian Shakespeare,* 2:84–99. New York: Palgrave Macmillan.

Decker, Christopher. 2003. "Shakespeare and the Death of Tennyson." In *Victorian Shakespeare,* 2:131–49. New York: Palgrave Macmillan.

———. 2009. "Tennyson's Limitations." In *Tennyson among the Poets: Bicentenary Essays,* edited by Robert Douglas-Fairhurst and Seamus Perry, 57–75. Oxford: Oxford University Press.

De Quincey, Thomas. 1848. "Alexander Pope" ["The Literature of Knowledge and the Literature of Power"]. Reprinted in *The Norton Anthology of English Literature,* 5th ed., edited by M. H. Abrams, 483–88. New York: Norton, 1986.

DeVane, William C. 1954. "Robert Browning." In *Major British Writers,* 2:467–79. New York: Harcourt, Brace.

Dickens, Charles. 1973. *Great Expectations.* London: Oxford University Press.

Donne, John. 1967. *The Complete Poetry of John Donne.* Edited by John T. Shawcross. Garden City, NY: Doubleday.

Donoghue, Denis. 1995. *Walter Pater: Lover of Strange Souls.* New York: Alfred A. Knopf.

———. 1998. *The Practice of Reading.* New Haven, CT: Yale University Press.

Drew, Elizabeth. 1933. *Discovering Poetry.* New York: Norton.

Drummond, William. 1791. *The Poems of William Drummond of Hawthornden.* London: Printed for E. Jeffrey.

Dryden, John. 1933. "An Essay of Dramatic Poesy." In *The Best of Dryden,* edited by Louis I. Bredvold, 377–459. New York: Ronald Press.

Dunn. T. A. 1957. *Philip Massinger.* Edinburgh: Oliver and Boyd.

Edel, Leon. 1985. *Henry James: A Life.* New York: Harper and Row.

Eliot, George. 1900. *Scenes of Clerical Life.* New York: R. F. Fenno.

———. 1956. *Middlemarch: A Study of Provincial Life.* Edited by George S. Haight. Boston: Houghton Mifflin.

———. 1961. *The Mill on the Floss.* Edited by George S. Haight. Boston: Houghton Mifflin.

———. 2008. *Adam Bede.* Oxford: Oxford University Press.

Eliot, T. S. 1932. "Dante." In *Selected Essays,* 237–77. London: Faber and Faber.

———. 1932. "George Herbert." *Spectator* (March 12): 360–61.

———. 1932. "*In Memoriam.*" In *Selected Essays,* 329–38. London: Faber and Faber.

———. 1935. *Murder in the Cathedral.* London: Faber and Faber.

———. 1943. *Four Quartets.* New York: Harcourt, Brace and World.

———. 1948. *Notes towards the Definition of Culture.* London: Faber and Faber.

———. 1958. *Collected Poems, 1909–1935.* New York: Harcourt, Brace.

———. 1960. "Shakespeare Criticism: From Dryden to Coleridge." In *A Companion to Shakespeare Studies,* edited by Harley Granville-Barker and G. B. Harrison, 293–305. Garden City, NY: Anchor Books.

———. 1961. "The Music of Poetry." In *On Poetry and Poets,* 17–33. New York: Farrar, Straus, and Giroux.

———. 1961. "Poetry and Drama." In *On Poetry and Poets,* 75–95. New York: Farrar, Straus, and Giroux.

———. 1961. "The Three Voices of Poetry." In *On Poetry and Poets,* 96–112. New York: Farrar, Straus, and Giroux.

Emerson, Ralph Waldo. 1965. "Self-Reliance." In *American Literary Masters,* edited by Charles R. Anderson, 1:555–71. New York: Holt, Rinehart, and Winston.

Empson, W. H. 1961. *Seven Types of Ambiguity.* Harmondsworth, UK: Penguin.

Ferrier, J. F. 1854. *The Institutes of Metaphysics: Theory of Knowing and Being.* Edinburgh: Blackwood.

Fish, Stanley. 2011. *How to Write a Sentence and How to Read One.* New York: HarperCollins.

Fitzgerald, Edward. 1968. *The Rubaiyat of Omar Khayyam.* 5th version. In *The Pre-Raphaelites and Their Circle,* edited by Cecil Y. Lang, 483–97. Boston: Houghton Mifflin.

Ford, George H. 1945. *Keats and the Victorians: A Study of His Influence and Rise to Fame.* New Haven, CT: Yale University Press.

Fossi, Gloria. 2003. "Filippo Lippi." In *The Great Italian Painters from the Gothic to the Renaissance,* 456–87. Florence: Scala.

Fox, W. J. 1972. Review of Tennyson's *Poems, Chiefly Lyrical.* In *Westminster Review* 14 (1831). Reprinted in *Victorian Scrutinies,* edited by Isobel Armstrong, 71–83. London: Athlone Press.

Frieden, Ken. 1985. *Genius and Monologue.* Ithaca, NY: Cornell University Press.

Frost, Robert. 1968. *Selected Prose of Robert Frost.* Edited by Hyde Cox and Edward Connery Lathem. New York: Collier.

Frye, Northrop. 1947. *Fearful Symmetry: A Study of William Blake.* Princeton, NJ: Princeton University Press, 1947.

———. 1957. *Anatomy of Criticism: Four Essays.* Princeton, NJ: Princeton University Press.

———. 1967. *Fools of Time: Studies in Shakespearean Tragedy.* Toronto: University of Toronto Press.

———. 1986. *Northrop Frye on Shakespeare.* New Haven, CT: Yale University Press.

———. 1990. *Words with Power.* New York: Harcourt Brace.

———. 2001. *The Diaries of Northrop Frye, 1942–1955.* Edited by Robert Denham. Vol. 8. Toronto: University of Toronto Press.

———. 2002. *The "Third Book" Notebooks of Northrop Frye, 1964–1972.* Edited by Michael Dolzani. Vol. 9. Toronto: University of Toronto Press.

———. 2004. *Northrop Frye: Wit and Wisdom from the Notebooks and Diaries.* Toronto: House of Anansi Press.

Fussell, Paul. 1965. *Poetic Meter and Poetic Form.* New York: Random House.

———. 1996. *Doing Battle: The Making of a Skeptic.* Boston: Little, Brown.

Gardner, Martin. 1996. *The Universe in a Handkerchief: Lewis Carroll's Mathematical Recreations, Games, Puzzles, and Word Plays.* New York: Copernicus.

Gielgud, John. 1991. *Acting Shakespeare.* New York: Applause Books.

Goddard, Harold C. 1951. *The Meaning of Shakespeare.* Chicago: University of Chicago Press.

Goode, John. 1969. "*Amours de Voyage:* The Aqueous Age." In *The Major Victorian Poets,* edited by Isobel Armstrong, 275–97. Lincoln: University of Nebraska Press.

Goodman, Nelson. 1976. *Languages of Art: An Approach to a Theory of Symbols.* New York: Hackett.

———. 1977. *The Structure of Appearance.* New York: R. Riedel.

———. 1978. *Ways of Worldmaking.* New York: Hackett.

———. 1984. *Of Mind and Other Matters.* Cambridge, MA: Harvard University Press.

Gough, J. W. Ben. 1895. "The Higher Criticism." In *Motley: Verses Grave and Gay,* 163–66. Toronto: William Briggs.

Granville-Barker, Harley. 1936. "King Lear." In *Shakespeare Criticism, 1919–1935,* edited by Anne Ridler, 19–51. London: Oxford University Press.

———. 1946–47. *Prefaces to Shakespeare.* Vols. 1 and 2. London: B. T. Batsford.

———. 1957. "The Merchant of Venice." In *Shakespeare: Modern Essays in Criticism,* edited by Leonard F. Dean, 37–71. New York: Oxford University Press.

———. 1960. "Shakespeare's Dramatic Art." In *A Companion to Shakespeare Studies,* edited by Harley Granville-Barker and G. B. Harrison, 44–87. Garden City, NY: Anchor Books.

Gray, Erik. 2009. *Milton and the Victorians.* Ithaca, NY: Cornell University Press.

———. 2010. "Victoria Dressed in Black: Poetry in an Elegiac Age." 272–88. In *The Oxford Handbook of the Elegy,* edited by Karen Weisman, 272–88. New York: Oxford University Press.

Green, T. H. 1874. Dissertations and Notes in David Hume's *A Treatise of Human Nature.* London: Longmans, Green.

———. 1929. *Prolegomena to Ethics.* 5th ed. Oxford: Clarendon Press.

Greenblatt, Stephen. 1989. *Shakespearean Negotiations: The Circulation of Social Energy in Renaissance England.* Berkeley and Los Angeles: University of California Press.

———. 1991. *Marvelous Possessions: The Wonder of the New World.* Chicago: University of Chicago Press.

———. 2004. *Will in the World: How Shakespeare Became Shakespeare.* New York: W. W. Norton.

Griffiths, Eric. 1989. *The Printed Voice of Victorian Poetry.* Oxford: Clarendon Press.

———. 2009. "Lines and Grooves: Shakespeare to Tennyson." In *Tennyson among the Poets: Bicentenary Essays,* edited by Robert Douglas-Fairhurst and Seamus Perry, 132–59. Oxford: Oxford University Press.

Gubar, Susan. 2009. *Judas: A Biography.* New York: W. W. Norton.

Hair, Donald S. 1991. *Tennyson's Language.* Toronto: University of Toronto Press.

Hallam, Arthur. 1968. "On Some of the Characteristics of Modern Poetry and on the Lyrical Poems of Alfred Tennyson." In *The Englishman's Magazine* (August 1831). Reprinted in *Victorian Poetry and Poetics,* edited by Walter Houghton and G. Robert Stange, 848–60. Boston: Houghton Mifflin.

Harbage, Alfred. 1963. *William Shakespeare: A Reader's Guide.* New York: Noonday.

Hardy, Barbara. 1969. "Clough's Self-Consciousness." In *The Major Victorian Poets: Reconsiderations,* edited by Isobel Armstrong, 253–74. Lincoln: University of Nebraska Press.

Hardy, Thomas. 1937. *The Complete Poetical Works of Thomas Hardy.* Edited by Samuel Hynes. 2 vols. Oxford: Clarendon Press.

———. 1983. *Tess of the d'Urbervilles.* Edited by Juliet Grindle and Simon Gatrell. New York: Oxford University Press.

Harrison, Antony H. 1993. "Christina Rossetti and the Romantics: Influence and Ideology." In *Influence and Resistance in Nineteenth-Century English Poetry,* edited by G. Kim Blank and Margot K. Louis, 131–49. London: Macmillan.

Harrison. G. B. 1947. *Introducing Shakespeare.* New York: Mentor.

Hartman, Geoffrey H. 1980. *Criticism in the Wilderness: The Study of Literature Today.* New Haven, CT: Yale University Press.

Heaney, Seamus. 2002. *Finders Keeper: Selected Prose, 1971–2001.* London: Faber and Faber.

Herbert, Christopher. 2001. *Victorian Relativity: Radical Thought and Scientific Discovery.* Chicago: University of Chicago Press.

Herbert, George. 1941. *Works.* Edited by F. E. Hutchinson. Oxford: Clarendon Press.

Hertz, Neil. 2003. *George Eliot's Pulse.* Stanford, CA: Stanford University Press.

Hill, Geoffrey. 1984. *The Lord of Limits: Essay on Literature and Ideas.* London: André Deutsch.

Hirsh, James. 2003. *Shakespeare and the History of Soliloquies.* Madison, NJ: Farleigh Dickinson University Press.

Hoggart, Richard. 1999. *First and Last Things.* London: Aurum Press.

Hollander, John. 1974. *Vision and Resonance: Two Senses of Poetic Form.* New York: Oxford University Press.

———. 1981. *Rhyme's Reasons: A Guide to English Verse.* New Haven, CT: Yale University Press.

Honan, Park. 1961. *Browning's Characters.* New Haven, CT: Yale University Press.

———. 1999. *Shakespeare: A Life.* New York: Oxford University Press.

Hopkins, G. M. 1938. *Letters of G. M. Hopkins.* Edited by Claude Colleer Abbott. London: Oxford University Press.

———. 1967. *Poems.* Edited by W. H. Gardner and N. H. Mackenzie. 4th ed. London: Oxford University Press.

Housman, A. E. 1994. *The Works of A. E. Housman.* Cumberland House, Hertfordshire: Wordsworth Poetry Library.

Huigzinga, Johan. 1949. *The Waning of the Middle Ages.* New York: St. Martin's Press.

Hume, David. 1888. *A Treatise on Human Nature.* Edited by L. A. Selby-Bigge. Oxford: Clarendon Press.

———. 2000. *An Enquiry Concerning Human Understanding.* Edited by Tom L. Beauchamp. Oxford: Clarendon Press.

Huxley, Thomas Henry. 1904–25. *Collected Essays.* 9 vols. London: Macmillan.

———. 1948. *Selections from the Essays of T. H. Huxley.* Edited by Alburey Castell. Northbrook, IL: AHM Publishing.

Hyland, Peter. 1996. *An Introduction to Shakespeare: The Dramatist and His Context.* London: Macmillan.

James, Henry. 1965. *The Wings of the Dove.* New York: Penguin.

James, William. 1993. *The Selected Letters.* Edited by Elizabeth Hardwick. New York and London: Doubleday.

Jannella, Celia, et al. 2003. *The Great Italian Painters from the Gothic to the Renaissance.* Florence: Scala.

Johnson, Samuel. 1908. *Johnson on Shakespeare.* Introduced by Walter Raleigh. London: Oxford University Press.

———. 1941. *The Poems of Samuel Johnson.* Edited by David Nichol Smith and Edward L. McAdam. Oxford: Clarendon Press.

Joseph, Gerhard. 1992. *Tennyson and the Text.* Cambridge: Cambridge University Press.

Kant, Immanuel. 1932. *Critique of Practical Reason.* Translated by T. K. Abbott. London: Longmans, Green.

———. 2005. *Critique of Judgment.* Translated by J. H. Bernard.Mineola, NY: Dover.

Karlin, Danny. 2003. "'The Names': Robert Browning's 'Shakespearean Show.'" In *Victorian Shakespeare,* 2:150–69. New York: Palgrave Macmillan.

Keats, John. 1958. *The Letters of John Keats, 1814–1821.* Edited by H. Rollins. 2 vols. Cambridge, MA: Harvard University Press.

———. 1978. *The Poems of John Keats.* Edited by Jack Stillinger. Cambridge, MA: Belknap Press of Harvard University.

Keble, John. 1912. *Lectures on Poetry, 1832–1841.* Translated by E. K. Francis. 2 vols. Oxford: Clarendon Press.

Kermode, Frank. 1966. *The Sense of an Ending: Studies in the Theory of Fiction.* New York: Oxford University Press.

———. 2000. *Shakespeare's Language.* London: Penguin.

———. 2010. "Eliot and the Shudder." *London Review of Books,* 13 May, 13–16.

Kierkegaard, Søren. 1964. *Repetition: An Essay in Experimental Psychology.* Translated by Walter Lowrie. Princeton, NJ: Princeton University Press.

Kooistra, Lorraine Janzen. 2002. "Poetry and Illustration." In *A Companion to Victorian Poetry,* edited by Richard Cronin et al., 392–418. Oxford: Blackwell.

Kuhn, Thomas S. 1962. *The Structure of Scientific Revolutions.* Chicago: University of Chicago Press.

Kushner, Harold S. 1983. *When Bad Things Happen to Good People.* New York: Avon Books.

———. 1996. *How Good Do We Have to Be?* Boston: Little, Brown.

Lamb, Charles. 1903. *The Works of Charles and Henry Lamb.* Edited by E. V. Lucas. London: Methuen.

Langbaum, Robert. 1975. *The Poetry of Experience: The Dramatic Monologue in Modern Literary Tradition.* New York: Norton.

———. 1995. *Thomas Hardy in Our Time.* New York: St. Martin's Press.

LaPorte, Charles. 2011. *Victorian Poets and the Changing Bible.* Charlottesville: University of Virginia Press.

Leavis, F. R. 1975. *The Living Principle: "English" as a Discipline of Thought.* New York: Oxford University Press.

Lever, J. W. 1966. *The Elizabethan Love Sonnet.* London: Methuen.

Lewis, C. S. 1942. *A Preface to Paradise Lost.* Oxford: Oxford University Press.

———. 1962. "Bluspels and Flalansferes." In *The Importance of Language,* edited by Max Black, 36–50. Ithaca, NY: Cornell University Press.

———. 2007. *The Collected Letters of C. S. Lewis.* Edited by Walter Hooper. Vol. 3. New York: HarperSanFrancisco.

Lyell, Charles. 1997. *Principles of Geology.* New York: Penguin. Originally published 1830.

Maclean, Norman. 1952. "Episode, Scene, Speech, and Word: The Madness of Lear." In *Critics and Criticism. Ancient and Modern,* edited by R. S. Crane, 595–615. Chicago: Chicago University Press.

Magee, Bryan. 1997. *Confessions of a Philosopher.* New York: Random House.

Mattes. E. B. 1951. *In Memoriam: The Way of a Soul: A Study of Some Influences that Shaped Tennyson's Poem.* New York: Exposition Press.
McGann, Jerome J. 1972. *Swinburne: An Experiment in Criticism.* Chicago: University of Chicago Press.
Meredith, George. 1919. *The Poetical Works of George Meredith.* London: Constable.
Merton, Thomas. 1960. *The Literary Essays of Thomas Merton.* New York: New Directions.
———. 1997. *Entering the Silence.* New York: HarperCollins.
Mill, J. S. 1938. "Nature." From *Three Essays on Religion.* In *English Prose of the Victorian Era,* edited by Charles F. Harrold and William D. Templeman, 727–51. New York: Oxford University Press.
———. 1965. *Utilitarianism.* In *Collected Works of John Suart Mill.* Edited by J. M. Robson. Vol. 10. Toronto: University of Toronto Press; London: Routledge and Kegan Paul.
———. 1974. *System of Logic: Ratiocinative and Inductive.* Edited by J. M. Robson and R. F. McRae. Vols. 7–8. Toronto: University of Toronto Press; London: Routledge and Kegan Paul.
Miller, J. Hillis. 1982. "*Tess of the D'Urbervilles:* Repetition as Immanent Design." In *Fiction and Repetition: Seven English Novels,* 116–46. Cambridge, MA: Harvard University Press.
———. 1990. *Versions of Pygmalion.* Cambridge, MA: Harvard University Press.
Milton, John. 1930. *The Student's Milton: Being the Complete Poems of John Milton with the Greater Part of His Prose Works.* Edited by Frank Allen Patterson. New York: Appleton Century-Crofts.
Montaigne, Michel de. 1958. *Montaigne Essays.* Translated by J. M. Cohen. Harmondsworth, UK: Penguin.
Morley, Sheridan. 2002. *John Gielgud: The Authorized Biography.* New York: Simon and Schuster.
Morris, William. 1914. *The Defence of Guenevere, The Life and Death of Jason, and Other Poems by William Morris.* London: Oxford University Press.
Murdoch, Iris. 1970. *A Fairly Honourable Defeat.* London: Chatto and Windus.
———. 1992. *Metaphysics as a Guide to Morals.* New York: Penguin Press.
———. 2009. *Iris Murdoch a Writer at War: Letters and Diaries, 1938–46.* Edited by Peter J. Conradi. Exmouth House, Pine Street: Short Books.
Nagel, Thomas. 1986. *The View from Nowhere.* New York: Oxford University Press.
Nelson, James G. 1963. *The Sublime Puritan: Milton and the Victorians.* Madison: University of Wisconsin Press.
Newman, John Henry. 1880. *Fifteen Sermons Preached before the University of Oxford, between A.D. 1826 and 1843.* New ed. London: Rivingtons.
———. 1906. *An Essay on the Development of Christian Doctrine.* New York: Longmans, Green.
———. 1959. *The Idea of a University.* Garden City, NY: Doubleday.
———. 1968. *Apologia Pro Vita Sua.* Edited by David J. DeLaura. New York: Norton Critical Edition.
Nietzsche, Friedrich. 1968. *Twilight of the Idols: The Anti-Christ.* Translated by R. J. Hollingdale. Harmondsworth, UK: Penguin.
———. 1989. *Beyond Good and Evil: Prelude to a Philosophy of the Future.* Translated by Walter Kaufmann. New York: Vintage.

Nowottny, Winifred. 1962. *The Language Poets Use.* London: Athlone Press.

O'Gorman, Francis. 2003. "'The Clue of Shakespearean Power Over Me': Ruskin, Shakespeare, and Influence." In *Victorian Shakespeare,* 2:203–18. New York: Palgrave Macmillan.

Ovid. 1955. *Metamorphoses.* Translated by Mary M. Innes. Harmondsworth, UK: Penguin.

Pater, Walter. 1938. *Appreciations.* Reprinted in *English Prose of the Victorian Era,* edited by Charles F. Harrold and William D. Templeman, 1424–69. New York: Oxford University Press.

Peterson, Linda H. 2009. "Tennyson and the Ladies." *Victorian Poetry* 47, no. 1: 25–43.

Poirier, Richard. 1987. *The Renewal of Literature: Emersonian Reflections.* New York: Random House.

Pope, Alexander. 1963. *The Poems of Alexander Pope.* New Haven, CT: Yale University Press.

Poole, Adrian. 2004. *Shakespeare and the Victorians.* London: Arden Shakespeare.

———, ed. 2011. *Great Shakespeareans: Scott, Dickens, Eliot, Hardy.* Vol. 5. London: Continuum.

Priestley, F. E. L. 1973. *Language and Structure in Tennyson's Poetry.* London: Andre Deutsch.

Prince, Kathryn. 2008. *Shakespeare in the Victorian Periodicals.* New York: Routledge.

Rader, Ralph. 1976. "The Dramatic Monologue and Related Lyric Forms." *Critical Inquiry* 3, no. 1: 131–51.

Rauh, Sister Miriam Joseph. 1947. *Rhetoric in Shakespeare's Time: Literary Theory of Renaissance Europe.* New York: Harcourt, Brace.

Richardson, James. 1988. *Vanishing Lives: Style and Self in Tennyson, Swinburne, and Yeats.* Charlottesville: University Press of Virginia.

Riede, David G. 1991. *Oracles and Hierophants: Constructions of Romantic Authority.* Ithaca, NY: Cornell University Press.

———. 2005. *Allegories of One's Own Mind: Melancholy in Victorian Poetry.* Columbus: Ohio State University Press.

Ricks, Christopher. 1963. *Milton's Grand Style.* London and Oxford: Oxford University Press.

———. 1972. *Tennyson.* New York: Collier.

———. 1984. *Keats and Embarrassment.* Oxford: Clarendon Press.

———. 1987. *The Poems of Tennyson.* Edited by Christopher Ricks. 3 vols. London: Longmans, Green.

———. 1987. *The Force of Poetry.* Oxford: Oxford University Press.

———. 1993. *Becket's Dying Words.* Oxford: Clarendon Press.

———. 2004. *Dylan's Vision of Sin.* New York: Penguin.

Rorty, Richard. 1979. *Philosophy and the Mirror of Nature.* Princeton, NJ: Princeton University Press.

Rossetti, Christina. 1979–90. *The Complete Poems of Christina Rossetti.* Edited by Rebecca Crump. 3 vols. Baton Rouge: Louisiana State University Press.

Rossetti, D. G. 1886. *The Poetical Works of Dante Gabriel Rossetti.* New York: Thomas Y. Crowell.

Ruskin, John. 1903–12. *The Works of John Ruskin.* Edited by E. T. Cook and Alexander Wedderburn. London: G. Allen, Longmans, Green.

———. 1938. "The Mystery of Life and Its Arts." Lecture 3 from *Sesame and Lilies.* In *English Prose of the Victorian Era,* edited by Charles F. Harrold and William D. Templeman, 968–86. New York: Oxford University Press.

———. 1972. *The Literary Criticism of John Ruskin.* Edited by Harold Bloom. New York: Norton.

Rylands, George. 1960. "Shakespeare the Poet." In *A Companion to Shakespeare Studies,* edited by Harley Granville-Barker and G. B. Harrison, 88–115. Garden City, NY: Anchor Books.

Rymer, Thomas. 1971. *Critical Works of Thomas Rymer.* Edited by Curt H. Zimansky. Westport, CT: Greenwood Press.

Sartre, Jean-Paul. 1966. *Being and Nothingness.* Translated by Hazel E. Barnes. New York: Washington Square Press.

Sawyer, Robert. 2003. *Victorian Appropriations of Shakespeare.* Madison, NJ: Farleigh Dickinson University Press.

Schoenbaum, S. 1977. *William Shakespeare: A Complete Documentary Life.* New York: Oxford University Press.

Shakespeare, William. 1941. *Antony and Cleopatra.* Edited by George Lyman Kittredge. Boston: Ginn.

———. 1999. *Antony and Cleopatra.* Edited by A. R. Braunmuller. Cambridge: Cambridge University Press.

———. 1999. *King Lear.* Edited by Stephen Orgel. New York: Penguin.

———. 2000. *Cymbeline.* Edited by Peter Holland. Oxford: Clarendon Press.

———. 2000. *Love's Labor's Lost.* Edited by Peter Holland. Oxford: Clarendon Press.

———. 2000. *The Merchant of Venice.* Edited by A.R. Braunmuller. New York: Penguin.

———. 2000. *Romeo and Juliet.* Edited by Jill Levenson. Oxford: Clarendon Press.

———. 2001. *The Sonnets.* Edited by Stephen Orgel: New York: Penguin.

———. 2001. *The Tragical History of Hamlet Prince of Denmark.* Edited by A. R. Braunmuller. New York: Penguin.

———. 2006. *Othello.* Edited by Michael Neill. Oxford: Clarendon Press.

———. 2008. *Macbeth.* Edited by A. R. Braunmuller. Cambridge: Cambridge University Press.

———. 2008. *A Midsummer Night's Dream.* Edited by Peter Holland. Oxford: Clarendon Press.

———. 2008. *The Tempest.* Edited by Stephen Orgel. Oxford: Clarendon Press.

———. 2008. *The Winter's Tale.* Edited by Stephen Orgel. Oxford: Clarendon Press.

Shattuck, Roger. 1996. *Forbidden Knowledge: From Prometheus to Pornography.* New York: Harcourt Brace.

Smith, Barbara Herrnstein. 1968. *Poetic Closure: A Study of How Poems End.* Chicago: University of Chicago Press.

Sparshott, Francis. 1982. *The Theory of the Arts.* Princeton, NJ: Princeton University Press.

Stokes, John. 2003. "'Shopping in Byzantium': Oscar Wilde as Shakespeare Critic." In *Victorian Shakespeare,* 1:178–91. New York: Palgrave Macmillan.

Steiner, George. 2003. *Lessons of the Masters.* Cambridge, MA: Harvard University Press.

Stevens, Wallace. 1996. *Letters of Wallace Stevens.* Edited by Holly Stevens. Berkeley: University of California Press.

Stevenson, Robert Louis. 1938. "On Some Technical Elements of Style." In *Contemporary Review* (April 1885). Reprinted in *English Prose of the Victorian Era,* edited by Charles Frederick Harold and William D. Templeman, 1501–11. New York: Oxford University Press.

Swinburne, A. C. 1918. *A Study of Shakespeare.* London: Heinemann. First published 1879.

———. 1925–27. *The Complete Works of Algernon Charles Swinburne.* Bonchurch edition. Edited by Edmund Gosse and Thomas James Wise. 20 vols. London: Heinemann.

Suzuki, Daisetz T. 1970. *The Field of Zen.* New York: Harper and Row.

Tennyson, Alfred. 1908. *The Works of Tennyson.* Edited by Hallam Lord Tennyson. Vols. 8 and 9. London: Macmillan, 1908. Only quotations from Tennyson's plays are taken from these volumes.

———. 1981. *The Letters of Alfred Lord Tennyson.* Edited by Cecil Y. Lang and Edgar F. Shannon Jr. Vol. 1: 1821–1850. Cambridge, MA: Harvard University Press.

———. 1987. *The Poems of Tennyson.* Edited by Christopher Ricks. 3 vols. London: Longmans, Green.

Tennyson, G. B. 1981. *Victorian Devotional Poetry: The Tractarian Mode.* Cambridge, MA: Harvard University Press.

Tennyson, Hallam. 1897. *Alfred Tennyson: A Memoir by His Son.* 2 vols. London: Macmillan.

Thackeray, W. M. 1963. *Vanity Fair: A Novel without a Hero.* Edited by Geoffrey and Kathleen Tillotson. Boston: Houghton Mifflin.

Thompson, Francis. 1913. *The Works of Francis Thompson.* Edited by Wilfrid Meynell. 3 vols. London: Burnes and Oates.

Tillyard, E. M. W. 1957. "*Richard II.*" In *Shakespeare: Modern Essays in Criticism,* edited by Leonard F. Dean, 138–58. New York: Oxford University Press.

Trollope, Anthony. 1936. *Barchester Towers* and *The Warden.* New York: Modern Library.

———. N.d. *An Autobiography.* Garden City, NY: Doubleday.

Tucker, Herbert F. 1980. *Browning's Beginnings: The Art of Disclosure.* Minneapolis: University of Minnesota Press.

———. 1988. *Tennyson and the Doom of Romanticism.* Cambridge, MA: Harvard University Press.

———. 1998. "Browning as Escape Artist: Avoidance and Intimacy." In *Robert Browning in Contexts,* edited by John Woolford, 1–25. Winfield, KS: Wedgestone Press.

Turner, Frank M. 2002. *John Henry Newman: The Challenge to Evangelical Religion.* New Haven, CT: Yale University Press.

Tuve, Rosemond. 1947. *Elizabethan and Metaphysical Imagery: Renaissance and Twentieth-Century Critics.* Chicago: University of Chicago Press.

Vendler, Helen. 1988. *The Music of What Happens.* Cambridge, MA: Harvard University Press.

———. 1997. *The Art of Shakespeare's Sonnets.* Cambridge, MA: Belknap Press of Harvard University.

Watkins, W. B. C. 1950. *Shakespeare and Spenser.* Princeton, NJ: Princeton University Press.

Weil, Simone. 1974. *Gateway to God.* Edited by David Raper. Glasgow: William Collins.

Weisman, Karen. 2010. Introduction to *The Oxford Handbook of the Elegy,* 1–9. New York: Oxford University Press.

Welsh, Alexander. 2001. *Hamlet in His Modern Guises.* New Haven, CT: Yale University Press, 2001.

Whitehead, Alfred North. 1933. *Adventures of Ideas.* New York: Free Press.

Wilde, Oscar. 1968. *Literary Criticism of Oscar Wilde.* Edited by Stanley Weintraub. Lincoln: University of Nebraska Press.

Willcock, Gladys. 1960. "Shakespeare and Elizabethan English." In *A Companion to Shake-*

speare Studies, edited by H. Granville-Barker and G. B. Harrison, 116–35. Garden City, NY: Doubleday.

Williams, Charles. 1936. "*Troilus and Cressida* and *Hamlet.*" In *Shakespeare Criticism,* edited by Anne Ridler, 188–208. London: Oxford University Press.

Williamson, George. 1951. *The Senecan Amble.* Chicago: University of Chicago Press.

Woolford, John. 1998. "Self-Consciousness and Self-Expression in Caliban and Browning." In *Robert Browning in Contexts,* edited by John Woolford, 86–100. Winfield, KS: Wedgestone Press.

Wollheim, Richard. 1984. *The Thread of Life.* Cambridge, MA: Harvard University Press.

Wordsworth, William. 1940–49. *The Poetical Works of William Wordsworth.* Edited by Ernest de Selincourt and Helen Darbishire. 5 vols. Oxford: Clarendon Press.

Wright, George T. 1981. "Hendiadys and *Hamlet.*" *PMLA* 96: 168–93.

———. 2001. *Hearing the Measures: Shakespeare and Other Inflections.* Madison: University of Wisconsin Press.

Yeats, W. B. 1960. *The Collected Poems of W. B. Yeats.* New York: Macmillan.

Index

Italicized page numbers indicate the location of major discussions.